Two Decades of Panchayat Raj in India

Two Decades of Panchayat Raj in India

Experiences, Issues, Challenges and Opportunities

Edited by
Yatindra Singh Sisodia
Ashish Bhatt
Tapas Kumar Dalapati

RAWAT PUBLICATIONS
Jaipur • New Delhi • Bangalore • Guwahati • Kolkata

ISBN 978-81-316-0927-9

Published by
Prem Rawat for **Rawat Publications**
Satyam Apts, Sector 3, Jawahar Nagar, Jaipur 302 004 (India)
Phone: 0141 265 1748 / 7006 Fax: 0141 265 1748
E-mail: info@rawatbooks.com
Website: www.rawatbooks.com

New Delhi Office
4858/24, Ansari Road, Daryaganj, New Delhi 110 002
Phone: 011 2326 3290

Also at *Bangalore, Guwahati* and *Kolkata*

Typeset by Rawat Computers, Jaipur
Printed at Chaman Enterprises, New Delhi

Contents

Part III
Changing Power Structure and Empowerment of Marginalised Groups

Part IV
Gender Issues and Empowerment of Women through PRIs

Preface

Decentralisation can take four major forms: deconcentration – dispersing decision-making authority to reach the entire territory; delegation – allocating decision-making authority to local governments; devolution – financial and legal establishment of government bodies at the sub-national level; and divestment – transfer of planning and administrative responsibilities from government to private or non-governmental institutions. Decentralisation is championed as a vehicle of democratisation. It should be recognised that decentralisation does not render central governments obsolete. Instead both should play complementary roles that can help bring about the most effective service. Decentralisation needs to be done in the context of existing cultural elements, be sensitive towards changing relationships, and seek to enhance mechanisms of participation and partnership.

From the Indian point of view, after independence, efforts have been made to meet the needs and expectations of the people. Special efforts have been taken up to address the rural multifaceted issues with massive investment but the results were not up to the expectations. The idea that produced the 73rd Amendment Act was not a response to pressure from the grassroots but to an increasing recognition that the institutional initiatives of the preceding decades had not delivered expected results, as the extent of rural poverty was still much too large and thus the existing structure of government needed to be reformed. It was a political drive to see panchayat raj institutions (PRIs) as a solution to the governmental crises that India was experiencing.

Panchayat raj, as a system of governance at the grassroots level in rural India has rightly been conceived as the most viable and proper mechanism of realising the goals of democracy and decentralisation. After Independence, efforts have been made to create the units of self-governance at grassroots level but all in vain since they could not produce the desired results. The persistent commitment of the Central Government to this cause finally resulted in bringing about the 73rd Amendment for the establishment of panchayat raj institutions in India.

Two decades of decentralised governance put forward many achievements and dilemmas. The states assured the peoples' participation in the local governance institutions with adequate gender, class and caste representation as per the need of the amendment package. Accountable administration and governance at local level is still an issue of serious concern. Efforts have been made to empower people through legislation but there are indications that the level of participation of people at grassroots level is very low. The political dynamics at grassroots level is different and has many players and they have their weightage in different context. As a matter of fact, it can be argued that despite the specific provision, there is a gap between macro level decisions and grassroots reality.

Keeping in view the significance of the issue, Madhya Pradesh Institute of Social Science Research, Ujjain (Madhya Pradesh) organised a National Seminar on *Two Decades of Panchayat Raj in India: Experiences, Issues, Challenges and Opportunities* to discuss threadbare the multi-faceted issues of panchayat raj in India. For articulation of views and presentation of papers in the seminar, the themes were as follows: Response of the State Government to the 73rd Constitutional Amendment Act; Devolution of Funds, Functions and Functionaries; Panchayat Elections and Emerging Profile of Representatives; Changing Power Structure, Leadership and Social Settings; Empowerment of Marginalised Section (Women, Dalits and Tribals) and their Participation; Community Assertion for Participation in Planning, Convergence, Implementation, Monitoring, Transparency and Accountability; Decentralised Planning and Finance; Emerging Conflicts between Public Representatives and Bureaucrats, Local Bodies and Civil Society Organisation and Parallel Bodies; Capacity Building Initiatives and their Problems; State-Specific Experiences in Structure and Functioning of PRIs.

This volume is an attempt to identify, document and comprehend the broad trends on the panchayat raj in India. It is important to understand and analyse the process and direction of macro vis-à-vis micro situation, which would have a significant impact and critical lessons for charting out the future course of action for effective people-centric local governance across the country.

First of all we would like to acknowledge ICSSR, Ministry of HRD, Government of India for providing financial support to organise this seminar. We would like to express our sincere thanks to Professor Nalini Rewadikar, President, MPISSR for inspiring us to edit this volume. We are thankful to our colleagues Professor Sandeep Joshi, Professor Y.G. Joshi, Dr Ashish Bhatt, Dr S.S. Chandel, and Dr Manu Gautam for their valuable suggestions and help extended during the editing of this volume.

Our sincere thanks are due to all the paper contributors, without their contribution this volume would not have been possible.

Finally, we would like to express our thanks to Mr Pranit Rawat of the Rawat Publications, Jaipur for showing interest in this manuscript and bringing out the volume in time.

Yatindra Singh Sisodia
Ashish Bhatt
Tapas Kumar Dalapati
MPISSR, Ujjain

Contributors

Yatindra Singh Sisodia, Director, M.P. Institute of Social Science Research, Ujjain (Madhya Pradesh).

Ashish Bhatt, Associate Professor, M.P. Institute of Social Science Research, Ujjain (Madhya Pradesh).

Tapas Kumar Dalapati, Assistant Professor, M.P. Institute of Social Science Research, Ujjain (Madhya Pradesh).

Alaknanda Shringare, Assistant Professor, Department of Political Science, Goa University, Bambolim (Goa).

Anuja, Assistant Professor, A.N. Sinha Institute of Social Studies, Patna (Bihar).

D.C. Sah, Professor Emeritus, M.P. Institute of Social Science Research, Ujjain (Madhya Pradesh).

G. Palanithurai, Professor, Gandhigram Rural Institute – Deemed University, Gandhigram, Distt. Dindigul (Tamil Nadu).

Gadadhara Mohapatra, Assistant Professor, Indian Institute of Public Administration, New Delhi.

Jitendra Wasnik, Assistant Professor, Department of Public Administration and Local Self-Government, Rashtrasant Tukadoji Maharaj Nagpur University, Nagpur (Maharashtra).

K. Gireesan, Faculty Head, School of Governance and Public Policy, Rajiv Gandhi National Institute of Youth Development, Sriperumbudur (Tamil Nadu).

M. Gopinath Reddy, Professor, Centre for Economic and Social Studies, Hyderabad (Telangana).

Narayan Billava, Research Associate, Centre for Multidisciplinary Development Research, Dharwad (Karnataka).

Nayanatara S. Nayak, Professor, Centre for Multidisciplinary Development Research, Dharwad (Karnataka).

Neeta Tapan, Assistant Professor (Economics), Girl's PG College, Ujjain (Madhya Pradesh).

Nilakantha Panigrahi, Associate Professor, Department of Anthropology and Tribal Development, Guru Ghasidas University, Bilaspur (Chhattisgarh).

Nupur Tiwari, Faculty, Indian Institute of Public Administration, New Delhi.

Ramkumar G., Research Scholar, Tata Institute of Social Sciences, Mumbai (Maharashtra).

Ruby Ojha, Associate Professor, Department of Economics, SNDT Women's University, Mumbai (Maharashtra).

S.K. Singh, Former Director, Centre for Panchayati Raj, NIRD, Hyderabad and Former Director, Training Division CIRDAP, Dhaka, Bangladesh.

S. Satyam, Assistant Professor, Council for Social Development, Hyderabad (Telangana).

S.N. Tripathy, Professor of Economics, Gokhale Institute of Politics and Economics, Pune (Maharashtra).

S.T. Shirsath, Associate Professor, Department of Public Administration, Dr Babasaheb Ambedkar Marathwada University, Aurangabad (Maharashtra).

Smita Agarwal, Assistant Professor Political Science, Amity School of Liberal Arts (Haryana).

V. Rama Krishna, Assistant Professor, Department of Political Science, Tumkur University, Tumkur (Karnataka).

1

Introduction

Yatindra Singh Sisodia, Ashish Bhatt and Tapas Kumar Dalapati

Decentralisation is a much-debated issue in India and other countries with federal system of governance. There are different arguments for and against decentralisation. However, the arguments in favour of decentralisation outweigh those against it because of the inherent potential of democratisation in the decentralised federal system through proper empowerment of people at the grassroots level. Deepening of democracy is an ideology as well as institution in the post-colonial societies like India. India has got a long history of the functioning of institutions at the grassroots for the existence and continuation of the social inequalities for centuries together. The institution of Panchayat Raj in its rejuvenated form tried to achieve the objectives of democratic decentralisation to accelerate socio-economic development and usher in equity and social justice. It was a political drive to see Panchayati Raj Institutions (PRIs) as a solution to the governmental crises that India was experiencing (World Bank, 2000). The enactment of the 73rd Constitutional Amendment Act in 1993 and the subsequent state-wise Panchayat Raj Acts in India brought to frontline significance of grassroots democratic processes. The new PRIs have the potential to usher in a new era of change and development in accordance with people's needs and priorities, and to revitalise a deeply troubled system of democracy (Behar and Kumar, 2002).

The execution of the Act was made mandatory for all the Indian states and panchayats have been provided a constitutional status. A special chapter has been added to the Indian Constitution on Panchayats. The 73rd Amendment Act provided uniformity and formal structure to these traditional institutions of self-governance for the sake of their effective functioning. The 73rd Amendment Act initiated a fundamental restructuring of governance and administrative system of the country, based on the philosophy of decentralisation and power to the people. This experience has brought the lesson that the success of the new panchayat raj system largely depends on the congruence of perception and commitment of people, their leaders and the officials, about the role to be played by them in the new system. The objective of decentralisation is to execute and implement schemes and programmes to meet the local needs, to mobilise people, to channelise their energies towards socio-economic reconstruction and to involve them in all the activities of the communities through the new institutions. United Nations Development Programme's experienced with decentralisation have demonstrated its significant contributions to improving the population's access to health, education, employment and sustainable livelihoods' opportunities, and various social services (UNDP, 2000).

After two decades, Panchayat Raj in India has been a matter of debate and speculation about its performance and impact. All the major states have completed at least four rounds of panchayat elections. Almost three million people including more than one million women and a sizeable number of SCs/STs took part in these elections. The sizeable presence of underprivileged and poor as representatives through reservations in the grassroots political institutions is a landmark development in the rural politics of the country. The experiences of the states are extremely rich and provide vital insights into the process of institutionalising panchayat raj. The crucial significance is also of the principle of accountability and regular social auditing of the performance and transparency in the form of information pertaining to all the activities of panchayats. A perusal of state profiles would show that panchayat raj reforms have certainly taken place with vigour and zeal in some western and southern parts of the country, which are relatively sound from the point of view of economy, are vibrant socially, and have active civil societies. On the contrary, the northern states with the greatest degree of poverty and inequality and deep schisms of caste and low pace of governance resulted in weak panchayats (Robinson, 2005). Looking into the relevance of new system, it is important to evaluate the ground reality and potentiality of the panchayat raj system in Indian States.

In this Volume

Keeping this background in view, M.P. Institute of Social Science Research, Ujjain organised a National Seminar on *Two Decades of Panchayat Raj in India: Experiences, Issues, Challenges and Opportunities*, to discuss threadbare the multi-faceted issues related to panchayats in India. It was aimed to understand the macro- and micro-dynamics of decentralised governance in India. This helped to find out the issues, challenges, opportunities and problems of governance at the grassroots level. The focal and subthemes of the seminar were as follows: Response of the State Government to the 73rd Constitutional Amendment Act; Devolution of Funds, Functions and Functionaries; Panchayat Elections and Emerging Profile of Representatives; Changing Power Structure, Leadership and Social Settings; Empowerment of Marginalised Section (Women, Dalits and Tribals) and their Participation; Community Assertion for Participation in Planning, Convergence, Implementation, Monitoring, Transparency and Accountability; Decentralised Planning and Finance; Emerging Conflicts between Public Representatives and Bureaucrats, Local Bodies and Civil Society Organisation and Parallel Bodies; Capacity Building Initiatives and their Problems; and State Specific Experiences in Structure and Functioning of PRIs.

This volume containing 21 papers has been divided into five thematic parts. The first part, *73rd Constitutional Amendment and Status of PRIs* has four chapters that review the Panchayat Raj in India. This part provides adequate details of the background and two decades of panchayat raj in the country. The second part, *Devolution of Funds, Functions and Functionaries in PRIs* has three chapters. One chapter is related to fiscal federalism and another on inclusiveness of panchayats. Third chapter of this part explains engagement of youth in panchayat raj. The third part, *Changing Power Structure and Empowerment of Marginalised Groups* has five chapters. Out of these, four chapters have analysed panchayats in the different tribal contexts. Remaining chapter has portrayed the Dalit leadership with empirical evidences gathered from the field. The fourth part, *Gender Issues and Empowerment of Women through PRIs* has five chapters. These chapters have primarily delved upon the issues of women in panchayat raj institutions. The fifth and last part *State Specific Experiences in Structure and Functions in PRIs* has four chapters. These four chapters deal with the specific four states of India.

73rd Constitutional Amendment and Status of PRIs

In this part, the first paper *Theoretical Nuances of Democratic Decentralisation in India,* by G. Palanithurai explains that people who have been in power so far and who are going to lose power in the new dispensation will create a new design and by which they will keep power with them. The dominant elites will capture power by using this new opportunities. Here, it is to be understood that in India, decentralisation of power is a top-down exercise and not bottom-up exercise. Yet the newly created institutions are put into action. It is an important question as to what extent the centralised drive for decentralisation yielded results. The centralised drive cannot go beyond certain limits as local governance is the subject of the state governments. Conceptually, it is a weak design of decentralisation of powers. It is a top driven strategy to reduce the power of the state government and equally the state governments adopt a strategy to retain their powers with them by creating a lose governance mechanism at the grassroots to fulfil the constitutional requirements. By this process one can see a governance arrangement at the grassroots in form but not in content and substance. In the two decades the institutions are functioning and for which huge expenditure has been committed and spent. The moot question is what impact it has created in Indian society and economy, more specifically, in the rural area by its functioning. Twenty years are methodologically sufficient to evaluate the functioning of any governance structure. Hence, an attempt is made to evaluate the process of decentralisation of powers in India. Decentralised governance, democratisation of communities, development management, delivering social justice and public goods, participatory development and empowerment of the marginalised groups are the subjects being looked at in this research article. It also highlights the missing links in the research areas already covered. The methodological nuances that have emerged in the research process are also highlighted in this work. Basically, it maps up the emerging trend in evolving theoretical nuances.

In the second paper by S.K. Singh on *Two Decades of Democratic Decentralisation in India: Some Reflections*, attempts to appraise the functioning of PRIs so as to reflect on critical issues that have emerged in the process of democratic decentralisation. While doing so, the author has selected parameters that are central to the effectiveness of panchayats as a conduit to a representative system, covered various facets of panchayats and reviewed whether panchayats have been effectively empowered and are delivering services. More so, this paper is based on and draws insights from various published reports of committees and commissions constituted after the amendment by different national level agencies dealing with panchayats and reviewing their functioning and impact.

Yatindra Singh Sisodia in his paper on *Two Decades of Democratic Governance at Local Level: Evidences from the Functioning of Panchayati Raj Institutions in Central Indian States*, explains that after almost two decades, panchayat raj in India has been a matter of debate and speculation about its performance and impact. All the major states have completed at least three rounds of panchayat elections. Almost three million people including one million women and a sizeable number of SCs/STs took part in these elections. The sizeable presence of underprivileged and poor as representatives through reservations in the grassroots political institutions is a landmark development in the rural politics of the country. This significant development has a special meaning because two decades earlier in most parts of rural India these groups were excluded from public life and political participation. This is also a matter of serious debate as how this excluded lot after their inclusion in active politics at grassroots would effectively tackle local power equation and set the agenda for development. The central Indian states have responded with innovativeness and remarkable commitment to making the system sustainable and successful. The experience of the states is extremely rich and provides vital insights into the process of institutionalising panchayat raj. Looking into the relevance of the new system, an attempt is made to evaluate the ground reality and potentiality of the panchayat raj system in central Indian States. The paper is dealing with the issues of people's participation through Gram Sabha; representation of marginalised sections of society; women's participation in panchayats; working of panchayats; panchayats and bureaucracy; devolution of powers; financial status of panchayats; decentralised planning in separate subheadings.

Nayanatara S. Nayak and Narayan Billava in their paper on *Decentralisation and the Empowerment of Women and the Other Marginalised Groups: Anecdote from the Review of Literature* examine the decentralisation process initiated through entry of women into politics to ensure through affirmative action, questions arising on whether this has resulted in their political participation, inclusive development or improvement in service delivery. Decentralisation is sought as panacea to all the problems of rural development and is linked to empowerment of the marginalised. Thematic review under this paper tries to look in to this holy nexus through the literature in the Indian context. The review suggests that the benefits are not reaching the marginalised to the expected level due to their low social status and lack of awareness. Unless awareness is created on a large scale they are likely to remain on the periphery on account of illiteracy, proxy candidature, poverty, dependence on dominant classes for work, etc. Decentralisation has helped women and the marginalised to come out of closed societies, work for their own upliftment and benefit of the society. It has compelled men and women from the dominant classes to accept the powers of the marginalised.

Devolution of Funds, Functions and Functionaries in PRIs

Neeta Tapan in her paper on *Fiscal Federalism and Panchayati Raj Institutions: Some Macro Issues*, narrates that decentralisation in the current development scenario emerges as a key strategy of governance to address the long-standing human development issues. Devolution of powers including fiscal powers to the Panchayati Raj Institutions (PRIs) is the most significant aspect that is reflected through the 73rd Constitution Amendment Act. It was suggested that the functions of 29 subjects under the 11th Schedule of the Indian Constitution will be devolved to the PRIs for ensuring effectiveness in functional aspects. Generally, the functional responsibilities are closely linked with the financial powers delegated to the local government; however, in practice there is a mismatch between the two, leading to a severe fiscal stress at the local level. Panchayats' own revenues are not enough even to meet their requirements; therefore they are dependent on the higher tiers of government to finance their activities. The role of State Finance Commissions (SFCs) in this context becomes critical in examining not only the revenue sharing arrangements between the state governments and their panchayats, but also the entire range of subjects concerning assignment of taxes, transfers of power and such other subjects for improving the financial health of the panchayats. At the same time, substantial funds are being transferred to the panchayats through the Centrally Sponsored Schemes (CSSs) and Additional Central Assistances (ACAs). Funds under this scheme are allocated to states and UTs in accordance with their performance as measured in the Panchayat Devolution Index and also the incremental panchayat devolution. These measures include parameters like functions, finances and functionaries, framework, capacity building and accountability to build the rating matrix. These indices reveal interstate variations across these parameters with substantial weightage given to finances. This paper thus attempts to unfold certain macro issues regarding fiscal decentralisation like the recommendations of SFC and National Finance Commission regarding share of Panchayats in state resources, revenue power of panchayats at each tier, inter-governmental transfers, and the Devolution Indices position with special reference to the state of Madhya Pradesh.

Nupur Tiwari in her paper on *How Inclusive are the Panchayats: The Future Stratagem*, states that India represents a paradox where on the one hand the GDP growth rate has been rising to 7–8 per cent in the last four years, while rural-urban divide, regional divide and rich-poor divide has become glaring. While the world and its financial hubs applaud the countries impressive annual GDP growth, other indicators such as poverty reduction, employment growth, health and education are less encouraging. The present pattern of growth has the potential of widening the inequality. If this inequality increases further, social displacement will result and it will be a major obstruction to higher growth. Large amounts of public funds are spent to address these issues but their implementation and the quality of services delivered leave much to be desired. Being closest to the people, the panchayats and their elected representatives have the feel of the pulse, the sufferings of the people and local conditions. The involvement of panchayats ensures greater transparency in working and fund utilisation than in execution carried out by central or state agency, many a times. It is important that local governance be brought centre-stage as the principal governance reform to reinforce economic reform in such a manner as to secure inclusive growth. Local self-government offers this opportunity, as communities, citizens, right from the Gram Sabha level can participate in the designing of the development in their area. When grassroots planning processes strikes deep roots, economic empowerment is both strong and sustainable.

K. Gireesan in his paper on *Mainstreaming Youth in Local Governance: Learning from an Indian Village*, presented that passing the 73rd and 74th Constitutional Amendment Act was a defining moment in the history of decentralisation of political power in India. Youth can play an important role in strengthening local governance as they constitute a significant and vital segment of the population in the country. It is essential that youth assume an important role in the systems, institutions and practices of local governance. The programmes and projects initiated and/or implemented by the local governments should take care of the specific needs, concerns, interests and priorities of youth. In addition, the local governments could utilise the competencies, dynamism, energy and skills of youth in planning, implementing and monitoring of programmes and projects. To make this happen, more and more youth should themselves participate in the activities of the local governments. The paper discusses the learnings from an action research project carried out in a Gram Panchayat of Himachal Pradesh. The paper brings out the status of youth, their needs, concerns, issues, problems and priorities from the study area. It also highlights the initiatives and interventions made by the local government and other organisations in the selected area, aiming at youth development.

Changing Power Structure and Empowerment of Marginalised Groups

D.C. Sah and Ashish Bhatt in their paper on *Governance and Multidimensional Poverty: Evidence from Central Tribal Belt of India*, argue that the changes in governance are postulated on three basic premises. First, traditional ways of tribal society could be integrated with decentralised governance. Second, the community would get an institutional space to govern its affairs in an accountable and meaningful manner. This means that the provisions would be able to level and homogenise the differences, leading to an informed decision-making by the people at the grassroots level. Lastly, the new system would usher in a regime of people's participation, where governance would be more responsible and fruits of development distributed more equitably. This paper examines this pertinent question in the context of developed and underdeveloped villages. This data base for the study is from 10 tribal districts of six states; Gujarat (Bharuch and Panchmahals), Rajasthan (Banswara), Madhya Pradesh (Jhabua and Badwani), Chhattisgarh (Bastar and Raigarh),

Jharkhand (Ranchi and West Singhbum) and Odisha (Koraput). The findings of this paper indicate towards the following two major conclusions: First, in one stroke, Panchayats (Extension to Scheduled Areas) Act 1996 (PESA) promised to give control of resources and decision-making to tribals. This has proved to be a false promise. Owing to the fact that rules of the line departments of states impinge upon the specific provisions of PESA, the community never got a chance to decide. Consequently, decision-making powers relating to land, water, forest and development still rest on bureaucracy. Secondly, decentralisation, it seems, has become an end in itself; this is true when one analyses the process of decision-making, which is still highly centralised, or with respect to fruits of development interventions, which are still highly iniquitous.

S.N. Tripathy in his paper on *Decentralised Governance through Panchayats PESA and Tribal Development*, argues that decentralisation can play a paramount role in enhancing the practice of democratic governance. It can contribute to the process of democratic development by expanding the scope of social, economic and political participation of the people and the corresponding responsiveness and accountability of the authority structures of the state. Ultimately, it can be an effective instrument of development policy to diminish inequality and poverty. The PESA Act, 1996 was extended to the tribal areas of nine states, namely Andhra Pradesh, Jharkhand, Gujarat, Himachal Pradesh, Maharashtra, Madhya Pradesh, Odisha, Rajasthan and Chhattisgarh. Under the Act, Gram Sabhas are endowed specifically with such powers and authority as to enable them to function as institutions of self-government. PESA is the single most important instrument for dealing with the economic and emotional alienation of the tribal people. Notwithstanding plethora of legislative and protective measures, with provisions of PESA, the socio-economic conditions of tribes in India are more deplorable. This theoretical paper focuses on decentralisation governance and PESA in tribal areas.

Nilakantha Panigrahi in his paper on *Impact of Decentralised Governance on the Implementation of MGNREGS in Scheduled Areas of Odisha: An Overview*, reflects that the status of tribal societies in Indian social structure is comparatively lagging behind in many respects. The basic premise behind PESA Act was to decentralise and entrust the financial and administrative powers with the panchayati raj institutions in scheduled areas of the country and thereby to bring the tribal communities to the level of the non-tribal communities of the nation. The paper firstly attempts to provide a brief profile of tribal population and the regions covered under PESA in the state of Odisha. Secondly, it critically analyses the operational status of decentralisation of power and programmes to the PRIs both in principle and in practice. Thirdly, while taking into account the implementation of Mahatma Gandhi National Rural Employment Guarantee Scheme (MGNREGS), the paper reviews the impact of decentralisation on the functioning of PRI bodies in schedule areas of the state. Finally, the paper concludes that the globalisation philosophy enthusiastically adopted by the state has partially affected the decentralisation processes promoted under PESA Act. As a result, the state is yet to establish inclusive processes of development which is really a concern for the development of tribal population and tribal dominated regions of Odisha, even after the adoption of PESA for two decades.

S.T. Shirsath in his paper on *Pattern of Local Governance for Tribes in Maharashtra: Analysis of Strategies and Policies for Inclusive Development,* says that tribal development is the key phenomenon to be chanted everywhere by every nation of the world. So, not only tribal development is a burning issue, but also a necessity of every nation. If every social element is empowered socially, politically and economically, it will play an important role in the national interest. Being a part of our social structure, tribal development is a mandatory function of governance. In this manner development of tribes through socio-political and economic empowerment is a crucial issue. These are major aspects in the functioning of local governance. Tribes in India present a significant degree of cultural and ethnic diversity. They differ in their socio-economic levels and behavioural patterns and they have distinct cultures, customary practices, dialects and economic pursuits in different ecological settings. The paper attempts to shed light on the condition of such excluded tribes and the inclusive efforts by the Government of India, especially in Maharashtra.

Ramkumar G. in his paper on *A Decade of Change through Dalit Leadership: Narratives from the Kuthambakkam Village Panchayat, Tamil Nadu,* reiterates that the 73rd Amendment in the Constitution provides opportunity for political participation of weaker sections in local governance. This political participation of the marginalised community (dalits) is not tolerated by the local dominant castes. Dalit representatives, therefore, run the risk of humiliation, being proxy candidates and even face violence. Such exclusions, however, have not restrained the dalits from being active in the panchayats and access development schemes. Kuthamabakkam is one such village, where the lives of dalits changed in terms of social infrastructure, education, and women empowerment due to the leadership of dalit candidate. This paper explores the dalit leadership and the nature of participation in local governance. Also, it charts the process of change in access to public amenities of dalits through local governance. This paper used the case study method to understand the changes that happened in Kuthambakkam village under the dalit leadership. This paper identifies that dalits in this village experienced caste-based discrimination. Also, they lived in a poor social and economic condition. The education level was also low. In that context, decentralised local governance brought in dalit reservation in Kuthambakkam village panchayat. Through the initiatives of dalit president, lives of dalit people have changed drastically. The schemes have reached the dalit people which resulted in improvement in social housing, road and drainage facilities, drinking water and other infrastructure facilities among dalit people habitation and the whole village. The village also improved in many other aspects such as education, involvement of women participation in the panchayat, increase in the people participation etc. through the innovative initiatives of panchayat and its leadership.

Gender Issues and Empowerment of Women through PRIs

V. Rama Krishna in his paper on *Decentralisation and Women's Development in India: An Institutional Perspective,* narrates that the idea of local self-government had existed in India even in ancient times. The 73rd and 74th Amendments, which were passed in 1992 and came into force in April 1994, have virtually revolutionised the idea of local self-government both rural and urban by bestowing constitutional status on them. These Amendments were passed in the light of the experience of the local self-government institutions in India. They have made a sincere attempt to overcome the limitations faced by these institutions. The paper discusses Panchayati Raj Institutions (PRIs) for the rural areas, created after a great and prolonged struggle, have given rural dwellers their self-governance structures and a fair degree of empowerment. Further, it elaborates about the participatory involvement of citizens and accountability of local self-governance structures which are almost totally absent. Finally, the paper makes an attempt to comprehend the revolutionary changes brought about by the 73rd Amendment, where it suffers from some serious limitations and offers a charter for more formally recognised structures that could be organised on a wider scale.

Ruby Ojha in her paper on *Empowerment of Women through Participation in Local Government in Maharashtra*, discusses the power relations that shape social, political, economic and cultural life that prevent women from participating fully in all areas of their lives, whether it is in the home, or in the public arena. While women's dedicated efforts to challenge the status quo have allowed more women to reach positions of power in recent years, women continue to be under represented in all areas of decision-making and still face significant barriers to their full and equal participation in the structures and institutions which govern their lives. One of the strategies to empower women and to overcome barriers preventing her equal participation in decision-making process is to allow her to obtain political power. Politics still continues to be a male bastion where self-made women are the exceptions rather than the rule. There can be no true democracy, no true people's participation in governance and development without equal participation of women and men. The inadequate representation of women in decision-making bodies has been a historical reality in our society. These Amendments have helped women not only in their effective participation but also in decision-making in the grassroots democracy. Women have shown how well they adapt to roles in governance and decision-making and all evidences show that their performance often far outshines that of men, while their concerns remain close to the ground and focus on real, survival issues. The quota strategy is a beginning which has the potential to kick-start other processes of empowerment of women but which cannot by itself be the answer to gender inequality.

S. Satyam in his paper on *Dalit Women in Power Politics: A Study of Gram Panchayats in Telangana*, argues that research on the representation of women and their leadership has burgeoned in recent years, with considerable attention given to the links between the descriptive and the substantive. Many of these analyses focus on women's political performances as elected leaders, the constraints and opportunities they face in seeking to advance women-friendly positions. Yet, recent studies have reached to an understanding that women's place in politics has become narrow in quantity and abnormal in political opportunity. But issues on existing and emerging dalit women leadership from grassroots politics with a view of societal constraints and political marginalisation and their existing limited or constrained political choices, opportunities at the bottom level with specific glimpse from academic research point of view has not seen much, though the recent academic studies were put to focus. It is clear that studies were conducted on women in panchayati raj but not from deep-rooted socio-political issues of dalits in general and women of dalit background in specific. In such both widespread and deep-rooted gaps, this paper is an attempt on grassroots leadership of dalit women in the context of Panchayati Raj Institutions in Telangana. It finds that even though the panchayati raj system brought about visible changes in the condition of villages, especially women, still there exist institutional, social and psychological obstacles.

Gadadhara Mohapatra in his paper on *Women's Empowerment through Panchayati Raj Institutions: A Sociological Study of Odisha*, explains that the Panchayati Raj Institutions (PRIs), through 73rd Constitutional Amendment have been designed to empower the people at three appropriate levels. The Amendment provided institutional mechanism and was meant to rekindle the flame of self-governance. The most important aspect of the widening democratic decentralisation has been the reservation of seats for the women and dalits. Extending reservation to women in PRIs has certainly led to the increased participation of women in panchayats as elected members of PRIs taking part in decision-making, planning, implementation and evaluation. There is evidence to show that in many areas, women attempt to address the more vital needs of women. As such, they work on schemes for bringing piped water into the village, inspect development works and nutrition centres under the Integrated Child Development Services (ICDS) and pay particular attention to children's education. They also take the initiative in a variety of family and matrimonial matters, from abusive or alcoholic husbands to settling land disputes. However, certain constraints which stem from traditional village institutions and familial and socio-cultural forces still remain. Social constraints feature patriarchal ordering of society that leads to tokenism and surrogate representation; illiteracy which deprives women participation in decision-making; and low caste position combines the oppression of caste and patriarchy. It is in this context, the paper attempts to analyse the emerging patterns of women leadership and the empowerment aspects among the dalit and tribal groups in the state of Odisha in Eastern India.

Anuja in her paper on *Representation, Inclusion and Empowerment of Women through Panchayati Raj Institutions: Bihar Perspective*, argues that empowerment of women is becoming an increasingly popular term in human rights and development discourses. It enables to challenge the skewed distribution of power relations in a society. Although women constitute half of the population, they are subjugated unequal in socio-economic and political status. Indian democracy has entered the next century but a large mass of women are still kept out of political arena. Empowerment also demands political inclusion of decision-making and changes in the existing power relations. Political inclusion of women is only possible through effective representation as voters and participation in PRIs' election. Therefore, empowerment and political inclusion through representation are essentially related. The 73rd Amendment Act is a major step towards political empowerment of women through panchayati raj institutions. This has resulted in the entry of large number of women into decision-making bodies in the rural areas, who were otherwise home makers. But equality and rights for women have always been claimed as crucial components in state policy. When one takes an example of Bihar state, the status of women is lower in terms of all development indicators such as education, health, justice and, of course, governance. But since 2006, the state took an important step in the realm of PRIs in Bihar which introduced 50 per cent reservation for women and became the first state to do so. The paper is an attempt to highlight through secondary sources that whether representation and inclusion in the political field are the most important factors for empowerment of women. It also tries to explore the reasons for this through theoretical assumptions and explain whether such representation leads on to empowerment of women as a collective group. The paper also examines effects of the two decades of panchayati raj in India on women.

State Specific Experiences in Structure and Functions in PRIs

M. Gopinath Reddy in his paper on *Status of Devolution of the Funds, Functions and Functionaries in United Andhra Pradesh: Task Unfinished?* elaborates that it is nearly two decades since Andhra Pradesh (composite) passed its Conformity Act in 1994 based on the 73rd Constitutional Amendment Act passed by the Parliament. AP's Act included all the key features of the Central Act. In addition, the institution of District Planning Committees (DPC) has been constituted duly (although belated), even though their functioning was found out to be lack lustre. The devolution status of the 3 Fs (funds, functions and functionaries) which is the key for strengthening the local self-government, is far from satisfactory in the State of Andhra Pradesh till date. This paper addresses the devolution position regarding 3 Fs, the various reasons for such a scenario and the implication of such scenario on the development of local self-government at the grassroots level. The basic reason for this tardy devolution position is the quite indifferent attitude of the respective governments both under Telugu Desam Party and the subsequent Congress Party for the last two decades. On the contrary, AP had earned dubious distinction of promoting a parallel structure in the form of Watershed Committees, Forest Protection Committees, Education Committees, Parents Teachers Committees etc. This policy of strengthening parallel bodies was done at the cost of bypassing the panchayati raj bodies. The paper presents a chronology of devolution status in AP and its implications for the development and service delivery in the rural areas.

Smita Agarwal in her paper on *Accountability of Mukhiyas: Strengthening of Panchayats in Bihar*, explains that the 73rd Amendment Act heralded a new era in the decentralisation process of India. It tried to bridge distance between the ruler and ruled by bringing governance at the door step. An emphasis was added on the aspect of involving people, so that holistic development of the area could take place. Along with it, accountability of the elected representatives became an important issue. Despite all its visions, decentralisation process in India met with hiccups as the system evolved itself. A close study of panchayats in Bihar reveals that it has not been able to free itself from the shackles of nepotism and nexus of vote and beneficiaries. This stems from the complexity involved in the larger process of decentralisation initiated in India. This is because programmes that are implemented by the panchayats lack autonomy. They are decided by the other tier of governance of Indian federal structure. There is a lack of independence in the sources of revenues and also in terms of allocation of money for various development programmes. Largely, they are administered on the guidelines issued by centre or state government with the aim of fulfilling yearly targets. This kind of targeted and quota development creates its own dynamics of voters turned into beneficiaries of these programmes. As a result, performance or non-performance of a panchayat is based on its success or failure to negotiate with this dynamics. These findings are based on detailed study of two panchayats in Bihar where personal interviews with elected representatives and people along with government data were used as evidence to highlight the challenges and prospects for local governance in India.

Alaknanda Shringare in her paper on *Rhetoric of Participatory Development: An Analysis of Functioning of PRIs in Goa*, narrates that in recent years when most of the political institutions are coming under criticism for losing their credibility whether PRIs are able to deliver effectively is the question one needs to analyse and debate. With the passing of 73rd Amendment Act, panchayat raj institutions received constitutional recognition to act as agencies to ensure participatory development. Participation of people is considered to be significant for development planning. However, whether PRIs have served the required purpose of ensuring participatory development is debatable. Keeping in view the significant role of PRIs, the paper analyses the functioning of PRIs in Goa. In 2013, Goa celebrated 50 years of panchayati raj institutions. Even before the 73rd Amendment Act was passed, panchayats were functioning in Goa. The first panchayat election was held in 1962. Unlike in other parts of India there is a thin line of separation between urban and rural areas in most parts of Goa. However, in recent years, the Goan villages came under the garb of mega housing projects and other developmental programmes and projects. These developments claimed to have changed not only the demography of the land but also put pressure on available resources. They also questioned PRIs being the agencies of decentralised development as in most cases people in the villages criticised panchayats of passing these projects without the knowledge of the people. The recent developments clearly indicated lack of trust of people in PRIs as institutions of village development. Present paper is an attempt to critically analyse the functioning of PRIs as agencies of decentralised planning and examine how far PRIs in Goa succeeded in ensuring participatory development.

Jitendra Wasnik in his paper on *Maharashtra Model of Panchayati Raj: Changes and Challenges after the 73rd Constitutional Amendment Act*, depicts that Maharashtra is one of the most important states in our country having its own roots of democratic decentralisation formed on 1 May 1960. After the 73rd Constitutional Amendment, the Maharashtra state government made necessary changes in its existing Act of 1961 and the Bombay Village Panchayat Act 1958 in 1994; as well as adopted the recommendation of 73rd Constitutional Amendment. In spite of this, Maharashtra model of panchayati raj has its own distinguish features. Some of them are: powerful district unit; weak intermediate unit; organically integrated three-tier structures with two comprehensive Acts; wider representation to varied interests groups; no association of MPs and MLAs and separate administrative machinery etc. With all the pronounced claims about decentralisation and devolution of power and authority at grassroots, the attempt is not sufficient and needs certain basic thinking about how to translate these principles into practice. Despite all thoughtful provisions the experiences of panchayati raj institutions over a period of two decades are not very encouraging. The prejudices emanating from caste, religion and sex are quite deep rooted, which also create obstacles in the successful working of the PRIs on democratic basis. Therefore, this paper discusses the major changes made in the structure and challenges before these institutions as per the aspiration of the people to meet the goals of 73rd Constitutional Amendment Act.

Looking Ahead

The papers of the volume in nutshell have put forward the fact that the establishment of panchayat raj system in various states is indifference to the provision of the 73rd Constitution Amendment Act. The State Acts have been amended from time to time to make it more effective in establishing PRI as genuine structure of grassroots democracy. Through a system of reservation, participation of the weaker sections has also been ensured. The three tiers have been empowered significantly to enable them to discharge their duties properly and fulfil the expectations of the people. Through PRIs, representative democracy at the grassroots has gone to direct democracy but the fact remains that despite this endeavour there is a clear-cut gap between macro level decisions and grassroots reality (Sisodia, 2005). However, much needs to be done as yet. Gram sabhas are yet to perform their desired role in the panchayat raj system. While state legislatures provided for the establishment of gram sabha, the statutes remained vague about procedures and power, resulting in dysfunctional instructions (Mander, 1999). Reservation has provided an opportunity to all backward classes to come out and play a significant role but the process of political socialisation is slow among these classes. Acute poverty, illiteracy and predominant position of rural elite have incapacitated them in discharging their duties effectively. Panchayats, which are 'institutions of self-governance', cannot function in a society that is ridden with caste, feudalism and poverty. Therefore, PRIs should be made effective instruments of social transformation through a vibrant democratic political process at the local level (Mathew and Nayak, 1996). Women representation in panchayats is a matter of some satisfaction but their performance is poor as compared to other classes of the society. Women's empowerment through the panchayats requires a sustained campaign and vigorous efforts for creating awareness about their rights and duties (Datta, 1997). The bureaucracy has to be made more responsive to the needs of the PRIs. Greater financial autonomy must be provided to the panchayats. Better coordination has to be established among the three tiers of panchayat. Greater clarity of roles and tier-wise division of functions is essential. Of no less importance is optimal direct participation of people in the developmental process. The central problem that has dogged the establishment of truly autonomous local governance through effective devolution to PRIs is the reluctance of state governments to part with the powers of governance that they enjoy (Banerjee, 2013). To generate this, the crucial significance is of the principle of accountability and continual social auditing of the performance and transparency pertaining to administrative activities. A drastic reorganisation and redesigning of the political and administrative system at the state level is required to accommodate strong district and lower-level PRIs on the principle of subsidiarity. There has to be greater political pressure from the people at the grassroots. Concrete efforts should also be made to reduce governmental interference in the day-to-day functioning of local self-government bodies and the process of their dissolution needs to be made more politics proof. Such measures will go a long way in establishing the panchayats as 'Village Republics'.

References

Banerjee, Rahul (2013), 'What Ails Panchayati Raj?', *Economic and Political Weekly*, Vol. XLV, No. 38, September 18.

Behar, Amitabh (2001), 'Madhya Pradesh-Gram Swaraj: Experiment in Direct Democracy', *Economic and Political Weekly*, March 10.

Behar, Amitabh and Yogesh Kumar (2002), 'Decentralisation in Madhya Pradesh, India: From Panchayati Raj to Gram Swaraj (1995 to 2001)', *Working Paper 170*, ODI, London.

Datta, Prabhat (1997), 'Political Empowerment of Rural Women in India', *Administrative Change*, Vol. 24, No. 2, January-June.

Mander, Harsh (1999), 'Towards Direct Democracy: The Legal Empowerment of Gram Sabha', *Kurukshetra*, New Delhi, Vol. 48, No. 1, October.

Mathew, George and Ramesh C. Nayak (1996), 'Panchayat at Work: What It Means for the Oppressed?', *ISS Occasional Paper Series–19*, Institute of Social Sciences, New Delhi.

Robinson, Mark (2005), 'A Decade of Panchayati Raj Reforms: The Challenge of Democratic Decentralisation in India', in L.C. Jain (ed.), *Decentralisation and Local Governance*, Orient Longman, New Delhi.

Sisodia, Yatindra Singh (2005), 'A Decade of Panchayati Raj System in Madhya Pradesh', in Yatindra Singh Sisodia (ed.), *Functioning of Panchayat Raj System*, Rawat Publications, Jaipur.

UNDP (2000), *Decentralised Governance: A Global Matrix of Experiences*, United Nations Development Programme, New York.

World Bank (2000), *Overview of Rural Decentralisation in India*, Vol. III, Washington, D.C., p. 24.

Part – I

73rd Constitutional Amendment and Status of PRIs

2

Theoretical Nuances of Democratic Decentralisation in India

G. Palanithurai

Twenty years have gone by after the enactment of the 73rd Amendment to the Constitution of India to establish a decentralised democratic governance structure at the grassroots in India. It has been considered as a remarkable transformative initiative to achieve democratisation of the communities and inclusive development. There are many theoretical assumptions on democratic decentralisation of powers. One dominant assumption is that this transformation will happen in Indian society through a prolonged struggle by the stakeholders who are substantially gaining benefits through capturing power. Theory on struggle for transformation unequivocally argues that unless people are mobilised consciously and organised firmly, there will not be any struggle and as a consequence, there will not be any worthwhile transformation in the society. People who are going to lose grip over the governing institutions at the ground due to these historic amendments will make all efforts to demonstrate that this new arrangement will be a failure. People who have been in power so far and who are going to lose power in the new dispensation will create a new design and by which they will keep power with themselves. The dominant elites will capture power by using this new opportunities. Here it is to be understood that in India, decentralisation of power is a top-down exercise and not bottom up exercise. Yet the newly created institutions are put into action. A centralised drive is on for decentralisation. It is an important question as to what extent the centralised drive for decentralisation yielded results. The centralised drive cannot go beyond certain limits as local governance is the subject of the state governments. Keeping this in the backdrop it was incorporated in the 73rd and 74th Amendments to the Constitution of India that the state government will decide the design of the decentralisation of powers while operationalising the framework of the constitutional Amendments.

The initiatives of Indian decentralisation process start from middle tier of governance (state government) and not from the top tier of governance (central government). Conceptually, it is a weak design of decentralisation of powers. It is a top driven strategy to reduce the power of the state government and equally the state governments adopt a strategy to retain their powers with them by creating a lose governance mechanism at the grassroots to fulfil the constitutional requirements. By this process one can see a governance arrangement at the grassroots in form but not in content and substance. When federal government is not in a position to decentralise powers from its institution how does it expect that state government would devolve or decentralise powers to local bodies. More than three million representatives are in the governance structure at grassroots at present in the two decades the institutions are functioning and for which huge expenditure has been committed and spent. The moot question is what impact it has created in Indian society and economy more specifically in the rural area by its functioning. State governments have constituted committees to study the impact and how decentralisation of powers worked and what are all the barriers and impediments for the functioning of local bodies. Twenty years are sufficient methodologically to evaluate the functioning of any governance structure. Hence, an attempt is made to evaluate the process of decentralisation of powers in India. While doing so, focus will be given on the theoretical nuances evolved in the process based on the studies conducted in India by the scholars and institution abroad and in India.[1] Decentralised governance, democratisation of communities, development management, delivering social justice and public goods, participatory development and empowerment of the marginalised groups are the subjects being looked at in this research article. Analysis will be made on varied perspectives mostly domain perspectives used in the wide canvass of research in decentralisation. The covered ground is limited and the uncovered is vast. The study will indicate the major areas to be covered in the research projects by the research institutions in the years to come. It will also highlight the missing links in the research areas already covered. The methodological nuances that have emerged in the research process will also be highlighted in this work. Basically, it maps up the emerging trend in evolving theoretical nuances.

New Federalism

Before the enactment of the 73rd and 74th Amendments to the Constitution of India, Indian federalism was seen and analysed in the backdrop of the relationship between the centre and the states. Discourses were on in the relationship between the two governments. It covers political, financial and administrative relationship between the centre and the states. By adopting different theoretical frameworks the relationship between the centre and the states has been analysed. Now, there is a third layer in governance arrangement which is called as local government. The new dispensation has come to operation as an institution of governance. It is not an implementing agency. It is incorporated in the constitution and it has got permanency. Hence, naturally a new discourse has to emerge and in which the relationship between centre and the state, and state and local has to be the focal points. In reality, the local governments are left to the discretion of the state governments but in practice they are to be developed in the backdrop of the framework given through the two historic amendments to the Constitution of India. Though the framework assures the institutional stability and sustenance, the design of the institution for governance at local level has been left to the discretion of the state government. There is a reason behind this discretion. Local bodies are in the state list as per the Constitution of India. State governments can evolve a design which is suitable to the requirements of the state, not to the requirements of the centre. There is no dispute over the design of the local government as envisaged by the state government. The concern here is to what extent the state governments are serious in designing local governments to deliver goods and services effectively and efficiently to the people. No doubt it is a top down initiative. There is no demand from the society for devolution of powers. Of course pressure has been exerted by the public on the governments for effective delivery of services and goods. Since it is a top town approach it is always being looked at by the state governments with suspicion. When the same amendments were introduced in Indian Parliament during Rajiv Gandhi's tenure as Prime Minister, they were defeated and the political parties which were committed on local government had opposed the amendments for creation of new local governments. Local governments have been created constitutionally. But the local governments have not been integrated in the system of governance as the other two governments are in a different footing and they do not have appropriate space to buckle the local bodies. While creating governments at the dawn of independence, clear responsibilities have been fixed between the central government and the state governments by creating lists (Central list, State list and Concurrent list). But, for the local governments, such list has not been created and instead 11th and 12th schedules have been incorporated. There is yet another argument for this arrangement. Centre and state governments are having the powers to enact legislations but local governments cannot enact legislation as there is no legislative body in local government. There is argument that it cannot be called as government. Local bodies are institutional mechanism to deliver goods and services. For the supply of goods and services, there is no ideological involvement.

There is yet another argument developed in India to project that local governments are delivery units of both central and state governments' development programmes and schemes for the people. So, they are mere implementing agencies of the state and centre governments. If the above argument is accepted, one has to question the role of District Planning Committee. In this context one has to remember the discussion on the same subject in the US. It was being discussed at every level about the role of federal government in designing the local government in the backdrop of the theory on federalism.[2]

Service Delivery

There are certain services to be delivered by the local bodies which are being mandated by the state Acts. No doubt one of the drawbacks of decentralisation is losing advantage of scale of operation. In the last twenty years certain services are delivered by the local bodies. To what extent services are effectively and efficiently delivered, whether the quality of service has been improved and to the level of satisfaction of the users, and whether the cost of services has been increased or reduced are the major questions to be investigated. It is necessary to compare interstate variations in terms of service delivery and the relationship between the capacity of the institutions and efficiency and quality in service delivery. It is imperative to test the theoretical propositions on service delivery by the local institutions. There are studies in India on this aspect. They are mostly location specific or state specific and they are not reflecting the scenario of service delivery in India. One important specific study covering seventeen states has been done by National Council of Applied and Economic Research (NCAER) with a huge funding of International Development Research Centre (IDRC) Canada. Now the report has been published.[3] From the conclusions, observations and interpretation a lot more studies can be conducted and the propositions evolved in the above study can be tested.

Representation vs Participation

Arguments have been projected that creating a constitutionally mandated local governments with Gram Sabha as a basic unit for people participation, an impression has been created that the character of our democracy will be changed from representative democracy to representative and participatory democracy. It has always been a myth that a limited representative democracy will enable a full fledged participatory democracy.

It is to be noted here that the representative democracy practised in India is confined only to a minimal democracy. Conducting periodical election, allowing the winners to take charge of governance and conducting the legislative institutions periodically are the minimum of functions of democracy carried out in India. Beyond that it has not moved and expanded. Even the minimal democracy has got severe limitations. Further, the social conditions are antithetical to democracy. The prevailing social hierarchy, feudal mindset, absence of social equality, patriarchical tendencies have contributed much for the ailment of Indian democracy. The representative democracy has not transformed the Indian society to practise social democracy. Now this responsibility has been shifted to the local bodies. Against this background, how a participatory democracy integrates into the representative democratic system and how it emerges has to be analysed and identify the new characteristic features of the new form of governance. As representative democracy, it exists in form, the participatory democracy also exists in form and not in behaviour. To create a participatory culture, enabling environment has to be created and otherwise it is only a ritual and symbol. Declining trend in representative democracy contributes for decline of participatory democracy also. There is always a close relationship between representative democracy and participatory democracy. These are the areas to be covered in the years to come in decentralisation studies.

Power Transfer and its Implications

The 73rd and 74th Amendments to the Constitution of India, essentially imply transfer of power from the dominant class to the oppressed and from men to women. Apart from this, it is a power transfer from bureaucracy to the people.

The whole design of devolution is with an objective of dismantling the power brokers. It aims to democratise the undemocratic society. Essentially it is a democratisation process. In the governance structure power brokers are so strong. To dismantle the whole edifice of the power broker structure a mass movement is needed.[4] In the absence of a popular movement, state will is necessary as it was exhibited by Kerala. In the absence of both public movement and will of the state, how power devolution will take place is a question to be investigated. It is unequivocal that possibilities are very high for the effective functioning of local bodies and yet local bodies are not given due importance, powers, functions, resources and functionaries. It is also proved that wherever powers are given to local bodies, they have created an everlasting impact.[5] Constitution grants equality but community and society rejects the constitutional sanctions through its behaviour and attitude. But, it is a major question whether the people, those who are going to get benefit out of the constitutional sanction are mobilised and sensitised to wage a relentless struggle to get their dues. Kerala is known for its struggle for social transformation and has taken steps to push this constitutional provision of decentralisation through its big bang approach.[6]

Lukewarm Attitude of the Federal Government

It has been argued that the central government is interested in strengthening local bodies by weakening the state government. Reality is that the central government is not firm in strengthening the Panchayati Raj system in India. If the central government is really interested in strengthening Panchayati Raj it will strengthen first the state government by devolving more powers to state government and thereby, it could direct the state government to devolve powers to Panchayats and thereby it will strengthen the local bodies. Reality is quiet opposite to the above argument. Central government's attitude towards the local bodies could be easily traced from its own activities towards local governance. The central government had introduced a plethora of development schemes with huge quantum of money allocated for them. But the role of local bodies in implementing the centrally sponsored schemes and programmes is very minimum. Had the central government taken initiatives to integrate the schemes with panchayats, by this time local governance mechanism would have been strengthened beyond anybody's imagination? The Ministry of Panchayati Raj, Government of India has been always limping. In such a way it has been created. The second Administrative Reform Commission through its report on local governance made certain detailed, operationable recommendations to both the central and state governments. Not even a single Ministry in the Government of India has agreed to the recommendations or taken earnest effort to implement the recommendations. Against this background how can the central government ask the state governments to devolve more powers to the panchayats? It is an irony that the amendment was passed by the Congress ministry and the same government led by the Congress party under the banner of UPA I and II has not made honest attempt in this regard. With great difficulty the Panchayati Raj Ministry persuaded the Rural Development Ministry to incorporate the Panchayats as the main agency to implement the Mahatma Gandhi

National Rural Employment Guarantee Scheme. Beyond this there was no significant move.

Issues in Conceptual Clarity

From the passage of the 73rd and 74th Amendments to the Constitution of India till date there is no clarity on the conceptual issues pertinent to the establishment of local governance institutions at the grassroots. Decentralisation, devolution and deconcentration are the concepts used interchangeably to refer to the new local body system in India. Devolution is totally different as it refers to transfer of power and authority from higher level of decision-making body to lower unit of decision-making body which is nearer to the people and the community. It further reiterates that the lower level units should have adequate powers, finance and functionaries to decide things at the level where they are. They should not be regulated or monitored or supervised or directed from above. The lower level units should have autonomy for their functions as other two governments. By keeping the above explanation and definition, analysis has been made as to what extent powers have been transferred and how they are transferred. As a result, they have concluded that devolution does not take place. There is yet another analysis, to what extent decentralisation of power took place in India? Decentralisation refers to transfer of power from highest decision-making bodies to the lowest unit of governance and administration. It is around administrative decentralisation. Even in decentralisation there should not be much regulation from the above. In the world, power transfer takes place in different forms in tune with the local requirement and ethos.[7] Focused attention is needed in research to bring clarity on the range of concepts based on the experience of the functioning of the local bodies in the backdrop of the two constitutional amendments.[8]

Law of Subsidiarity

Law of subsidiarity means that things that could be done at the lowest level could be allowed to be done at that level and things that could not be done at that level should be allowed to be done at the next higher level. In this order, activities have to be done in the governance orbit from the lowest unit to highest unit of governance. It needs extreme clarity to demarcate the powers, functions, roles and responsibilities to be discharged by the units of governance from the lowest unit Gram Sabha to Lok Sabha and Rajya Sabha. It is necessary here that to what extent clarity was brought in among the three-tier rural governance arrangement through activity mapping. For example, agriculture is a subject dealt with the Union Ministry, State Ministry and local government. In local government there are three tiers. How activities are divided among the three tiers have to be explained with clarity for governance and administration. By doing so, the complicated governance issues can be simplified and in fact it will help ordinary citizens to understand governance. The operationalisation of law of subsidiarity has to be analysed.[9]

Humanising the State

When decentralisation of powers was in full discourse in Indian politics, there was an argument projected from the left that it is also a plan of the World Bank to make the state to relinquish certain basic responsibilities. It should be in the name of giving power, communities are asked to take responsibility for their life and livelihood through panchayats. State is relieving itself from certain major responsibilities. A counter argument was projected by a section of the scholars that it is not reducing responsibilities of the state and instead it expands the role of the state in the sense that the whole process is humanising the state by involving the stakeholders in the process of governance and development. The state governments have got one more support agency for effective delivery of services and by which an organic linkage with the community is established. Hence, it is only the expansion of state and humanising state machinery for development.

Deliberative Democracy

In order to orient and train our communities in democratic practices, Gram Sabha has been created constitutionally where every adult has to participate in the process of decision-making on the issues affecting their life. This decision-making is based on the deliberation of the members of Gram Sabha. The deliberative process is the soul of grassroots democracy. It is not a number game. Decisions have to be taken on the basis of the deliberations. Decisions are taken on the basis of consensus evolved over deliberations. It is not based on numbers. Deliberative process has to lead the community to fairness, justice and truth. It is fairness, and logic should be the basis and not majority for decision-making process. It is a time consuming process and yet it brings maturity, understanding and equipoise. This process has to lead the community to respect the dissent voice. Respecting the dissent voice is the hallmark of democracy. Ultimately it has to lead the community to reach the highest level of tolerance. All the above cannot be achieved without a thorough preparation of the communities. It needs proper training and orientation. People have to be oriented to discuss, deliberate, debate and discourse on issues affecting their life. People have to be oriented to raise issues and discuss on all the issues from the perspective of inclusiveness and more specifically inclusiveness of the last rung of the society. Gram Sabha is capacity building[10] and it is a place where information has to be disseminated, is a place where logical debate on issues has to be developed, and is a place where discourse has to take place on matters pertinent to development. It needs a sober leader to enable the members of the community to participate. It needs rules for debate, discourse and discussion. As in Parliament and Legislature, guidelines have to be prepared to have a meaningful debate, discourse and discussion in Gram Sabha meetings. It should not be a crowd management but it should be a joyful and passionate exercise in which everybody has to participate in discourse both as speaker and listener. Both are participants. Apart from the above, a conducive environment has to be created for passionate discourse or debate on issues which will lead to decision-making.[11] How enabling environment was created in different states over two decades of deliberative democracy has to be analysed.

Beneficiary vs Citizens and Stakeholders

Since independence, both centre and state governments in the name of development have taken responsibility and proliferated development schemes and programmes. As per the reasonable estimate of the World Bank, it was more than 2,000 development schemes evolved and implemented over a period of time. Even at present in Tamil Nadu one can see 369 development schemes operated through 37 agencies both government departments and civil society organisations.[12] As a result, government departments and employees have been increased in their strength. The services are delivered through their schemes. People have been classified as beneficiaries according to the criteria fixed for each and every scheme. Since this practice has been continued for long in our development practice, people have been made to relinquish their responsibilities. Subtly, poor are disempowered and their dignity is at stake as they have been branded as beneficiaries. Even the benefits have been distributed through politicians and bureaucrats. Now through the creation of local governments, it is reiterated that people should be the stakeholders and they should have responsibilities. By taking up responsibilities, people become active social citizens and take responsibilities to get works done through the departments of the governments. Because of the new local government, whether the beneficiary syndrome has been changed to active citizenry, has to be probed. Citizenship building is yet another key responsibilities of the local governments. This will enable the citizens to participate in common social transformation.[13]

Transformative Process

When representatives are elected to the local bodies, they have to equip themselves to perform their duties and responsibilities. It is to be noted here that the federal government and state governments have created this new local body system with an understanding that the existing problems at the ground cannot be addressed without a responsible, responsive and representative governance and administrative arrangement at the grassroots. The task and its volume are huge and it requires enormous skill, capacity and capability to attend to them. Unless their skill, capacity and capability are enhanced, the delivery of services would be poor. Hence, the elected representatives both men and women have to be oriented to be leaders. It is not an auto process of transforming the elected representatives as leaders. Individuals become leaders after a long process of orienting themselves formally and informally in the institutional and field setting. They build the skill, capacity and capability consciously in the process of learning by doing. They are not ordinary individuals. They should become transformative leaders. In order to bring such transformative leaders, we need more of leadership schools and not training institutions. If they become transformative leaders, they will make the panchayat as peoples panchayat and development will be the perspective for them. Basically the local bodies have to do only the development functions. Hence, there is no ideology or party politics involved in the process. It is a space only for development. Hence, development should be the perspective. To orient the elected representatives as transformative leaders, it requires enormous preparation on the part of the leadership schools. This issue has to be seen in a context and a culture. We are a largest, popular and populous democracy with distinct characteristics. We have around 7,000 elected representatives both in Parliament and State Legislatures. Till date we do not have training institutions to training our Members of

Parliament and Members of state Legislative Assemblies. We do not have any training policy or framework. In our budget, there is no allocation of resources for training our representatives. Nobody is at a higher level is conscious of such issues of orienting our legislators to enhance their skill and capability. It is a culture in which our representative democracy is rooted and as a result we could not find any innovation in our parliamentary democracy. Instead of innovation and improvement, degradation sets in our representative form of government. Researchers started lamenting on the decline of parliamentary democracy in India. In this culture we develop local democracy. It has to be nurtured and cultured. But there is no policy perspective on this issue of building the capability of the elected representatives of the people. It needs a solid work. It is in the area of leadership and that too on transformative leadership.[14]

Accountability and Responsiveness

So far, communities found that they were not able to fix accountability and responsibility on the part of the state and central governments for their services to the people through their institutional mechanism namely the departments. Both governments have accepted the failures in ensuring accountability and responsiveness. Accountability is nothing but answerability. For the activities carried out by the government departments, they are responsible for the outcome and the consequences created through the actions. Benefit receivers have powers to fix responsibility on the benefit providers. It is nothing but taking ownership of the activities. Equally, the responsiveness of the institutions which are involved in delivery of services and goods, assumes significance as both the federal and state governments far away from the people, ensuring both are difficult. When governance mechanism is created at the doorsteps of the communities, it is easier for the people to fix responsibility, responsiveness and accountability on the part of the local governments. At the grassroots, accountability system has not been developed in the light of the basic objectives of decentralisation of powers. At present the accountability system works for the grant giver or resource giving agency. This system of accountability has to be turned towards the stakeholders or citizens. This accountability is downward accountability system. This is yet another area to be investigated.

Constitutional Provision vs Community Practices

When power goes down to the community level, one could see the interaction between the constitutional provisions and community practices. Whenever the communities are in the transformative process firstly, the communities allow the constitutional provisions to act without any resistance. As a result, community will witness delivery of services. This is not the case in all the places. There are places where communities are rigid and not having access to transformative process where one will find an intense conflict between the constitutional provisions and community practices.[15] All constitutional sanctions will be resisted by the communities. As a result, the panchayats are always in conflict with traditional panchayats and not in the path of development. The state governments are facing and tackling those issues in its own perspective. In order to create an enabling environment to have a democratic culture at the grassroots, people have to be mobilised by the state. Social mobilisation has to be done with the active involvement of the state, as state is the drive engine of development. The state has to involve the civil society organisations and media for such a transformative work. Unless state adopts the big bang approach the task is very difficult. Kerala is the best model in this regard. Socio-political movements have to be used for this purpose. How these problems are to be sorted out in India is a question to be seen. This is yet another area for research in future.

Social Justice and Gender Justice

Of the three governments, local government is inclusive as it has got representatives in adequate number to bring transformation in the society. Reservation of seats for SC and ST proportionate to their population and reservation of seats for women not less than one-third of total seats in all positions of local bodies are revolutionary steps from the perspective of social justice and gender justice. It is a matter to be investigated to what extent the presence of women and Dalits in local bodies has changed the nature and course of governance at grassroots.[16] How social justice and gender justice issues are dealt with in the decision-making process in local governance has to be researched. It is a well known fact that Indian society being a hierarchical one which denies social justice and being a patriarchical one which denies gender justice, has to face volley of problems when these issues are taken up in local governance because of the presence of critical mass of the elected representatives from Dalits and women. Where is local governance on social justice and gender justice at present?[17]

State Local Body Relations

In the federal governance arrangement focus was always given to centre and state relations. After the establishment of local bodies constitutionally struggle is on for appropriate powers, finance, functions, functionaries, freedom and facilitation from the state government. Local bodies are functionally linked with the state governments. Hence, the local bodies expect support from the state governments even though substantial resources are coming from the central government for development activities at the ground. In the absence of the above strategies have been evolved by the elected representatives of local bodies to form a forum or an association to exert pressure on the state government to facilitate them to empower the local bodies.[18] How local bodies are treated and facilitated to function as institutions of governance and administration is a major subject of debate and discourse. It is not focused so far. This is a major area of concern in academic research but a neglected area.

Decentralisation not Defined

It is an argument for a long in Indian politics that the state governments are not having adequate powers to deal with issues as state government faces the wrath of the people. Many of the regional parties made it a major issue for debate and discourse. There are commissions and their reports on this issue for more powers to state governments. In the meanwhile, powers have been taken away from the states by the centre. For development grants the states have to rely on the federal government as state governments have revenue to manage only the state government machinery and not for development. Only a few governments are having adequate resources to manage their development programmes. Having understood the resource conditions of the state governments, the central government treats the state governments as it likes. In such a way, relationship between the centre and the state governments has been developed. In this context, decentralisation of powers has been thought of and it refers to transfer of power from the highest policy making and decision-making body to lowest decision-making body. But in India, it is argued that powers have to be devolved from the state government to local government and not from the centre to state government. In the absence of transfer of power from the centre to state, how can one expect power from the state government to local government. There is no meaningful debate and discourse on this subject, either in political platform or in academic domain. It needs a meaningful debate in the academic domain. It is a known fact that Indian federal government has got enormous powers and powers are concentrated at the centre. The above issue needs intense debate. Hence, state governments design a structure of local governance in such a way that it acts as an agent of the state government to implement its decisions, schemes and programmes. Everywhere, decentralisation is explained from power from the topmost decision-making body to the lowest unit of government. But only in India it is defined ambiguously or partially defined.

People's Preference and Local Needs

It is an assumption that when local governance mechanism is created very near to the community, preference of the local people on the goods and services will be considered and acted upon.[19] The service providers and the agencies both governmental and non-governmental will work on the needs of the communities. While articulating the need there will be competition among the groups within the area as preference and needs are not uniform. How harmonisation is being done among the competing groups over the expression of local needs. Further, the federal and state governments have proliferated more number of schemes and programmes and left very little space for local bodies to work on the preference. In this context, the resources available with the local bodies are limited and powers with them are also limited and in this backdrop how local needs are fulfilled and people's preferences are being met is to be probed.

Rural Urban Continuum

In India, local bodies are being perceived as rural and urban distinctively, as a mechanism to deal with issues of development separately. In reality, the rural urban issues are mostly emanating from the rural urban migration nexus. The fast urbanisation process due to economic globalisation triggers migration which brings plethora of problems to urban governance. Equally, the consumeristic culture coupled with fast urbanisation of rural areas brings whole lot of problems to rural governance also. Unless they are approached in an integrated fashion, there will not be any solution to the growing problems in the rural and urban areas. It needs only one local governance arrangement. It is to be analysed whether the life of the people in the rural areas is seen with proper perspective, as rural areas are being exploited right from the colonial days to the present. Unless the issue of rural reality is seen from a proper perspective further exploitation will continue. Hence, rural local governance is not only to deliver services but also to protect the people and the resources in the rural areas.

Participation Denied

When an opportunity is being given to the rustic folks in the rural areas to participate in the decision-making process, why is it not being given to the people in the urban areas even though they also have local bodies. Even in larger rural local bodies, instead of Gram Sabha, ward sabhas have been created. In the same way, ward sabhas can be formed for urban areas also. Unless ward sabhas are created for urban local bodies participation has no meaning and inclusive development has no meaning, because the ultra poor from the rural areas have migrated to urban areas for want of livelihood. They are on the roads and below the shades of bridges and trees. They do not have any basic facilities to lead a decent life. They do not have any channel to communicate their demands to the government. They are allowed to live there as their services are required but they are not being provided with minimum basic facilities. They do not have a forum to articulate their grievances.[20] Against this background it is being mooted that there should be a forum in different wards of the municipalities and different regions of the corporations to hear the views, opinion, demands and preference of the local people. Appropriate design has to be created in the urban areas to elicit the participation of people in the decision-making process.

Where is the Planning?

In India, there are three planning institutions, namely Central Planning Commission (now functioning) and State Planning Boards or Commissions and District Planning Committees. Of the three planning bodies, only the District Planning Committee is created through the Constitution of India. Yet the other two planning boards are powerful and they have huge machinery at their disposal, whereas the District Planning Committee do not have adequate planning machinery (exception in Kerala). The District Planning Committee's mandatory function is to evolve a plan for the whole district by adopting a participatory approach. Till date, planning at the bottom with the participation of people was not taking place barring the state of Kerala. It is a mandatory exercise which has to be done by the District Planning Committee. There is no question or debate over the neglect of micro plan from below even though it is mandated constitutionally. Why nobody bothers about this micro plan? It is strange to note that nobody has gone to the courts get a direction from the court to initiate the planning process at the grassroots. There is yet another argument that micro level planning will be effective and efficient only when adequate resources are devolved to local bodies. In the absence of resource allocation, planning exercise is only a preparation of wish list.[21]

Reduction of Corruption

In the rural development sector corruption became a key issue which prompted Rajiv Gandhi to make an open statement that when Delhi sends one rupee while it goes to the village, it becomes only fifteen paise. This became a subject for debate and discourse for a long period. To find answer to this malady, local governance institution was considered as remedy which will reduce corruption. There are arguments for both increasing number of people involved in corruption and decreasing the amount of corruption due to local governance arrangement. In Kerala, there are studies which portray the role of the local bodies in reducing corruption. There are national studies on Mahatma Gandhi National Rural Employment Guarantee Act (MGNREGA), which portray the role of local bodies in increasing corruption. There is no clarity on which aspect triggers corruption and which reduces corruption at grassroots level.[22]

Public Action

The new local bodies have created certain institutional arrangement for mobilising people for public action. Gram Sabha and other committees are institutional mechanism to bridge the information gap between the people and the government. The right to information has provided yet another strength to local bodies to demand information from the central and state governments' departments to feed the people. This continuous mobilisation of people for Gram Sabha meeting and continuous engagement of Gram Sabha members in the Gram Sabha meeting by providing needed information about development activities which are being initiated by the departments of government through their schemes and programmes will empower them and make them more responsible to take responsibility for their life. Gram Sabha and the other committees can conduct social audit also. In this process, government Departments can be made accountable to the people. It requires only understanding. If the local body leaders have leadership qualities, by using the powers given to Gram Sabha and the committees people can be mobilised and social audit could be done. Local body performance depends on active citizenry. Active citizenry can be created only through a process of continuous social mobilisation.[23] It is a culture in Indian society that leaders never want participation as it will empower the people to question the leaders if they drift away from the main process. Hence, they want to keep the citizens away from the governance orbit. It is an area to be investigated.

Leader Centric or People Centric

The 73rd Amendment to the Constitution of India unequivocally argues for empowerment of people. It is power to the people but that power goes to people through Panchayats. In reality, power stops with panchayats. Even in panchayat, power rests with panchayat leader. The whole functioning of panchayat is centering around Panchayat leader. That is why arguments have been projected that our Panchayats are leader centric and not people centric. Normally, democracy enables only collegial governance, not individual governance. Collective decision-making is designed but while functioning they are always relying on the leader, as society is feudal and hierarchical. Why in Indian democracy whether it is in central government or in state government or in local government an individual gets supremacy rather than the group.

Decency in Governance

We have three layers of governance. First layer is local government. Second one is state government and the third one is federal government. All the three governments have got the earmarked roles and responsibilities constitutionally delineated. Everyone is important in his or her domain of activities. No one is superior or inferior. Everyone is working for the people. But in reality, everyone is trying to establish superiority over the other. Of the representatives, local body leaders are the most affected as they are not respected either by the MLAs and MPs or the bureaucrats unless their socio-economic background is sound. As if they are working under central government, state government and the bureaucracies and by which decency of governance is the casuality. Decency of a government can be accessed on the basis of the respect given to the citizens when they come to government office to get some assistance. Central government and state government Departments treat the ordinary poor citizens as beneficiaries as if their life and livelihood are depending on the assistance given by them. In such a way poor men and women are deprived of their dignity. In India, decency in governance happens only in local bodies.[24]

Structuring of Government

Mere passing of the confirmative legislation and operationalising the Act by passing government orders is not enough. It has to go through series of steps by designing and structuring the local government. Of the three-tier structure functions, finance and functionaries have to be clearly demarcated. Functional freedom has to be ensured instead of establishing control over them. Framework of devolution has to be in place for bringing clarity. Formula has to be evolved for devolution of funds. Designing of the structure will be more important for effective functioning of the local bodies. It is to be understood here that in the name of structuring government at grassroots, steps should not be taken to proliferate rules and regulations. It should be a simple structure and less rules and regulations. Governance and administration has to be simplified. The existing gap between the government and the people is due to complicated and complex process of governance. This has to be changed. The whole process has to be made people friendly. It should be understandable and operationable to the ordinary citizen.

Conclusion

Old theories argue that decentralisation of powers will be very effective in creating impact on the society if land reforms are done, presence of the active middle class in the society, higher literacy rate in the areas, presence of a neutral media and active civil society. All the above factors are imperative for effective functioning of local bodies to make expected impact. All the factors are not present in all the provinces. A few factors may be present and a few may be absent and in this context what impact have local bodies created in the society at present. All the larger and extensive studies that covered the whole country though limited concluded that despite limitations, weaknesses, barriers and obstacles, the local bodies have delivered services and goods. It is also demonstrated that in India all the factors which are necessary for the success of local bodies are present yet the state governments are not devolving powers adequate to the local bodies. But in the new context it has to be seen in the backdrop of centre-state relationship, new federalism, fiscal federalism, law of subsidiarity, deliberative democracy, humanising the state, democratisation of communities, how local bodies conducted themselves and delivered goods and services. Only government documents are available with wider coverage. There are other studies funded by IDRC and World Bank which looked at from the perspective of service delivery. It is high time to evaluate the performance of the local bodies and they are to be done from the perspective of governance, empowerment and service delivery. At present, available studies are very limited for covering the entire country. These stats-specific studies will not reflect the trend in India. It is high time to form research consortium among the scholars and conduct studies on the areas discussed in this paper and discuss the theoretical aspects on those areas studied.

Notes

1. Government of India, *State of Panchayati Raj Report 2008–2009*, New Delhi: Ministry of Panchayati Raj, 2010; George Mathew (ed.), *Status of Panchayati Raj in the States and Union Territories of India 2013*, New Delhi: Concept Publishing Company, 2014.
2. Neal R. Peirce, 'The State of American Federalism', *Civic Review*, January 1980, p. 32; James Macgregor Burns, J.W. Peltason and Thomas E. Cronin, *State and Local Politics: Government by the People*, New Jersey: Prentice-Hall Inc, 1984.
3. Hari K. Nagarajan, Mads P. Bisnuwanger-Mkhize and S.S. Meenakshisundaram, *Decentralization and Empowerment for Rural Development*, New Delhi: Foundation Books, 2015.
4. George Mathew, *Panchayati Raj from Legislation to Movement*, New Delhi: Concept Publishing Company, 1994; Jayaprakash Narayan's Presidential Speech in All India Panchayat Parishad, National Conference Speech in Bangalore. Details can be seen in All India Panchayat Parishad, *Panchayati Raj: Perspectives and Programmes*, New Delhi: All India Panchayat Parishad, 1964.
5. James Manor, 'Local Governance', in Niraja Gopal Jayal and Bhanu Mehta (eds), *The Oxford Companion to Politics in India*, New Delhi: Oxford University Press, 2010.
6. S.M. Vijayanand, *Kerala: A Case Study of Classical Democratic Decentralisation of India*, Thrissur, Kerala: Kerala Institute of Local Administration, 2009.
7. James Manor, *The Political Economy of Democratic Decentralisation*, Washington, D.C.: The World Bank, 1999.
8. Manishankar Committee report deals with this issue see, *Towards Holistic Panchayati Raj*, New Delhi: Ministry of Panchayati Raj, 2013.
9. Anwar Shah, 'Fiscal Decentralisation in Developing and Transition Economies: An Overview', in L.C. Jain (ed.), *Decentralisation and Local Governance*, New Delhi: Orient Longman, 2005, p. 172.
10. Niraja Gopal Jayal, Amit Prakash and Pradeep K. Sharma (eds), *Local Governance in India: Decentralisation and Beyond*, New Delhi: Oxford University Press, 2006.

11. G. Palanithurai (ed.), *Deliberative Democracy: Functioning of Gram Sabha in South Indian States*, New Delhi: MJP Publications, 2015.
12. G. Palanithurai, *Three Tier Panchayati Raj System in Tamil Nadu: Acts, Rules, Schemes* (in Tamil), Chennai: South Vision, 2006.
13. John Gaventa and Rosemary Mcgee (eds), *Citizen Action and National Policy Reform*, London: Zed Books, 2010.
14. B.M. Bass and R.E. Riggo, *Transformational Leadership*, New Jersey: Lawrence Erlbaun, 2006.
15. Kripa Ananth Pur, 'Selection by Custom and Election by Statute: Interfaces in Local Governance in Karnataka', in Niraja Gopal Jayal, Amit Prakash and Pradeep K. Sharma (eds), *Local Governance in India: Decentralisation and Beyond*, New Delhi: Oxford University Press, 2006, pp. 27–46.
16. G. Palanithurai, *Evaluation of Process and Performance of Gram Panchayat Women and Dalit Presidents in Tamil Nadu*, New Delhi: Concept Publishing Company, 2003; Government of India, *Study on Elected Women Representatives in Panchayati Raj Institutions*, New Delhi: Ministry of Panchayati Raj, 2008.
17. G. Palanithurai, *Status of Dalits and Dalit Representatives in Rural Local Bodies*, New Delhi: Concept Publishing Company, 2013.
18. G. Palanithurai, *Federating Elected Women Representatives in India*, New Delhi: Concept Publishing Company, 2014.
19. Pranab Bardhan and Dilip Mookherjee (eds), *Decentralisation and Local Governance in Developing Countries*, New Delhi: Oxford University Press, 2007, p. 4.
20. Arvind Kejriwal, *Swaraj*, New Delhi: Harper Collins Publishers India, 2012, p. 139.
21. G. Palanithurai (ed.), *Dynamics of New Panchayati Raj System*, Vol. V, New Delhi: Concept Publishing Company, 2006.
22. N. Narayanasamy, M.P. Boraiyan and M.A. Jayaraju (eds), *Corruption at Grassroots: The Shades and Shadows*, New Delhi: Concept Publishing Company, 2000.
23. D. Dalton, *Building National Campaign: Activists, Alliances and How Change Happens*, Oxford: Oxfam, 2007.
24. S.M. Vijayanand, Keynote address in the International Conference on Gandhi, Gram Swaraj and Democratic Decentralisation on 27 November 2014.

3

Two Decades of Democratic Decentralisation in India

Some Reflections

S.K. Singh

In the changing global scenario, development paradigms require decentralised local government system to stimulate democracy, improve efficiency through people's involvement, communicate civic voice in governance and increase empowerment. Present local governments play a dynamic role in preserving the social fabric, effectively addressing local interests and placing checks on operations at higher levels of authority. Thus, democratic decentralisation and involvement of people in decision-making has been an important thrust in the development discourse and many countries have opted for it from 1980s onwards using diverse systems, so is the case with India.[1] The 73rd and 74th Constitution Amendment Acts, 1992 marked a watershed in the history of democratic governance in the country. The Panchayati Raj Institutions (PRIs) were introduced in rural areas as a distinct third tier of the government to realise the progressive intent of national policy and to strengthen local democracy.

Historically, local self-governments have had a long and esteemed institutional set-up in India. It is not a new phenomenon, rather it has deep roots. Democratic decentralisation is an affirmed national policy for governance and was verbalised by giving it the constitutional status in 1992. The reforms intended panchayats as a constitutional body that will be a vehicle to deliver services and respond to local needs and diversity. They will establish and maintain responsive, transparent and accountable government and accelerate the democratic process. In addition, they are at an appropriate level for effective government intervention to provide social welfare measures and to stimulate economic efficiency.[2]

General Accomplishments and Status

As a sequel to the 73rd Constitution Amendment, all States and Union Territories to which Part IX applies have enacted Conformity Act (CA) within the stipulated period and mandatory provisions were incorporated. The new dispensation of panchayat has completed two decades of journey started from 1993 and four rounds of regular elections in most states (in abeyance in Andhra Pradesh and Puducherry). The State Finance Commissions were constituted and five-year recommendations also made. Three Union Finance Commissions (11th 2000–05; 12th 2005–10; and 13th 2010–15) emphasised on local government finances, allocated grants and suggested several measures to strengthen their financial position. As per the provision of Article 243 SD of the 74th Constitutional Amendment, the District Planning Committees have also been established, by and large. However, as it appears at the operational level, panchayats have been encumbered with several problems. Their functioning in several states have been impeded due to various reasons such as structural pattern, composition, organic linkages among different tiers, electoral process, concept of rotation for reserved seats, devolution of powers and function, bureaucratic control, etc.[3] It is therefore, useful to analyse some of the legal issues encompassing the implementation of the Act and suggest suitable measures to revitalise and make them vibrant. Nevertheless, it is appropriate to examine the status.

Considering the importance of the subject and to take panchayats forward during this period, several high-level committees were constituted to examine various issues. A few important reports dealing with panchayats are: Task Force Report, 2001, Planning Commission and Ministry of Rural Development; the report of the National Commission to Review the Working of the Constitution, 2002; Second Administrative Commission Report, 2007; and Expert Committee on Leveraging Panchayats for Efficient Delivery of Public Goods and Services, 2013.

In addition, a separate Ministry of Panchayati Raj (MoPR) was created to take the panchayats forward. The MoPR arranged seven Round Table Conferences of Ministers in charge of Panchayati Raj (July–December, 2004) to evolve a nationwide consensus on how to take forward the Panchayat Raj agenda. The Ministry has also guided the states in activity mapping with regard to devolution of powers. All these reports had a common concern that panchayats have not risen to the expected. We will briefly discuss important observations and recommendations of these reports to understand the progress and the pitfalls.[4]

Progress and Pitfalls

The Ministry of Rural Development had set up a Task Force (recommendation submitted in September 2001) to examine the question of demarcation of functional responsibilities between different tiers of the PRIs for the subjects listed in the Eleventh Schedule of the Constitution. The committee found that though States have enacted Panchayati Raj legislation, real devolution of powers and responsibilities that empower panchayats as institutions of self-government is yet to happen. Progress in this respect has been uneven. In many states, panchayats have not been able to become effective instruments of economic development and social justice as devolution of functions, funds and functionaries have remained largely on paper.

The taskforce adopted the principle of subsidiarity which postulates that any function which can be performed by a lower tier should be handled by that tier alone and not by any higher tier of PRI, as their guiding principle for functional demarcation. The taskforce also reiterated that different tiers of PRIs are not subservient to each other in a hierarchical fashion. They form an organic structure where higher tiers play a supportive role towards the lower tiers.[5]

The report of the National Commission to Review the Working of the Constitution (NCRWC) observed, 'more than eight long years have passed, but the change brought about by the Amendment has not been radical, nor its implications are found to be far reaching. For, Panchayats have, till now, failed to emerge as governments at the third stratum, up to the expected level'. The commission has identified gaps and recommended several amendments to Part IX of the Constitution to further strengthen it. Some recommendations made were: to amend Article 243G by substituting the word 'endow' with 'vest'; restructure the Eleventh and Twelfth Schedules in a manner that creates a separate fiscal domain for panchayats and municipalities; confer on the panchayats full powers of administrative and functional control over staff transferred to them and the power to recruit staff required for service in their jurisdiction; and establish a State Panchayat Council under the chairmanship of the Chief Minister and Comptroller and Auditor-General of India conducting the audit and lay down accounting standards for panchayats.[6]

The second Administrative Reforms Commission (ARC) appointed by the Government of India, in its sixth report titled, Local Governance – An Inspiring Journey into the Future (2007) revealed that the growth of local self-governing bodies as the third tier of governance has been 'uneven, halting and slow'. In implementing the rural development policies, the local bodies are poorly empowered and they experience various institutional barriers. Also, they have been starved of funds as the political and bureaucratic corruption lets only few drops to reach the bottom of the chain, though gallons of water is pumped on the top. The ARC made wide ranging recommendations, inter alia, that: state should ensure that Gram Panchayats are of an appropriate size to make the viable units of self-government; the ward Sabha should provide a platform where people can directly discuss their needs and prepare area-specific local plans; state government should not have power to suspend or rescind any resolution passed by the PRIs or take action against the elected representatives or to supersede/ dissolve the panchayats; the power to investigate and recommend action should lie with the local Ombudsman; the flow of funds for all public development schemes in rural areas should exclusively be routed through panchayats with local area development authorities and other organisations having similar functions should be wound up and their function and assets transferred to the appropriate level of panchayat; Members of Parliament Local Area Development (MPLAD) and Members of Legislative Assembly Local Area Development (MLALAD) should be abolished; and the centrally sponsored schemes have to shed their vertical identity and be part of the overall development plan of the panchayat raj system.[7]

In the twentieth anniversary year of Constitutional Panchayat Raj, the Ministry of Panchayati Raj constituted an expert committee to examine how

PRIs might be leveraged to secure the most efficient delivery of public goods and services. The committee examined a wide range of issues and submitted their report in April 2013. This is the latest report on Panchayati Raj and provides exact status and position of the system. The committee observed, 'the implementation of the operative core of Part IX relating to devolution of 3Fs – Functions, Finances, Functionaries – has been far from in accord with the letter and spirit of the Constitution Amendments, notwithstanding numerous directives from the Prime Minister downwards and the interventions of Planning Commission'. Further, the committee felt, 'there could be several reasons for such failure of which important ones are: lack of political will to devolve power to lower level elected governments; lack of administrative will to bestow authority by the bureaucracy; state's inability to create required posts in panchayats and reluctance and even opposition by state government employees to work under the panchayats; departmental opposition to part with their budgetary allocation in favour of the panchayats for carrying out functions which have been devolved to panchayats, which is partly due to the compulsion of bearing the share of Centrally Sponsored Scheme (CSS) out of their own budget'. As a result of these factors, devolution has been very scanty in most states and whatever functions have been devolved, the same have not been done in most cases through supportive legislation. With regard to finances of panchayats, the committee observed, 'adequate funds have not been provided to panchayats to meet the task assigned to them, whatever funds that are provided have not always been on time and with no assurance through specific budgetary provision and manpower to the panchayats in carrying out whatever has been devolved'. The report further mentions, 'local governments are still considered subordinate entities to states, largely entrusted with agency functions, predominantly funded by tied revenue transfers from above and critically dependent upon deputed state government staff with little accountability to the panchayats for implementation of their schemes'. It was further observed, 'panchayats are subordinated or by passed by other state institutions to which the bulk of local governance responsibilities are entrusted. Such faulty design of devolution, practised so far in most states, is the main reason for the weakness in the present panchayat system'. The committee rightly pointed out that 'without correcting these systemic defects, the panchayats cannot be leveraged to improve delivery of local goods and services, comparable to a local government'.

The committee further examined a larger issue of federalism and felt, 'the local government framework has typically been considered in isolation of and as standing apart from the issue of federalism. They believe that the local government system should be considered an integral part of a larger inter-governmental federal framework. Indeed, strengthening the federal structure would be an essential prerequisite for a strong local government'. The committee jotted down advantages of such arrangement, 'it will lay down the rules of engagement between the central, state and local governments. Secondly, it will also lay down with greater precision the role and responsibilities of the state and central governments in fostering and nurturing an effective local government system. Thirdly, it will undoubtedly strengthen the local government to perform an effective role in the delivery of goods and services to the people'.[8] The committee's analysis is pragmatic on the prevailing situation and recommendation deserves serious consideration.

Restating the Problem and Emerging Issues

The post-amendment panchayat bodies have sustained structure and composition but the main crux of the problem is devolution of powers, functions and functionaries. The process of devolution emanates from Article 243-G and reads, 'subject to the provisions of this constitution, the legislature of a state may, by law, endow the panchayats with such powers and authority as may be necessary to enable them to function as institutions of self-government and such law may contain provisions for the devolution of powers and responsibilities upon panchayats at the appropriate level, subject to such conditions as may be specified therein, with respect to (a) the preparation of plans for economic development and social justice (b) the implementation of schemes for economic development and social justice as may be entrusted to them, including those in relation to matters listed in the Eleventh Schedule'. The provision is discretionary in nature and retained by the State Legislature (Government) so far as the devolution of powers and responsibilities to the panchayats are concerned. The Eleventh Schedule lists 29 items in respect of which specific schemes along with necessary powers and resources are expected to be transferred to the domain of the panchayats. Several states have provided for a plethora of responsibilities which pertain to these subjects. But unfortunately, many such provisions have not been given effect to, reducing the efficacy of panchayats in the process. In fact, real devolution has not taken place and progress is uneven. In the absence of appropriate devolution, panchayats, as envisaged, have not been able to become an institution of self-government and instrument of economic development and social justice.

Some important principles should be kept in view while devolving responsibilities on lower levels of governance. Firstly, the principle of 'subsidiarity' needs to be given due consideration. Secondly, the state government should not unilaterally withdraw the responsibilities and powers already devolved to the panchayats, without adequate justification and prior consultation with them. Thirdly, responsibilities, authority and powers assigned to the panchayats should be extremely specific, clear and simple so that they are easily comprehended by the panchayats. In other words, the state governments should bear in mind the principle of specificity/itemisation of responsibilities and powers devolved. Fourthly, whenever functions or responsibilities are transferred to the panchayats, it should be accompanied with the necessary funds, functionaries and freedom in decision-making.[9]

Similarly, Article 243 H and Article 243-I of the Indian Constitution provide for financial devolution to the PRIs. Article 243-H empowers the state legislatures (a) to authorise, by law, to levy, collect and appropriate specified taxes, duties, fees and tolls on panchayats; (b) to assign State taxes, duties, fees and tolls to panchayats specific for purposes; (c) to provide for making grants-in-aid to the panchayats from the Consolidated Fund of the State; and (d) to constitute specified Funds for crediting all moneys received by or on behalf of the panchayats and for their withdrawal. This provision endows the state legislatures with the discretionary power to strengthen the finances of the panchayats through assignment of certain revenue powers to and sharing of state revenues with panchayats and payment of grants-in-aid to them. Article 243-I which is a mandatory provision for the States requires the state Governor to appoint a Finance Commission at the state level within one year from the date of commencement of the 73rd Amendment Act and at the expiry of every fifth year, thereafter, to review the financial position of the panchayats and to make appropriate recommendations to improve their finances. Another far-reaching mandatory provision of the 73rd Amendment Act relates to enlargement of the functional domain of the National Finance Commission constituted every five years by the President of India under Article 280. After 73rd Amendment Act, the commission is required to suggest measures for augmentation of the Consolidated Fund of the States with a view to supplementing the resources of the panchayats, on the basis of the recommendations made by the State Finance Commissions (SFCs).[10]

Devolution

A pertinent question arises whether such powers and authority has been devolved to panchayats in the state or there is a need for enlarging functional domain. In that case, state should endeavour to entrust specific activities/functions/schemes to make them unit of self-governance and allow them to function properly and deliver services to people. What appropriate administrative measures are required to operationalise the intent of the legislature?

Similarly, inadequacy of staff is one of the major problems of panchayats. Functionaries should be posted in corresponding to the devolved subjects, activities and schemes. This needs to be examined for further action. Moreover, it has been observed that many gram panchayats do not have a full-time secretary, rather one secretary looks after work of two or three gram panchayats. It has been suggested to have a separate panchayat cadre of employees. How can the problem of staff inadequacy be tackled?

Article 243-H and Article 243-I of the Indian Constitution provide for financial devolution to the PRIs. Panchayats are empowered to levy certain taxes, fees, duties, etc. The experience gained so far points out that panchayats do not exercise their powers to levy taxes due to obvious reasons and do not have proper machinery to collect revenue. Therefore, own sources of revenue is limited which leads to dependency syndrome. What steps could be taken to mobilise own resources and make panchayats economically viable and self-sufficient?

According to Article 243-I and 280 of the Constitution, the State Finance Commission and the National Finance Commission are mandated to improve not only the finances of the panchayats but also to make them an integral part of both State and Union Government finances. The experience reveals that financial devolution is not much effective. It warrants improvement and this aspect need more attention. What could be the modalities of intergovernmental transfer of funds to ensure panchayats to get their due share?[11]

Decentralised Planning

Economic development with equity and justice to all sections of society has been a guiding principle of Indian planning. Though there is a general perception that planning in India has always been top down with reliance on a trickle down approach for percolation of fruits of economic development to the poorer sections of the society, the Five-Year Plans have consistently advocated decentralised planning as a means to involve local community in the planning process. Successive Five-Year Plans have reinforced the concept of planning from below and their integration both in the State and National Plans.

The process of decentralised planning was given greater impetus with the passing of the 74th Constitutional Amendment Act, 1992. Article 243-ZD of the amendment mandates for setting up of District Planning Committee (DPC) in every district. The constitutional provisions (Article 243-G and 243-W) envisage planning for economic development and social justice by panchayats for the rural areas and municipalities for the urban areas in the district and prepare the draft development plan for the entire district. While consolidating the district plan, the DPC will consider the matters of common interest between panchayats and municipalities including spatial planning, sharing of water and other physical and natural resources, environment conservation, integrated development of infrastructure, and extent and type of resources available whether financial and otherwise. Indeed, it has paved the way for grassroots participation and people's direct involvement in the governance and local level planning with bottom-up approach. According to the Bihar Panchayat Act, District Planning Committees (DPCs) were established. However, the experience gained so far is not very encouraging. How to make optimal use of DPC, as envisaged?

In some states, the Zilla Parishad President is ex-officio chairperson of DPC. This has resulted in smooth functioning of DPC. Why not a system of District Minister be dispensed with the Zilla Parishad President as the Chairperson of DPC? To have an organic link and an adequate representation of the lower tier of panchayats, should elected representatives of village and intermediate panchayats be given representation in the DPC?[12]

Process of Empowerment

The 73rd Constitution Amendment has a revolutionary provision for political empowerment of the women and marginalised communities in the rural society. It has thrown open political opportunities in the panchayats to these disadvantaged sections. Skeptics argue against it making a case out of certain deficiencies such as illiteracy, family responsibilities, poverty, lack of experience and exposure, awareness, communication skills, etc. These are inhibiting factors for effective participation of women and weaker sections in the decision-making process and holding political offices at the local level. Political empowerment of women and weaker sections is bound to face such opposition. In fact, women and the marginalised communities in rural areas were not initially confident of their abilities to assume leadership in panchayats. Nevertheless, the leadership that emerged after panchayat elections had to cope with several problems due to their traditional social conditioning. Entrenched rural power structure was reluctant to share power with newly emerging groups. But the situation is encouraging with more than 50 percent women being elected. However, there are several instances where the elected women chairpersons, particularly at the village panchayat, had to depend exclusively on their family members to perform their official duties. Many women members and sarpanches did not know the nuances of panchayat administration and had to depend on their men for transacting official business. What is the situation now? Are women now independently transacting official business?[13] Are the capacity building efforts making them independent?

There were attempts and instances where feudal individuals fixed their 'men' or their 'wives' for the seats and offices of chairpersons reserved for women, Scheduled Castes and Scheduled Tribes. What is the situation now? Has the awareness and perception level of women and marginalised groups improved and has it created an urge in them to assert their rightful share in the decision-making process at the local level? Has the process of political empowerment gained momentum and is it giving expected results? Are they comprehending that political empowerment in the ultimate analysis holds the key for their social and economic betterment?

Realising Potential of Gram Sabha

Gram Sabha is the soul of the Panchayati Raj system and the centre of democratic power in the village. It is the repository of all powers and responsibilities bestowed on PRIs through the 73rd Amendment Act. The Gram Sabha as a collective body discusses issues and problems, needs and aspirations of the village, including problems faced by special groups. Gram Sabha-based comprehensive planning is the basis of local self-governance. Gram Sabha consists of people themselves and an institution of participatory democracy. It functions as a watch dog and enhances accountability and transparency in the system.

Gram Sabha is a forum for deliberative democracy and to discuss issues related to the village. However, owing to political, social and other reasons, it is not functioning as expected. They are yet to become operational entities and realise their full potential in making the panchayat system truly self-governed and a grassroots participatory structure. The experience gained thus far, tends to suggest that Gram Sabhas need further empowerment.

Some states are holding Gram Sabha at ward level owing to the problem of population size, quorum and territorial jurisdiction of village panchayats. Is holding gram sabha at ward level suitable? Should beneficiaries to all development programmes be selected in the gram sabha? Should the decisions taken by the gram sabha not be meddled with by any higher level body? Gram sabha has to play a prominent role in participation of villagers in the planning to meet their needs and requirements. How do we activate gram sabha?

Representative System

The framework for representation and the electoral process are among the most important mechanism that shape local democracy. The objective of the 64th Amendment Bill (May 1989) was to ensure that panchayats have a democratic character and function as representative institution of the people. Therefore, some important issues relating to it need consideration.

Political parties are among the main actors in governance, influencing the nature of democratic polity in the country and the coherence of their programmes, ideologies and leadership has a major impact on local democratic development. Political parties play an important role in enabling and limiting representation at the local level and have important implications for centre-local relations. Moreover, the growth in political parties over a period of time coincided with the increase in elections.[14] This is a pertinent issue to consider whether political parties can take part in local government.

It is said that directly elected members are more accountable to their constituents than indirectly elected. Direct election also has cost concern.[15] Panchayats have directly elected members at all levels. Chairperson at the district and intermediate level is indirectly elected. What should be the organic link between the upper and lower tier? What could be a more appropriate mode of election to Chairperson? Whether other categories of membership like ex-officio, nominated, etc. may be considered for the local government. Experience shows that frequent rotation of reservations led to adverse effect. What should be the criteria for rotation of reserved seats in the panchayats?

Recently, a new issue of educational qualifications for candidate seeking election to local bodies has come up in view of ordinance of the Rajasthan Government to amend the Act. It has legal, social, and broader implications. Literacy rate in rural area is low and it will debar a huge chunk of the population. What would be the suitable option in this regard?

Panchayats vis-à-vis Rural Development

Over a period of time, the portfolio of rural development has multiplied substantially in terms of policy, programmes, financial allocation, etc. More so, several centrally sponsored schemes pertaining to 29 subjects are in vogue, but panchayats are not involved. It has been observed that many such programmes are not properly implemented due to various reasons and inadequate institutional and structural arrangements. Some of the flagship programmes like MGNREGA have a distinct role for panchayats but such programmes are not fully entrusted to them. The ministries/departments have not taken concrete steps to integrate panchayats in their strategy of planning and implementation of programmes under their purview.

Considering the existing situation and available institution of panchayats, should all development programmes and schemes be entrusted to panchayats and put under one umbrella? The institutional capability should be built to take up new assignments so as to deliver services to rural people to become a unit of self-governance.[16]

Conclusion

In Indian context, democratic decentralisation has led to the promotion of local democracy. The new dispensation has given younger generation democratic rights at local level. Experiences by now reveal that decentralisation is good both for democracy and efficiency. The process of decentralisation requires redefining structure, procedures and practices of governance which is closer to citizenry, gives importance to a general sensitisation of the public, and creates a heightened awareness.[17] Based on the existing provisions of the Constitution and Conformity Acts of the states, and recommendation of the Second Administrative Commission and other expert groups, is there a need to have further amendment in the provisions of the Constitution to revitalise panchayats as to make them vibrant?

Notes

1. Axel Hadenius (ed.), *Decentralisation and Democratic Governance: Experiences from India, Bolivia and South Africa*, Uppsala, Sweden: Almqvist and Wiksell International, 2003.
2. Government of India, *Local Governance: An Inspiring Journey into the Future*, Sixth Report, Second Administrative Reforms Commission, 2007.
3. Various reports of Ministry of Rural Development and Ministry of Panchayati Raj.
4. Task Force on Panchayati Raj, Ministry of Panchayati Raj, August 2001.
5. National Commission to Review the Working of the Constitution, New Delhi, 2001.
6. Government of India, *Local Governance: An Inspiring Journey into the Future*, Sixth Report, Second Administrative Reforms Commission, 2007.
7. Government of India, *Towards Holistic Panchayat Raj*, Report of the Expert Committee on Leveraging Panchayats for Efficient Delivery of Public Goods and Services, New Delhi: Ministry of Panchayati Raj, 2013.
8. UNDP, *Local Democracy in Asia: Representation in Decentralised Governance*, United Nations Development Programme, Regional Centre in Bangkok, 2006.
9. Government of India, *Roadmap for the Panchayati Raj (2011–16): An All India Perspective*, New Delhi: Ministry of Panchayati Raj, 2011.
10. *Status of Panchayati Raj in the States and Union Territories of India*, New Delhi: Institute of Social Sciences, 2013.
11. UNDP, *Local Democracy in Asia: Representation in Decentralised Governance*, United Nations Development Programme, Regional Centre in Bangkok, 2006.
12. Government of India, *Local Governance: An Inspiring Journey into the Future*, Sixth Report, Second Administrative Reforms Commission, 2007.
13. Ibid.
14. Local Governance, UNDP Document, 1996.
15. Axel Hadenius (ed.), *Decentralisation and Democratic Governance: Experiences from India, Bolivia and South Africa*, Uppsala, Sweden: Almqvist and Wiksell International, 2003.
16. *Status of Panchayati Raj in the States and Union Territories of India*, New Delhi: Institute of Social Sciences, 2013.
17. Government of India, *Local Governance: An Inspiring Journey into the Future*, Sixth Report, Second Administrative Reforms Commission, 2007.

4

Two Decades of Democratic Governance at Local Level

Evidences from the Functioning of Panchayati Raj Institutions in Central Indian States

Yatindra Singh Sisodia

After independence persistent efforts have been made to make rural local self-government viable and self-sustainable on the lines portrayed by Mahatma Gandhi. Unfortunately, the response of the state governments was of very different nature and as a result the pace and pattern of establishment of rural local political institutions was not very enthusiastic in the initial phase. The state governments showed very little interest to empower these institutions and transfer of power to the representative institutions was almost negligible. However, the political leadership of some Indian states like Kerala, Karnataka, Maharashtra and West Bengal came forward to establish panchayats at local level but, on the whole, the pace of development was restricted that left much to be desired. Champions of local self-government debated and argued that the development planning was faulty, that the results did not reach the people concerned despite plethora of schemes and massive investments in rural sector. It was also realised that the infrastructure at the local level was in a very bad state and one of the obvious reasons was poor delivery system through local bureaucracy. People's participation was rarely seen and the development model was of 'top-down approach'. Accountability of the delivery mechanism was nominal as it rested with the bureaucratic hierarchy that looked at rural mass(es) as mere recipients.

Almost after forty-five years of Independence, the Central Government realised this hard truth that the delivery system was not effectively operational; it realised at last that without making people's direct and responsible participation through panchayat raj, development in the desired manner was not possible. As a result, the introduction of 73rd Constitutional Amendment Act was made in 1993. The execution of the Act was made mandatory for all the Indian states and panchayats have been provided a constitutional status. A special chapter has been added to the Indian Constitution on panchayats. The

73rd Amendment Act has provided uniformity and formal structure to these traditional institutions of self-governance for the sake of their effective functioning. The 73rd Amendment Act has initiated a fundamental restructuring of governance and administrative system of the country, based on the philosophy of decentralisation and power to the people. Policy planners have realised by now that the new Panchayat Raj Institutions (PRIs) have the potential to usher in a new era of change and development in accordance with people's needs and priorities, and to revitalise a deeply troubled system of democracy (Behar and Kumar, 2002).

The idea that produced the 73rd Amendment Act was not a response to pressure from the grassroots but to an increasing recognition that the institutional initiatives of the preceding decades had not delivered, that the extent of rural poverty was still much too large and thus the existing structure of government needed to be reformed. It is interesting to note that this idea evolved from the Centre and the State Governments. It was a political drive to see PRIs as a solution to the governmental crises that India was experiencing (World Bank, 2000). The Institution of panchayat raj in its rejuvenated form seeks to achieve the objectives of democratic decentralisation to accelerate socio-economic development and usher in equity and social justice.

The enactments of the 73rd Constitutional Amendment Act and the subsequent state-wise panchayat raj acts in India have brought to frontline the significance of grassroots democratic processes. This change in the Indian political system is the result of a growing conviction that the big government cannot achieve growth and development in a society without people's direct participation and initiative. This experience has brought the lesson that the success of the new panchayat raj system largely depends on the congruence of perception and commitment of people, their leaders and the officials, about the role to be played by them in the new system. Contextually and theoretically too, the new panchayat raj system has been created as a model of self-governance (Sisodia, 2005). The objectives of decentralisation are to execute and implement schemes and programmes to meet the local needs, to mobilise people, to channelise their energies towards socio-economic reconstruction and to involve them in all the activities of the communities through the new institutions. Its objectives include also to reduce the size of work of the higher level government and leaving the responsibility to the people to decide their destiny as per the new dispensation. Decentralisation is a much-debated issue in India and other countries with federal system of governance. Though there are various arguments for and against decentralisation, arguments in favour of decentralisation far outweigh those against it because of the inherent potential of democratisation in the decentralised federal system through proper empowerment of people at the grassroots level.

Two decades of panchayat raj in India has been a matter of debate and speculation about its performance and impact. Almost three million people including more than one million women and a sizeable number of SCs/STs took part in these elections. The sizeable presence of underprivileged and poor as representatives through reservations in the grassroots political institutions is a landmark development in the rural politics of the country. This significant development has special meaning because two decades earlier in most parts of rural India these groups were excluded from public life and political participation. This is also a matter of serious debate as how this excluded lot after their inclusion in active politics at grassroots would effectively tackle local power equation and set the agenda for development. Yet, the fact remains that these backward and so far ignored classes have heralded their arrival on the political stage of the country in the countryside. The responses of state governments to the implementation of panchayat raj varied significantly and it is very difficult to generalise about this issue on the basis of their functioning for the last two decades or so.

A perusal of state profiles would show that panchayat raj reforms have certainly taken place with vigour and zeal in some western and southern parts of the country, which are relatively sound from the point of view of economy, are vibrant socially, and have active civil societies. On the contrary, the northern states with the greatest degree of poverty and inequality and deep schisms of caste and low pace of governance resulted in weak panchayats (Robinson, 2005).

In this mixed scenario of development, exemplary reforms have taken place in Kerala and Madhya Pradesh due to the strong political will of the political leadership of these states after the implementation of the 73rd Amendment Act. In Kerala, the people's planning campaign was predicated on a high level of popular mobilisation that was made possible by high level of literacy and professional support with a mass base social movement (Issac and Franke, 2000). Initially, in Madhya Pradesh, a series of reforms and amendments in panchayat raj were taken to strengthen the grassroots institutions, specially the Gram Sabha. The example of West Bengal is well known where the CPM government used the PRIs as a political support base in rural areas with a significant degree of success. The land reforms in West Bengal could take place due to panchayat raj (Webster, 1992).

Evidences from the Field

State governments (evidences are from the states of Madhya Pradesh, Chhattisgarh, Rajasthan, Gujarat and Maharashtra) have been doing remarkable work for the strengthening of panchayat raj system since its inception. The state governments have responded with innovativeness and remarkable commitment to making the system sustainable and successful. The efforts of states to institutionalise the system are evident in the number of amendments that have been made to the State Panchayat Acts as a dynamic response to the problems at the ground level. During the implementation of panchayat raj system, Indian states have faced several opportunities and difficulties. The experience of the states is extremely rich and provides vital insights into the process of institutionalising panchayat raj. On the one hand, the story is of bureaucratic resistance, functional problems, political and institutional challenges, financial inadequacy and mismatch of capacities and roles. On the other hand, it involves the grassroots level in a democratic and participative governance system and therefore, potentially unleashes its considerable energy. Looking into the relevance of new system, an attempt is made to evaluate the ground reality and potentiality of the panchayat raj system in Indian states. The paper is dealing with the issues of Gram Sabha (village assembly), reservation, women representatives, working of panchayats, panchayats and bureaucracy, devolution of powers and finance in separate sub-headings.

People's Participation through Gram Sabha

The legislative empowerment of the Gram Sabha in India is a political development of utmost importance, because it marks the clearest break from the most dominant political orthodoxy of this century (Mander, 1999). This recent faith in gram sabha is based on the belief that the objective conditions of the poor are directly involved in the process of formulation and implementation of decisions affecting their lives.

It is important to recognise that this faith in the gram sabha is based on several extremely important but largely untested assumptions. It is assumed firstly that even in a village society with deep schisms of caste, class and gender, an organic community still exists and that given appropriate legal and institutional spaces, it can act cogently and responsibly as a community. The second assumption is that the collective of the gram sabha would be a more reliable vehicle of good governance than a relatively unencumbered bureaucracy or local elected representatives.

The experience of panchayat raj in various states indicates that the State Acts have been amended from time to time to make it more effective in establishing gram sabha as genuine structure of grassroots democracy. It is evident from the experience of panchayat raj that the level of participation of people at grassroots level was very low and gram sabhas were almost a formal institution with no role in various assigned works related to rural development. Limited and confined role of people in gram sabha has been a significant reason for the increased status of village head at local level.

Gram sabha or people's forum has always been an integral part of the concept of a gram panchayat. Rajni Kothari visualises gram sabha as 'watchdogs' coming between the politician-bureaucratic nexus (Kothari, 1998). It is unfortunate that both grassroots leadership and grassroots bureaucracy could not strengthen the gram sabha as expected. The institution of gram sabha is dysfunctional due to the lack of leverage of local leaders to initiate meaningful participation in the sabha and their incapability to persuade people to support local initiatives (Fernandes, 1999). It has been evident that meetings called were mostly without prior and adequate notice. In most places, only a formality was observed; proxy meetings, at time were convened and proceedings were written even without the knowledge of those who attended. Meeting, if arranged, either proved to be abortive or unsuccessful because of thin attendance with the panchayat or discussion (Mander, 1999). It is certain that unless we have a vibrant gram sabha, we cannot have empowered and accountable panchayats (Nambiar, 2001).

Legislation by itself is not adequate for correcting a wrong. The experience of the last two decades has revealed a general indifference towards the functions of gram sabha and its meetings. The significance of gram sabha has not as yet rubbed upon the villagers. Their eyes are still focused on the gram panchayat as the hub of all activity. Not only this, even panchayat officials and the local elite have evinced little interest in the functioning of the gram sabha.

Gram sabhas are to be made effective, active and creative so that the expected result could be accessible to the rural society. It is foremost responsibility of the panchayat raj representatives to convey to the people the real nature, function and the real spirit of gram sabha. Meeting of gram sabha can be a good platform for the solution of various day-to-day problems pertaining to the village society. This platform can also be used for the initiation of community work. Most of the basic rural problems, which have hardly any cost effect, can be solved through motivation among the villagers and the gram sabha is the right forum to discuss all such issues. The vibrancy and efficacy of gram sabha will remain dismal if it does not possess the capacity to perform assigned roles and responsibility. This question becomes more pertinent in a socio-cultural milieu where human resource development is low and society is deeply fragmented and hierarchical. And therefore, it is urgently needed that marginalised sections of society, which have been remained out from the process of decision-making, have to be taken in mainstream through sensitisation and capacity building.

Representation of Marginalised Sections of Society

The state legislations have made provisions for the reservation of Scheduled Castes, Scheduled Tribes and Other Backward Castes. All these groups had negligible presence in the rural politics before this statutory provision. It is definitely a very important step through which largest political recruitment has become possible.

The Scheduled Castes have been provided reservation in proportion to their population. A basic difference between the SC and the ST is that while the latter reside in specific habitats, the former live along with the people of the general category. As a result, they face more difficulties because of social deprivations. Acute poverty, illiteracy and predominant position of rural elite have incapacitated them in discharging their duties effectively. Panchayats, which are 'institutions of self-governance', cannot function in a society that is ridden with caste, feudalism and poverty. Therefore, PRIs should be made effective instruments of social transformation through a vibrant democratic political process at the local level (Mathew and Nayak, 1996). The initial dissent and non-cooperative attitude towards SC leadership is gradually changing.

The tribals have also been given reservation in proportion to their population. When one examines the degree of their participation in the panchayat raj system, it emerges that much needs to be done to equip them for facing the new task. Many reasons can be pointed out for this situation: illiteracy, poverty, lack of awareness, socio-cultural deprivations, lack of experience and training etc. The new Acts provided respectable space to the tribal people in the working of the panchayat raj system, such legislation could not make the tribal communities the sole masters of their socio-political destinies in their homelands. The need was always felt that the institutional structures within the Scheduled Areas were to be in consonance with the tribal needs, ethos and tribal institutions with which these people were familiar for ages (Purohit, 2002). Accepting the felt needs, Union Government passed an amendment known as

Panchayat (Extension to the Scheduled Areas), 1996 and accordingly the state governments have also made Amendments in respective state legislations. A perusal of catalogue of powers of scheduled area panchayats convinces that they have been equipped with special powers for the preservation of tribal identities. The gram panchayat in scheduled areas shall work under the general superintendence, control and direction of the gram sabha.

Panchayat raj system in scheduled areas of Indian states has empowered gram sabhas with all such powers and duties to become the real unit of self-governance. As a result, there has been a growing concern for the speedy development of tribal areas. The state governments transferred nearly all powers previously exercised by gram panchayats to gram sabha. It has thus gone from representative democracy at the grassroots to direct democracy, but the fact remains that despite this endeavour, there is a clear-cut gap between macro level decisions and grassroots reality.

At the micro level, the gram sabha is a peoples' institution and has been made a statutory body through a Constitutional Amendment. Panchayat raj system in scheduled areas has provided all powers and duties to gram sabha. The resource flow to gram sabha and its ever-increasing powers and authority has generated a lot of interest in people. It is expected that this interest is likely to be translated into a more broad based and participative leadership at grassroots level. However, a gradual process of change can be discerned. The tribal leadership is getting increasingly involved in understanding the system and coming to grips with it (Sisodia, 2002).

OBC, hold a position different from that of the SCs and the STs. Even before reservation they had representation in the panchayats as well as in other institutions. Their social position in the traditional social set-up was also more respectable. The same can be said about their economic standing. As a result of these factors they have made use of the new panchayat raj system more effectively.

It is, therefore, essential that while the position of the OBCs needs further consolidation, that of the SCs and the STs should be ameliorated a great deal. In this endeavour though legislation is important, much more important is attitudinal change on part of the administration and also of the society at large. The weaker sections need more training and experience in the exercise of their powers. Equally important are concrete measures to remove illiteracy and poverty from amongst them.

Only political recruitment of all the sections of society will never attain the desired goal. The basic idea behind the reservation was to provide an opportunity to the depressed classes to come forward and be a part of the total development process. In spite of all bottlenecks, gradually the changes are taking place. It happens so in a new system where representatives are not familiar with the working of the system. Even then, slowly and steadily changes are visible. Taking lessons from the working of the panchayats, the leadership is getting skilled. At the same time the other persons of the society are sharing several experiences as well. This process of decentralised governance will provide opportunity to rural people, particularly the persons of backward classes, to involve in development activities and several other works for the betterment of their life. The common man of the society will gradually become aware about day-to-day functioning and in that way the coming generations will be well acquainted with the processes of development. This will certainly enthuse younger people to participate in the political process in the larger interests of the community.

Women's Participation in Panchayats

Women representation through 73rd Constitutional Amendment Act is a landmark decision through which 33 per cent of the seats were reserved for women. Women are being considered as a backward class because of their negligible representation in political process. As a result of this statutory provision for reservation for women, situations have dramatically changed. It is generally believed of the rural women that their responsibilities are confined merely up to kitchens and farms. This prolonged myth has changed. Big number of women are joining the panchayat elections.

To ensure adequate and effective participation of women in the panchayat raj system, the Panchayat Raj Acts, after an amendment many states reserved half of the seats for women in all the three tiers. Most of these women representatives have entered in the political process for the first time. However, many of them in general and the OBC category belonged to the families which had traditional political base. Yet the situation of women leadership and its working is not very encouraging. The reasons of their poor performance are more or less because of their overall backwardness. Other important bottlenecks among women representatives are interference by male members of their families vis. of the husband, brother, father, son etc. However, in many cases now such interference is gradually declining. The reasons behind involvement of male members are very clear: first, rural women do not have the required exposure; secondly, lack of experience of working in panchayats; thirdly, there is a non-cooperative attitude of other panchayat raj representatives and government officials.

If an evaluation of their functioning is done, it becomes clear that with the passage of time the women leadership became more assertive and independent as well as aware of the systemic processes. However, to strengthen this segment it is necessary to do away with illiteracy, socio-economic deprivations and many other complexes. It is equally important that to equip these women properly, sufficient training programmes should be organised for them. There should also be a change in the attitude of their menfolk and the administration. If women's empowerment has to be successful, then the existing feudal patriarchal structure in most parts of the country has to be dismantled. Moreover, women's empowerment through the panchayats requires a sustained campaign and vigorous efforts for creating awareness about their rights and duties (Datta, 1997).

It cannot, however, be denied that as a result of reservation for women their participation in the political process has been ensured and they are playing a constructive role in development and welfare activities now. This will lead to positive changes in the entire social system. These problems are, of course, initial hurdles. With the passage of time and gaining of experience, it is believed, women leadership will become more mature and effective. Regular training of this class, cooperative attitude of males and government officials will definitely provide strength to the leadership to work with perfection.

Working of Panchayats

The Panchayati Raj Institutions (PRIs) have been made the units of self-governance and they have been empowered to perform various powers and duties. However, certain issues are very important in respect to the working of panchayats.

The PRIs have been established as units of self-governance. There are many dimensions to the functions performed by the panchayats. The meetings have predetermined agenda. For discussion, new subjects can be taken up with the permission of the chair. Personal issues, which are directly related to some members, are often debated at length. On many occasions themes, which pertain to comprehensive rural development, are overlooked due to involvement of vested interests. In decisions taken by the panchayats, the acceptance or approval of people's representatives or those in power is a must. This process of decision-making fails to fix correct priorities. Although elected on a non-party basis, the functionaries are influenced by political affiliations in debates and in the decision-making process. It would be more meaningful if party politics brings about greater politicisation and participation rather than socio-political fragmentation. The influence of factors such as caste, class, community, religion cannot be wholly denied as these do have a role to play. However, occasions have not been few where panchayats have, in fact, played a cementing role.

As the panchayats have been saddled with a plethora of activities, a lot of paper work obviously becomes necessary. While these records are maintained properly at the Janpad Panchayat and the Zilla Panchayat levels, the situation is not so rosy at the Gram Panchayat level due to inexperience of the panchayat raj representatives and lack of staff support. There is also an increasing need to inform the people about the meetings of panchayats, their decisions and policies. The panchayat functionaries are also not too keen about ensuring transparency and informing people about their activities. Efforts should, therefore, be made to make the people more vigilant.

PRIs have been given the responsibility of implementing different governmental schemes. For this the gram sabhas select the beneficiaries and also examine panchayats as well as control the objectives of such schemes. The beneficiaries are selected through the gram sabha. The gram sabha has to try to select people on economic basis so that the genuinely needy person should get the benefits on a priority basis.

Thus, the functioning of the different panchayat bodies, though it is improving, still needs further streamlining. It has, however, to be understood that it is still their infancy period. Things will definitely get better with more training, experience and increasing awareness about powers and duties. Their efficiency and effectiveness will surely infuse greater confidence among the people at large in their activities. Active participation of the members, cooperative response of the community and a spirit of selfless dedication to panchayat work are necessary for the successful working of Panchayati Raj Institutions.

Panchayats and Bureaucracy

In the period prior to the implementation of the Panchayat Raj Acts, the control of bureaucracy over rural development was complete. However, now all the responsibilities relating to rural development have been handed over to the panchayats. This has necessitated fundamental changes at the bureaucratic or technocratic level also.

There is thus a widespread feeling of fear, mistrust and insecurity among the panchayat representatives regarding their staff. A clear-cut need exists for greater understanding between the two sets of functionaries to remove misperceptions and apprehensions regarding each other. The bureaucracy has to understand its position and responsibilities in a democratic system. A system has to be developed where accountability informs the upper echelons of administration and our understanding shows that authority resides with the lower levels.

The panchayats at all the three levels must be provided with a separate and autonomous cadre, which should be delinked from the states. Responsibilities relating to recruitment, promotion, transfer etc. should be handled by the panchayats themselves or through some relevant agency. Posting at local levels should be permitted on permanent basis. This would solve the problem of transfer and officials will have wide knowledge of his area. Misuse of power should be checked through a system of checks and balances. There is also a need of simplification of procedures so that usual and routine matters do not cause confusion, delay and deadlocks. A Panchayat Manual should be prepared as an authentic and ultimate source of eliminating all confusion or possible misunderstanding. Multiple and periodically recurring orientation programmes should be organised for both the groups.

Devolution of Powers

The Constitution of India vide Schedule 11 has laid down 29 subjects related to social justice and economic development. These have been devolved upon the panchayats for planning and implementation. It is on the basis of this Schedule that important powers of all departments have been handed over to panchayats. Importantly, these departments are: social welfare, agriculture, mineral resources, food and civil supplies, sports and youth welfare, rural development, village industries, livestock, dairy and poultry development, revenue, public health and engineering, forest, school education, labour etc. All these departments have been vested with different types of powers and responsibilities to the three tiers of panchayat. However, most panchayat representatives do not possess adequate knowledge about the functions and responsibilities entrusted to them by the various departments. As a result, their role as regard to number of such departments is negligible. Such devolution, therefore, would be fruitful only when the representatives are made aware of their role and encouraged to perform such roles.

The elected representatives have been provided with many administrative powers, which relate to recruitment, supervision and control. However, many of them have no experience of such jobs and find it difficult to handle them judiciously. As a result in the exercise of these powers, the importance of administrative officials and influential people has increased. For proper use of these functions, the panchayat representatives should be given proper training.

Members of Parliament and State legislators are *ex officio* members of different tiers of the panchayat raj. They take part in the meetings. Though denied by the Act, in practice they exercise undue influence in the functioning of these bodies due to their political clout and access to centres of power. Even the panchayat representatives become subservient to them to seek favours from them. The MPs and MLAs have often shown disinterestedness in successful functioning of the PRIs as in their perception this would limit their own area of influence. The feeling is growing that if direct elections were held to all positions in the PRIs, the influence of representatives would get augmented. It has also been suggested that the development fund available to MPs and MLAs should be spent in consultation with the panchayat raj functionaries. Separate development funds should be provided to the panchayat representatives enabling them to spend it in accordance with the felt needs of the people. To streamline the division of functions between the three tiers, a suggestion has been made to establish State Commission to distribute the 29 subjects judiciously and also provide a 'local list' in the Constitution along with the Union, State and Concurrent lists.

Financial Status of Panchayats

Finance is the first and foremost necessity of any institution for its successful working. It is important to make PRIs financially sound and self-sufficient. Panchayats of Indian States have two resources – funds from government and local tax collection. It is observed that majority of the panchayats depend on funding from state governments but do not levy local taxes for political reasons. The state governments allocate the money to the three tiers meant for rural development. These bodies are provided finances to implement government schemes.

The state governments have been attentive to the need of financial efficacy of the PRIs. These have been empowered by the Act to levy many new taxes i.e. market fee, property tax, land tax, private toilet tax etc. The governments also constituted State Finance Commissions from time to time and many of their recommendations were accepted with regard to distribution of financial powers to the panchayats. Yet the PRIs cannot be regarded as financially self-reliant. Their dependence on the state governments for grants is not conducive to their successful functioning. Not many panchayats have utilised the powers given to them to levy local taxes. The functionaries have expressed the view that most of the people living in rural areas are poor and it would be improper to levy more taxes on them. Moreover, such new taxes would make them politically unpopular among the people. As such, the taxes should be levied only on those who are able to pay. The rural leadership should also realise the significance of tax collection, as these constitute the major source of their income. They have to establish examples of devoted and transparent work so that people do not mistrust them when new taxes are levied. Greater participation of the people in the whole process should be ensured.

Despite all these efforts one would not be in a position to state that the panchayats are financially self-sufficient. Dependence of panchayats on state government for funds is not good for the health of the new system. The leadership will have to come forward to meet the financial needs locally. Various provisions are available to generate resources. This way alone, the scheme of decentralisation will bear fruits.

Decentralised Planning

Indian states are continuously devolving powers and authority to the panchayats and initiated innovative measures to empower, strengthen and institutionalise the PRIs. It is based on the premise that in a village people can assemble and sit collectively, and decide the local issues. The new system intends to give power to the people and therefore, all the powers previously exercised by gram panchayats are transferred to gram sabhas. The approach of decentralised planning is 'bottom-up'. The planning starts from village itself. These local plans are sent to intermediate panchayat (Janpad Panchayat) through Gram Panchayats. After scrutiny and compilation, it goes to Zilla Panchayat. A consolidated plan for the district is prepared at District Planning Committees and percolation of resource flow to downward panchayats is done from here. However, the panchayat planners do not enjoy autonomy with regard to plan formulation. There is absence of coordination between governance and planning at different levels. There is very little people's participation in the planning process (Aziz, 1998).

The decentralised planning is need of the hour. The development and desired goals can only be achieved through it but it seems that at village level the plans lack the vision for the multifaceted and balanced development due to variety of reasons. It is, therefore, important to initiate special orientation, sensitisation and training of the local people for better decentralised planning.

Conclusion

The establishment of panchayat raj system in various states is in deference to the provision of the 73rd Constitution Amendment Act. The State Acts have been amended from time to time to make it more effective in establishing PRI as genuine structure of grassroots democracy. Through a system of reservation, participation of the weaker sections has also been ensured. The three tiers have been empowered significantly to enable them to discharge their duties properly and fulfil the expectations of the people. However, much needs to be done as yet. Gram sabhas are yet to perform their desired role in the panchayat raj system. Reservation has provided an opportunity to all backward classes to come out and play significant role but the process of political socialisation is slow among these classes. Women representation in panchayats is a matter of some satisfaction but their performance is poor as compared to other classes of the society. The bureaucracy has to be made more responsive to the needs of the PRIs. Greater financial autonomy must be provided to the panchayats. Better coordination has to be established among the three tiers of panchayat. Greater clarity of roles and tier-wise division of functions is essential. Of no less importance is optimal direct participation of people in the developmental process. To generate this, what is of crucial significance is the principle of accountability and continual social auditing of the performance and transparency in the form of right to information pertaining to administrative activities. The panchayats should be given the power to form organisations like neighbourhood groups to stimulate and direct people's participation in administration and development. Concrete efforts should also be made to reduce governmental interference in the day-to-day functioning of local self-government bodies and the process of their dissolution needs to be made more politics proof. Such measures will go a long way in establishing the panchayats as 'Village Republics'. The panchayat raj system has provided opportunities for wider political recruitment to all sections of the society, which should lead to achieve the goals of social justice and economic development in the years to come.

References

Aziz, Abdul (1998), 'Process of Decentralised Governance and Planning', *Prashasnika*, Vol. 25, No. 2, July-December.

Behar, Amitabh and Yogesh Kumar (2002), 'Decentralisation in Madhya Pradesh, India: From Panchayati Raj to Gram Swaraj (1995 to 2001)', *Working Paper 170*, ODI, London.

Datta, Prabhat (1997), 'Political Empowerment of Rural Women in India', *Administrative Change*, Vol. 24, No. 2, January-June.

Fernandes, A. (1999), 'Reconnecting the Sabha to Gram', paper presented at the National Conference on Gram Sabha, National Institute of Rural Development, Hyderabad, 28–29 July.

Issac, T.M. Thomas and Richard W. Franke (2000), *Local Democracy and Development: People's Campaign for Decentralised Planning in Kerala*, Leftword, New Delhi.

Kothari, Rajni (1998), *State Against Democracy: In Search of Human Governance*, Ajanta Publications, Delhi.

Mander, Harsh (1999), 'Towards Direct Democracy: The Legal Empowerment of Gram Sabha', *Kurukshetra*, New Delhi, Vol. 48, No. 1, October.

Mathew, George and Ramesh C. Nayak (1996), 'Panchayats at Work: What It Means for the Oppressed?', *ISS Occasional Paper Series–19*, Institute of Social Sciences, New Delhi.

Nambiar, Malini (2001), 'Making the Gram Sabha Work', *Economic and Political Weekly*, Mumbai, August 18.

Purohit, B.R. (2002), 'Panchayat Raj System in Scheduled Areas of Madhya Pradesh', in G. Palanithurai (ed.), *Dynamics of New Panchayati Raj System in India*, Vol. I, Concept Publishing Company, New Delhi.

Robinson, Mark (2005), 'A Decade of Panchayati Raj Reforms: The Challenge of Democratic Decentralisation in India', in L.C. Jain (ed.), *Decentralisation and Local Governance*, Orient Longman, New Delhi.

Sisodia, Yatindra Singh (2002), 'Decentralised Governance in Madhya Pradesh: Experiences of the Gram Sabha in Scheduled Areas', *Economic and Political Weekly*, Mumbai, October 5.

—— (2005), 'A Decade of Panchayati Raj System in Madhya Pradesh', in Yatindra Singh Sisodia (ed.), *Functioning of Panchayat Raj System*, Rawat Publications, Jaipur.

Webster, Neil (1992), 'Panchayati Raj in West Bengal: Participation for the People or the Party?', *Development and Change*, Vol. 23, No. 4.

World Bank (2000), *Overview of Rural Decentralisation in India*, Vol. III, Washington, D.C., p. 24.

5

Decentralisation and the Empowerment of Women and the other Marginalised Groups

Anecdotes from the Review of Literature

Nayanatara S. Nayak and Narayan Billava

There is widespread agreement that empowerment (facilitated through decentralisation in this context), as understood and promoted in the context of development and poverty reduction, is a multidimensional and interdependent process involving social, political, economic and legal changes that will enable people living in poverty and marginalisation to participate meaningfully in shaping their own future (Pettit, 2012). Democracy ensures empowerment, while decentralisation of democratic process ensures participation of all segments of society in this process. Empowerment and participation, presumed to be the outcomes of decentralisation, are deeply complementary and can be considered both as means and ends, processes and outcomes. Some approaches to empowerment focus on enabling individuals to gain access to assets, information, choices and opportunities so that they are able to improve their own situations. Decentralisation is argued on the grounds of allocative efficiency, as the public expenditure at the local level taken up by local self-government agencies are likely to reflect the demand for local services. Decentralisation also builds and nurtures social capital, which is essential to bring in changes in the society. Social scientists have argued that decentralisation builds a sense of community feeling, enhances capacities, paves way for freedom, permits meaningful participation of self-government (Kalin, 2003; Sen, 1999). J.S. Mill visualised democratic decentralisation as a school of political capacity, which makes citizens capable of genuine and informed participation (as quoted by Chhetri, 2012: 5). Empowerment becomes not a means to achieve development goals, but an end in itself, and a process 'by which those who have been denied the ability to make strategic life choices acquire such an ability' (Kabeer, 1999).

Many argue that decentralisation has not brought in desired results in practical terms. As put forth by Bardhan and Mookherjee (2007: 9) 'due to the absence of prerequisites like; educated and less aware citizens, social and economic equality (the absence of which inhibits political participation of poor and minorities), law and order, the ability to run free and fair elections, reliable and trustworthy information channels and, oversight by an active and effective civil society, local governments in developing countries may be more vulnerable than central system to problems of accountability'. For example, social audit, which is considered as an important accountability tool contributing to transparency and effective governance, was found to have excluded poor labourers in Karnataka for whom the scheme was designed due to village elites (Rajasekhar et al., 2013). Mohanty (2009) from his study of three panchayats in Orissa (now Odisha) generalises that although the provision of inclusion for marginalised groups has enhanced their participation in the decision-making process at the local level, it is inadequate for their empowerment. His study reveals that the dominant castes had co-opted loyal and faithful members from the reserved category and enjoyed major share in gram panchayat (GP) budget, while women from reserved category remained faithful to their party than their castes and class. This phenomenon has been identified by Jairath and Sajja (2009) also from their study on three selected GPs in Telangana district of Andhra Pradesh. According to their study 'Inclusion of excluded committees does not take place automatically through passage of bills in the legislature, giving them rights and power, it depends on factors such as social discrimination, economic dependence, control over means of violence, access to information and the nature of social movements to mobilise the excluded committees and groups'. Chakrabortty and Bhattacharyya (1993) conclude from their study on party politics into panchayat system in West Bengal that 'PRI will prove to be sheer ritualism, which is totally ineffective in fighting corruption, favouritism, inefficiency, if the spirit for real change is lacking' within the political parties, which fail to 'rise above the limitations of narrow and immediate interests'.

There is enormous flow of literature on the process of decentralisation, its inception, factors enabling its foothold, its influence on empowerment of women and vulnerable social groups, best practices in local self-government, political interests interfering in its process, lack of power to perform the duties, etc. We discuss below decentralisation in terms of inclusive development, political participation, service delivery, etc. in the background of the affirmative action with specific reference to empowerment of women and the marginalised; the motives credited to decentralisation in the literature.

Decentralisation and Affirmative Action

The constitutionally mandated reservations in Panchayati Raj Institutions (PRIs) brought in through 73rd Amendment have ensured women in general, and those from the marginalised groups in particular, to participate in the decentralisation process and thereby in the village and community development. Over and above the region-specific several Acts enacted by state governments, the 73rd Amendment to the constitution brought in 1992 was a major strengthening pillar to decentralised process. Government of India has been trying to achieve empowerment of women through various programmes and constitutional safeguards. Economic empowerment has been targeted or recognised through women component plan, financial assistance to self-help groups, establishment of women operated bank, colleges and universities specifically established for women and, social empowerment is being cherished through free education to girls up to certain levels, provision of housing with entitlements to women, access to services, etc. Political empowerment is assured through reservation of seats for contesting elections at different levels, earmarking of funds to panchayats under reserved category, etc. In Gram Panchayat (GP), the provision of seats has been increased from 33 per cent to 50 per cent for women in Karnataka. Although the experiences in grassroot politics over the past two decades do not give us rosy pictures, there are credible incidences of change in rural area due to women's empowerment. These incidences may be a few, but a beginning seems to have been made. In the caste and class ridden society that prevailed for long in India, women's empowerment is emerging in different fields as a result of induced process or affirmative action (Makwana, 2012). According to Aiyer (2002), reservations for Scheduled Castes/Scheduled Tribes (SCs/STs) are generally working well. And, although there is a long way to go in changing the apparent empowerment of women in to a real and genuine empowerment, he feels that reservation for women has opened the door to revolutionary changes of a political, social and cultural nature by empowering more than one million women through free and fair elections, a unique feature in the world. But, using data of gram sabhas followed by household survey in Tamil Nadu, Karnataka, Andhra Pradesh and Kerala, Ban and Rao (2009) recall that in villages where the presidency is reserved for lower caste, the dominance by landowners is higher suggesting that political reservation could produce weak leaders. However, through their earlier study they presume that women could acquire more experience via reservation system and with time they are expected to become effective leaders (Ban and Rao, 2008). Absence of affirmative action excludes disadvantaged groups and women, as a result of which existing divisions may continue (Mansuri and Rao, 2013). Due to affirmative action, women empowerment is coming by default making men to accept the change and giving boost to girl education (Singh, 2009: 404). The role played by political reservations for women and disadvantaged castes (SC/ST) in local governance has been documented by many. The strategy of reservation has ensured representation for deprived groups in PRIs. However, the evidence on the role of women's reservations is mixed. A few studies found that reservations for disadvantaged castes yielded benefits to the members of these castes in the village (Chattopadhyay and Duflo, 2004; Besley, Pande and Rao et al., 2004). According to Sudha Pai (2001), reservation is helpful to disadvantaged groups and other backward classes (OBCs) to identify themselves in the local governance and control the upper caste and middle caste dominance. Patnaik (2005) found that elected representatives were not able to properly articulate interests specific to their group or even exercise their own judgment in panchayat decision-making, which Patnaik asserts will question the very notion of representation of the marginalised groups through affirmative action. Based on the study of four GPs in Dhekanal district of Odisha, Patnaik concludes that affirmative action has not ensured the effective representation of the disadvantaged groups in the panchayats in terms of their participation, responsiveness to the interests of villagers and accountability to panchayats. Das (2013) in his study on Dalit and tribal leadership in Gujarat found that only one-third of the Dalit women were able to win the panchayat elections with freedom and, independently. He finds education, experience in social issues, motivation to bring development to their community, prior performance in panchayats, family support, personal relation with villagers, economic stability and family's political contacts as factors responsible for women to access panchayat positions, which indicates that the road to success is not easy for those without such background. Thorat (2002) also feels that despite several constitutional provisions, the problem of caste based violations of human rights in modified form continues to persist leading to exploitation of Dalits, especially in rural India as they are yet to be fully politically mobilised against the dominant class.

Mishra (1997) observes that the reservation of seats for women in PRIs will provide them with an opportunity to air their grievances and to take active part in the formal political arena which deals with social and economic problems. Palanithurai's study (1994) revealed that the participants had a fear that the upper caste and affluent sections of their communities would not tolerate the increased number of women representatives from the SC and ST to local government bodies. The study also pointed out that women members face a lot of problems in the panchayat as male members sometimes do not cooperate with elected women ward members and it is generally a difficult task for women to balance their housework and their duties as an elected representative. Baviskar and Mathew (2009) narrating the status of weaker sections in different states opine that affirmative action has helped SCs in West Bengal, in Uttar Pradesh they have started asserting their rights in panchayats and women show courage to hit back and money earmarked for SC welfare is spent for them. Further, they point out that in Maharashtra SC (New Buddhists) men and women exercise their full rights in panchayats and are treated respectively by dominant castes in panchayats and in Kerala political parties tend to ignore the role of women in panchayats, while in Manipur women panchayat leaders are found to be more effective, work oriented and not corrupt (as against views of Brara (2009) who states that women zilla adhyakshas in Manipur are not different from their male counterparts in matters of corruption as they spend lakhs of rupees on elections to remain in power). Reddy (2012) opines that reservation of the seats by rotation to SCs and STs according to their proportion and one-third each for OBC and women had advanced the pace of the political mobilisation among the disadvantaged groups.

From their study of three GPs in Haryana, Ahlawat and Ahlawat (2009) opine that 73rd Amendment to the Constitution of India has given a sense of identity and dignity to the Dalits and women, forcing the dominant castes to renegotiate their relationships with them. They had started asserting themselves, although the decision-making was found largely in the hands of dominant castes, which controlled the panchayat with the help of government officials. Bhargava and Subha (2009) in their study on three GPs in Bangalore (Bengaluru) rural district – one headed by a female SC woman, one by a male SC and the other by a male from general category – found that the policy of inclusion is being followed in PRIs of Karnataka as the reservations had increased the participation of women, but, lack of education, short tenure of president and money required for contesting for election had been the hurdles in their continued participation. Suresh (2009) presents a comparative analysis of three GPs in Kerala in terms of their role in empowering the excluded communities, wherein 10 per cent of the plan outlay is earmarked for special women component plan and, 75–80 per cent of special component plan (SCP) and tribal sub plan (TSP) are transferred to local bodies encouraging execution of schemes for the excluded groups. Women members were found to be involved in solving local problems and creating awareness. He finds that reservation has opened up the possibility of becoming an instrument of social justice and mobilisation of depressed groups, although the social empowerment of women and other disadvantaged groups remains far from adequate and their role in decision-making is minimal.

According to Poornima and Vyasulu (1999), women from the poorest and oppressed sections of the population have gained political experience and have held elective office because of reservations, which has an impact on the whole of rural society. They illustrate a case from Malgudi in Karnataka showing that reservation for women and for the oppressed is working at its best by referring to a story of rural SC woman who gradually climbed the ladder from GP president to mandal panchayat member and then to zilla panchayat (ZP) president and had plans to contest for Assembly elections. They felt it was not just a power ladder as the lady also set up mahila mandal (women's club) and had access to government grant for self-help groups (SHGs) and ran literacy classes for women. However, we do not agree with Vyasulu's other statement that 'since women who came to power under caste reservations have come with their social and economic disadvantages, illiteracy, little productive assets, wage labour in a society that has fixed places for various assets and gender, constitutional amendment cannot change their position'. Although this statement matches with the statement of Martin Luther King who said that 'in reality you cannot have economic and political equality without having some form of social equality...' (as quoted by Singh, Santosh, 2009: 353) and the concern expressed by Dr B.R. Ambedkar who did not favour panchayat system as he felt they were captured and governed by dominant castes or elites; one could be pessimistic about the changes that are taking place in governance structure of India, whether they are induced or spontaneous. It is 16 years since the publication of Vyasulu's study that the reservation quota for women in Karnataka has been increased from 33 per cent to 50 per cent. Many new cases of positive actions by women and their involvement in the progress of villages are reported across the country. Men have started to accept the reality of listening to the instructions of women.

Through affirmative action there is much improvement over the years in the status of women, their involvement in politics and rural development is emerging slowly and, the progress is gradual.

Decentralisation and Inclusive Development

Inclusive development is a process of development that includes every citizen in any country (Conceicao et al., 2001). Following Sen's concept of development with human face, Chatterjee (2005) defines inclusive development as that, which generates broad based participation and specifically reduces poverty and social exclusion and addresses deprivation arising due to caste, racial category and minority status. According to UNDP, 'development can be inclusive – and reduce poverty – only if all groups of people contribute to creating opportunities, share the benefits of development and participate in decision-making' (www.undp.org). Inclusive development ensures the participation of marginalised and excludes groups in the development process, wherein they become one of the stakeholders. According to Muddiman (2000), the concept of exclusion captures the processes of disempowerment and alienation, say some social groups and neighbourhoods becoming more detached and alienated from the mainstream society. Joshi (2009: 430) states that 'the objective of PRIs is to share political power in the society so as to tilt balance of power in favour of larger masses, enhance their political participation in the decision-making process and thereby bring social transformation for a just and egalitarian social order'.

Decentralisation fits into inclusive development structure as it itself is a model of development, which enables empowerment and upliftment of the marginalised and the poor guaranteed by institutional framework. The affirmative actions of the governments enable their participation. The very purpose of decentralisation is to develop plans for activities at the local level with the participation of all the sections of the community represented through the voices, for example Gram Sabha in India. Since decentralisation facilitates democratic governance that is representative, accountable, transparent and accessible to the public, it is likely to embrace inclusive development. It has been introduced in countries across the world as a mechanism to improve governance and service delivery.

The 73rd Amendment to Constitution of India is a major step initiated with respect to promoting inclusive development through mandatory participation of disadvantaged groups including women. It specifies that; 'Seats are reserved for Scheduled Castes (SCs) and Scheduled Tribes (STs) at all level according to their population at each level. Not less than one-third of seats are reserved for women and these may be allotted by rotation. The office of chairperson will also be subject to this provision'.

Distinguishing between formal inclusion of excluded communities and the real empowering inclusion, Jairath and Sajja (2009) state that there is a relationship between the nature of inclusion/exclusion in civil society and the way democratic institutionalisation of inclusion, functions during elections and meetings. They quote Andhra Pradesh's experience wherein the social and economic empowerment of women in some parts was possible through awareness campaigns and mass mobilisation, which led to anti-liquor movement by women in coastal Andhra and large scale organisation of women's SHGs which helped women to manage and save crores of rupees respectively. The review of literature suggests that affirmative action by the government across the world has brought in significant changes in rural political life (Aziz, 2000; Chattopadhyay and Dufflo, 2007) though there are a few studies, which claim that reservation or affirmative action has not resulted in desired result either because women are made proxies by their spouses or children or by powerful political interests in the case of SC/ST candidates and due to differences that exists between communities at local level (Pai, 2001). However, in cases where there is limited influence of decentralisation on women's empowerment, upliftment of reserved categories and minorities, overtime the affirmative actions are expected to enable these groups to assert themselves more effectively (Manor, 1999). In Kerala, Kudumbshree, a network of organisation of women with a focus on the poor has contributed to the effectiveness of decentralisation by generating social capital needed for influencing the course of local development (Vijayanand, 2012: 242). The Expert Committee on leveraging panchayats for efficient delivery of public goods and services opines that 'Reservations have combined political empowerment with social empowerment such that the earlier fears about elite groups capturing these institutions have been allayed'. This argument is supported by the study of Desposato and Norrander (2005) on Latin American countries. They observe that restrictions on political participation and the social norms, which discouraged participation for the older generation, are likely to disappear with time as new generation's experience has been different and, suggest for institutionalising political rights and descriptive representation for increasing participation.

Deshpande and D'Souza (2009) observe that, PRIs while being accountable and transparent offer possibilities for making local governance and the rural development process more need based, participatory and productive. Their study in 12 villages of Vidarbha, Marathwada and Western Maharashtra carried out in 2007 reveals that the rural government had become proactive in governance and development, which had become participatory and accountable. Reservations had given women a space in public and political field, which is necessary for inclusive development. Prud'homme (1995) argues that decentralisation increases disparities for the reason that while central government redistributes income from richer areas to deprived areas, local governments will collect taxes from all and spend on activities for the benefit of all. He concludes based on his review of both analytical and empirical research that national budgets tend to reduce regional disparities and any reduction in the importance of national budgets relative to those of subnational level increase disparities. But, Kalin (2003) argues in favour of decentralised governments for the reason that they are capable of attending to local problems like leakage in pipes, absence of teachers in local school, etc.

Lalita's study (2009) on an inquiry into the inclusion of excluded groups including women in social and political life of villages as against their formal inclusion by affirmative action of the government reveals mixed results. While women and SCs were active in one of the three panchayats of her study, their inclusion was minimal in other two panchayats. Discrimination in terms of non-entry to temples and sitting on the floor was practised by SCs themselves as followers of tradition, while they were discouraged by non-SCs in their economic empowerment. In Tamil Nadu, Thara Bhai (2009) found the dominance of caste and money in local politics, as a result of which Dalit members and presidents and women did not get the respect and power that was due to them. But, women were found to be doing well through Self-Help Groups

(SHGs). Although affirmative action has enabled representation of women and SCs their participation in real terms seems to be far away and Thara Bhai feels that to initiate this gradual process there is a need for the support from civil society and government.

Based on their study in Chitradurga district of Karnataka, Nagaraja and Pallavi (2013) have found that reservation in PRIs had increased the number of women members and had helped the development of tribal women in knowing about their voting power, duties and responsibilities of panchayat members, and were being supported by their family members. As per the analysis made by Crook and Alan (2001) decentralisation contributed to increased participation and representation in India and Columbia with mixed outcome in Phillippines and poor outcomes in Brazil, Chile, Bangladesh, Ghana, Kenya and Nigeria. They observe that the decentralisation process in West Bengal and Karnataka had helped women, SCs and STs to participate in the panchayat activities although the men tended to dominate, and both uneducated and SCs and STs were found engaged in meetings, contacting officials, joining associations, sending petitions, etc. An assessment of women's empowerment through Gram Panchayats (GPs) made by Chandrashekhar and Kadam (2012) in 25 GPs of Shimoga district in Karnataka reveals entry of young and educated women into panchayat elections most of them wanting to recontest. Further, there was improvement in women's social and family status, their contribution to society in terms of public services and developmental initiatives. But, Craig (2001) argues that although decentralisation had improved levels of public participation and accountability, it had done little to reduce rural inequality and poverty. Similarly, Behar and Kumar (2002) based on their study of five districts in Madhya Pradesh opine that though constitutional provisions had helped women to move forward and demonstrate their capacities, any attempt to go against male dominance resulted in usurping of their power.

Despite many efforts to include the weaker sections in to the main stream, discrimination exists in many villages of the country. As put forth by Baviskar and Mathew (2009), although the scenario is changing, discrimination does exist and it is sometimes making the president and panchayat members sit on the floor, keeping aside cup and plates for their use (which are required to be washed by them), creating rift between them and supporting weak SC candidates in election to control him/her after the elections. These were some of the tactics used by dominant castes. This is because the "formal institutional arrangements may not adequately reflect the democratisation of a society as there is distinction between making of a democracy and deepening of a democracy (Jairath and Sajja, 2009: 79, quoting Patrick Heller, 2000: 485). They therefore, assign successful implementation of panchayati raj in Kerala and West Bengal to social and land reforms and mass mobilisation movements. Kumar (2012) in his study of two villages in Nellore district of Andhra Pradesh finds caste as a hurdle to the democratic spirit of decentralisation of powers and inclusion of the marginalised groups. So, it is the social power that has been identified as the element that tries to pull down the very idea of decentralisation of political power. Palanithurai (2012) lists around thirty types of discrimination and practice of untouchability against Dalits in four sample villages of

Tamil Nadu selected for his study. He found that Dalit women panchyat leaders were not allowed to visit GP office nor preside over the gram sabha. Their husbands were attending to office work as proxies.

The study on dynamics of exclusion and inclusion by Singh, Santosh (2009) covering panchayat members, officials and villagers in Agra district of Uttar Pradesh reveals that women in Uttar Pradesh have always remained on the periphery, which is due to illiteracy, proxy candidature, low status of women in family and society, early marriage, poverty, burden of domestic chores, etc. His study states about a woman president in a sample village who did not know about the number of households in her village, whether panchayat collects taxes, name of block panchayat, her panchayat area, etc. all due to her illiteracy, inability and the low status that she faced in her village. However, Singh concludes that reservation had improved the bargaining power of SC women who have been using panchayats for socio-political gains and are approachable to village women for their problems.

The Citizens' Report on Governance and Development, 2010 (National Social Watch, 2011) concludes that governance is far from effective and there is a long way to go before decentralised local governance can produce real gains for the marginalised sections of the society, produce inclusive development and facilitate democratic practice. In many cases, inclusive development is not possible because of lack of awareness about panchayat activities.

Decentralisation and Political Participation

Political participation rates are an indicator of governmental legitimacy, citizens' support for a democratic form of government, and the sense of collective responsibility and civic duty that are associated with consolidated and stable democracies as expressed by Desposato and Norrander (2005). According to Mansuri and Rao (2013) decentralisation strengthens citizens' participation in local government by instituting regular elections, improving access to information by fostering mechanisms for deliberative decision-making on the demand side and enhances the ability of local governments to provide services by increasing their financial resources, strengthening the capacity of local officials and streamlining and rationalising administrative functions. The study on the background of women representatives by the Department of Panchayati Raj (2010) in West Bengal reveals that 47 per cent of the women panchayat members belonged to political family and 40 per cent of the women presidents and vice presidents had their husband involved in active politics. Another study in West Bengal (Beaman et al., 2009) shows that prior exposure to a female leader is associated with electoral gains for women and is likely to improve perceptions of female leader effectiveness. The share of female president was 11 per cent in panchayats where the pradhan's position had never been reserved and was 18.5 per cent in panchayats, which were continuously reserved for female pradhans for almost a decade. However, mere reservation does not ensure an easy ride for them. Due to differences in socio-economic status, occupational choice and family responsibilities in comparison to men, women candidates are likely to have greater difficulties in becoming eligible and aspiring political candidates (Alexander, 2007). And mere numerical representation itself does not ensure empowerment of weaker sections unless and until it is transformed into effective participation (Patnaik, 2005). Kundu (2009) with reference to West Bengal finds that the issue of powerlessness of the women has been neglected by the political party that ruled West Bengal (left front) for many years. According to Sivanna (2012) the asymmetries of information, inability to lobby and to be articulate on the part of women act as constraints in getting the decisions in their favour. According to Singh, Santosh (2009) women in Uttar Pradesh find it difficult to participate in PRIs due to traditional and weak organisational factors. And even if they are elected under reservation quota, they remain behind the walls of the house while male members look after GP matters. Poornima and Vyasulu (1999) also opine that women face hurdles in political participation due to limited mobility, domestic responsibilities and historical prejudices. A dismal picture of panchayati raj emerges from the statement of Bandyopadhyay and Mukherjee (2004) as they found that intended benefits of PRIs had not flown to empower the truly disempowered, the poor Dalits, minorities women, disabled, old aged and socially marginalised groups. Das (2013) investigates Dalit women's inroad into political system in terms of their access to panchayat posts, factors inhibiting their access giving thought to what state institutions can do to prevent such obstructions from his study in Ahmedabad district of Gujarat. Proxy politics was found to be observed taking advantage of low gender status of Dalit women, illiteracy, old age, widowhood, livelihood dependency and lack of financial resources. 'In spite of constitutional rights and positive outcomes reported elsewhere, there are reports about continued resistance to women's power with incidences of backlash and violence and efforts to unseat them through no confidence motions' (Sharma, 1998; Ramesh and Ali, 2001). Vijayalakshmi and Chandrashekar (2002), based on their study on participation of women in Karnataka, reveal that although there was enhanced representation and improvement in political status of women in local government, it had not translated into effective outcomes due to gender and other social differences. In the sense, they lacked power to execute works as active participation of women was not tolerated by men. Mathew (2013: 11) traces this phenomenon to inferiority complex among male members as elected women prove to be more responsive, sympathetic and caring than male members. Chhetri (2012) in his study on Sikkim found low participation of women in gram sabha, but as per the perceptions of the officials he assumes that there was no proxy representation. The level of awareness about panchayati raj is also not widespread as a study by Vaidya (1997) shows that female representatives in Karnataka were better informed as compared to representatives in Haryana. However, everything is not dismal. Despite the social resistance, Das (2013) identifies Dalit panchayat functionaries who used their rights to grow into role models in many villages across India.

Brara's study (2009) on GPs in Manipur reveals that the representation of Meira Paibis (torch-bearing women) a strong women's organisation are more popular among people than elected women GP members and presidents. Women presidents had taken up developmental works despite meagre funds and special provision under Tribal Sub Plan (TSP) had enabled development works in tribal areas. Brara observes that 73rd Amendment had resulted in sharing of power with excluded groups. Other communities were found to be tolerant of the reservation system as they were aware of the rotation system, which gave them a chance to contest for elections and compete for the seat of president. Patil (2009) studied the power structure and participation of SCs, STs, OBCs and women in rural local government in Kolhapur district of Maharashtra and found that although women who were housewives had entered politics due to reservations, their role in administration was nominal and they were found to be dependent on their husbands for such activities. Lack of education and knowledge about panchayat administration, poor economic status of weaker sections made dominant caste people to control GP administration. The other main reason for submissive nature on the part of excluded groups was their dependence on dominant castes for agricultural work.

Women's Political Empowerment and Service Delivery

The linkage between decentralisation and efficiency in service delivery without specific reference made to gender can be traced in the work of Tiebout (1956) who guessed that people move to places which provide services and fiscal sops according their preferences. According to his theory, elected representative who cannot keep costs or taxes low in comparison to those in similar communities will be out of his position. Empowerment has different dimensions. For women it could be attaining financial autonomy, decision-making power on household matters, political participation and decision-making power in administration, improvement in health and social status, educational attainment and well-being of self and family members. The reservations were given to women to bring their presence in the panchayats to contribute to good financial management and honest, corruption-free services and positively affect the role and place of women in public life with ultimate impact on the household (Government of India, 2013). Duflo and Topalova (2004) point out in their study of 24 Indian states that female presidents of GPs performed better than male leaders in providing public services, such as water supply and sanitation. Similar studies (Chattopadhyay and Duflo, 2004; Rajasekhar and Manjula, 2011) indicate that the representation of women has resulted in better service delivery. Female members were also found to be more effective leaders when they had spent a longer time in power, and they were more effective in states where a reservation system had been in place for a longer time (Ban and Rao, 2008). Chattopadhyay and Duflo (2004) in their study on West Bengal and Rajasthan found that women leaders bring benefits to their villages by providing public goods preferred by women. For example, the war against insanitation is reported to be fought by women in Haryana by placing a simple condition before the bridegrooms that the household should have a toilet before they marry their daughters (Water and Sanitation Programme, 2010). Bhargava and Subha (2009) in their study of GPs with SC, ST and women presidents in Bangalore (now Bengaluru) rural district, found that women approach female president with their problems relating to widow pension, access to drinking water, housing, sanitation, family fights, disputes with neighbour, etc. and many of these problems were solved through various programmes for the weaker sections.

Participation is seen as a key component to the process of decentralisation (Kulkarni, 2011). In order to enable the women to participate in local governance, women have to be given positive incentives in the form of appropriate reservation system. But, Ban and Rao (2008) feel that women presidents are less likely to meet higher level officials than men, although they are knowledgeable about political activities. Their study found that the presence of women leaders did not have significant impact on women's participation in gram sabha and their participation in women's organisation, but helped them at least to talk in the gram sabha. Contrary to this argument Buch (2000) in her study of three states viz. Madhya Pradesh, Uttar Pradesh and Rajasthan in India documents about women presidents feeling improvement in their status, self confidence, life style and awareness. And more than 50 per cent of the respondents in the study had positive views about women representatives and felt satisfied with their work though they felt that many of the works were carried out by presidents' husbands or other male members.

However, political journey is not smooth for women in a patriarchal and caste-ridden society, which poses challenges to come out to speak in open and participate in public activities (Kulkarni, 2011). Kulkarni notes that the following factors constrain women to participate in the local governance' viz., design of the programmes taken up by GPs, which are handled comfortably by men rather than women; the rules for membership of associations, which allow more male participation; lack of support from the household; the social expectations of the society that define women's roles and behaviour; women's own under estimation of their skills and capacities to perform; holding meetings when women are at work in the field or when they are busy with domestic work and, holding meeting at GP's office (where women are not comfortable due to presence of large number of men) other than at Anganwadi centres or schools preferred by women. Although women representatives are largely dependent on their husbands to run panchayat activities, as observed by many studies, some of them are able to put forward their views and agenda (Joshi, 2009) for the benefit of their community and self. Craig (2001) drawing from the relevant review of literature and the existing policies states that while democratic decentralisation has improved levels of public participation and government accountability, its ability to address rural inequality and poverty has been relatively modest. This could imply that while those in power could improve their political and social status, the system failed to translate this empowerment into benefits flowing to the rural poor. Blair (2000) points out that 'increased representation offers significant benefits in itself' and participation in local, democratically elected bodies can lead to improvements in self-identity and worth, which can help to break down customs of inequality and discrimination. He also states that membership in local administrative bodies can provide important skills (e.g. bookkeeping, leadership, etc.) that can be transferred to other walks of life.

Sathe et al. (2013) examine the performance of women members in service delivery and participation in democracy in the background of mandatory reservations for women. Using multistage sampling with representation of both male and female presidents from 32 villages and 640 respondents from Sangli District of Maharashtra the study found that the availability of basic services was higher in villages headed by female presidents who had served for more than three years as compared to villages headed by male presidents. Political participation was also found to be higher in villages headed by female presidents. The study by Bhat and Venkata Ravi (2012) also found that the presence of SCs/STs and women representatives in panchayats encouraged people to participate actively in development matters. Their study identified successful cases of administration by female presidents in Himachal Pradesh, Orissa (Odisha), Madhya Pradesh, Andhra Pradesh, Maharashtra and Karnataka where there was greater efficiency and transparency in the running of public affairs. The welfare of women, water supply and sanitation, maternal care, fight against alcohol consumption, improving mid-day meals, attending to school dropout cases, creation of garden for children, construction of toilets, roads, etc. were taken up by female presidents in the sample GPs of the above districts, while in some cases the priorities and felt needs of SCs and STs were not considered as SC/ST leaders joined hands with upper caste men. Further, the study found that in Kerala and Andhra Pradesh, political parties selected women of their choice for GP president.

Conclusions

Earlier studies on rural administration (Hiramani, 1979; Mukhopadhyay, 1982; Sharma, 1985; Rao, 1989; Iyer, 1989) largely indicate the influence of elite and upper caste in politics, which used power for protecting their self-interests and that of their community denying decision-making power to the downtrodden and common man, thereby failing to sustain or achieve the objectives of decentralisation. However, the traces of transition are seen across the country with many women taking the lead and taking the benefit of affirmative action set in by the Constitution of India and respective state governments.

The review of literature on decentralisation carried out with specific reference to women's participation and the other marginalised groups in general, points out that women are largely proxies of their husbands or other influential persons in the village (Mohanty, 2009; Singh, 2009; Jairath and Sajja, 2009; Kumar, 2001; Bhargava and Subha, 2009 (in some cases); Sivanna, 2012; Das, 2013), but they are less corrupt (Baviskar and Mathew, 2009) as against its high prevalence or failure to prevent it in earlier system (Chakrabortthy and Bhattacharyya, 1993; Poornima and Vyasulu,1999) and they try to provide basic services in the villages and attend to the needs of women (Chattopadhyay and Duflo, 2004; Sivanna, 2012). Their participation in the local government facilitated by affirmative action has led to inclusiveness and empowered them politically (Jairath and Sajja, 2009; Das, 2013) though only a minority of them have benefitted over and above mere representation and economically improved their self-confidence and social status (Buch, 2000). Due to such action the number of women in panchayats has also increased although it does not guarantee their participation (Kundu, 2009). Education and social background of the members are found to be the factors motivating empowerment and participation while poverty and continuity of faithfulness to the dominant castes are obstacles (Baviskar and Mathew, 2009; Jairath and Sajja,

2009). There are also evidences that political interests and social influences restrict entry of some women into politics, affect decisions on who should participate and their continued participation (Ananthpur, 2004; Mukhopadhyay, 2005). The literature indicates that real empowerment is possible only when the marginalised viz. SCs/STs and women influence decision-making, which is a sign of their being included overcoming their earlier state of exclusion (Baviskar and Mathew, 2009). However, no major improvement was found in the living conditions of the Dalit in GPs with Dalit presidents (Palanithurai, 2012) and their inclusion in political sphere did not make much difference to their individual or community lives (Kumar, 2012).

The fact that the dependence of weaker sections on the dominant castes in village for labour and financial needs, making them submissive and non-asserting in the case of panchayat activities has been discussed and identified by researchers (Joshi, 2009; Patil, 2009). There is a demand for creating employment avenues, distribution of land rights, creating capacity to learn and participate, organising and networking among women members, etc.

Many studies indicate that reservation has given the marginalised communities a sense of empowerment though they are yet to reach an equilibrium level. In the next decade or so the SCs, STs and women are bound to make further progress in their social status, leadership role, economic position, educational level and political awareness (Baviskar and Mathew, 2009). A majority of the studies stressed the need for capacity building among elected representatives as many members are new entrants and illiterates (Bhat and Venkata Ravi, 2012; Rao, 1989; Aiyer, 2002; Raghunandan, 2012; Palanithurai, 2012; Sivanna, 2012). Unless awareness is created on a large scale, they are likely to remain on the periphery on account of their illiteracy, proxy candidature, low status, poverty, dependence on dominant classes for work, etc. The short tenure of the president and money required for contesting elections have also been the hurdles in their continued participation.

Finally, as put forth by Crook and Manor (2000) 'where they are, democratic decentralisation tends not to damage programs to promote equity and to erode social exclusion'. Although the process is slow, the motion has been set in. Decentralisation has helped women and the marginalised to come out of closed societies, work for their own upliftment and benefit of the society. It has compelled men and women from the dominant classes to accept the powers of the marginalised. It is a holy nexus that is being manipulated for political gains also. But, linking decentralisation to every panacea of rural development without financial and functional autonomy could dilute its significance.

References

Ahlawat, S.R. and N. Ahlawat (2009), 'On the Floor and Behind the Veil: The Excluded in the Panchayati Raj in Haryana', in B.S. Baviskar and George Mathew (eds), *Inclusion and Exclusion in Local Governance: Field Studies from Rural India*, Sage Publications, New Delhi, pp. 137–67.

Aiyer, Mani Shankar (2002), 'Panchayati Raj: The Way Forward', *Economic and Political Weekly*, Vol. 37, No. 31, pp. 3293–97.

Alexander, Amy C. (2007), *Empowering Women: Four Theories Tested on Four Different Aspects of Gender Equality*, Conference Paper/Unpublished Manuscript, University of California, USA.

Ananthpur, Kripa (2004), 'Interfaces in Local Governance: A Study in Karnataka', *Working Paper No. 187*, Madras Institute of Development Studies (MIDS), Chennai.

Aziz, Abdul (2000), 'Democratic Decentralisation in Karnataka: Past and Future', International Conference on Democratic Decentralisation, Thiruvanthapuram, Kerala, India, 23–27 May, http://decwatch.org/files/icdd/044.pdf

Ban, R. and V. Rao (2008), 'Tokenism or Agency? The Impact of Women's Reservations on Village Democracies in South India', *Economic Development and Cultural Change*, Vol. 56, No. 3, pp. 501–30.

—— (2009), 'Is Deliberation Equitable? Evidence from Transcripts of Village Meetings in South India', *Policy Research Working Paper*, WPS4928, Development Research Group, World Bank [available at elibrary.worldbank.org/doi/pdf/10.1596/1813-9450-4928 accessed on 21 July 2014].

Bandyopadhyay, D. and A. Mukherjee (2004), *New Issues in Panchayati Raj*, Concept Publishing, New Delhi.

Bardhan, P. and D. Mookherjee (2007), *Decentralisation and Local Governance in Developing Countries: A Comparative Perspective*, Oxford University Press, New Delhi.

Baviskar, B.S. and George Mathew (2009), 'Introduction', in B.S. Baviskar and George Mathew (eds), *Inclusion and Exclusion in Local Governance: Field Studies from Rural India*, Sage Publications, New Delhi, pp. 1–17.

Beaman, Lori, Raghabendra Chattopadhyay, Esther Duflo, Rohini Pande and Petia Topalova (2009), 'Powerful Women: Does Exposure Reduce Bias?', *Quarterly Journal of Economics*, Vol. 124, No. 4, pp. 1497–540 [available at http://hdl.handle.net/1721.1/57903 accessed on 27 August 2013].

Behar, Amitabh and Yogesh Kumar (2002), 'Decentralisation in Madhya Pradesh, India: From Panchayati Raj to Gram Swaraj (1995 to 2001)', *Working Paper No. 170*, Overseas Development Institute, London.

Besley, T., R. Pande and V. Rao (2004), 'The Politics of Public Good Provision: Evidence from Indian Local Governments', *Journal of the European Economic Association*, Vol. 2, No. 2–3, pp. 416–26.

Bhargava, B. and K. Subha (2009), 'Including the Excluded through Panchayati Raj in Karnataka', in B.S. Baviskar and George Mathew (eds), *Inclusion and Exclusion in Local Governance: Field Studies from Rural India*, Sage Publications, New Delhi, pp. 169–97.

Bhat, K.S. and R. Venkata Ravi (2012), *Empowerment of SCs, STs and Women in Panchayati Raj Institutions*, Kanishka Publishers, New Delhi, pp. 1–136.

Blair, Harry (2000), 'Participation and Accountability at the Periphery: Democratic Local Governance in Six Countries', *World Development*, Vol. 1, No. 28, pp. 21–39.

Brara, Vijayalakhsmi (2009), 'Brushed Under the Carpet: Inclusion and Exclusion in Manipur', in K.S. Bhat and R. Venkata Ravi (eds), *Empowerment of SCs, STs and Women in Panchayati Raj Institutions*, Kanishka Publishers, New Delhi, pp. 285–316.

Buch, Nirmala (2000), 'Women's Experience in New Panchayats: The Emerging Leadership of Rural Women', *Occasional Paper No. 35*, Centre for Women's Development Studies, New Delhi.

Chakrabortty, K. and S.K. Bhattacharyya (1993), *Leadership, Factions and Panchayati Raj: A Case Study of West Bengal*, Rawat Publications, Jaipur.

Chandrashekhar and Ravindranath N. Kadam (2012), 'A Study on the Grama Panchayat Women Members' Participation in Developmental Initiatives: With Special Reference to Shivamogga District', *International Journal of Advanced Research in Management and Social Sciences*, Vol. 1, No. 3, September.

Chatterjee, S. (2005), 'Poverty Reduction Strategies: Lessons from the Asian and Pacific Region on Inclusive Development', *Asian Development Review*, Vol. 22, No. 1, pp. 12–44.

Chattopadhyay, R. and E. Duflo (2004), 'Women as Policy Makers: Evidence from a Randomised Policy Experiment in India', *Econometrica*, Vol. 72, No. 5, pp. 1409–43.

—— (2007), 'Impact of Reservation in Panchayati Raj: Evidence from a Nationwide Randomised Experiment', in Satyajit Singh and Pradeep K. Sharma (eds), *Decentralisation: Institutions and Politics in India*, Oxford University Press, New Delhi, pp. 223–44.

Chhetri, Durga (2012), *Decentralised Governance and Development in India with Special Reference to Sikkim*, Mittal Publications, New Delhi.

Conceicao, P. Gibson, D.V. Heitor and M.V. Sirilli (2001), 'Knowledge for Inclusive Development: The Challenges of Globally Integrated Learning and Implications for Science and Technology Policy', *Technological Forecasting and Social Change*, Vol. 66, No. 1, pp. 1–29.

Craig, Johnson (2001). Local Democracy, Democratic Decentralisation and Rural Development: Theories, Challenges and Options for Policy, *Development Policy Review*, 19(4), pp. 521–532.

Crook, Richard C. and Alan Sturla Sverrisson (2001). Decentralization and Poverty-alleviation in Developing Countires: A Comparative Analysis or is West Bengal Unique, *Working Paper No 130*, Institute of Development Studies (IDS), Sussex, England.

Crook, Richard and James Manor (1998), *Democracy and Decentralisation in South Asia and West Africa*, Cambridge University Press, Cambridge.

—— (2000), 'Democratic Decentralisation', *OED Working Paper Series No. 11*, The World Bank, Washington, D.C. [available at www.worldbank.org/html/oed accessed on 18 June 2014].

Das, Narayan (2013), *Dalit Leadership in Panchayats*, Centrum Press, New Delhi.

Department of Panchayati Raj (2010), *Information on West Bengal Panchayats, Their Members and Functionaries*, Panchayat and Rural Development Department, Government of West Bengal.

Deshpande, Ravi and Marcella D'Souza (2009), *Panchayat Raj on the Ground Issues in Village-Level Panchayat Raj Operation*, Watershed Organisation Trust (WOTR), Pune.

Desposato, Scott and Barbara Norrander (2005), *The Participation Gap: Systemic and Individual Influences on Gender Differences in Political Participation* [available at www.plataformademocratica.org/publicacoes/6612_cached.pdf accessed on 23 July 2014].

Duflo, E. and P. Topalova (2004), 'Unappreciated Service: Performance, Perceptions and Women Leaders in India', Mimeo, MIT [available at economics.mit.edu/files/793].

Government of India (2013), *The Expert Committee on Leveraging Panchayats for Efficient Delivery of Public Goods and Services*, Vol. I, New Delhi.

Hiramani, A.B. (1979), 'Dynamics of Factions in a Maharashtra Village', *The Eastern Anthropologist*, Vol. 32, No. 3, pp. 177–83.

Iyer, Krishna (1989), 'Panchayati Perestroika?', *Economic and Political Weekly*, Vol. 24, No. 37, pp. 2051–54.

Jairath, V.K. and Srinivas Sajja (2009), 'Negotiating with Empowerment', in B.S. Baviskar and George Mathew (eds), *Inclusion and Exclusion in Local Governance: Field Studies from Rural India*, Sage Publications, New Delhi, pp. 79–106.

Joshi, Satykam (2009), 'Local Governance and Social Change in Gujarat', in B.S. Baviskar and George Mathew (eds), *Inclusion and Exclusion in Local Governance: Field Studies from Rural India*, Sage Publications, New Delhi, pp. 407–32.

Kabeer, Naila (1999), 'Resource, Agency, Achievements: Reflections on the Measurement of Women's Empowerment', *Development and Change*, Vol. 30, No. 3, pp. 435–64.

Kalin, W. (2003), *Decentralisation: Why and How?*, Department of International Public Law, University of Berne.

Kulkarni, Seema (2011), 'Women and Decentralised Water Governance: Issues, Challenges and the Way Forward', *Economic and Political Weekly*, Vol. XLVI, No. 18, April 30.

Kumar, G.M. Ramesh (2001), 'Local Government for Good Governance: Experience in Andhra Pradesh', in Hasnat Abdul Hye (ed.), *Governance: South Asian Perspectives*, The University Press Ltd., New Delhi, pp. 247–68.

Kumar, Satish (2012), 'Marginalised Groups and Their Decision-making Power in PRIs: A Case Study from Andhra Pradesh', in K.S. Bhat and R. Venkata Ravi (eds), *Empowerment of SCs, STs and Women in Panchayati Raj Institutions*, Kanishka Publishers, New Delhi, pp. 187–202.

Kundu, M. (2009), 'Panchayati Raj or Party Raj', in B.S. Baviskar and George Mathew (eds), *Inclusion and Exclusion in Local Governance: Field Studies from Rural India*, Sage Publications, New Delhi, pp. 229–62.

Lalita, C. (2009), 'Caste and Politics in Rural Tamil Nadu', in B.S. Baviskar and George Mathew (eds), *Inclusion and Exclusion in Local Governance: Field Studies from Rural India*, Sage Publications, New Delhi, pp. 107–36.

Makwana, Ramesh (2012), *Women Empowerment through Panchayati Raj*, ABD Publishers, New Delhi.

Manor, James (1999), *The Political Economy of Democratic Decentralisation*, The World Bank, Washington, D.C.

Mansuri, Ghazala and Vijayendra Rao (2013), *Localizing Development: Does Participation Work?*, The World Bank, Washington, D.C.

Mathew, George (2013), 'Panchayati Raj in India: An Overview', in *Status of Panchayati Raj in the States and Union Territories of India*, Institute of Social Sciences, New Delhi, pp. 3–32.

Mishra, Sweta (1997), 'Women and the 73rd Constitution Amendment Act: A Critical Appraisal', *Social Action*, Vol. 47, No. 1, pp. 16–30.

Mohanty, B.B. (2009), 'Power to the Excluded Groups and Panchayati Raj in Coastal Orissa', in B.S. Baviskar and George Mathew (eds), *Inclusion and Exclusion in Local Governance: Field Studies from Rural India*, Sage Publications, New Delhi, pp. 43–78.

Muddiman, Dave (2000), 'Theories of Social Exclusion and the Public Library', in Muddiman et al., *Open to All? The Public Library and Social Exclusion*, Resource, London [available at eprints.rclis.org/7118/1/vol3wp1.pdf].

Mukhopadhyay, Maitrayee (2005), 'Decentralisation and Gender Equity in South Asia: An Issue Paper', The International Development Research Centre, Canada [available at www.idrc.ca/...decentralisation.../maitrayee-mukhopadhyay-decentralis... accessed on 1 December 2014].

Mukhopadhyay, R. (1982), 'Resource Distribution and Power Structure: A Case Study of a West Bengal Village', *The Eastern Anthropologist*, Vol. 35, No. 1, pp. 63–72.

Nagaraja, S. and S. Pallavi (2013), 'Political Inclusion and Schedule Tribe Women: A Case Study in Karnataka', *International Journal of Scientific Research (IJSR)*, Vol. 2, No. 10, pp. 1–2.

National Social Watch (2011), *Citizens' Report on Governance and Development 2010*, Sage Publications, New Delhi.

Olsen, Hans (2007), 'Concept Paper on Decentralisation and Local Governance', Swiss Agency for Development and Cooperation, Bern [available at http://www.deza.admin.ch/ressources/ resource_en_167288.pdf accessed on 18 July 2014].

Pai, Sudha (2001), 'Social Capital, Panchayat and Grassroots Democracy', *Economic and Political Weekly*, Vol. 36, No. 48, pp. 645–54.

Palanithurai, G. (1994), *Empowering People for Prosperity: A Study in New Panchayat Raj System*, Kanishka Publishers, New Delhi.

—— (2012), 'Status of Dalit Gram Panchayat Leaders in Tamil Nadu', in K.S. Bhat and R. Venkata Ravi (eds), *Empowerment of SCs, STs and Women in Panchayati Raj Institutions*, Kanishka Publishers, New Delhi, pp. 203–33.

Patil, R.B. (2009), 'Changing Power through Panchayats in Maharashtra', in B.S Baviskar and George Mathew (eds), *Inclusion and Exclusion in Local Governance: Field Studies from Rural India*, Sage Publications, New Delhi, pp. 1–13 and 18–51.

Patnaik, Pratyusna (2005), 'Affirmative Action and Representation of Weaker Sections: Participation and Accountability in Orissa's Panchayats', *Economic and Political Weekly*, Vol. 40, No. 44/45, pp. 4753–61.

Pettit, Jethro (2012), *Empowerment and Participation: Bridging the Gap between Understanding and Practice*, Institute of Development Studies, Sussex, UK.

Poornima, V. and V. Vyasulu (1999), 'Women in Panchayati Raj: Grassroots Democracy in Malgudi', *Economic and Political Weekly*, Vol. 34, No. 52, pp. 3677–86.

Prud'homme, Remy (1995), 'On the Dangers of Decentralisation', *The World Bank Research Observer*, Vol. 10, No. 2, pp. 201–20.

Raghunandan, T.R. (2012), *Decentralisation and Local Governments: The Indian Experience*, Orient Blackswan, New Delhi.

Rajasekhar, D. and R. Manjula (2011), 'Decentralised Governance and Service Delivery Affordability of Drinking Water Supply by Gram Panchayats in Karnataka', Monograph 23, Institute for Social and Economic Change (ISEC), Bangalore.

Rajasekhar, D., Salim Lakha and R. Manjula (2013), 'How Effective are Social Audits Under MGNREGS? Lessons from Karnataka', *Working Paper No. 294*, Institute for Social and Economic Change (ISEC), Bangalore.

Ramesh, Asha and Bharti Ali (2001), *33-1/3% Reservation Towards Political Empowerment*, Books for Change, Bangalore.

Rao, C.H. Hanumantha (1989), 'Decentralised Planning: An Overview of Experience and Prospects', *Economic and Political Weekly*, Vol. 24, No. 8, pp. 417–26.

Reddy, Krishna (2012), 'On Mapping Rural Governance in India', in K.S. Bhat and R. Venkata Ravi (eds), *Empowerment of SCs, STs and Women in Panchayati Raj Institutions*, Kanishka Publishers, New Delhi, pp. 164–70.

Sathe, Dhanmanjiri, Stephen Klasen, Jan Priebe and Mithila Biniwale (2013), 'Can the Female Sarpanch Deliver? Evidence from Maharashtra', *Economic and Political Weekly*, Vol. 48, No. 11, pp. 50–57.

Sen, A. (1999), *Development as Freedom*, Oxford University Press, New Delhi.

Sharma, Kumud (1998), 'Transformative Politics: Dimensions of Women Participation in Panchayati Raj', *Indian Journal of Gender Studies*, Vol. 5, No. 1.

Sharma, S.K. (1985), 'Revitalisation of Panchayati Raj', *The Indian Journal of Public Administration*, Vol. 31, No. 2, pp. 745–54.

Singh, S.B. (2009), 'Devolution of Power through Panchayats in Rajasthan', in B.S. Baviskar and George Mathew (eds), *Inclusion and Exclusion in Local Governance: Field Studies from Rural India*, Sage Publications, New Delhi, pp. 379–406.

Singh, Santosh (2009), 'Dynamics of Inclusion and Exclusion', in B.S. Baviskar and George Mathew (eds), *Inclusion and Exclusion in Local Governance: Field Studies from Rural India*, Sage Publications, New Delhi, pp. 353–77.

Sivanna, N. (2012), 'Women in Local Governance: Issues for Discussion', in K.S. Bhat and R. Venkata Ravi (eds), *Empowerment of SCs, STs and Women in Panchayati Raj Institutions*, Kanishka Publishers, New Delhi, pp. 247–56.

Strulik, Stefanie (2003), 'Against the Notion of "Proxies": Women Prada's Inimical and Uttar Pradesh', in Bidyut Mohanty (ed.), *A Decade of Women's Empowerment through Local Government in India*, Institute of Social Sciences, New Delhi.

Suresh, T.G. (2009), 'Understanding Grassroots Power and Excluded Communities in Kerala', in B.S. Baviskar and George Mathew (eds), *Inclusion and Exclusion in Local Governance: Field Studies from Rural India*, Sage Publications, New Delhi, pp. 199–228.

Thara Bhai, L. (2009), 'Gender, Caste and Politics in Rural Tamil Nadu', in B.S. Baviskar and George Mathew (eds), *Inclusion and Exclusion in Local Governance: Field Studies from Rural India*, Sage Publications, New Delhi, pp. 263–84.

Thorat, S. (2002), 'Oppression and Denial: Dalit Discrimination in the 1990s', *Economic and Political Weekly*, Vol. 37, No. 6, pp. 572–78.

Tiebout, Charles M. (1956), 'A Pure Theory of Local Expenditures', *Journal of Political Economy*, Vol. 64, No. 5, pp. 416–24.

UNDP (2000), 'Decentralisation in India: Challenges and Opportunities', HDRC discussion paper, United Nations Development Programme, New Delhi [available at http://www.undp.org.in/hdrc/resources/dissrs/challenges/ accessed on 1 June 2014].

—— (undated), 'From Reservation to Participation: Capacity Building of Elected Representatives and Functionaries of Panchayati Raj' [available at www.in.undp.org content/dam/... /from_ reservation_to_participation.pdf].

Vaidya, V.C. (1997), *Political Empowerment of Women at the Grassroots*, Kanishka Publishers, New Delhi.

Vijayalakshmi, V. and B.K. Chandrashekar (2002), 'Authority, Powerlessness and Dependence: Women and Political Participation', *Working Paper No. 106*, Institute for Social and Economic Change, Bangalore.

Vijayanand, S.M. (2012), 'Local Governments and Socially Disadvantaged Groups: Learning from the Kerala Experience', in K.S. Bhat and R. Venkata Ravi (eds), *Empowerment of SCs, STs and Women in Panchayati Raj Institutions*, Kanishka Publishers, New Delhi, pp. 234–46.

Water and Sanitation Programme (2010), 'From Dreams to Reality: Compendium of Best Practices in Rural Sanitation in India' [available at www.wsp.org/sites/wsp.org/ files/.../wsp_compendium_india.pd].

Part II

Devolution of Funds, Functions and Functionaries in PRIs

6

Fiscal Decentralisation and Panchayati Raj Institutions

Some Macro Issues

Neeta Tapan

Decentralisation in the current development scenario has emerged as a key strategy of governance to address the long-standing human development issues. In a federal system, functions are divided across different levels of government i.e. central/national, states/provinces and local governments. The economic rationale for decentralisation is based upon the limited geographic extent of the benefits of public goods and the relatively high costs of decision-making if everything is centralised. Thus, fiscal decentralisation as an important subset of decentralisation has attained significance, as it is believed that fiscal transfer to local self-governing institutions can produce effective result in addressing the development needs. In the context of India, the emergence of third tier governments (PRIs) and their fiscal issues have provided enough scope to relook into the existing pattern of fiscal decentralisation, as it is argued that without fiscal devolution, the spirit of self-governance may be floundered.

During the post-independence period, the Indian Constitution adopted the Panchayat Raj system as a part of the 'directive principles of state policy' in an effort to decentralise the administrative powers to the grassroots. However, at the same time, the constituent assembly adopted a federal structure with an intention to create a strong centre. The Third Five-Year Plan (1961–66) laid considerable stress in rural sector to make India self sufficient for food products. Particular attention had been given to the administrative and functional aspects of Panchayati Raj in the initial two years. To carry out the responsibilities entrusted to them, PRIs at each level were in a position to secure adequate resources both from the State Government and at the local level (GoI, 1963). In the Fourth Five-Year Plan (1969–74), an outlay of ₹ 115 crore was provided for the schemes of Community Development and Panchayats. Out of this amount, ₹ 98 crore were allocated for the plan schemes of various States and Union Territories. Among all the central sector schemes, the progress of expenditure had been very slow in many schemes particularly (i) composite programme for women and pre-school children, (ii) orientation of school teachers in Community Development. In the centrally sponsored sector, the scheme relating to the Applied Nutrition Programme was making satisfactory progress (GoI, 1969–74).

The Ashok Mehta classified post-1959 panchayat experience into the following 3 phases:

(i) Panchayat Ascendancy (1959–64)
(ii) Panchayat Stagnation (1965–69)
(iii) Panchayat Decline (1969–77)

The factors including (a) absence of political will, (b) resistant bureaucracy, (c) lack of involvement in planning, (d) ambiguity with respect to the role and status of panchayats, and (e) the domination of rural elite on panchayats were considered responsible to undermine PRIs (GoI, 1978). However, the absence of panchayats could not even be noticed in the Seventh Plan (1985–90) document. About 9,000 crore outlays was allocated for rural development in the 7th Plan and no role was assigned to *panchayats* even in the Minimum Needs Programmes (MNP) related to rural sanitation, rural roads, rural health, rural housing, rural energy, etc. (GoI, 1985–90).

In keeping with the global pattern, in India too there has been a trend towards greater devolution of powers to urban and rural local governments particularly since 1990. Keeping in view the historical blunders committed in the earlier experiments and the need for decentralised governance system in the globalised era, the Central Government in 1992 introduced the 73rd and 74th Amendments to the Constitution. The former Amendment relates to rural local governments, i.e. Panchayati Raj Institutions (PRIs) and the latter to urban local bodies (ULBs). Many provisions were incorporated under the 73rd Amendment Act with the intention of making panchayats self-governing institutions. The important provisions of the 73rd Amendment Act are: compulsory elections to PRIs once in five years, reservation of seats and executive positions for Scheduled Castes/Scheduled Tribes (SCs/STs), backward classes (optional) and women, the constitution of Finance Commission and District Planning Committees. These have made the panchayats one of the permanent political structures in India. Although this was done not as a component of structural reform, the attempt to decentralise allocative decisions was in conformity with the change in the development strategy towards a more open and market friendly economic regime.

The 73rd Constitution Amendment Act provided impetus to the local self-government (LSGs) in India by devolving requisite powers and functions, which are political and economic in nature. It is argued by the proponents of decentralised governance in India that the 73rd Constitution Amendment Act has ushered a greater degree of uniformity in structure (three-tier), composition (reservation for SCs, STs and women), powers and functions (financial and planning) of these institutions with an objective to achieve faster social and economic development.

Decentralisation is perceived as an important means to enable efficient allocation of resources, improve governance, accelerate economic growth, reduce poverty, achieve greater gender equity and empower weaker sections of society. In contrast, arguments against decentralisation have focused on weakening the capacity of the central governments to undertake macroeconomic stabilisation, efficiency loss due to poor administrative capacity of local governments to undertake the functions assigned to them and potential for increased corruption. However, the fact is that the fiscal decentralisation envisaged in the Constitutional amendments has the potential to significantly improve the efficiency of public services delivery in the country. Devolution of powers to the panchayats is done under Article 243-G of the constitution which states, ... the Legislature of a State *may*, by law, endow the Panchayats with such powers and authority as may be necessary to enable them to function as institutions of self-government ... . An important feature of this provision is the discretionary nature of the devolution. The fact that a State may endow powers to the panchayats implies that the devolution of functions is to be done at the discretion of the state governments.

Schedule XI to the Constitution specifies a list of 29 areas for the *panchayats*. The important areas include agriculture, land improvement, minor irrigation, development of water bodies and watershed development, education, healthcare, water supply and sanitation, rural housing, poverty alleviation, rural roads, women and development and social welfare. In respect of these areas, the state legislature is required to devolve the functions, functionaries and assign revenue bases or transfer funds to carry out these functions satisfactorily. The extent of devolution of powers as stated above, however, is at the discretion of the state government and the latter undertakes the functions in these areas concurrently with panchayats.

The political theories make out the case for federalism on the basis of freedom and representation, safeguarding group identities and ensuring security and stability through bargains. On the other hand, economic theories of federalism focus on creating multilevel public sector governance systems to improve efficiency. Hence, a fair degree of financial autonomy, in the true spirit of decentralisation of power, is a sine qua non for local governments to function more effectively as self-governing institutions. By financial autonomy we mean that they should have their own taxation and borrowing powers as well as a share in the state's taxes and duties and grants-in-aid from higher levels of government. The local governments should not only have the power to raise revenues but the own source of revenues should constitute a very significant share in the total revenues (Bahl, 1999). However, it is a general perception that panchayats are financially and technically underequipped to perform even the core functions, much less the welfare functions and other economic functions related to agriculture and industries. Hence, many of the core functions that traditionally belonged to panchayats – drinking water, rural roads, street lighting, sanitation, primary health, and so forth – have not been transferred fully in some states; they are being performed by the line departments of the state government or the parallel parastatals. As a result, the per capita total expenditure of *panchayats* remains abysmally low in all states except Andhra Pradesh, Chhattisgarh, Goa, Gujarat, Karnataka, Kerala, Maharashtra, and Tamil Nadu.

An important implementable rule of fiscal decentralisation is the clear assignment of revenue handlers to effectively implement the functional responsibilities (Bahl, 2000). Finances should follow functions so that the subnational governments can vary the public services across jurisdictions according to the preferences of the people by varying tax payments on them. Assignment of revenue sources is necessary for a strong link between the decision to spend and the decision of raising revenues to finance the spending, imparts greater efficiency and accountability in public service provision. Thus, proper assignment of functions and sources of finance, consequences arising from their overlap and the mechanism to match their functions and finances both vertically among different levels of government and horizontally among different governmental units constitutes the subject matter of fiscal federalism.

Major revenue raising powers assigned to the village panchayats comprise of (i) tax on land and buildings not subject to agricultural assessment; (ii) taxes on entertainment other than cinematograph shows; (iii) taxes on vehicles other than motor vehicles; (iv) taxes on advertisements and hoarding; (v) pilgrim fees on persons attending *jatras*, festivals etc. where the village panchayats make arrangement for water supply and sanitation; (vi) market fees; (vii) fees for registration of cattle brought for sale to the market; (fees on buses and taxies and auto stands if the panchayat provides facilities for travellers and (ix) fee for grazing cattle in the grazing lands. Of these, only the tax on land and buildings other than agricultural land has some revenue significance. Other taxes are not important, either because the tax base is negligible or the local bodies do not have the capacity to administer them. In respect of taxes on land and buildings too, the village panchayats can levy and collect this tax subject to the specified exemptions and ceiling rate specified.

Thus, revenue bases assigned to the local governments in all multilevel fiscal systems are inadequate to meet their expenditure requirements because although local governments have comparative advantage in implementing expenditures due to their lowest transaction costs but have comparative disadvantage in raising revenues for all; broad based, mobile and redistributive taxes can be effectively levied only by the higher level governments. Besides, there are significant differences between different local bodies in their capacity to raise revenues and costs of providing public services. These vertical and horizontal fiscal imbalances have to be offset through a system of intergovernmental transfers. Consequently, the provision for the appointment of the State Finance Commission every five years is essentially to assess the expenditure requirements of Panchayats for carrying out the functions devolved to them at all the three levels, assess their capacity to raise revenues from the sources assigned to them and recommend grants to meet the remaining requirements for the five years under their consideration. In addition to the state transfers to the panchayats based on the recommendations of the State Finance Commissions (SFCs), the central government also gives grants based on the central Finance

Commission. One of the terms of reference to the Central Finance Commission is to make recommendation on the '... measures need to augment the Consolidated Fund of a State to supplement the resources of the panchayats in the State on the basis of the recommendations made by the Finance Commission of the State'.

In India, Article 280 of the Constitution empowers the President to constitute a Finance Commission (FC) at the central level once in five years. The FC is to make recommendations on the distribution between the Union and the states of the net proceeds of taxes, allocation between the states, the principles which should govern the grants-in-aid of the revenues of the states out of the Consolidated Fund of India etc. Similarly, Article 243(I) of 73rd Amendment Act provides for constitution of a FC by the states once in five years to look into the resources of both state and local governments.

Many state governments transfer the functions to the *panchayats* along with the employees and estimated finances to pay the salaries of the employees and meet non-salary components of these functions. However, in order to make the system implementable and ensure compliance of the employees to the new plan, the transfers have been tied to several schemes that were originally implemented by these state government employees. With state governments continuing to exercise the powers of transfers and promotions of these employees, the accountability of the employees to the panchayats is totally lost. Devolving functions in terms of schemes has robbed the advantages of fiscal decentralisation altogether. The basic advantage of fiscal decentralisation is to enable the local governments to provide public services according to the preferences of people. By devolving the functions in terms of schemes, autonomy and flexibility required to implement expenditure programmes have been denied to the panchayats.

In addition to the state schemes, there are a number of central schemes which are passed on to the *panchayats* for implementation. These include schemes on poverty alleviation, education and nutrition, health, water supply and sanitation, women and child development, rural housing, rural roads and rural electrification. Devolving functions segmented into various schemes and prioritising them has meant that the rural local bodies do not take any decisions, but simply implement the schemes designed by the State/Central governments. Second, rural local governments do not have the incentive to raise revenues. Overwhelming proportion of the transfers is scheme based and the preoccupation is with implementing them – particularly those involving contractors.

The recommendations of the State Finance Commissions can be divided into three categories: (i) assignment of taxes, duties, levies and tolls to local bodies; (ii) sharing of revenue proceeds; and (iii) transfers on account of grants-in-aid and other financial assistance.

So far, four National Finance Commissions (the 10th, 11th, 12th and 13th) have made their recommendations.[1] As per the SFC recommendations, many of the State Governments have agreed to give PRIs a specific percentage of share in some of the State taxes like land revenue and cess on it, additional stamp duty, entertainment tax, royalties on minerals and mines, forest revenue and market fees; these taxes are less buoyant in nature and have no relation to the powers and functions to be devolved upon panchayats. More buoyant taxes like sales tax and excise are kept out of the purview of PRIs. States where panchayats exist have constituted their respective State Finance Commissions (SFCs). Except for Sikkim and Goa, SFCs have submitted their reports to respective State Governments. Recommendations of the SFCs have been accepted in toto by ten States, viz; Karnataka, Kerala, Madhya Pradesh, Manipur, Punjab, Rajasthan, Tamil Nadu, Tripura, Uttar Pradesh and West Bengal. All these commissions were severely constrained for reasons emanating partly from the practice and partly from the design of the new fiscal arrangement: the lack of synchronisation of the periods covered by the SFCs with those covered by the National Finance Commission; the absence of a timeframe for action by the state government on the recommendations of the SFC; a lack of clarity in assigning functions, finances, and functionaries to local governments; and heterogeneity in approach, content, and period covered by the various SFCs.

All SFCs have put great emphasis on internal revenue mobilisation, but none has suggested any effective mechanism for PRIs to generate their own revenue. SFCs do not recommend or foresee any noticeable change in the tax (including the non-tax) jurisdiction of local bodies. However, the SFCs suggest better use of the existing tax jurisdiction by referring the system of property taxation and giving greater autonomy to local bodies in matters relating to tax rate setting. SFCs place greater reliance on transfers for bridging the gap between the local bodies' revenue and expenditure. In real terms, no improvement in local resource base is likely as a result of the recommendations of SFCs. Moreover, the SFC reports have paid far less attention to issues of autonomy, financial management and auditing procedures.

Apparently, all the Commissions except the 13th Finance Commission recommended ad hoc lump sum grants to panchayats. The Thirteenth Finance Commission made a major departure from the ad hoc practice adopted by the previous commissions of recommending lump sum grants to local governments, both panchayats and municipalities. According to the recommendation of the 13th Finance Commission, the grant would be calculated from the volume of the Union divisible pool of the previous year. In this context, the percentage share would gradually increase from 1.5 per cent in 2010–11 to 2.28 per cent in 2010–15. The respective population of panchayats and municipalities would determine their share in the grant. The grant as recommended by the Commission has two components – a basic component and a performance-based component. The basic is equivalent to 1.50 per cent of the previous year's divisible pool. All states are entitled to have access to this grant for all the five years, as per the criteria and weights recommended by the Commission. The performance grant effective from 2010–12 was 0.50 per cent for the year 2011–12 and one per cent thereafter, upto 2014–15.

The State-wise Thirteenth Finance Commission's General Basic Grant for *Panchayati Raj* Institutions in 2010–11 and 2011–12 is as shown in Table 1.

Table 1

State-wise Thirteenth Finance Commission's General Basic Grant for Panchayati Raj Institutions (₹ crore) (2010–11 and 2011–12)

States	*2010–11*			*2011–12*		
	Allocation	*Release*	*Release to Allocation Ratio*	*Allocation*	*Release*	*Release to Allocation Ratio*
Andhra Pradesh	481	481	100	616	305	49
Arunachal Pradesh	25	25	100	32	16	50
Assam	145	73	51	186	165	89
Bihar	456	456	100	584	584	100
Chhattisgarh	154	154	100	197	197	100
Goa	8	4	51	11	4	39
Gujarat	215	217	101	275	272	99
Haryana	100	101	101	128	127	99
Himachal Pradesh	51	51	100	66	66	100
Jammu & Kashmir	84	0	0	108	108	100
Jharkhand	139	139	100	179	179	100
Karnataka	414	419	101	531	526	99
Kerala	179	179	100	230	230	100
Madhya Pradesh	378	378	100	485	485	100
Maharashtra	506	506	100	648	648	100
Manipur	20	20	100	26	0	0
Meghalaya	29	29	100	37	37	100
Mizoram	19	19	100	24	12	50
Nagaland	28	14	51	36	14	39
Odisha	238	238	100	305	305	100
Punjab	104	104	100	133	0	0
Rajasthan	362	367	101	464	460	99
Sikkim	17	9	51	22	30	139
Tamil Nadu	284	287	101	363	360	99
Tripura	27	27	100	35	35	100
Uttar Pradesh	900	911	101	1153	1142	99
Uttarakhand	54	54	100	70	70	100
West Bengal	381	381	100	488	242	49
Total	5,799	5,645	97	7,429	6,616	89

Source: Ministry of Panchayati Raj, Government of India, website (http://www.panchayat.gov.in).

Besides these basic grants for PRIs, substantial tied funds are being transferred to the panchayats through the centrally sponsored schemes (CSSs) and additional central assistance (ACAs). For long, the CSS transfers were administered and utilised mainly by the line departments. In recent years, the panchayats are being increasingly recognised as implementing institutions for the plan schemes of line ministries. The most important of these is the

Mahatma Gandhi National Rural Employment Guarantee Act (MGNREGA), where the panchayats at the district, intermediate and village levels have been given specific responsibilities as principal authorities for planning and implementation. Village panchayats are required to take minimum 50 per cent value of the works.

Over a period of time panchayats evolved differently across states with respect to its structure, achievements and accountability. Since panchayat is the derivative of the state, it is the responsibility of the subnational governments to devolve its power and authority, functions and functionaries, rights and duties, and the funds to the structure below, and thus bring the government to the doorstep of the people. It has been done in a variety of ways since states vary in their complexion. The system of decentralisation, whether it is related to functioning of PRIs or about promoting accountability or capacity building, there is no uniformity since patterns of their evolving vary from one state to another.

Improvement of service delivery at the local level has become one of the most important goals in recent time. In pursuance of inclusiveness in the growth process, the 11th Plan recognises the criticality of involving Panchayati Raj Institutions (PRIs) in planning, implementing and supervising the delivery of services at the local level that would require functional, fund and staff devolution to them. The government of India has committed to accelerate the ongoing decentralisation as one of the important means for successful implementation of its Centrally Sponsored Schemes and hence articulated important roles for PRIs in implementation of these schemes. Yet simply providing greater responsibility onto PRIs without systematic reform and capacity building is unlikely to lead to dramatic improvements in service delivery.

All said and done, the PRIs have a poor fiscal base. While resource mobilisation by the PRIs is generally limited, it is imperative to provide PRIs with revenue raising powers of their own in order to reduce their excessive dependence on the State and Central Governments. But till such time that they are financially dependent on funds from the State Governments, the State Budgets should specify the amount earmarked for district sector plans under Panchayati Raj as also their distribution among the three tiers. In addition, a part of the finances should be in the form of untied funds so that the funds can be utilised as per the felt needs of the panchayats. Training and capacity building of PRI functionaries is essential and devolution of financial resources must be accompanied by suitable strengthening of PRIs through transfer of departmental functionaries.

Finally, the panchayats should be given a respectable place in the scheme of Indian public finance and planning. They cannot raise adequate resources to meet their responsibilities, and hence transfer of resources is inevitable. The real challenge is to make the sub-state transfers, and the mechanisms designed for them, truly rational in terms of efficiency, equity, predictability, transparency, and adequacy.

Note

1. The 10th National Finance Commission was not mandated to make recommendations for local governments. Because the CAA became effective before the commission submitted its report, it made recommendations for the newly inserted sub clauses of Article 280(3) regarding local government.

References

Bahl, Roy (1999), 'Implementation Rules for Fiscal Decentralisation', paper presented at the International Seminar on Land Policy and Economic Development, organised by Land Reform Training Institute, Taiwan, 17 November 1998.

—— (2000), Intergovernmental Transfers in Developing and Transition Countries: Principles and Practice, *Urban and Local Government Background Series No. 2*, Washington DC: World Bank.

Government of India (1957), *Report of the Team for the Study of Community Projects and National Extension Service* (Chairman: Balvantrai Mehta), Vol. I and II, Committee on Plan Projects, National Development Council, New Delhi.

—— (1963), *Report of the Study Team on Position of Gram Sabha in Panchayati Raj Movement* (Chairman: R.R. Diwakar), Ministry of Community Development and Cooperation, New Delhi.

—— (1969–74), Fourth Five Year Plan, Planning Commission, Yojana Bhawan, New Delhi.

—— (1965), *Report of the Committee on Panchayati Raj Elections* (Chairman: K. Santhanam), Ministry of Community Development and Cooperation, New Delhi.

—— (1978), *Report of the Committee on Panchayati Raj Institutions* (Chairman: Asoka Mehta), Department of Rural Development, Ministry of Agriculture and Irrigation, New Delhi.

—— (1985–90), Seventh Five Year Plan, Planning Commission, Yojana Bhawan, New Delhi.

—— (2000), *Report of the Eleventh Finance Commission for 2000–05*, Akalank Publications, New Delhi.

—— (2001a), *Report of the Task Force on Panchayati Raj Institutions*, Planning Commission, New Delhi.

—— (2001b), *Report of the Working Group on Decentralised Planning and Panchayati Raj Institutions*, Ministry of Rural Development, New Delhi.

—— (2009), *Report of the Thirteenth Finance Commission for 2010–15*, Finance Commission, New Delhi.

7

How Inclusive are the Panchayats

The Future Stratagem

Nupur Tiwari

Panchayati Raj in India is designed to strengthen the totality of our democratic institutions and practices. The system of governance inherited by India has its roots in the feudal-imperial legacy of the past, largely modified and adapted by the British to meet their colonial ends. The efforts of leaders of freedom struggle who upheld the principle of self-reliant villages did not reflect much in the new Constitution framed after Independence. In India, the local governance system had no constitutional backing till the 73rd and 74th Constitutional Amendments of 1993. With the passing of Conformity Act all the states and union territories are expected to initiate activities for decentralisation. The devolution of powers to the Panchayati Raj Institutions (PRIs) in different states has not been uniform. A few states like Kerala, Karnataka and West Bengal did much to devolve 3Fs (funds, functions and functionaries) at the grassroot level. But in most of the states a great deal of confusion as regards the nature of the transfer itself, prevailed.

Experience over a decade and a half shows that the decision to devolve and the trigger to do so has always been driven politically. However, since in different states, the impetus has come from different political parties, it is difficult to say that one or the other party has been more panchayat friendly than the other. It would be more accurate to say that within each political party, there are divided views on Panchayati Raj. However, no party today can openly question Panchayati Raj; that would be political suicide.

The other lesson that can be drawn from States that have devolved or are currently devolving with reasonable success is that in all of them, the bureaucracy has played its part in proper design of systems, when backed by the political signal to devolve. Most such states brought out a road map on devolution, which was widely discussed in public, before going ahead with a devolution plan. Behind successful devolution, there have always been a cabal of champions, from politics, the bureaucracy and civil society, who have contributed collectively to its success. Politically driven decisions to devolve, without sufficient backing in terms of changes in administrative and executive design have tended to flounder, with adverse consequences on those who motivated such changes.

In India it has now been accepted that higher GDP rates during the recent years have not helped the larger masses in getting integrated with the process of development. It is important that Local governance be brought to centre-stage as the principal governance reform, to reinforce economic reform in such a manner as to secure inclusive growth. Inclusive Growth 'is growth pro-poor', the bulk of the population of this country feel that they have not benefited in any obvious way from the development of the last decade'. There is need to reconceptualise inclusion as not only recognising the usual marginalised communities or sections of society as beneficiaries but by including them as thinkers who think and 'know' differently, and whose presence in designing is the real inclusion. There is need to give the excluded agency inclusion – to include knowledge and analysis and experience of minority groups, women and other excluded and deprived sections of society, in development design. 'Inclusion' needs to be reconceptualised, as 'agency', the think side of action.

Local self-government, offers this opportunity, as communities, citizens, right from the Gram level, can participate in the designing of the development in their area. With the arrangements that have been made in the constitutional amendment to give voice to historically discriminate against groups such as women and the SCs and STs, this is the space where inclusion can really take place. Local self-government makes the link between political and economic governance, and could lead to the alternative paradigm. The Panchayati Raj system, the movement to devolve power, to deepen democracy in India, is a movement for economic and social justice, and provides the vehicle to implement the vision of inclusive growth in India. It is necessary to recognise that we cannot secure inclusive growth without inclusive governance. And it is this, fundamental conundrum which local government in our system is attempting to address. If Gram Sabhas are largely non-functional and most elected representatives (other than panchayat Presidents) left uninvolved and, therefore, frustrated, this is because even as they see more and more money being poured into rural areas, they also see that much of it is beyond their control or responsibility. But it is critically important that over the next decade and not much longer than that we actually succeed in empowering our institution of local self-governance with the functions, the finances and the functionaries that are essential to running of effective local self-government.

In India, the participatory planning that has been institutionalised in the state of Kerala has been accepted as a good practice to emulate. Besides, functioning of Gram Sabhas capacity building activities, gender mainstreaming, grievance redressal mechanism, Nyaya Panchayats and poverty reduction strategies have been highlighted as innovative models for replication.

Transition to the New System Underway

In India, constitutionally mandated PRIs have moved into the second stage so the need is to set in motion second-generation reforms. Elections have been held (thrice in most places) and the relevant functions have also been devolved, as intended, in most states. Considering activity mapping as the foundation for sound Panchayati Raj, various states have prepared it on the principle of subsidiary. This involves identification of functions, within a given sector and desegregations of these functions into tasks, activities and responsibilities for the devolution for the three levels of panchayats. However, there has been much less action in devolving funds and functionaries, which are the other two legs on which the structure must rest. The extent of financial devolution varies from state to state. While some have devolved a significant proportion of the state budget to the PRIs, many others have not yet done so. It was expected that local bodies would become financially independent along with a constitutional guarantee of existence breathed through five yearly elections. But there are doubts and financially local governments are largely dependent on state governments. State governments have a large number of powers to inspect, dissolve, remove and audit the functioning of local governments. Bureaucratic stranglehold may not be absolute but functioning of local government has been restricted.

By contesting and getting elected to PRIs, women have shattered the myth of their own passivity – that women are not willing to enter politics. For women, successful grassroots experience has meant a chance to form coherent voice, to be heard and to make a difference in their communities. However, women's representation in the decision-making positions with monitoring power is still negligible. The present rules of the game and decision-making procedure do not allow a greater participation of women and in the absence of women, there is no effort to recognise or change the game. The very absence of women at these levels thus leads to preservation and reinforcement of male-oriented and male benefiting types of decisions. The reservation in panchayats has provided for the erosion of the traditional gender, caste, class roles and hierarchy but it has still to cover a long and difficult process. Women not only have to fight for their right to be more than proxy members but also to break the barriers of gender division of labour, illiteracy, low level of mobility, seclusion, lack of training and information, which still continue to exist without enough support from the power structure. Women's low self-esteem at the household level and their new role in local politics where they are now expected to function as leaders, creates a contradiction between women's role at home and in local government. The fact is that the participation of women could be better if they had functional education and also training on the various intricacies involved in the political field.

There is much importance of Information and Communication Technology (ICT) in enhancing panchayat capacity so that they can perform their constitutionally and legislatively mandated functions better. When it comes to e-governance Gram Panchayat has unique importance for the reasons of primacy of Gram Sabha and its impact on the Gram Panchayat (GP) and requirement of keeping the Gram Sabha (the citizenry) well informed, by the GP. E-governance can help in aiding Gram Sabhas to take better informed decisions. E-governance can help in dissemination of internal processes of Gram Panchayats (agendas, resolutions, voting record); Proceedings of Gram Sabhas and action taken, Progress reports, Dissemination of data (family surveys, property lists, BPL lists, pensions, censuses); Services data (education, health, water and sanitation); Natural resources and biodiversity data; Databases on panchayat members and staffing details; Availability of government and private infrastructure and village habitat planning. It is important to position IT as decision-making support system for panchayats.

There is much to do – and much to Learn

Cynics are fond of pooh-poohing decentralisation in India on the ground that all that is decentralised is corruption, and therefore, one needs to analyse why such a widespread negative impression about PRIs has taken root. Much of it is a matter of selective memory and autosuggestion – ignore the good stories and highlight the bad. However, the functioning of panchayats is quite distinct from that of higher level governments. First, being closer to the people, a lot more corruption gets exposed to public view as compared to corruption at higher levels. Second, while grassroot level institutions have distinct advantages in localising government, they also face proximate political and social pressures that make traditional virtues of public administration such as impartiality, neutrality and anonymity difficult to realise locally. Third, regardless of whether PRIs are elected on a party basis or otherwise, they are political institutions. Elected members have constituencies both in the geographical and socio-political sense. One cannot avoid legitimate aspirations to nurse constituencies in today's context of highly competitive electoral politics and one must accept that there is bound to be a tendency to favour a region, a group of people or even individuals in developmental decision-making. Fourth, unlike legislators, PRI elected representatives are vested with executive authority and are empowered to take decisions having financial implications and authorise expenditure from public funds, decide levels of taxation, exercise power of collecting taxes and regulatory powers which are of a quasi-judicial character.

Two things need to be done to make panchayats more inclusive and effective as local governments. First, inclusiveness has meaning only if panchayats are given responsibilities in the letter and spirit of the Constitution. Unfortunately, Panchayati Raj is often a charade in several States and political rhetoric hides their marginalisation. Both the centre and the states need to bring in real devolution, which can be differentiated from the charade that Panchayati Raj has often become, as follows:

Real Devolution:	Not-so-real devolution
Clear role assignment	Somebody else (above or below) responsible for Panchayat performance
Power to spend money	
Power to tax	Limited power to collect resources
Discretion in spending money,	Scheme bound expenditure
Power to hire fire and control staff.	
Direct Accountability.	Somebody else (above or below) acting for the panchayats

Second, decision-making processes in panchayats need to be better defined, to diminish the possibility of elite capture, proxy participation, single point decision-making and corruption. The formula for improving PRI functioning would follow a four-fold path; simplify, inform, review and hold accountable for non-performance or mal administration. Some key steps in this regard are as follows:

(a) Well functioning Gram Sabhas are essential.

(b) Just as in the case of most government offices, a thick veil of secrecy hides inefficiencies, arbitrariness, corruption and nepotism from public gaze in PRIs too. An example of the secrecy that surrounds executive action in PRIs is seen in the selection of beneficiaries for various schemes. The logical transparent sequence ought to be the laying down of the selection criteria, publicising them, calling for applications through the Gram Sabha, processing them with reference to the criteria, making selections and ending with publicly explaining the rationale of the selection made. When there is a great deal of arbitrariness in decision-making at the local level, records will not show how the choice was arrived at or whether various options and possibilities were analysed and on which criteria the final decision was made. Fairness at the cutting edge will need to be seen and corroborated by full disclosure, whatever may be the inconvenience and cost involved for the administration. Therefore, systems that ensure easy access for the citizen to information must be put into place. If the right to information is to have any meaning, information will have to be systematised and packaged in a manner that makes sense to those who seek it.

(c) We need to sytematise the process of recording decisions, to ensure the democratic functioning of panchayats There are seven linked aspects of ensuring that PRIs work more democratically as described below:

  (i) The emphasis on consensus in decision-making should be approached with caution, while true consensus is appreciable, an unnecessary emphasis on consensus could stunt the growth of democracy. Consensus undermines democracy in two ways. First, in a consensus, the strongest voices prevail automatically. Thus it is easier for a situation of elite capture to prevail if business rules of representative bodies expressly prefer consensus in decision-making. Reservations in favour of women and the socially disadvantaged do not make much sense in a consensus situation because one can just as easily silence the poor. The second disadvantage of a consensus situation is that elected representatives can hide behind a consensus decision to avoid responsibility and accountability to their voters. Therefore, votes have always to be recorded. This is an important aspect of democratic PRI functioning. If there is a consensus or unanimity, even this should be recorded. The record of voting by individual members in PRI meetings could become the most important mechanism of opening up the proceedings to the public, particularly if there is express provision in the law for disclosing the voting pattern to the public. Mandatory public display of resolutions of the PRIs along with the record of members voting for or against them will enable the public to know what their members are doing for them. They will know how their member has articulated their concerns in meetings. More than anything else, this alone will be an effective mechanism of downward accountability

  (ii) Procedures for conduct of meetings will have to be laid may be necessary, in order to ensure that those who do not feel up to articulating their concerns in an open meeting can still make their presence felt in decision-making.

(iii) A strict quorum requirement will diminish the scope of marginalisation in decision-making.

(iv) Ensure that the body is collectively responsible for its actions. The requirement of collective responsibility is another method of increasing accountability of the body to the people. Once a member knows that his position is also in jeopardy as he is also vicariously responsible for wrong acts of his colleague-members in the body, there is a greater price to be paid for being a passive spectator to the proceedings. Members will be induced to participate meaningfully and there will be peer pressure on each other not to take wrong decisions.

(v) Make decision-making committee based. Most panchayat legislations provide for Standing Committees in Panchayats, but these provisions are neglected and hardly operatonalised. Committee based decision-making diminishes the scope for elite capture and allows for the articulation of all voices.

(vi) Put in place mechanisms to open up the process of decision-making which is opened up to public gaze. Ordinarily, meetings shall be open to the public. There must be full disclosure of facts in meetings, so that reasoned decisions can be taken. One method of doing this is to ensure a prior circulation of the agenda for a meeting and if necessary, allow one meeting to intervene before a decision is made. Thus a resolution can be introduced in a particular meeting and discussed, but voting could be held in the next meeting of the body.

(vii) Intervals between the rotation of reservations for women and SC and ST representatives need to be extended. If reservations are rotated after every 5 year term, it leaves very little incentive for the member elected on a reserved seat to perform, because he or she knows that next time around, there will only be a remote chance of being elected as she will not have the benefit of reservation in the same seat.

(d) Provide a right to recourse to an independent institutional mechanism that gives speedy relief to the aggrieved which effectively bolsters empowerment through panchayats. With greater devolution and decentralisation there will be a need to investigate independently, complaints made by individuals, groups and even the Government relating to defective administration by local bodies. An Ombudsman system could provide a convenient and relatively low-cost mechanism to deal with complaints of mal administration.

Conclusion

Panchayati Raj is a silent revolution and most importantly, this system has included the marginalised sections, in the process of governance and these groups have found a place in Indian polity and a new broad-based political leadership and wisdom is emerging. A large number of women and other marginalised classes have come to power as a consequence of reservation provided to them in panchayats and it has rekindled the hopes of the local citizenry.

The Constitutional specification of the role of Panchayats in 'planning for economic development and social justice' and 'implementation of schemes' towards these ends, and further, the critical role assigned to the 'Gram Sabha' and district planning are but the building blocks for creating a more just, equitable and vibrant society. It is here, in imagining the locality where lives are lived and everyday experiences are produced and reproduced, that the conceptions of state, civil society and market must intersect privileging the democratic ideal of citizenship.

We can conclude that the present pattern of growth has the potential of widening the inequality. Such unequal opportunity structure weakens the positive role of growth in reducing poverty and making growth inclusive. If this inequality increases further, social displacement will result and it will be a major obstruction to higher growth. To achieve inclusive growth, it is crucial that the poor are integrated with the dynamic sectors of growth. We cannot overlook the fact that being closest to the people, the panchayats and their elected representatives have the feel of the pulse, the sufferings of the people and local conditions. The effectiveness of providing services through local bodies cannot be overemphasised as they know their real requirements, and are familiar with every nook and corner of the village and, above all, they are answerable to the people.

The PRIs are eminently suited for service delivery as they can ensure equity and/or equitability in the provision of services (in view of their nearness to the people), inclusiveness (in view of the assured representation available to all sections of the society in the Panchayati Raj Institutions), accessibility, transparency, local participation, accountability and sustainability of services.

The involvement of Panchayats ensures greater transparency in working and fund utilisation than in execution carried out by central or state agency, many a times. Panchayats should be given powers to decide on technology, cost, location, infrastructure and beneficiary selection; and since they have a role in rural housing, primary health care, water and sanitation in many states, should be given these functions by the coordinating authority. Adequate resources should be provided to PRIs to build up their capacities and sensitisation and training of PRI members on related areas will have to be promoted and capacity for the same should be institutionalised in the existing institutional framework in the states.

In a mature and responsible administrative system where power is in the hands of the people and their democratically elected local government institutions, relief operations, day-to-day running of civic services, providing medical assistance, etc. could best be done by the local government. Gram Sabhas can play a very meaningful role in selecting the beneficiaries, prioritising the beneficiaries to ensure gender and equity concerns and also in deciding the appropriate rehabilitation or reconstruction programme that is needed for the communities.

Moving from a model of central provision to that of decentralisation to local governments introduce a new relationship between national and local policy makers, while altering several existing relationships such as that between the citizens, elected politicians and the local bureaucracy. Such inclusive governance, besides ensuring political empowerment, through enabling people to control their own destiny, would also yield significant inclusive growths. Social empowerment through inclusive governance would help safeguard social, ethnic and cultural values of people, which in turn would lead to building trust of their governments in tribal communities. Active participation of people in the political processes and in grassroots planning will bring about the desired transformation of the region by establishing peace and setting in motion the wheels of progress towards prosperity. When grassroots planning processes strike deep roots, economic empowerment is both strong and sustainable.

References

Fifteenth Anniversary Charter on Panchayati Raj (April 2008), It is important to position IT as decision making support system for Panchayats.

Government of India (2007), *Local Governance: An Inspiring Journey into the Future*, Second Administrative Reforms Commission, New Delhi.

Ministry of Panchayati Raj (MoPR) (December 2004a), *Compendium of Resolutions of the Seven Round Tables of Ministers in-Charge of Panchayati Raj.*

—— (December 2004b), *Report of the Task Force of Officials in Charge of Panchayati Raj in States to Examine the Centrally-Sponsored Schemes.*

—— (March 2006), *Report of the Expert Group on Grassroots Level Planning.*

—— (August 2006), *National Capability Building Framework.*

—— (November 2006a), *Guidelines for the Backward Regions Grant Fund.*

—— (November 2006b), *The State of Panchayats Report 2006–07.*

—— (August 2007), *Report of the Expert Committee on Grassroots Level Planning in Areas Not Covered by Parts IX and IXA of the Constitution.*

MoPR, Government of India (2008), *Note on Devolution of Powers to Standing Committee on Rural Development*, New Delhi.

MoPR, IRMA (April 2008), *The State of Panchayats Report 2007–08: An Independent Assessment.*

MoPR, Planning Commission (2006), *Report of the Working Group on Democratic Decentralisation and PRIs*, New Delhi.

—— (November 2008), *Report of the Empowered Sub Committee of NDC on Financial and Administrative Strengthening of PRIs.*

—— (January 2009), *Manual on District Planning.*

MoRD (August 2001), *Report of the Task Force on Devolution of Powers and Functions Upon Panchayati Raj Institutions.*

Planning Commission (August 2007), *Report of the Committee to Review Modifications to be Made in the Existing Guidelines of Centrally-Sponsored Schemes on Identifying a Domain for the Panchayati Raj Institutions.*

—— (2007–2012), *Eleventh Five Year Plan*, Vol. 1, Inclusive Growth-Chapter 10 Governance (Decentralization and Strengthening of PRIs).

Rao, M.G. and U.A. Vasanth Rao (2008), 'Expanding the Resource Base of Panchayats: Augmenting Own Revenues', *Economic and Political Weekly*, January.

Sethi, Geeta (2004), *Fiscal Decentralisation to Rural Governments in India*, The World Bank, Washington, D.C.

Vijayanand, S.M. and T.R. Raghunandan (August 2004), *Note on Parallel Bodies*, Second Round Table of State Ministers of Panchayati Raj, Mysore.

8

Mainstreaming Youth in Local Governance

Learnings from an Indian Village

K. Gireesan

The freedom movement in India was that of a struggle for acquiring political power in terms of 'Own rule' interlaced with the social, economic and psychological aspects of a 'Republic'. The freedom struggle in India inspired the spirit of nationalism and sense of unity across the length and breadth of the country. During the freedom struggle, along with elder political leaders and social reformers, lot of young leaders, revolutionaries and activists from diverse background were also plunged into action. They were inspired by the progressive thinkers, political leaders, social reformers, writers, etc. like Swami Vivekananda, Maharshi Aurobindo, Gurudev Tagore, Gopal Krishna Gokhale, Mahatma Gandhi, Jawaharlal Nehru, Maulana Azad, Annie Besant, Sarojini Naidu, Subramania Bharati, etc. It is noted that several young warriors like Ashfaqulla Khan, Bipin Chandra Pal, Bhagat Singh, Chandra Sekhar Azad, Jhansi Rani Lakshmi Bhai, Khudiram Bose, Mangal Pandey, Ram Prasad Bismil, Subhash Chandra Bose, Shivaram Rajguru, Sukhdev, etc. contributed their part to the freedom movement of India. The mesmerising words and reverberating actions of the young leaders of the past along with the sufferings and struggle undergone by them is a point of inspiration for youth forever.

Passing the 73rd and 74th Constitutional Amendment Act was a defining moment in the history of decentralisation of political power in India. The constitutional amendments have resulted in changing the dynamics and equations of power significantly in the country at the cutting edge levels. These amendments have enabled the Local Government Institutions (LGIs) to function with power and authority as units of self-government, though the devolution of 'Functions, Funds and Functionaries' (3Fs) vary significantly both in letter and spirit in different parts of the country. Devolution of powers and responsibilities enabled the LGIs to formulate plans aiming at local economic development and social justice. And, LGIs have started assuming the centre stage in ushering in people-centric governance as they are more responsive, effective, efficient and people-friendly.

According to Census reports, the proportion of population in the productive age group 15–59 years increased from 53.3 per cent in 1961 to 56.9 per cent in 2001 with a rise of 3.6 percentage points. However, the proportion of population in the age group below 14 years showed a decline of 5.7 percentage points during the same period when the figures dropped from 41 per cent in 1961 to 35.3 per cent in 2001. And, the proportion of population above 60 years showed a minor rise from 5.6 per cent to 7.4 per cent during the reference period, showing a rise of 1.8 percentage points. The data on demographic transition during the period proved beyond doubt that there is a clear advantage in favour of the productive age group in the country, which may be termed as 'demographic dividend'.[1] It is reported that the youth population in many developed countries is fast shrinking with higher dependency ratio; however, India is blessed with 70 per cent of her population below the age of 35 years.

India, owing to its demographic dividend, has the potential to grow more quickly than that of many other countries, including China, Japan and USA. Demographers report that in the year 2020, the average age of an Indian will be 27 years only. On the contrary, the average age of a Chinese and American will be 37 years, a West European 45 and Japanese 48 years (Saraswathi, 2008). It is visualised that youth form the basis of progress and social mobilisation in any country and, aiming at youth development is the most cost-effective strategy for achieving growth and development in a country characterised by demographic dividend (Gireesan, 2012).

There is no doubt that youth can play an important role in strengthening governance in the country as they constitute a significant and vital segment of the population. This is possible and can be realised only when the political system in the country is able to attract more and more youth towards it. And to transform the demographic dividend into development dividend, there is a need for mainstreaming youth in governance.

It is imperative that youth assume an important role in the systems, institutions and practices of local governance. The programmes initiated and implemented by the local governments should take care of the specific needs, concerns, interests and priorities of youth from the geographical area. In addition, the local governments could utilise the competencies, dynamism, energy and skills of youth in planning, implementing and monitoring of programmes/projects. To make this happen, more and more youth should themselves participate in the activities of the local governments. Youth organisations, both political and non-political, could play a crucial role of recruiting able youth to the development politics of local governance system. In addition to extending support to the local governments in its functioning, youth can also become the 'change agents' aimed at bringing 'good governance at the grassroots' (Gireesan, 2013).

However, interactions with the elected members and other key functionaries of local governments, deliberations with the experts and practitioners, discussions with the representatives of youth organisations and reflections from the field indicate that youth participation in local governance is not happening to the desired extent.[2] However, a positive trend has been noted in the recent years regarding the rise in percentage of young members getting elected to local leadership in many parts of the country. Elections to the 'local governments' in many states in the country indicate that there is a significant rise in the percentage of voting by the youth also. It is widely acknowledged that youth are in the fore front of many activities at the local level. However, it is yet to be ascertained whether the rise in percentage of young elected members and rise in voting share of young citizens have genuinely resulted in 'Mainstreaming Youth in Local Governance'.

According, to the Commonwealth Youth Programme, the word 'mainstreaming' refers to the systematic integration of youth affairs into the work of all relevant stakeholders. For governments, this means:

- Allocating a proportion of all relevant departmental budgets to youth development;
- Introducing a youth empowerment perspective to the work of all relevant departments;
- Setting up appropriate mechanisms for youth participation in policy making;
- Systematically monitoring and reporting progress made in youth development; and
- Building the body of knowledge on youth affairs.

Mainstreaming youth in local governance 'refers to the activities for empowering youth to play an active role in Gram Sabha and other participatory structures at the local level, equipping them to make active contributions in the functions of local government and other local institutions, giving them a space and responsible positions in different committees and other decision-making forums and equipping them with personal and social skills to function as change agents in the society' (RGNIYD, 2013).

In operational terms, mainstreaming refers to '*Engage, Enable, Ensure and Empower*' the target population in the development programmes, projects and other activities. 'Mainstreaming Youth in Local Governance' is operationally viewed as:

(a) *Engage* the youth to play an active and constructive role in the functioning of local government institutions with special reference to 'gram sabha and other participatory structures'; and, 'Critical engagement' of youth in local governance as observers, analysts, critics, facilitators, supporters, etc.

(b) *Enable* the youth with knowledge, skills, attitudes and values aiming at 'deepening democracy'; enable to enhance their voluntary spirit and develop social capital among them; and, enable them to perform as 'change agents' in the society.

(c) *Ensure* that their needs, concerns, issues and problems are addressed on priority; ensure that they have access to resources, able to make their own choice and enhance their capability; ensure that they are given due space and responsible position in decision-making forums; and, ensure a youth development perspective in the initiatives and interventions leading to 'Youth Budgeting'.[3]

(d) *Empower* the youth to assume leadership towards bringing Inclusive governance, sustainable development, e-governance, transparency and accountability in the system; and, empower the local government institutions and other institutions for ushering local economic development and social justice towards realising 'Good Governance at the Grassroots'.

The operational aspects of 'Mainstreaming Youth in Local Governance' discussed above are only suggestive in nature and subjected to appropriate variations in the changing context. In brief, every attempt, effort, initiative and intervention aimed at empowering youth by enhancing their capacities and strengthening local government and other institutions, can be viewed as 'Mainstreaming Youth in Local Governance'.

Areas of Study

Rajiv Gandhi National Institute of Youth Development (RGNIYD) initiated the action research project 'Mainstreaming Youth in Local Governance' in the selected Gram panchayats/villages across the country in 2011. The pilot study was taken up in 27 States and one Union Territory (UT). The basic operational unit of Government, Gram Panchayat/Village Panchayat/ Village Council, was selected as the area of intervention in each State/UT. Necessary consultation was carried out with the District Administration/Department for the selection of the study area. And, the following points were considered during the selection of the operational units for the study: (a) To be headed by a young President/Chairperson/Sarpanch. (b) Presence of more young elected members[4] in the selected area. (c) Interest and willingness of the elected members and officials in the area to cooperate with the project. (d) Active presence of youth organisations like Youth wings of political parties, Youth Clubs, Mahila Mandals, etc. in the area.

The project was taken up in 27 States and one UT in the country and it was scaled up in three phases – six states and one UT in the first phase; eight states in the second phase; and the remaining 13 states in the third phase. Details regarding the areas selected for operationalisation of action research project in different States/UT are indicated in Table 1. The details are indicated in alphabetical order.

Towards focusing the discussions and analysis of the study, this paper has been limited to the operationalisation of the project in one village of a State. Asrang village is situated in Pooh Block of Kinnaur district in Himachal Pradesh. The area of the village is around 2.87 sq. km. The village has a total population of 542 that includes 294 male and 248 female as per the 2001 census. The village has 75 children below the age of 13 years, and the number of youth in the age group of 13–35 years is 180. The main religion practised in this village is Hinduism, and Buddhism has been simultaneously adopted by many families. About four-fifths of the villagers (80%) are Scheduled Tribes (ST) and the remaining are Scheduled Castes (SC).

Table 1

Areas of Interventions for the Action Research Project

Sl. No.	State/ UT	District	Block/ Mandal/ Taluk/ Circle	Gram Panchayat/Village Panchayat/Town Panchayat/ Village Council
1.	Andhra Pradesh	Chittoor	Tirupati Rural Mandal	Paidipalle Gram Panchayat (GP)
2.	Arunachal Pradesh	Lohit	Tezu Block	Changliang Village Panchayat (VP) and Khoraliang VP
3.	Assam	Kamrup Rural	Chhamaria Block	48 No. Chhamaria GP
4.	Bihar	Bhojpur	Agiaon Block	Khoipira GP
5.	Chhattisgarh	Rajnandgaon	Dongargaon Block	Mathaldabri GP
6.	Gujarat	Kheda	Nadiad Block	Bhumel GP
7.	Haryana	Mewat	Tauru Block	Utton Village
8.	Himachal Pradesh	Kinnaur	Pooh Block	Asrang GP
9.	Jammu and Kashmir	Ganderbal Kashmir	Wakura Block	Halqa B/GB 88 Kondabal
10.	Jharkhand	Garhwa	Garhwa Block	Ranka Boullia GP
11.	Karnataka	Bangalore Rural	Devanahalli Taluk	Kundana GP
12.	Kerala	Wayanad	Mananthavadi Block	Edavaka GP
13.	Madhya Pradesh	Ujjain	Ujjain Block	Kasampur GP
14.	Maharashtra	Latur	Nilanga Block	Panchincholi GP
15.	Manipur	Thoubal	Thoubal CD Block	Charangpat GP
16.	Meghalaya	Ri Bhoi	Umsning C & RD Block	Umsohlait Village
17.	Mizoram	Aizawl	Tiangnuam Block	Sihphir Venghlun and Sihphir Villages
18.	Nagaland	Wokha	Wokha Circle	Wokha Village Council
19.	Odisha	Keonjhar	Saharadpada Block	Digposi GP
20.	Puducherry	Puducherry	Villiannur Commune Panchayat	Pillayar Kuppam VP
21.	Punjab	Hoshiarpur	Hoshiarpur II Block	Chaggra GP
22.	Rajasthan	Jaipur	Chaksu Taluk	Chandelkalan VP
23.	Sikkim	South Sikkim	Sumbuk Block	Mellidara Paiyong 22 GPU
24.	Tamil Nadu	Vellore	Arakkonam Block	Thakkolam TP
25.	Tripura	Tripura West	Dukli RD Block	Malaynagar GP
26.	Uttarakhand	Almora	Dwarahat Block	Rana GP
27.	Uttar Pradesh	Barabanki	Banki Block	Khaspariya GP
28.	West Bengal	Purba Medinipur	Shahid Matangini Block	Santipur II GP

Source: Records maintained by RGNIYD.

Asrang village is situated at an altitude of 4,000 metres and it experiences mild summers and severe winters. The average summer temperature rises to a maximum of 30°C and during winter, it falls below –10°C. Road is the only means of connectivity to the village. The road connects Asrang to Reckong Peo, the district headquarter of Kinnaur by a bus which plies once in a day. Reckong Peo is at a distance of 55 km from Asrang. The road is not motorable in almost 4–6 months during winter owing to heavy snowfall. There is no mobile tower around 15 km and hence telecommunication is a major problem in the village. The extreme winters often leads to snowfall of 15 feet and avalanches have often caused loss of life and property. The landslides, avalanches and earthquakes make the inhabitants of the village highly vulnerable. The situation gets further worsened by lack of infrastructural facilities and telecommunication facilities.

Varying trends in rainfall, declining water level in rivers, variations in the extent of snowfall and other aspects of climate change have been affecting the agricultural productivity of the village on which the entire economy and sustainability of the people depend. Results of the climate change are seen in the depleting grasslands, forest resources and the biodiversity of flora and fauna.

The village has two schools – one primary and one high school. There are two health institutions in the village – a health subcentre and an Ayurvedic hospital. The village is supplied with pipe water by the Irrigation and Public Health Department of the State Government. There are four public water supply taps for the village. But the water supply gets completely disrupted during winters as a result of freezing. The alternative source is Chasma (springs) for which people have to trek for 4–5 km.

For the purpose of pilot study in Himachal Pradesh, Asrang village was chosen by the PRAGYA, the development organisation collaborated with RGNIYD.[5] The collaboration was made with the conviction that such linkages would not only be beneficial for enhancing the breadth and depth of the interventions, but also for ensuring sustainability of the interventions in the field. The selection of GP was made in consultation with the officials of Panchayati Raj Department, keeping in view the criteria mentioned earlier. This was done specifically towards ensuring their ownership, cooperation and support during the project, in addition to aim at the possibilities of scaling up.

This paper discusses about the status of young people in the selected area of Himachal Pradesh. It analyses the needs, concerns, issues, problems and priorities of youth from the study area. In addition, the initiatives and interventions made by the local government and other organisations from the selected area, aiming at youth development, were also taken up for analysis. The paper makes a unique attempt to suggest the outline and steps for carrying out 'Youth Budgeting at the local level'.[6] In addition, it put forward the suggestions for enhancing the effectiveness and efficiency of such interventions and possible scaling up of the project in other parts of the state and country.

Methodology

The study was taken up as a Participatory Action Research (PAR) in the selected area, which includes different elements of a community action planning similar to the methods of participatory appraisal. This approach was chosen deliberately because the research was initiated in a rural area and it requires a participatory assessment strategy to look at the existing situation, analyse them, explore different approaches and strategies, and then take up the needed and appropriate interventions.

The following components were included in the PAR:

(a) Community mapping of the area.
(b) Participant observation.
(c) Informal interviews with the youth leaders.
(d) Interviews with the young citizens.
(e) Designing of a seasonal activity calendar for youth.
(f) Initiation of capacity building sessions for youth.
(g) Organising demand-driven and need-based skill development programmes for youth.
(h) Networking of local government with academic institutions and other social organisations to ensure sustainability.

Discussions and Analysis

This section discussed the profile of youth from the selected area of Himachal Pradesh. The needs, concerns, issues, problems and priorities of youth from the study area were analysed. Initiatives and interventions made by the local government and/or other organisations in the area for youth development were also examined. An attempt for formulation of the outline for taking up youth budgeting at the local level was also made towards the end of this section. Subsequently, certain visible outcomes of the study were documented.

Profile of Youth from the Study Area

As part of the project, almost every youth from the village were contacted as part of the study and necessary information collected from them. A brief profile of the young population from the study area, in terms of their gender, age, community status, educational status and occupational status, is given below. In addition, patterns of migration, health status, skills and career interests, participation in sports, games and leisure time activities, associational life of youth, linkage with bank and insurance, spirit of voluntarism and survival skills, and participation in local governance also have been analysed.

Table 2

Age-Group of the Respondents

Age-Group	*No. of Respondents*			*Percentage*
	Male	*Female*	*Total*	
13–18 Years	25	20	45	31.47
19–24 Years	22	15	37	25.87
25–30 Years	21	17	38	26.57
31–35 Years	19	04	23	16.08
Total	87	56	143	100

Source: Data collected from the youth of Asrang village.

Table 3

Community Status of the Respondents

Community Status	*No. of Respondents*			*Percentage*
	Male	*Female*	*Total*	
Scheduled Tribes (STs)	68	50	118	82.52
Scheduled Castes (SCs)	18	06	24	16.78
General	01	00	01	00.70
Total	87	56	143	100

Source: Data collected from the youth of Asrang village.

Table 4

Educational Status of the Respondents

Educational Status	*No. of Respondents*			*Percentage*
	Male	*Female*	*Total*	
Illiterates	01	02	03	02.09
Primary Education	11	10	21	14.68
Secondary Education	48	24	72	50.30
Higher Secondary	16	08	24	16.78
Higher Education	11	12	23	16.08
Total	87	56	143	100

Source: Data collected from the youth of Asrang village.

Table 5

Status of Computer Proficiency among the Respondents

Educational Status	*No. of Respondents*	*Percentage*
Sending and receiving e-mails	13	09.09
Browsing the internet	39	27.27
Accessing the job sites	37	25.87
No computer proficiency	54	37.76
Total	143	100

Source: Data collected from the youth of Asrang village.

Table 6

Occupational Status of the Respondents

Occupation	*No. of Respondents*	*Percentage*
Government Job	1	00.70
Self-employed (Agriculture/Business)	93	65.00
Student	49	34.00
Total	143	100

Source: Data collected from the youth of Asrang Village.

It is noted that men outnumber women youth in the study area, which is in line with the population pattern of the District and the State. About the community status of youth from the area, it is noted that more than four-fifths (82.52%) of the population in the village are STs, followed by SCs (16.78%). Regarding the educational status, it is noted that only a very small section of the youth (2%) from the area were illiterates. Nearly one-third of the youth population (32.86%) was educated up to Higher Secondary or above. Majority of the respondents from the area (62.24%) were computer literate who could send-receive e-mails, browse internet and/or surf job sites. About the employment status, just less than two-thirds of the youth (65%) were self-employed, either engaged in the field of agriculture or running their own business like shop, hotel, car driving, etc.

Needs, Concerns, Issues, Problems and Priorities of Youth

In this section, needs, concerns, issues, problems and priorities of youth from the study area in different dimensions like educational, social, economic, political and cultural, will be discussed and analysed.

Educational Dimensions

Needs

Standard of educational attainment affects the economic potential of youth as well as their effectiveness to play major role in socio-economic development and democratic governance. It is noted that a very small segment (2%) of youth from the study area were illiterates and nearly two-thirds of the youth from the area (65%) were self-employed. It is observed that among those self-employed, most of them (90%) work in the field of agriculture and only a small segment (4%) run their own business like shop, hotel and car driving. And a significant segment of youth from the area migrate to Reckong Peo, Rampur and Shimla, in addition to Chandigarh and Delhi, primarily in search of better educational and employment avenues.

Some of the important needs identified from the study area were: Computer literacy programmes need to be started at the Primary level. Necessary efforts are to be made to bring in cent-per-cent computer literacy among the youth. Scholarship need to be provided to children from BPL families for secondary, higher secondary and higher education to enable them to continue studies as per their interests and choice. Special funds need to be earmarked for girls for pursuing higher education. Necessary awareness sessions be organised in the schools about various scholarships and other educational schemes. School buildings should be made earthquake, avalanche and landslide resistant in order to avoid long break in studies. Special classes for weaker students should be arranged in the schools. Educational tours to different institutions, government offices and historically important places may be arranged in educational institutions, as that will enable them to have first-hand information about various aspects. Programmes and activities of Scouts and Guides, NCC cadets and NSS volunteers in the educational institutions need to be enhanced towards developing discipline, personality, community work and voluntarism among the youth. Playground and indoor games with proper equipment need to be made available in the educational institutions. Library should be initiated/developed in the educational institutions. Standard of education should be improved with proper emphasis on English as well as local language. Culture, values, ethics and indigenous history should be part of the curriculum, setting examples through biographies of local ideal and great men. Job information kiosk/job sites should be available/accessible in the higher educational institutions. Mobile tower and internet facility should be provided for exposure to opportunities and knowledge updation. The demand for education in the area seems to be low, which further indicates the need for counselling and guidance to the students as well as parents.

Concerns

It is noted that only a small segment of youth from the study area (16.08%) opted for higher education even though majority of them (68.53%) were above 18 years. Some of the important concerns noted from the study area were: Outmigration in search of good education and job is observed among youth especially in the age group of 13–20 years. Education gained from the school is perceived to be not job-oriented because of its low quality and absence of linkage with the field realities and requirements. Extinction of local/indigenous knowledge, literature, folklore, language is as a result of outmigration and exclusion from school curriculum.

Issues

Lack of adequate number and efficient teachers at primary level weakens the knowledge base of the students. Discouragement of female education was prevalent till the recent past. Poor families lack funds for providing proper education to their children, especially for higher education. Though there are provisions for scholarship and other support systems for students, especially from SCs/STs, to pursue education, the issue of 'information disconnect' remains. Lack of thrust in English as the medium of instruction even in the institutions of higher education and the low of quality of education have lead to demoralisation in job market. On several occasions, persons who can communicate in English are preferred during the interviews. Lack of fluency in spoken English minimises their chances in getting better jobs. Lack of information about employment opportunities in the Higher Secondary School/Colleges.

Problems

Lack of facilities and encouragement in sports and other extra-curricular activities minimises their opportunity to play in state level and national level sports though they are physically more capable. Even the employment opportunities on the basis of sports quota could not be received by many potential youth, which by itself is a demotivating factor. Misutilisation of funds provided for Sarva Siksha Abhiyan (SSA) has also been observed. Seminars are being held and speakers from outside the area and unaware of the field realities were invited for lectures by which no benefit could be available to the stakeholders from the region.

Priorities

The need for providing quality education and employability skills to the student-youth must come as a top priority. Providing requisite information about the educational scholarships and other welfare schemes to socially and economically backward, girls and minorities must come as the priority. Preference should be given to the youth from poor socio-economic status, illiterate/low literate households and girls. Vocational education to all those interested need to be given priority over others. More quality educational institutions and vocational education facilities be made available in the area.

Social Dimensions

Needs

Equal access and opportunities to education, employment and other social facets of life to different gender categories is an important need. In addition, adequate recreational facilities and leisure time activities are necessary as they contribute significantly for holistic development of the youth.

Some of the important needs of the youth noted from the study area were: Female education needs to be promoted through awareness programmes. Special schemes needed to educate girl children. Awareness programmes and active surveillance by the youth on child marriage and its health impacts need to be carried out in collaboration with Local Government Institutions. Discrimination in distribution of resources must be checked towards bringing equitable growth and development. Talents/ skills/ abilities of the youth need to be channelised for development of the village. Superstitions prevailing in society can be abolished through education and campaigns in which the youth need to be actively involved.

Concerns

Female education is highly neglected, and girls are mostly sent to school only till primary level. Though not in large numbers, child marriage is still prevalent among illiterate families. Alcoholism among the youth has degraded the work culture in the region. In addition, it indirectly influenced the agricultural, socio-economic and cultural milieu. Casteism inhibits people from taking active participation in local governance and other socio-cultural activities.

Issues

Lack of female education, marriage at an early age, and superstitions combine to create an adverse impact on the maternal and child health in the region. Conservative mindset of men towards women and not viewing them as equal partners in development are noted here. Social discrimination is highly prevalent in the area. The ST population in the region consider themselves as Rajputs and often treats the SC population in a derogatory manner.

Problems

Lack of proper medical facilities has often led to mortality of mother and child. Consumption of liquor among the youth on regular basis is leading to misutilisation of human resources as well as serious health and social problems. Alcoholism also results in domestic violence in some households to a certain extent.

Priorities

Focused efforts for realising gender equity in all spheres of life must be formed on top of the agenda for youth. Necessary efforts be made towards nullifying the discriminatory practices prevailing among STs and SCs in the area.

Economic Dimensions

Needs

There is a need for more facilities for the skill building of the youth in different trades and towards enabling them to take up self-employment. Special facility for girls/young women is required to be initiated in the area to make them more confident and self-reliant. Conduct of a skill-gap study among the youth in the State is an important need of the hour.

Some of the important needs of the youth noted from the study area were: Soft loans for improvement of apple orchards, with focus on improving the quality of land and enhancing the yield need to be made. Such loans should be provided to marginal farmers on a priority basis. Necessary aid for setting up farmer's cooperative and weavers' cooperative need to be provided together along with developing linkages with buyers of agricultural and handloom produce and initiation of market information system. Grameen Bank needs to be set in the village towards facilitating savings and investment, both for individuals and cooperatives. Vocational training and absorption into various employment sectors need to be provided, especially in trades like carpentry, car mechanic, mobile repairer, computer mechanic, repair of alternative energy equipment, traditional wood carving and weaving. Necessary training on pruning and other advanced techniques in horticulture need to be initiated. Linkages with agricultural research institutes and availability of climate resilient varieties of seeds and saplings for high yielding need to be made available to the farmers. Information kiosk for employment opportunities need to be set up in the area. Implementation of Mahatma Gandhi National Rural Employment Guarantee Scheme (MGNREGS) needs to be modified according to the necessity of the region and feasibility options. Necessary technical, financial and marketing support need to be provided for setting up of mineral water bottling plant in the area. This will generate lot of employment options for the youth. Support for Beekeeping needs to be provided to develop it on a large scale.

Concerns

Scanty rainfall, declining snowfall trends and rampant soil erosion have reduced the agricultural productivity, especially of apple, peas, potato and other cash crops which are the major source of income from the area. Low quality and small sized apples and grains fetch low price in the market. Alternative livelihood options are quite less in the area. Enterprises like dhaba/hotel, automobile workshops and vehicles for transportation of goods and passengers are some of the areas of concern in the area. Employment opportunity is not adequate in the area. MGNREGS, a flagship programme which provides assured employment of 100 days in a year for each family, could not attract many unemployed youth from the area.

Issues

Non-availability of improved variety and drought-resistant seeds, sprinkler irrigation, alternative agricultural practices hinders production and limits income from agriculture. Increasing number of type of pests and insects and decrease in pollinator species have resulted in more demand for procurement of fertilisers, pesticides and bees. As a result of which, the input cost has increased. The inflation in cost of agricultural inputs has collectively taken a toll on the economic conditions of the people especially the marginalised sections. Absence of banking services for savings and investment in the village has been an important economic issue. Out-migration by the youth in search of alternate livelihoods is also hampering the agricultural sector significantly. Younger generation does not take interest in agriculture which is also diminishing the income from this sector in many households.

Problems

Lack of proper Market Information system and interference of middle men for selling the products cause significant loss to the apple growers. Lack of marketing facilities for handicrafts, woolen shawls, traditional jewellery and woodwork has deprived the villagers from alternate livelihoods.

Priorities

Provision for skill development suited to the needs and demands in the field is a priority area in this dimension. Imparting vocational training to the youth along with career guidance and support for taking up self-employment is another priority area.

Political Dimensions

Needs

There is a need for enhancing political awareness to encourage youth participation in the political process. It is not only necessary to inculcate the 'right type of political education' to the youth but also important to develop leadership qualities among them enabling them to contribute towards the society and nation.

Some of the important needs of the youth documented from the study area were: Youth of 13–18 years age hardly participate in the proceedings of the Gram Sabha. Hence, convening of Bal Sabha and Yuva Sabha in the area need to be made before the conduct of Gram Sabha towards understanding the aspirations, needs and demands of children and adolescents. Periodical conduct of Gram Sabha with active participation of all elected representatives of the village and the citizens is necessary. Political parties need to enhance representation of youth in the Panchayati Raj Institutions (PRIs) towards encouraging their active leadership in developmental activities. Appropriate reforms need to be made to free politics from criminals, tainted and corrupt people. That can happen only by bringing in more youth towards politics and governance.

Concerns

Criteria for the selection of the candidates during the elections do not happen considering their qualification, honesty, character, commitment, dedication and simplicity. Influence of money, muscle power and caste/community factors are some of the important features figured in the selection of candidates. Voter's awareness about the candidates is very low to enable them to elect good candidates.

Issues

False promises by politicians discourage involvement of youth in the political arena. Prevalence of corruption at different levels has led to misuse of funds and has tarnished the image of politicians. Hence, many youth do not want to be directly involved in political affairs.

Problems

Youth of age 13–17 years generally do not attend the Gram Sabha, political meetings and rallies, even though their involvement and participation in such matters is crucial for development politics. Many elected members of PRIs, especially women, are not independent and assertive because of their ignorance, lack of self-confidence, economic dependence on others, etc. Many of them were not even aware of the basic features, provisions and scope of the Panchayati Raj system in the State to play an active leadership role in local governance. For various political activities like rallies, campaigns, etc. youth are widely used by all the political parties. However, while assigning positions and responsibilities, their potentials and contributions were generally overlooked and claims ignored. Politicians usually visit the village during elections only, in order to seek votes. Due to sparse population and small size of voters, their thrust on developmental activities in the area is very low.

Priorities

Youth need to be given due weightage to hold key positions in the political parties and other institutions of power. Voter awareness campaigns, 'Meet the candidate programme', etc. can be organised in the area towards sensitising the youth. Capacity building sessions on the prospects and possibilities of Panchayati Raj system with special reference to the role of youth in local governance need to be organised on priority.

Cultural Dimensions

Needs

There is a need for protection and promotion of culture and with the active involvement of youth, youth clubs and youth organisations in cultural programmes and other recreational events in the area.

Some of the important needs of the youth identified from the study area were: Training classes for potential youth on weaving, drawing, painting, clay modelling, etc. will not only help in preservation of the culture but it can also prove to be an alternative livelihood option for them. Promotion of handicrafts through showroom facilities in Reckong Peo is necessary. Classes in school need to be initiated for preservation of Kinnauri language, dance and folk songs. Troupes/ individuals for music and dance need to be given impetus, with involvement of youth. Training classes on folk dance and folk songs need to be initiated. Cultural events need to be held during festivals and other celebrations, as they can be viewed as occasions for promoting tourism. Hoot (Chilta), Namkeen chai, Jow ki sattu, Chultelang, Bakchamarku, Lungthupa are examples of traditional food items from the area, which need to be promoted through tourism. This would enable income generation for the youth. Necessary efforts be made to document, preserve and market the indigenous medicines. Traditional dress-making would be source of income generation. Tailoring and weaving classes need to be provided. Woodcraft and carpentry should also be encouraged among youth as a means of earning as well as promotion of culture.

Concerns

Television has captured the arena of entertainment as a result of which the local festivals, melas and events are vanishing fast. Local folklore, songs, stories, cuisine, etc. are disappearing at a fast pace. Transfer of these traditions from one generation to another is becoming weak.

Issues

The children of the emigrants do not even know how to speak, read or write Kinnauri dialect/Bhoti language. Giving and taking dowry for marriage in the disguise of traditions or family prestige is another important issue. It cannot be looked at merely as a social issue. Lavish expenditure during marriage and other social functions, even beyond the capacity of the family due to societal pressure, is also noted. Increasing use of liquor and other drugs during the cultural events, social gatherings and recreational activities among the youth is also crucial as they become irrational in their behaviour, thought and action.

Problems

Lot of traditions during wedding or any such occasions have become adulterated as a result of influx of western and external influence. The younger generation is losing their touch of their culture and historical moorings. There has been loss in the traditional knowledge of weaving, craft, folklores/songs, handicraft, carpentry and if this persists for some more time, they would completely disappear in the future.

Priorities

Awareness sessions to develop scientific temper among the youth and to keep them away from superstitions can be organised on priority. Moral education can be given to the youth to realise the significance of values and principles in life. Specific thrust on programmes and activities should be organised towards enabling the youth to understand the culture and heritage of the country and its glorious past. Such programmes will help to strengthen the character building of youth, leading to their holistic development.

Initiatives and Interventions for Youth Development

In this section, initiatives and interventions for youth development by the local government and other organisations in the area will be examined and analysed.

It is noted that Asrang village has no specific agenda to deal with the needs, concerns, issues and problems of the youth. Preparation of agenda at the panchayat level is generally influenced by the programmes and schemes of the government at Central and State Governments. Most of the programmes and schemes have common objectives to cover beneficiaries in general and no specific thrust has been given to the youth. It is also noted that the absence of adequate funds, especially untied funds, inhibit the GP from planning and implementation of youth-specific projects, in line with the needs and demands of the local youth. Lack of own funds generated by the GP is also crucial which discourage the PRIs to take up special programmes and projects for the youth. It is noted that lack of sufficient funds at their disposal, either through grants from the State Government or generation of own funds, is a serious matter which does not enable the GPs to take up initiatives and interventions for youth development.

As a result of lack of funds and awareness, the LGIs have not been able to fully implement various programmes and schemes for the development of the village. The major developmental programmes that have been undertaken in the village are Mahatma Gandhi National Rural Employment Guarantee Scheme (MGNREGS), Pradhan Mantri Grameen Sadak Yojana (PMGSY), Indira Awas Yojana (IAY), National Social Assistance Programme (NSAP), Integrated Watershed Management Programme (IWMP) and Mathru Shakti Bima Yojana (MSBY). As a result of implementation of the above schemes, 12 people were provided employment through MGNREGS, especially to those from the economically backward sections; 10 households were assisted with funds for housing and construction purposes through Indira Awas Yojana; 55 people were facilitated with pension scheme through NSAP; the initiatives for afforestation and conservation of traditional water resources were done through IWMP which helped the entire village; and, around 4 widow mothers were financially supported through the MSBY.

The major hurdle was noted during the implementation of MGNREGS. The MGNREGS is generally put to use during the summer months, because during winter, for almost 4–6 months, there is extreme low temperature and snowfall resulting in complete out-migration of the villagers to warmer locations. And during summer, the villagers cannot be involved in the MGNREGS work to a great extent, as that is the season for several agricultural activities. Moreover, the wages paid per day for a MGNREGS worker is around ₹ 175 which is much less than the amount paid to a wage labourer working in agriculture in the area. Thus, apathy towards participation in MGNREGS is observed in the village. Some alternative possibilities and solutions need to be devised for developmental programmes like this.

However, there is some degree of flexibility at the level of Local Government in the planning and implementation of the programmes. For example, the GP could construct a 'Sanitary Complex for Women' within the provisions of Total Sanitation Campaign (TSC), which will significantly benefit the young women in the village. Similarly, the GP can take up 'development of a new playground' or 'levelling of an existing playground for youth' within the specified guidelines of the MGNREGS. Even the labour component for construction of a 'Youth Club building' or 'Village Knowledge Centre' or 'Information Kiosk' could be met from the MGNREGS funds. But such youth-perspectives in the operationalisation of programmes and schemes could not be seen in the place.

Most of the development programmes (central and state sponsored) have 'rigid guidelines' which do not allow the PRIs to adopt a flexible approach. They find it very difficult to incorporate the specific agenda of youth in those programmes. It is also noted that in many programmes and schemes, the GP is not even considered as a unit for implementation as the responsibility is vested in the Government Departments at different levels. It is noted that in certain cases, the GPs are not even consulted in the planning and implementation of the programmes. In this respect, there is a need for ascertaining the devolution of Functions, Funds and Functionaries (3Fs) by the State Government to the Local Government Institutions (LGIs) is to be made.

Specific efforts were made to sensitise the young persons from the area on the significance of Gram Sabha and the need for youth participation in local governance. A group discussion was organised in the area towards enabling them to involve in the planning exercise, based on the resources (both human and natural) available in the area.

Youth Budgeting at the Local Level

Budget is one of the main instruments of the Government/Institution/Organisation/ Agency to achieve its goals/objectives. It represents the preferences and priorities of the Department/Institution. The process of arriving at a budget involves difficult political decisions regarding how resources should be raised and allocated over a specified time period. Generally the term 'Budgeting' refers to financial aspects like anticipated revenues and expenses within a specific time period and could be even regarded as 'Financial Budgeting'.

However, unlike the features of financial budgets, 'Youth budgeting' is visualised here as 'Social Budgeting'. It denotes the process by which the goals, interests, aspirations and priorities of the entire population or a specific social category are better reflected through budgeting. In Youth Budgeting, the thrust is on understanding and gathering the details about the needs, concerns, issues, problems and priorities of youth; mapping of the initiatives and interventions for addressing them; and then, develop an operational model for process documentation and analysis. And by specifically limiting the functional domain to the field unit of the government (i.e. Gram Panchayat/Village Panchayat/Village Council), the purview of this budgeting has been confined to the Local Government only. Hence, it is visualised as 'Youth Budgeting at the local level'. However, the analysis has been limited to a specified duration only.

The budget cycle covers formulation, analysis, execution, monitoring and evaluation. And, towards carrying out a meaningful analysis of the budget, the entire process shall be focused, rather than limiting the analysis to allocations and expenses. The latter may or may not be carried out, nor result in the expected benefit/influence/ impact as visualised. In addition, the feedback from the target group of population on the initiative/intervention is also essential towards making necessary changes wherever necessary.

The framework for youth budgeting has been visualised through the following aspects:

(a) Resource mapping and planning in participatory manner.
(b) Spatial mapping of the resources – physical and human-made.
(c) Review of initiatives and interventions by the local government and other agencies.
(d) Review of existing programmes, schemes and projects, aiming at youth development.
(e) Appraisal of new programmes, schemes and projects from the youth perspective.

Towards a focused appraisal of youth budgeting in a locality, an outline has been suggested, which will delineate the process threadbare. Table 7 provides the outline for youth budgeting at the local level, where a qualitative analysis could be made through different stages.

Table 7

Youth Budgeting at the Local Level – Outline

Description	*Stage-wise Information*
Conduct of youth status study in the field	Documenting the needs, concerns, issues, problems and priorities of youth from the field
Documenting the initiatives and interventions for youth development in the area	Initiatives and interventions for youth development will be documented and examined in the following stages:
	Stage I: To examine whether the needs, concerns, issues and problems of youth have come to the agenda of the LGI and other organisations functioning in the area?
	Stage II: To examine whether these aspects have been crystallised into any project?
	Stage III: To examine whether administrative and technical sanction for these projects have been obtained?
	Stage IV: To examine whether these projects have been launched?
	Stage V: To examine whether these projects have been implemented?
	Stage VI: To examine whether these projects have been implemented completely?
	Stage VII: To examine whether the project interventions have reached to the youth?
	Stage VIII: To examine whether the youth are satisfied with the interventions?

Note: Framework developed by the author.

It is noted that in the process of 'Youth Budgeting', the analysis needs to be done right from the entry of the specific item/aspect in the agenda of the local government, up to the recording of feedback from the youth. It is visualised that though this mode of analysis appears to be a long drawn one, it is expected to provide a comprehensive assessment of each item/aspect, in addition towards identifying the current stage of travel, aiming at its successful execution. As no special provisions or funds are available or allocated for the purpose of youth development in the area during the period of study, youth budgeting could not be ascertained.

Summing up

The action research project initiated in 27 States and one Union Territory on a pilot basis enabled the researcher to understand, analyse and document the status of youth. And the 'Learning Journey' through the Asrang village in Kinnaur District of Himachal Pradesh enabled the researcher to realise, revisit, refine, redefine and rejuvenate the measures adopted in the area for mainstreaming youth in local governance. And on similar lines, the inputs gathered from different parts of the country could also provide sufficient evidences from the field about this pioneering initiative.

Experiences of Asrang village, realised during the action research project 'Mainstreaming Youth in Local Governance' definitely enabled to document the needs, concerns, issues, problems and priorities of youth on various important dimensions. At the same time, the initiatives and interventions for youth development in the area also could be examined at a micro level. The outline developed for ascertaining youth budgeting at the local level could be suitably used subsequently towards taking up appropriate policy initiatives and operationalisation of programmes for youth development. Such micro level initiatives for 'Mainstreaming Youth' have the latent potentials towards realising 'Good Governance at the Grassroots' with more active involvement and participation of youth. This could be scaled up to other parts of the State and the country, by making necessary temporal and spatial changes as per the local context.

Notes

1. Demographic dividend is characterised by the rise in working age population, out of which largely consists of youth, which is an indicator of the potentials of a country to grow more quickly than other countries. This clearly points towards the advantage of having a sizeable youth population which could be tapped properly aiming at the nation-building. However, this dividend could be translated into positive direction only by providing proper education, adequate health care, capacitating with skills and competencies, and enabling them to secure suitable employment in line with their interests, aptitude and skills. Only such an approach to the youth is expected to enable them to contribute towards the growth and development of the country.
2. Panchayati Raj Institutions and Youth Affairs Division of RGNIYD carried out a research study titled 'Knowledge, Attitude and Practice of Youth in Panchayati Raj' in 10 states across the country during 2008–2009. The field studies revealed that

youth participation in local governance is not happening significantly even in politically active states like Kerala and West Bengal.

3. 'Youth budgeting' is visualised here as 'Social Budgeting' in which the needs, concerns, issues, problems and priorities of youth are analysed with regard to the initiatives and interventions for youth development over a specified period.
4. According to the National Youth Policy of India, 2003, the term 'youth' refers to the persons within the age group of 13–35 years. The National Youth Policy, 2014 revised the target age group to 15–29 years. However, the term 'Young elected members of PRIs' in this study refers to the elected members between the age group of 21–35 years.
5. Panchayati Raj Institutions and Youth Affairs (PRIYA) Division of Rajiv Gandhi National Institute of Youth Development, Sriperumbudur has taken up the action research project, Mainstreaming Youth in Local Governance in Jharkhand in collaboration with the PRAGYA, a development organisation with its registered office at Gurgaon by signing a Memorandum of Understanding in 2012. For more details, look into the website: www.pragya.org
6. Here the thrust is given to the 'Youth Budgeting at the Local Level' as the exercise has been limited to a small geographical area only.

References

Commonwealth Secretariat (n.d.), *The Commonwealth Plan of Action for Youth Empowerment 2007–2015*, Commonwealth Youth Programme, Commonwealth Secretariat, London, p. 13.

Gireesan, K. (2012), *Demographic Dividend and Policy Priorities: A Discourse in the Select Papers of the Seventh Annual International Conference on Public Policy and Management*, Centre for Public Policy, Indian Institute of Management, Bangalore, pp. 67–74.

—— (2013), 'Knowledge, Attitude and Practice of Youth in Panchayats, Kerala', *KILA Journal of Local Governance*, Vol. I, No. 2, July-December, pp. 19–30.

Planning Commission (n.d.), *Report of 11th Five Year Plan (2007–2012)*, Vol. 2, Chapter 2, Government of India, New Delhi, p. 41.

RGNIYD (2013), *Handbook of the National Colloquium on Mainstreaming Youth in Local Governance*, Panchayati Raj Institutions and Youth Affairs Division (PRIYA), Rajiv Gandhi National Institute of Youth Development, Sriperumbudur, pp. 1–2.

Saraswathi, S. (2008), *Indian Youth in the New Millennium*, Rajiv Gandhi National Institute of Youth Development, Sriperumbudur, p. 8.

Part III

Changing Power Structure and Empowerment of Marginalised Groups

9

Governance and Multidimensional Poverty

Evidence from Central Tribal Belt of India

D.C. Sah and Ashish Bhatt

Sah et al. (2008) have established that the quantum of public expenditure, in the form of benefits to individuals from panchayats and government programme are not directed equitably and the group that does not necessarily deserve, the always-non-poor, receive the benefits that should have gone to poor and chronic poor. Poverty, in this sense, is a product of unequal power relations in the community. Powerful political elites control the public resources and govern the manner in which these resources will be utilised. Poor are not only unable to participate in this process but also are ill-equipped to influence the wasteful distribution of public resources. The Panchayat Extension to Scheduled Areas (PESA) Act of 1996 empowers the tribal community to take hold of its land, water and forest resources and empowers the community by involving it directly in all the decision-making processes – a power that was earlier enjoyed by the bureaucracy and Sarpanch.[1] The Act extends panchayats to tribal areas of eight States namely, Andhra Pradesh, Bihar, Gujarat, Himachal Pradesh, Maharashtra, Madhya Pradesh, Orissa (Odisha) and Rajasthan; it will enable tribal society to assume control of its own destiny to preserve and conserve the traditional rights over natural resources.

These political reforms have thrown up a new dominant group that controls financial resources and challenge the existing hierarchy. This may disturb the apparent homogeneity of the tribal society. The emerging heterogeneity may curtail the participation of the community in governance. On the other hand, the provisions of the PESA have come in direct confrontation with the earlier Acts and the then existing state departmental rules that governed the natural resources in the tribal regions. This has made the Act redundant in relation to management of the natural resources of the region. The objective of this chapter is to understand the impact of these changes. More specifically, the chapter addresses to the following three sets of propositions. First, if villages were socially, politically and economically divided, dominance of any one of the groups in decentralised governance would influence the distribution of the development gains as well as participation of the community. Second, political reforms that give management of natural resources to the community would create expectations that would be frustrated by the existing departmental laws. Consequently, the community may resist state development programmes that curtail their access to natural resources. Lastly, decentralised governance, as a process, may not necessarily be an infallible mechanism to tackle political unfreedom of the community.

These changes in governance are postulated on three basic premises. First, traditional ways of tribal society could be integrated with decentralised governance. Second, the community would get an institutional space to govern its affairs in an accountable and meaningful manner. This means that the provisions would be able to level and homogenise the differences, leading to an informed decision-making by the people at the grassroots level. Lastly, the new system would usher in a regime of people's participation, where governance would be more responsible and fruits of development distributed more equitably. Did this happen? This paper examines this pertinent question in the context of developed and underdeveloped villages of our sample. This data base for the study is ten tribal districts of six states; Gujarat (Bharuch and Panchmahals), Rajasthan (Banswara), Madhya Pradesh (Jhabua and Badwani), Chhattisgarh (Bastar and Raigarh), Jharkhand (Ranchi and West Singhbum) and Odisha (Koraput). The selected districts represent high concentration of tribal population in the respective state. Two tribal dominated *Janpad* from each of the ten selected districts, one developed and other underdeveloped, were selected purposively. The selection of the villages was done on the basis of the following two criteria: high incidence of poverty represented by extent of dryness or lack of irrigation; and remoteness. Two villages, representing an average 'remoteness' in each of these twenty *Janpads* in the ten districts, were purposively selected for the detailed study. The micro-study, thus, involves collection of primary and secondary data from the sample villages. This includes group discussions to get familiarised with villages and their people. This was followed by a survey of randomly selected sample of 50 households from each of the forty villages. The quantitative database thus, was randomly selected sample of 1,614 households from the six states.

Panchayat Raj in Central Tribal Belt

The experience, argues Upadhayay (2004), reveals that even after eight years of its enactment, PESA has not had an impact on the ground. All the states with tribal areas were to adopt this law within one year after it came into being. Almost all these states have done that but without internalising the spirit of the law. First, there are critical omissions of some of the fundamental principles behind PESA, Second, the States have invariably twisted certain words in the Central PESA, which has resulted in powers being taken away from the Gram Sabha. Third, even while affirming some provisions of the law in principle, the states have made their applicability subject to framing of rules/orders. Such enabling rules are not yet in place in most cases.

In order to make the Central Act effective, it is necessary for the State Governments to make appropriate amendments in their State Laws which impinge on specific provisions contained in the Central Act namely: (i) Land Acquisition Act; (ii) Excise Act; (iii) State Irrigation Act; (iv) Minor Forest Produce Act; (v) Mines and Minerals Acts; (vi) Land Revenue Code/Act; (vii) SC/ST Land Alienation Act; (viii) Money Lenders Act; and (ix) Regulated Market Act. No doubt, some State Governments (like Madhya Pradesh) have already amended some of the relevant Acts; others are yet to follow suit.

Table 1

Review of the State Acts

Components	*Mandatory Provision*	*Status*
Definition of Village	A village consists of a habitation or a group of habitations or a hamlet or a group of hamlets, comprising a community and managing its affairs in accordance with traditions and customs	All States adopted this definition
Status and Functions of Gram Sabha	Every village will have a Gram Sabha which will be competent to safeguard and preserve the traditions and customs of the people, their cultural identity.	All State Acts follow the Central Act. The Orissa Act adds that it should be consistent with the relevant laws in force and in harmony with tenets of the Constitution and Human Right.
Acquisition of land for development projects and resettlement of displaced persons	Prior consultation with Gram Sabha or Panchayats at the appropriate level shall be made mandatory	MP, CG and Rajasthan State Acts follow the Central Act. Gujarat assigned this power to Taluka Panchayat, however, no provision relating to coordination of such projects at state level. Orissa assigned the power to Zilla Panchayat with no role for the Gram Sabha/Gram Panchayat
Planning and Management of Minor Water Bodies	Entrusted to Panchayats at the appropriate level	MP, CG and Rajasthan State Acts follow the Central Act. Orissa assigned power to Zilla Parishad instead of Gram Sabha/Gram Panchayat
Grant of Prospecting licence or mining lease for minor minerals	Prior recommendation of Gram Sabha or Panchayats at appropriate level shall be made mandatory.	Gujarat does not make mention of it. Madhya Pradesh – No mention in the Madhya Pradesh and CG Panchayat Act but the relevant subject act Mines and Minerals (Regulation and Development Act) 1957 amended to assign powers to Gram Sabha and Panchayats at appropriate level. Orissa gives powers to Zilla Parishad.
Grant of concession for exploitation of minor minerals by auction.	Prior recommendation of Gram Sabha or Panchayats at appropriate level shall be made mandatory.	Gujarat - No mention of it. Madhya Pradesh - Madhya Pradesh Panchayat Act does not make mention of it but the subject Act Mines and Minerals (Regulation and Development) Act, 1987 amended to assign the power to Panchayat at appropriate level. Orissa- assigned the power to Zilla Parishad.

Cont'd...

...*Cont'd*

Enforce prohibition/regulate or restrict sale and consumption of any intoxicant	Panchayats at the appropriate level and the Gram Sabha to be endowed with the powers	All State Acts followed the Central Act except Madhya Pradesh which does not make provision for it in its PR Amendment Act. However, the Subject Act Madhya Pradesh Excise Act 1915 has been amended to give powers to Gram Sabha.
Ownership of Minor Forest Produce (MFP)	Panchayats at the appropriate level and the Gram Sabha endowed with the powers of ownership	All State Acts follow Central Act by assigning this power either to Gram Sabha or to the Gram Panchayats.
Prevention and Restoration of Tribal Alienated Land	Panchayats at appropriate level and the Gram Sabha to be endowed with this power.	Gujarat, Madhya Pradesh Panchayati Raj Amendment Acts do not make provision for this. However, in case of Madhya Pradesh, the Madhya Pradesh Land Revenue Code, 1959 has been amended to give power to Gram Sabha.
Manage Village Markets	Panchayats at appropriate level and the Gram Sabha to be endowed with this power.	MP, Rajasthan, CG and Orissa follow Central Act. Gujarat Amendment Acts is silent on this matter.
Money lending to the Scheduled Tribes	Panchayats at appropriate level and the Gram Sabha to be endowed with this power.	Madhya Pradesh Amendment Act does not make a mention of this subject.
Exercise control over institutions and functionaries in all social sectors.	Panchayats at appropriate level or the Gram Sabha to be endowed with this power.	All State Acts except Madhya Pradesh assign this power either to Gram Panchayat or Panchayat Samiti/Mandal Parishad. The Madhya Pradesh Amendment Act has given this power to the Gram Sabha and the Janpad Panchayat or the Zilla Parishad.
Control over Local Plans and Resources including Tribal Sub Plans	Panchayats at appropriate level and the Gram Sabha to be endowed with this power.	State Acts of Gujarat, Orissa have assigned the power to Panchayat Samiti/Taluka Panchayat/Mandal Parishad while the Madhya Pradesh and CG Acts assign this power to Gram Sabha.

Source: Planning Commission (2005).

A review of the state Acts (Table 1) shows that most states have assigned a less prominent role to Gram Sabhas/panchayats in the Scheduled Areas than was intended by PESA. In Orissa, Gram Sabhas or panchayats have been given very few powers. In many states like Gujarat and Rajasthan, powers earmarked for Gram Sabha/panchayats have been entrusted to Janpad and zilla parishads. In Madhya Pradesh Chhattisgarh, Grams Sabhas have been given powers of control only on forests located within the revenue boundaries of the village and not on all forests (including reserved forests) in the vicinity of the village. Forest products such as cane, bamboo and *mahua* seeds have been excluded from the category of minor forest produce in order to keep them under the control of the Forest Department. The brief description brings out the dismal impact of PESA on empowering Gram Sabha.[2]

Representation and Participation in Panchayat

The present political leadership is the third generation PRI leadership that has emerged after Panchayat elections. Community participation in panchayats starts from elections of PRI representatives. Discussions with villagers in tribal area reveal that people participation in these elections were large. Election process, whether for state assembly or for parliament, has its own importance in tribal areas. In order to encourage people to come out and exercise their franchise, distribution of money, in cash or kind, by candidates is common in this area. The same malpractice was seen in Panchayat elections, especially in the election of Sarpanch in the area. Consequently, the community participation in the PRI elections was high.

About 5 per cent of the households have some representatives in Panchayat either as Sarpanch, Up-Sarpanch, Panch or committee members. Such representation among always non-poor households is about 8 per cent, whereas among chronic poor it is only 4 per cent. In tribal areas, *Panch* and such inclusions are generally in consultation with socially influential people of *falia*. Economic condition is an important criterion for identification of potential political elite. Election of Panch, Sarpanch and Committee members in the village is generally unopposed; selected by social hierarchy.

Although required quorum for the meetings of Gram Sabha is one-third of all adults in the village, at least a third of them should be female members. The quorum in the Gram Sabha meetings was never present, except on the first meeting when various committees were constituted. Villagers believe that Gram Sabha meetings are irregular, informal and information of such meetings is never given to them. The community does not cooperate fully with panchayat and its operations, as it feels that programmes and developmental works are undertaken to favour the people belonging to the *Sarpanch* group. People are also critical of the fact that discussions in the earlier meetings did not get any place in the programmes of the panchayat. The first two meetings of newly constituted Gram Sabha, recall villagers, did take place with large participation. All the committees under the Gram Sabha were formed. But after that, neither the Gram Sabha nor any of its committees met. According to the villagers, Gram Sabha, the most potent social institution of the panchayat system in tribal areas, is ineffective so far as development of village is concerned. It seems that decentralised governance and people's participation remained only on paper; the political elites of the village control the activities of the Panchayat. Thus during the last year, as a matter of protest, community members have reduced their participation in Gram Sabha meetings.

Community by and large (92 per cent) is aware about Gram Sabha but is unaware about how often the Gram Sabha meets. As high as two-thirds of the respondents did not know how often Gram Sabha meets. Only 28 per cent respondents have attended Gram Sabha meetings in last one year. Lack of participation in Gram Sabha meetings is a problem faced since its inception. About 92 per cent of respondents who did not participate in Gram Sabha did so because of their preoccupation, agriculture and labouring, or owing to lack of knowledge about the meeting. Lack of quorum is a problem faced by Gram Sabha even after a decade of its functioning. In study villages, about 56 per cent of chronic poor and 43 per cent always non-poor never participated in Gram Sabha meetings.

Community and Polity

Villages in this tribal belt have a close network of clans living in hamlets. They are governed by informal but traditional social norms and are led by hereditary leaders. These traditional leaders are chosen ones, whom the community considers well acquainted with their problems and capable of solving them. These traditional leaders receive support from old and wise men from each of the hamlets. In the study villages, the traditional leaders have stronghold on the community, especially with respect to social and religious affairs of the village.

Decentralised governance has created another set of elites in the village, which is strongly challenging the existing power structure in the village. The emerging political leadership has economic superiority, understands well the tribal as well as non-tribal customary practices and is fully conversant with government programmes. They are also skilled public speakers. This new class of political leaders has posed strong challenge to the traditional leaders. A third set of emerging leaders is a group of young educated (up to class 10) tribals who have some understanding of laws that govern the Panchayat, know weaknesses of the existing system of decentralised governance, and the pattern of fund flow to Panchayats.

But villages have internal contradictions; social power is still with traditional leaders, whereas economic power is with political leaders. In underdeveloped villages, this divide is not very apparent, for villagers are not intensely fermented owing to relative homogeneity of agricultural income. Income in these villages is not only low but is less varying across households (₹ 8,598 with standardised SD 135%). In developed villages with relatively higher irrigation not only the agricultural income is high (₹ 10,415) but the variations in income are high (standardised SD 168%); indicating an intensely segregated village on economic lines. In developed village, political elites have created a buffer that absorbs criticism and discontent of the community. This coterie of *Sarpanch* also corners a sizeable part of development benefits. Political leadership operates uncontrolled when it comes to development intervention. They are neither answerable to the community nor to the social leaders in relatively developed villages.

People's Participation and Accountability

Efficiency and impact of PRI intervention largely depends on people's participation. A meaningful participation in local affairs, it could be argued, would improve quality and reach of services, especially meant for the chronic poor. But the evidences from study villages reveal that participation is confined to participating in election and registering their presence in Gram Sabha. In this tribal community, social networking and dependency on economic and social elites is still an important mechanism of meeting crisis. Disgruntled with the machinations and politicking of the social elites the poor prefer to remain away from participation in Gram Sabha and from free discussions about development issues. However, because of the overriding presence of secretary (*Sachiv*) and his knowledge of rules and regulations, many of the decisions taken by Gram Sabha or by *Sarpanch* are forced to be changed. Although, *Sarpanch* takes the final decision, the secretary is generally overpowering. In fact, the *Sachiv* has usurped the powers that belong to the community. Moreover, the client-protégée relationship and economic stratification have created a negative environment where people's participation is not feasible and accountability of people's representatives towards Gram Sabha is eroded. The net result is that corrupt practices continue to thrive in the local panchayat system.

In order to improve accountability of political elites and increase transparency in the affairs of Panchayat, the Gram Sabha is the appropriate forum. The scrutiny of accounts and monitoring of the progress made in implementing schemes and programmes by the community could check the ways of *Sarpanch* and make them accountable. But in the absence of community participation, the planning, execution and monitoring of the activities of the Panchayat are controlled by a small coterie. The community under the burden of client-protégée relationship does not demand explanations. On the other hand, due to a nexus between the bureaucracy, the political elites and the middleman, corruption has become systemic. Neither the provision to recall nor the provisions to recourse to higher authorities has any relevance here.

Perception of the Community

The community has expressed that Gram Sabha meetings are not organised on regular basis and consequently their participation in Gram Sabha has significantly reduced in the last few years. Unfulfilled expectations and livelihood struggles (migration) also do not create conducive environment for larger participation of the community in Panchayat affairs. The community feels that programmes and developmental works are unequally distributed. General perception is that benefits accrue mostly to that group of the people of the village to which the *Sarpanch* belongs. Local demands and needs are thus ignored in the interests of the powerful persons of the Panchayat. According to the villagers, *Jati Panchayat*, the most potent social institution in tribal areas, has been rendered ineffective so far as development issues of the village are concerned.

If nothing, political decentralisation has at least given rise to a new set of political elites, some of whom are corrupt and self-serving. On the other hand, as the local bureaucracy has been replaced by local political elites, the expectations of community participation in decision-making have remained a distant dream. Community openly points out to the irregularities committed in the allotment of benefits under welfare schemes like *Indira Awas Yojana*, prioritising the asset transfer beneficiaries, *Jeevan Dhara* loan, and *Jawahar Gram Samridhi Yojana.* Coterie of Sarpanch, and not the genuine persons, is the beneficiaries. These are the village people of the Sarpanch who get lion's share in building link roads, school buildings, hand pumps and construction of houses under *Indira Awas Yojana*; these are the reserved benefits for the people living in Sarpanch's *falia* (village). The only benefit the community has received is ration cards from Panchayat for subsidised food. Sarpanch, say the villagers, would never say 'no' to their requests, but would never fulfil any. The lame excuse given by the *Sarpanch* is that his hands are tied as prioritisation is done under instructions of the government officials. Moreover, a large part of fund flow is predetermined by state-run schemes and untied allocation to meet local needs is inadequate to meet the expectations of the community.

State Interventions and Development

Decentralisation has redefined the scope of development by transferring 29 items directly to be implemented by Panchayat. Community does acknowledge the programmes implemented by Panchayat under the new dispensation (Table 2).

Table 2

Main Work Done by Panchayat as Reported by the Community

	Chronic Poor	*Non-chronic Poor*	*Transitory Non-poor*	*Always Non-poor*
	Percentage			
Approach Road	65	61	61	65
Water Harvesting	14	17	9	12
School	4	3	3	3
Electricity line	4	–	–	–
Health	4	1	–	1
Building and construction	1	2	1	3
No work undertaken	20	14	26	16

Apart from creating physical infrastructures like link-roads, Panchayat building, schools, Anganwadi etc. the two most important programmes are disbursement of loan for asset transfer to the vulnerable sections, and employment generation. While the target group for asset transfer programme – known as *Swarn Jayanti Gram Sawrojgar Yojana* – are economically poor households, the beneficiaries of the employment generation schemes are marginal farmers and labouring households. The employment generation schemes usually take up works that add to tribal infrastructure especially relating to digging wells, small check dams, water harvesting devices, construction and deepening of tanks and link roads etc.

Discussions with the villagers reveal that Panchayats have done precisely little in order to fulfil the needs of the community. According to the villagers, the major benefits of assets transfer have accrued to only the influential families of the village. Gram Sabha has played no role in identifying the beneficiaries. Over 85 per cent of the respondent either do not know how the beneficiaries are selected or believe that it is Sarpanch who selects them. The Sarpanch decides who would get what, when and how the benefits of the asset transfer programmes. In the last few years, this support is in the form of different schemes like irrigation asset transfer to a few well-to-do households, intensification of investment in their farms after some time, and then meeting their replacement demands. Important loans given are for (a) diesel and electric pumps; (b) water distribution pipes, in undulating topography; (c) crop productivity enhancement schemes and (d) loan for animal purchase. Sarpanch plays a critical role in the identification of beneficiaries and loan disbursement process. In both Developed (74%) as well underdeveloped villages (77%) significant proportion of respondents believe so.

An analysis of the priorities of the community and work undertaken by Panchayat reveals that there is serious mismatch between need of the community and programmes undertaken by Panchayat (Table 3). Overemphasis by Panchayat in developing the infrastructure and agriculture at the cost of employment and services like health and education is evident.

Table 3

Mismatch of Community Needs and Panchayat Work

Work desired by Community	*Infrastructure*	*Water Harvest*	*School and Health*	*No Work*	*All*
	Number of Households				
Infrastructure[a]	392 (24)	64 (4)	9 (1)	103 (7)	568 (36)
Water Harvesting and agriculture	252 (16)	73 (5)	15 (1)	67 (4)	407 (26)
School, Health and Other services	381 (24)	91 (6)	14 (1)	87 (55)	573 (36)
Employment	26 (2)	3 (0)	-	3 (0)	32 (2)
All	1,051 (66)	231 (15)	38 (3)	260 (16)	1,580 (100)

[a] Includes construction and electrification.

Figures in parentheses are percentage of total respondents.

Principal causes for the mismatch between the demand of the community and supply of programmes by Panchayat are poor representation of chronic and non-poor in the PRIs, their lack of participation in decision-making and lack of accountability of elected representatives. What is worth noting is the fact that corruption is rampant at all levels, public as well as private, of Panchayat system: for illustration, to receive these loans, the common belief in the tribal areas is, one needs to grease the palms of the concerned officials, without which loan is not possible. Clearly, the asset transfer programme of Panchayat has failed to reach the poorest, because the well-connected rich tribals corner bulk of the benefits.

Villagers in general are unaware of when and where any public works programme would be taken up by the Panchayat. These decisions are never openly taken in Gram Sabha but are always taken by the Sarpanch. The only employment the villagers get is from deforestation, that too mainly for seedling transplanting. This is the only time when a large number of villagers are employed. In severe drought years, *Janpad/taluka* Panchayat, stopping all other programmes, diverts large part of its resources in creating community water conserving structures in the area. Villagers, however, complained that they did not know about work progress schedule. The unfortunate result was that they were deprived of much needed employment.

Table 4

Number of Beneficiary of Different Schemes

	Chronic Poor	*Non chronic Poor*	*Transitory Non-poor*	*Always Non-poor*
	Number of Households			
Pension	6 (2075)	16 (2340)	3 (2559)	11 (2754)
Indira Awas Yojana	21 (19571)	50 (19145)	10 (17850)	38 (19806)
SJGSY	1 (2)	3 (4550)		10 (5159)
SGRY	5 (960)	12 (993)	3 (1271)	7 (1371)
Food for work	30 (980)	104 (759)	30 (839)	84 (2754)
Crop Improvement		3 (22000)		1 (25000)
Livestock	1 (10000)	4 (20000)		5 (1001)
Irrigation	4 (17750)	5 (8900)	3 (17333)	5 (2754)
Other Schemes	15 (7328)	96 (9411)	16 (10394)	75 (11837)

Figures in parentheses are benefit per beneficiary.

The other complaint of the villagers is that employment and agricultural programmes have benefited the *falia* or the village where Sarpanch lives. The beneficiaries of employment generation schemes did confess that they received stipulated wages in the food for work programme – ₹ 15 plus 5 kg wheat – but the total quantum of work provided by Panchayat (per annum 15 days work per family) was inadequate. The food for work programme although did not provide adequate employment to the villagers, it did manage to establish new power relations and reinforce economic exchange to perpetuate these power relations. Villagers complain by way of an example that while only a few villagers received some employment in the construction of water conservation structure, friends of *Sarpanch* and his close relatives were employed in these programmes.

The above discussion should not give an impression that marginalised group were totally ignored in receiving benefits of employment-oriented schemes like SGRY and drought relief work. What is evident from our analysis is that it was not the chronic poor and poor who benefited alone, the always non-poor also equally benefited from such schemes (Table 4). Evidence shows that in programmes like pension scheme, Indira Awas Yojana, SJGSY, SGRY and Food for Work programme, the benefits to always non-poor were significantly more compared to chronic poor. In poverty-ridden areas, welfare schemes like pension, *Indira Awas Yojna*, irrigation development are meant to transfer public resources to most vulnerable sections. Resources redistribution did take place but, as evidences show, such redistribution was not done equitably; the always non-poor received more resources from redistribution and a larger section of this community benefited from this (Table 5). While the average sum transferred was ₹ 6,631 per beneficiary to about 35 per cent of the community, in developed villages and in the case of always non-poor such resource transfers were twice as much in comparison to underdeveloped villages and chronic-poor.

Table 5

Benefit of Accruing to Community across Groups

	Number of Beneficiary	Benefits ₹ per Beneficiary
All	559 (35)	6,631
Across villages		
Developed villages	331 (40)	7,426
underdeveloped villages	248 (29)	5,633
Across Poverty Profile		
Chronic Poor	64 (26)	9,327
Non-chronic poor	242 (35)	6,191
Transitory non-poor	56 (40)	5,641
Always non-poor	197 (38)	6,576

Figures in brackets are percentage beneficiaries in the group.

Evidences further reveal that Jharkhand has done relatively much better in terms of resource transfer to poor (Table 6). While on an average 35 per cent of households were benefited from various programmes to a tune of ₹ 6,631 per beneficiary, in Jharkhand chronic poor as a group was benefited to a tune of ₹ 16,538 and over 33 per cent households among chronic poor received these benefits. In other states, the intensity of support was low either in terms of proportion of households covered (Madhya Pradesh, Gujarat and Rajasthan) where 12 to 16 per cent of the chronic poor received benefits or the amount was much lower (Madhya Pradesh, Chhattisgarh, Odisha and Rajasthan where the amount was ranging from ₹ 1160 to ₹ 8,170). Clearly without a representative democracy in Jharkhand, the poor were gainers while in Madhya Pradesh, Rajasthan, Chhattisgarh and Odisha despite a so-called vibrant decentralisation, the interest of the most deserving; the chronic poor could not be protected. This is not to imply that one should do away with Panchayati Raj. It only indicates that there is something very wrong with the decentralisation process.

Table 6

Benefits to the Community across Poverty Profile in States

	Chronic Poor	Non-Chronic Poor	Transitory Non-Poor	Always Non-Poor
	₹ per Beneficiary			
Madhya Pradesh	(16) 3,807	(19) 7,993	(6) 5,700	(22) 11,623
Chhattisgarh	(55) 8,170	(65) 2,252	(61) 3,499	(63) 3,195
Odisha	(37) 5,142	(27) 2,085	(50) 4,562	(57) 4,328
Jharkhand	(33) 16,538	(34) 14,049	(18) 11,588	(24) 15,437
Gujarat	(12) 14,000	(19) 14,757	(19) 14,116	(12) 14,013
Rajasthan	(12) 1,160	(23) 5,617	(40) 1,460	(43) 1,732

Figures in brackets are percentage of beneficiary in each group.

It seems that decentralisation has become an end in itself. Whether the process is able to bring decision-making near to people or whether the fruits of decentralisation are equitably distributed, no one in the bureaucracy and policy circles is concerned. The process of decision-making is still highly centralised and the fruits of development interventions are highly iniquitous. Unless all the programmes and schemes are rooted through Gram Sabha, the decentralisation as a panacea has little future.

Commons and Community

Depletion of tribal resources – land, forest and water – has a history. After independence, tribals lost control over the forest because of the Forest Laws. The PESA transferred back the power to manage natural resources, including land, water and forest, to the community in accordance with its traditions in harmony with the provisions of the constitution and with due regard to the spirit of other relevant laws for the time being in force. This section argues that even after reforming political governance, the existing forest laws have not allowed the control of forest to pass to the community.

The whole tribal belt had dense forest about 100 years back. Today a large part of it is a depleted thin forest. Depleted though, the remains are still sufficient for meeting the timber, fodder and fuel needs of the villages around the forest. As the forest falls under control of forest department, the administration of the forest does not fall within the purview of Gram Panchayat. Entry to the forest has been restricted and any community use – in the form of wood, minor forest produce, fuel and fodder – is deemed as illegal by the forest department. The forest department is trying to rejuvenate this forest by creating undisturbed natural rooting environment and also by sapling plantation. The upper hills and a part of the villages are under the administration of forest department, whereas the lower reaches, including the valley, are administered through Panchayat. The lower reaches are the only land that can be brought under agriculture. The community in a number of villages, a few years back, had access to upper reaches of the hills for grazing animals as well as for wood but now the entry to the upper hills has been restricted. This was, according to officials, done mainly to restrict the entry of the cattle that destroyed forestation, as unrestricted movements helped gully formations and erosion of thin topsoil that holds the vegetative growth.

In these villages, the institutional forest and watershed committees, as a part of Gram Panchayat, are in place. But the committees are not empowered to control the structure created by different departments. These resources, though being within the villages, are out of the reach of the community. Though the control of these resources should have been with the Gram Panchayat and its committees, forest laws govern their management. The community is, nonetheless, using the forest resources, illegally. The villagers are not too resentful of this access loss to forests. Community, however, is agitated about the restrictions and more aware about its rights. The process of converting the administration from *Van Gram* to Panchayat was initiated over 25 years back. The measurement and demarcation of individual holdings and settlement was also done. Individual agricultural land rights, *Patta,* were prepared but were not distributed. But the villagers in *Van Gram* often face wrath of forest officials on issues like quanta of land they could cultivate, their rights to land, tresspassing and access to commons, and forest protection. Often the community has to bribe the forest officials in such disputes. The distress also provided support to protest against access failure to natural resources. Their inability to manage their resources is, however, neither because of their illiteracy nor lack of awareness about the laws. In a sense, PESA is as an Act that has no *locus standi* of its own; the overlapping power of the various departments is a crucial impediment in passing control of forestland to the community; without reforming it the grassroots situation may not change.

Environment and Sustainability

A large number of villages in the tribal area are forest villages. For example, about half of hundred villages falling in the *Pati* Janpad in Badwani district of Madhya Pradesh are outside the control of decentralised governance. These types of villages are also present in other states. These villages, called *Van Gram*, are administered by the forest department and should have been converted to usual administrative Panchayat villages long back. Still the state Forest Department is controlling these *Van Grams*. Unlike Panchayat administered villages that get a lifelong lease of the land, agricultural land in a *Van Gram* is allocated to individual households for 15 years and the lease is renewed afresh by the forest department. The forest officer of the range manages land, water and forest in these *Van Grams*. Community's access to forest for timber, fodder and fuel is much better in *Van Gram* than forests falling under Panchayat administered villages. Community is aware about the denial to control their resources and the consequent hardships caused by it. But it accepts the superiority of laws of the Forest Department.

The access failure to natural resources needs to be viewed within the context of the efforts of PESA to empower the community as well as in relation to the discredit the what state receives due to its repressive ways. Discrediting of the state originated due to a flux of tribal migration into these virgin hills, even as late as during early 1950s, in search of arable land that has put the community as well as the commons into an impasse. Both the questions of livelihood and the commons have transformed over the years into a new politics of environment. Tribals who cleared areas under the control of the Forest Department for cultivation now face the charge of being encroachers and destroyers of forests. Control over land, especially forestland, is highly challenged by the left-oriented civil society organisations (Sah, 2004). On the other hand, the process of empowering community was a new approach of managing the commons; it was meant for changing laws to accommodate community participation in governance of the commons. The theoretical strength to these steps has been provided by the seminal work of Gadgil and Guha (1992):

That (a) the use of natural resources with a monopolistic command by a few influential castes in the society was in fact a prudent way of natural resource use, for it provided checks against overexploitation by others; (b) the traditional societies had non-exploitative and harmonious relationship with nature, whereas modern society has subordinating relationship with it; (c) the fissures in a traditional society are naturalised by non-competitive nature of their interests; (d) any violation in the traditional use of nature is an aberration rather than the traditions; and (e) an opportunistic behaviour by traditional communities is an infection of modernity. Implicit in the formulation are first, variations of uses and abuses of commons arising from the binary nature of local, traditional, women and tribal versus outsider, global, state and market. The traditional amounts to sustainable use of commons, whereas commercial exploitation by the state is implicit in the arguments (Agrawal and Sivaramakrishnan, 2001). Secondly, the naturalising non-competitive behaviour of the society reflects that conflicts over the resources were actually conflicts over sustainability of resources. The dichotomy, thus provided strength in two differing ways. The civil society took a leaf out of the ecological history of India and attributed powerlessness of tribals before the state and market as the cause of tribal access failure to natural resources. This resulted in the left-oriented NGOs mobilisation of tribals against repressive markets and the state. The other process influenced by the construct was the appealing aspect of traditional communities with conservation; and so started joint management where communities have become equal partners in management of natural resources like forest and water or in areas that PESA gave control of commons to the community.

The above frame, however, delinks the environmental politics from communities' livelihood struggles. The uniform tribal character as protector of nature artificially homogenises and hides the social identities and conflicts. On the other hand, treating livelihood and environment simultaneously could provide understanding on how both apply to each other, so that one can ask what do we mean by sustainable, sustainability of livelihood, or environment.

It can be argued that economic growth adversely affects the natural resources because of critical interactions between livelihood, technology and nature. But the implications of environmental degradation are conceptually different in Central tribal belt than in the dynamic rural areas. In the former situation (tribal belt), the livelihood processes influence nature not because of overuse per se but because of sheer survival of different participants. Stagnation and low level of economic activities are, thus, the cause of degradation. This calls for developing new opportunities that create interest for protecting nature. In the latter situation (rural areas), nature degrades owing to uncertainty of availability of natural resources to various segments of the society. Overuse of nature is not because of availability of resources per se but owing to mistrust and uncertainty about their availability. In order to maximise his or her returns in this uncertainty, everyone overuses the nature. Regeneration rests on sharing information with trust between community, classes and social groups that have varying perceptions about the access to commons. Sustainability of both environment and livelihood is possible then.

Political Unfreedom

Adverse Incorporation and Political Exclusion

Positive discrimination in the form of retained places in public office like universities, the civil service and the legislature, appears to provide opportunities for individuals rather than for the systematic advancement of Adivasi as a whole.

There is a widespread belief in the majority Hindu population that the Indian nation-building measures have attempted tribal integration through a culturally imperialist form of cooption and assimilation.

Non-tribal populations cling to a set of beliefs concerning Adivasi, which justify their income poverty, low literacy rates, and socio-political exclusion. Non-tribals, particularly in the (non-tribal majority) towns in majority tribal areas are fearful of the tribals. They fear what might happen to their own dominance if tribals become educated and demand their rights. Even amongst the educated upper class and amongst government officials, tribals are regarded as unruly, ignorant, dirty and drunken. They are dismissed as polygamous, and having too many children; as not having a savings culture; as desiring to live hand to mouth, being lazy and stopping work when they have enough money to buy food for the day; as retaining 'backward' agricultural practices; and as having no idea of society and so living in widely spread nuclear families rather than tightly clustered joint families. Tribals who 'make good' and become political or administrative leaders are seen as being 'the worst', as they treat 'their own kind' badly and threaten non-tribal colleagues with legal action for discrimination and defamation.

Within tribal communities, there is evidence of both political exclusion and adverse incorporation. In terms of adverse incorporation, villagers are incorporated into local political interactions, but in a set of feudal relationships with the traditional leaders, Sarpanch and asymmetric, extractive, not so transparent and unpredictable relationships with the local police and forest officials.

Tribal communities are strongly heterogeneous, with economic stratification reinforced by patriarchal and political differentiation. Patron-client relationships are strong with non-tribal moneylender *bania* who engages tribals in highly extractive interlocked market relationships; with widespread share-cropping and leasing relationships; and with the potential for power asymmetries in the forward contracting of agricultural produce, as part of debt payments and for cash crop produce. Perhaps the most notable example of patron-client relationships is between the Sarpanch and villagers.

In terms of exclusion, poor households and women from all households are excluded from decision-making and negotiations. Men from poor tribal households and from the *harijan* households in the village will not attend public meetings. Women are largely absent from all such meetings; we assume that widows and the socially excluded – e.g. the mentally handicapped – have no access either directly or through male representation to village governance structures.

Political Economy of Panchayat

Decentralisation in this tribal area has neither brought decision-making closer to the community nor equity in delivering the benefits. It has, nevertheless, replaced the traditional bureaucracy by a new class of political elites who have control on decision-making as well as resources. People's participation has not yet undergone the stages of critical evaluation of local priorities and strategies to meet them. The work done by Panchayat is not congruent with what the community needs. The work done by Panchayat also helps in sustaining the well-being of non-poor. The political economy of decentralisation has engendered a nexus between the political elites, the bureaucracy and the contractor for furthering their own interests. This nexus has defied the basic objective of decentralisation, empowering the chronic poor and non-poor. It is true that Panchayats are implementing all those schemes and programmes that earlier were done by the bureaucracy. But the financial control of upper echelons of the elected representatives and bureaucracy keeps the village Sarpanch under their dependence. A substantial part of time of the Sarpanch is spent in meeting and entertaining the officials and the elected representatives at the *Janpad*. Despite Sarpanch and Gram Sabha being introduced as the agencies for implementing the development programmes, these agencies have become an add-on to the old chain of corruption. Sarpanch has become a medium in this chain of corruption. Redistribution of resources do take place but with considerable leakage and misdirection.

Unfreedom

Sen (1999) has conceptualised that unfreedom – economic, political, social, transparency and security – can pull people into poverty. Sen's proposals of unfreedom include both inability of the community to exercise its rights freely as well as opportunities of individuals to operate freely, for poverty can manifest by unavailability of services at the macro level as well as access denial at the micro level. Political unfreedom can surface by micro processes of lack of freedom to choose who governs as well as macro principles of how to govern. Political freedom, it can be argued, could create an environment that helps community to participate freely in the process of governance, choose the leaders who are committed, plan and manage their resources for local development and criticise the approach and monitor the functions of those who are governing. If the political process is free, it can help fulfil the expectations of the community. Political freedom, thus, can be operationalised as freedom to individuals to (a) choose who governs them; (b) be governed in a participatory process; (c) plan and manage their natural resources; and (d) be able to criticise and organise protests against uniformed decisions so that gains are equitably distributed within the community. One can use the findings of this chapter to evaluate the extent to which each of these freedoms has successfully been attained.

Findings of the chapter reveal that the process to choose those whom the individuals want them to govern is free and fair. People have used their franchise in deciding who would govern them freely. But the process created fissures in a homogenous community with social, political and economic interests. Once the political leaders took over their responsibility, the process of decentralised governance, instead becoming participatory, became highly centralised. The gains of the decentralised governance have been too few and highly iniquitous. Community's expectations remained unfulfilled and participation slowly dwindled. The role of Sarpanch, and the exclusive group of his people sharing interest, has made people lose their faith on Panchayat. Political decentralisation has not only fractured the homogeneity of the tribal society but has also made governance highly centralised.

The community does monitor how the governance is neglecting it. But it, however, does not get enough opportunity to register its protest about this governance. There are provisions of recall a corrupt Sarpanch but the tribal community is unaware of these remedial measures. It is only once in five years that they get the freedom to punish bad governance by rejecting those involved in the governance. Nevertheless, the community has no freedom in the process of planning programmes it needs. The blame for this unfreedom to decide what and how the local development should take place falls at various levels. First, the process of centralisation at the Panchayat level is too overpowering for community to exert pressures for participatory process to begin. Second, the quantum of financial allocation is too thin to meet the demands of the community. Third, the desire of the bureaucracy and the elected representatives, at higher echelons, to control the activities and finances of the Gram Panchayat, does not allow independence to the Panchayat. Lastly, existing laws that govern the natural resources obstruct the process of giving their control to the community.

Summing Up

The findings of this paper indicate towards the following two major conclusions: First, in one stroke, PESA promised to give control of resources and decision-making to tribals. This has proved to be a false promise. Owing to the fact that rules of the line departments of states impinge upon the specific provisions of PESA, community never got a chance to decide on its own. Consequently, decision-making powers relating to land, water, forest and development still rests with bureaucracy. Secondly, decentralisation, it seems, has become an end in itself; this is true when we analyse the process of decision-making, which is still highly centralised, or with respect to fruits of development interventions, which are still highly iniquitous.

Notes

1. PESA is a unique legislation; it gives radical self-governance powers to the tribal community and recognises its traditional community rights over natural resources. Prior to passage of this Act, laws passed by central and state governments were applied mechanically to tribal areas even when these contravened traditional tribal practices and institutions. However, under PESA the law focuses on settlements, which the tribal people themselves perceive to be traditional and organic entities. In fact, this is the first law that empowers people to redefine their own administrative boundaries. PESA provides that the tribal Gram Sabha so defined would be empowered to approve all development plans, control all functionaries and institutions of all social sectors as well as control all minor water bodies, minor minerals and non-timber forest resources. It would also have the authority to control land alienation, impose prohibition, manage village markets and resolve internal conflicts by traditional modes.
2. State-specific development in empowering Gram Sabha is as follows:

   Rajasthan

   In Rajasthan though knowledge of the details of PESA has been minimal, a serious concern is that the elected representatives and officials of various departments of scheduled areas do not seem to be aware of the state's adoption of the PESA or at least they considered that such a law would not be really beneficial for them. PESA does not talk about a hamlet-based village. One panchayat includes average 3 to 4 villages and a village includes 1.5 to 2 Ward Sabha. Ward Sabha's power and functions overlap with the Gram Sabha and creates conflicts. A parallel jurisdiction with no clear definition of responsibilities aggravates these differences in perceptions. Sometimes, even the lack of awareness has resulted in not exerting vital powers that have been granted under PESA as applicable in the state. There have been several reasons why the process of implementation fails. It ranges from political will to the attitudes of line functionaries, to clear lack of awareness. Besides, one of the key problem areas is the fact that powers of the Gram Sabha envisaged under the state PESA is not recognised by different line agencies such as Forest, Land and Revenue Department etc.

Madhya Pradesh

An important feature of PESA in Madhya Pradesh is that the Gram Panchayat would act under the direct supervision of the Gram Sabha. This is significant because it at least places the hierarchy of the power structure at the village level and in that sense it is perhaps a very significant move in the empowerment of Gram Sabha. But because of lack of awareness as well as lack of legislative activism, community had very little information of the specific law under PESA. Moreover, as the Laws on Forest Produce in MP have still not been amended to grant ownership rights to the Gram Sabha especially in Scheduled Areas. While there is a JFM scheme in the state of MP, the role of Gram Sabha in relation to the Forest Protection Committee under the JFM is still unclear at the local level. Gram Swaraj Act of 2001 has taken up a number of provisions that were specially enacted for scheduled areas and made it applicable in the entire state the distinction between Gram Sabha in non-scheduled areas and scheduled areas are now blurred and the political will to implement PESA is lacking.

Gujarat

Various amendments of the Act in Gujarat have significantly reduced the role of Gram Sabha. Most of the powers that were originally intended to be given to Gram Sabha or the panchayat have been given to the various tiers of the Panchayat rather than the Gram Sabha. PESA is just a mechanism of the state to retain control by introducing these in blurred legal terms, which are used in accordance with convenience.

Chhattisgarh

Chhattisgarh did not enact any new legislation after it became a separate state. Not only that, even the implementation of the laws enacted after PESA, leaves a lot to be desired. However, due to its association with Madhya Pradesh, it has some devolution of power to the village level functionaries. In Chhattisgarh the new poverty eradication programme funded by World Bank has some positive effect upon the livelihood of the tribals.

Orissa (Odisha)

The new act came into existence in 1997, but so far only Orissa Excise Act and Land Alienation Act has been amended. The rule regarding the Gram Sabha control own forest produce and the rule about moneylending are awaiting approval. In the case of land acquisition, mining lease, management of water bodies in place of Gram Sabha it is assigned to Zilla Parishad. True devolution of power is not percolated to village due to lack of awareness among the functioning. Most of the implementation works are handled by Panchayat secretaries who are also unaware about the real power of Panchayat assigned to them under PESA.

Jharkhand

The most unfortunate fact is that in Jharkhand, Panchayat elections are not held since 1978. In the absence of panchayat, the act provides for an Aam Sabha (similar to Palli Sabha of Orissa) to implement development programmes in the state. In the Palli Sabha, villagers assemble to decide development strategies of the concerned village, which is presided over by the Block Development Officer. In absence of PRIs, practically all the development work has been implemented by a panchayat Sewak, who has more than one panchayat under his jurisdiction. Therefore, it is very difficult for him to supervise the works efficiently. However, weekly meetings are held in the village where only development contractors and influential people of the village participate. However, development works are carried out without participation of the villagers.

References

Agrawal, A. and K. Sivaramakrishnan (2001), 'Introduction: Agrarian Environment', in A. Agrawal and K. Sivaramakrishnan (eds), *Social Nature: Resources, Representation and Rule in India*, Oxford University Press, New Delhi.

Gadgil, M. and R. Guha (1992), *This Fissured Land: An Ecological History of India*, Oxford University Press, Oxford.

Planning Commission (2005), *Decentralisation and Panchayati Raj Institutions*, Government of India, New Delhi, www.planningcommission.nic.in:80/plans.mta-9702/mta-ch10.pdf

Sah, D.C., A. Bhatt, Tapas K. Dalapati (2008), Chronic Poverty in Remote Rural Areas, Report submitted to Planning Commission, Government of India, MPISSR: Ujjain.

Sah, D.C. (2004), 'Continuity and Change: Tribal Society in Southwestern Madhya Pradesh', *Madhya Pradesh Journal of Social Sciences*, Vol. 8, No. 1, January-June.

Saxena, N.C. (2003), 'Issues in Panchayat', www.panchayat.org.

Sen, Amartya (1999), *Development as Freedom*, Oxford University Press, Oxford.

Upadhyay, S. (2005), 'Impact of State Legislation on the Empowerment of Gram Sabha in Schedule V Areas', in R. Singh (ed.), *Empowerment of Gram Sabha and Social Audit*, NIRD, Hyderabad.

Upadhyay, V. (2004), 'Tribal People and the Law', *Frontline*, Vol. 21, No. 10, 9–22 October.

10

Decentralised Governance through (PESA) Act and Tribal Development

S.N. Tripathy

In recent years, there has been growing focus on governance issues at global, national, regional and local levels. Governance is an efficient and effective public participation process in discharging governing functions and can be seen as method of distribution of power and management of public resources. Problems of governance is the joint responsibility of the state and people to mobilise and utilise public resources and promote public decision-making towards the improvement of common public good. The Government of India, since the early 1990s has undertaken several initiatives for decentralisation in rural and tribal governance.

Democratic decentralisation refers to the programmes and techniques which imply devolution of governmental powers and responsibilities, decentralisation of political institutions, development of local leadership and strengthening the efforts for economic modernisation.

Decentralisation means transfer of planning, decision-making or administrative authority from the central government to its field organisations, local administrative units, semi-autonomous organisations, local governments or non-governmental organisations.

Democratic decentralisation envisages association of more and more people with government at all levels. Democratic decentralisation stands for people's right to initiate their own projects for local well-being and the power to execute and operate them in an autonomous manner. Decentralisation is seen as a theory of development, which requires a variety of institutions for empowering and uplifting the marginalised and the poor. It is expected to work for the building up of an administrative space at the cutting edge level where the felt needs of the poor could be ventilated. Decentralisation is a prime mechanism through which democracy becomes truly representative and responsive.

Decentralisation can play a paramount role in enhancing the practice of democratic governance. It can contribute to the process of democratic development by expanding the scope of social, economic and political participation of the people and the corresponding responsiveness and accountability of the authority structures of the state. Ultimately, it can be an effective instrument of development policy to diminish inequality and poverty.

Since last three decades, the idea of decentralisation has become increasingly popular and most countries have placed it on their development policy agenda. In many countries, policymakers have considered it as a panacea for various ills concerning development and implemented it as a way of reducing the role of the state as the centralised state has lost a great deal of legitimacy on account of its many disappointments (Bardhan and Mookherjee, 2002). However, action to empower local governments with substantial taxing powers and increased expenditure autonomy has not always matched plans and promises.

Decentralisation is the transfer of political, administrative and fiscal responsibilities to locally elected bodies and empowerment of communities to apply control over these bodies. The economic justification that supports decentralisation is that local governments being closer to their constituencies, may be more responsive to local needs, and consequently, provide various services more efficiently.

The advantages and disadvantages of decentralisation as a strategy are well recognised (Oates, 1972; Tiebout, 1961), as we saw earlier, good governance is accepted as the key to efficient and welfare enhancing key, of which decentralisation is one of the constituent best practices. Indeed, there is a fair consensus that decentralisation is a challenging and complex process that requires dedicated participation by all stakeholders, and promises to be a mechanism for improved democratic governance and sustainable human development. In any case, the process of decentralisation has been institutionalised through constitutional amendment.

In recent years, globalisation has been accompanied by tremendous increase of prosperity, but ironically in the midst of large islands of abject poverty. Even where the poverty has been dented, inequality has increased. These are clearly warning signals for sustained human development.

India has a federal structure, essentially a union with a strong centripetal bias with the constitution ensuring an overwhelming and overriding power to the central government. The political climate in recent times has been such that more and more ground has had to be yielded to the states. The days of single party domination are past and coalitional politics are to continue and therefore, regional parties have been gaining ground.

Panchayati Raj System

The institutional arrangement for the policy of democratic decentralisation in India is known as 'Panchayati Raj'. The 73rd Constitution Amendment Act brought historic power to the grassroot bodies recognising them as the third tier of government and creating a channel for effective decentralisation.

The word 'democratic' explains the nature and purpose of the concept as also its basic claims in an institutional set-up. The word 'decentralisation' is essentially indicative of the method to realise the end as contained in the word 'democratic'. In general sense, decentralisation is the transfer of power from a central authority to lower levels in a territorial hierarchy. The main objective behind such a process is to empower the people at the grassroots by accessing power and utilities.

In Panchayati Raj system of local self-government wherein the people take upon themselves the responsibility for development. It is a system of institutional arrangement for achieving rural development through people's initiative and participation. Panchayati Raj involves a three-tier structure of democratic institutions at district, block and village levels namely, Zillah Parishad, Panchayat Samiti and Gram Panchayats respectively. These institutions are considered as training ground for democracy and gives political education to the masses. These institutions were established in 1959 based on the philosophy of decentralisation and Gram Swaraj (village self-rule). Rural development plans and programmes are implemented at this level so that fruits of development can accrue directly to the community.

In the current context of Panchayati Raj Institutions (PRIs) getting effectively empowered, especially because many of the public goods have to be provided and serviced locally (below state level), the continued differentiated mandate (so far as party political strength is concerned) means that the situation is full of potential issues. More than ever before, the 'political feasibility' in the heterogeneous domain of polity presents a sobering reality. Such a situation, however, can be turned on its head to bring more progress rather than less on the front of empowerment of PRIs.

The 73rd Amendment made a sea of change in the status of the Panchayats because the Constitution made it mandatory for all the states to set up three-tier Panchayats and to hold direct elections to all the tiers at the regular interval of five years and imposed a political uniformity on the structure and workings of the third tier.

The radical features of the 73rd Amendment tried to address some of the problems encountered by the PRIs in previous years are: granting PRIs constitutional status; uniform three-tier PRI structure with village, block/taluka and district levels; direct elections to all seats for all members at all levels; empowering socially and economically disadvantaged groups such as Scheduled Castes, Scheduled Tribes and women; one-third of the total seats and chairperson offices reserved for women; ensuring free, fair and regular elections; keeping terms fixed; identifying a list of subjects to come under the jurisdiction of the PRIs; addressing the issue of PRI finances; and establishing the Gram Sabha (village assembly) as the electorate body to which the panchayat would be accountable.[1]

The Indian Constitution defines PRIs as institutions of self-government. This clearly implies that there must be unambiguous administrative, fiscal and political devolution so that in the local governments, all three tiers are empowered to deal with local development issues. However, our discussion above shows that this is not the case. While political decentralisation seems to have progressed quite well, with elections held relatively regularly and with good participation, there has been only limited administrative and fiscal decentralisation. As a consequence, PRIs control few resources and cannot make relevant decisions and, lack the capacity to implement assigned functions, which remain de facto under the control of the state administration (World Bank, 2000).

Fiscal Performance of PRIs: An Inter-State Comparison

Data on rural local bodies in the diverse states are available from the Central Finance Commissions (CFCs) both 11th and 12th and also from the State Finance Commissions. The State Finance Commission data are somewhat more comprehensive. It is revealed from the Table 1 that Andhra Pradesh, Karnataka, Punjab, Rajasthan and Tamil Nadu have been gainers from the allocations by the 12th Finance Commission vis-à-vis their relative positions in the 11th Finance Commission allocation. Assam, Goa, Madhya Pradesh, Rajasthan, Uttar Pradesh and West Bengal have been unaffected in their relative rankings. Gujarat, Haryana, Kerala and Maharashtra have been losers. Most programmes are implemented at the block/village level, where local bodies and Panchayati Raj Institutions (PRIs) play a significant role together with NGOs.

Table 1

State-wise Allocations to PRIs in the 11th and 12th Finance Commission

States	*11th Finance Commission*		*12th Finance Commission*		*Changed Rank*	*Relatively Changed Position*
	Shares	*Ranks*	*Shares*	*Ranks*		
Andhra Pradesh	152.04	2	317.4	4	2	Gainer
Assam	46.68	12	105.2	12	0	Unaffected
Goa	1.85	15	3.6	15	0	Unaffected
Gujarat	69.61	9	186.2	8	–1	Loser
Haryana	29.42	14	77.6	13	–1	Loser
Karnataka	78.82	8	177.6	9	1	Gainer
Kerala	65.92	11	197	7	–4	Loser
Madhya Pradesh	143.09	3	332.6	3	0	Unaffected
Maharashtra	131.35	4	396.6	2	–2	Loser
Orissa (Odisha)	69.11	10	160.6	11	1	Gainer
Punjab	30.92	13	64.8	14	1	Gainer
Rajasthan	98.18	6	246	6	0	Unaffected
Tamil Nadu	93.22	7	174	10	3	Gainer
Uttar Pradesh	263.83	1	585.6	1	0	Unaffected
West Bengal	115.55	5	254.2	5	0	Unaffected

The enactment of the 73rd and 74th Amendments of the Constitution have provided a framework for decentralisation of governance and local participation in the formulation and implementation of plans for economic development and social justice including environmental protection and provision of basic services like water supply, sanitation and solid waste management.

Decentralised Governance in Tribal Societies

According to the 2011 Census, tribes in India constitute 8.6 per cent of the total population of our country. Constitutional and legal history of the formation of Scheduled Areas in India can be traced back to the colonial period. As the policy of the British government was solely directed and dominated by the colonial interests, it was based on isolation and exploitation of the tribes. Since the policy was in the interest of the vested interests, i.e. non-tribal landlords, contractors and moneylenders, they not only took possession of tribals' land, but also brought the tribes into perpetual bondage (Ratho, 2007: 4).

The traditional tribal bodies – tribal councils/tribal Panchayats- are one of the oldest known institutions of a local self-government nature. In recent years these traditional institutions have become inactive or lost their influence or have generally weakened in such areas and amongst such communities which have had continuous close interaction with other communities or where statutory Panchayat have been introduced. Situation in tribal areas in respect of self-governing institution was quite different from the general areas. The tribal people have a strong community organisation. Therefore, the introduction of formal Panchayats created an anomalous situation. These formal institutions have been largely ignored by, the people. They did not have much significance for their day-to-day life. In those cases, where the new leadership of formal Panchayat tried to assert its authority, there was confrontation.

Article 244(1) and 244(2) of the Constitution of India enables the government to enact separate laws for the governance and administration of the tribal areas. In pursuance of these articles, the President of India had asked each of the states in the country to identify tribal dominated areas. Such areas which have been identified by the states were declared as Fifth Schedule areas. Such areas have special rights and the Governor of the respective states have powers to make regulations for better governance and for protecting the rights of the tribal community.

The Parliament of India passed Provisions of the Panchayats Extension to the Scheduled Areas (PESA) Act, 1996 to extend the provisions of the 73rd Constitutional Amendment 1993 to the Fifth Schedule areas of the country. This Act is quite significant as it accords statutory status to the Gram Sabhas in Schedule V areas with wide ranging powers and authority. States having Fifth Schedule areas, namely, Andhra Pradesh, Chhattisgarh, Gujarat, Himachal Pradesh, Jharkhand, Madhya Pradesh, Maharashtra, Orissa (Odisha) and Rajasthan have amended their respective Panchayati Raj Acts to give effect to the provisions of the PESA Act.

The most important feature of the 1996 Panchayat Act is to make the people in scheduled areas to govern themselves. It is impossible for this law to be successfully implemented without the participation of the people. Thus, the 'People's Participation' has gained much significance in the above context. But the purpose of the extension act has not been completely understood, either by the political leadership or by the bureaucracy. People at large are not aware about the system of Tribal self-rule except in those areas where NGOs are working with the people, and where tribal people are also working in these NGOs as social activists.

The democratic form of government with decentralised planning committed to the well-being of the people particularly the poverty stricken, isolated and vulnerable sections of our country can thrive only when there is room for expression of their legitimate grievances. As such, in the local plan or grassroot plan we found a rationale in terms of participation of the people for whom plans are actually meant. A practical planner has been entrusted with the responsibility of solving localised problems, development of certain segments of the population, striking a harmonious blending between mobilisation of resources and optimum utilisation of social overhead capital.

Under the PESA Act, Gram Sabhas are endowed specifically with such powers and authority as to enable them to function as institutions of self-government.

These Powers are

Ownership of Minor Forest Produce, power to enforce prohibition, power to prevent alienation of land, power to control local plans and resources including the Tribal Sub-Plan, power to manage village markets, power to control money lending to STs, power to control institutions and functionaries in all social sectors.

Right to Self-rule under PESA

Section 4(b) of the PESA Act defines a village as a habitation or a group of habitations or a hamlet or a group of hamlets comprising a community and managing its affairs in accordance with tradition and customs. In the section the term 'community' seems to have been used in a micro-territorial sense. Tribal communities do not live in isolation. The tribal community, which lives in isolation, inhabits in more than one habitat. Moreover, there is also the problem of authentication of tradition and customs. As the tribal areas are scattered, with many languages, different cultures, traditions and customs, it is not possible to define the village. There is no uniform pattern of tribal rule with this cultural diversity. Most of the tribal villages survive in their current habitats with their respective territorial jurisdictions. This does not mean that status quo must be maintained in all cases. But rather than creating new territorial entities through legal instruments, the best course would be to recognise the existing villages and village boundaries, and leave it to the people as a whole to formally pass a resolution indicating, with reasons, the changes they want in their spatial jurisdiction. It is quite likely that there will be conflict in this matter among adjoining villages. In such cases intermediate level Panchayats rather than the state bureaucracy may be vested with the power of arbitration and reconciliation.

Section 4(m) endows Panchayats in the Scheduled areas with powers and authority to function as institutions of self-government. Such powers are essential to enforce prohibition/regulate the sale and consumption of any intoxicant, the ownership of Minor Forest Produce, prevention of land alienation, managing village markets, control over moneylending and implementation of social sector schemes, local plans including tribal sub-plans. The powers mentioned in the section are of two categories: (a) powers which are of executive nature and can be delegated by the concerned state governments, (b) law-making powers which can be exercised by various entities only by conforming to the basic structure of the Constitution.

However, the above two categories cannot be seen in isolation from each other. The Panchayats to be effective in discharging responsibilities like prohibition, curbing the evils of moneylending, etc. will require law-making powers, judicial power and control over the law enforcing machinery. In view of the famous judgment by Justice Mahajan in 1950, the state legislatures are unlikely to vest law-making powers in Panchayat bodies. The state legislature can, of course, delegate judicial and police powers up to a point to local bodies, but to expect more will require radical transformation of political climate in the country.

In fact, conferment of all the powers mentioned not only in Section 4(m) but also in 4(k) and (1) will require political mobilisation on a massive scale. It is doubtful whether the political culture in the country is ready for such a radical transformation. There is also another danger that as and when a state government delegates certain executive powers to the Panchayats, it will render the latter its subordinate organs. This is a far cry from the ideal of tribal self-rule.

To cite an illustration when Vedanta started its alumina project two decades back in Kashipur block of Rayagada district, Odisha, cohesive measures were adopted to obtain the signature of the villagers in the Gram Sabha for the implementation of the project. 'Agragammee' – an NGO fought for the tribal rights at Kashipur. But the Orissa Gram Panchayati Act has bestowed power to the district collector to summon the records of the 'Gram Sabha' and to make changes. This is a mockery to the PESA Act as the State Act has over-riding power to circumvent the Central Act.

Right to Control over Land and Natural Resources

Section 4(i) provides that the Gram Sabha or the Panchayats should be 'consulted' before making the acquisition of land for development projects and before resettling or rehabilitating persons affected by such projects. This is a very weak framework of tribal self-governance. It does not require the 'approval' or 'consent' of the Gram Sabha or the Panchayat. Moreover, it makes a vague stipulation that the actual planning and implementation of the projects be coordinated at the state level. It does not make it clear, either, among whom and through which mechanism will the coordination at the state level be done.

Section 4(j) provides that planning and management of minor water bodies in the Scheduled Areas be 'entrusted' to Panchayats at the appropriate level. Ethnographers know that water body management among many tribes is a dimension of village moral economy and the entire community is involved in the decision-making process. But the PESA Act constricts this process. Who will entrust the planning and management of minor water bodies in the Scheduled Areas?

Sections 4(k) and (1) lay down that the recommendations of the Gram Sabha or the Panchayat at the appropriate level are made mandatory prior to grant of prospecting license or mining lease for minor minerals in the Scheduled Areas as well as for their auction. There may positive or negative recommendation and hence, the license could be granted even if the Gram Sabha sends a negative recommendation. The word 'recommendation' in this section seems to be inappropriate. The appropriate word should have been 'consent.'

It is essential to present an instance depicting the significance of PESA Act and role of 'Gram Sabha' for tribes. Since a decade, the thickly forested and riverine region of Lanjigarh in Kalahandi (Odisha) was under severe pressure from mining development for bauxite deposits and alumina processing, by the British Vedanta Group, in collaboration with State of Odisha, Orissa Mining Corporation (OMC) and also, Ministry of Environment and Forests. The proposed mining would have severely degraded the Niyamgiri hills ecosystem. It is a rich wildlife habitat and an important and recognised elephant corridor. Mining would have endangered the Dongaria Kondh's self-sufficient forest-based livelihoods, leading to the extinction of their culture over a period of time. More than 7 square kilometres of the sacred undisturbed forest land on top of the mountain that has been protected for ages by the Dongaria Kondh as sacred to their deity, Niyam Raja, and essential for the region's fertility; would have been stripped off its vegetation, soil and rendered into a vast barren exposed land. Mining would have built roads through the Dongaria's territories, opening the area to outsiders, a trend that is already threatening the rich biodiversity of the hills.

In the context of PESA Act it is pertinent to note that the Union Ministry of Environment and Forests in August 2010 rejected the forest clearance to the bauxite mining project as its against the rights of the tribes. OMC later challenged the ministry's denial in the Supreme Court. However, the Supreme Court ruled out the Vedanta Group's bauxite mining project and ordered the Gram Sabha to examine the mining proposals, juxtaposing them with the community, individual as well as cultural and religious claims by the tribals and forest dwellers, including their rights of worship over the Niyamgiri hills. The villagers living in Rayagada and Kalahandi districts unanimously passed resolution held in twelve Gram Sabhas; vehemently resisting bauxite mining in Niyamgiri claiming that they worshipped the whole of it as their revered God Niyamraja.

Thus, in the context of inclusive decentralised governance; this is the victory of Niyamgiri villagers in the frame of democratic institutions of 'Panchayati Raj' guaranteed under India's Constitution, and more abundantly spelt out in the Panchayat Extension to Scheduled Areas (PESA) Act 1996, and the Forest Rights Act.

Right to Protect Culture and Cultural Identity

Section 4(d) stipulates that 'every Gram Sabha shall be competent to safeguard and preserve the traditions and customs of the people, their cultural identity, common property resources and the customary mode of dispute resolution.'

It may be noted that there is hardly any tribe, which lives in isolation from its compeers inhabiting in more than one habitat. Otherwise continuous inbreeding within a single habitat would lead to genetic aberrations and ultimate extinction. There are hierarchies of behavioural norms, which are regulated at different levels.

Right to Development

Development is about improving the well-being of the people. Raising living standards, improving education, health and equality of opportunity are all essential components of economic development. It is basically a continuous process of change that involves the whole society, its economic, socio-cultural, physical structure as well as the value system. A single indicator cannot capture it, as it is necessarily multidimensional.

'Development must be conceived as a multidimensional process involving major changes in social structures, popular attitudes and national institutions, as well as the acceleration of economic growth, the reduction of inequality and the eradication of absolute poverty. Development, in its essence, must represent the whole gamut of change by which an entire social system, tuned to the diverse basic needs and desires of individuals and social groups within that system, moves away from a condition of life widely perceived as unsatisfactory towards a situation or condition of life regarded as materially and spiritually better (Todaro, 1994).'

Amartya Sen (1999), has remarked development as a process of expanding the real freedoms that people enjoy, focusing on human freedoms contrasts with narrower views of development, such as identifying development with the growth of GNP, or with the rise in personal incomes, or with industrialisation, or with the technological advancement or with social modernisation. According to him, freedom is central to the process of development for two distinct reasons: (i) the evaluative reason that states assessment of progress has to be done primarily in terms of whether the freedoms that people have are enhanced; (ii) The effectiveness reason states that achievement of development is thoroughly dependent on the free agency of people.

Growth of Gross National Product or of individual incomes can of course be very important as a means of expanding the freedoms enjoyed by the members of the society. But freedom also depends on other determinants, such as social and economic arrangements (e.g. facilities for education and health care) as well as political and civil rights (e.g. the liberty to participate in public discussion and scrutiny).

For Sen, freedom (not development) is the ultimate goal of economic life as well as the most efficient means of realising general welfare. Overcoming deprivation is central to development. Unfreedoms include hunger, famine, ignorance, an unsustainable economic life, and unemployment, barriers to economic fulfilment by women or minority communities, violation of political freedom and basic liberty threats to environment. Moreover, freedom of exchange, labour contract, social opportunities, and protective security is not just ends or constituents of development but also important means to development and freedom.

Thus, according to Sen, 'Development requires the removal of main sources of Unfreedoms: poverty as well as tyranny, poor economic opportunities as well as systematic social deprivation. Economic growth cannot be sensibly treated as an end in itself. Development has to be more concerned with enhancing the lives we lead and the freedoms we enjoy.'

In the context of tribal development, Section 4(e)(i) of PESA inter alia provides that every Gram Sabha (i) approves the plans, programmes and projects for social and economic development before such plans, programmes and projects are taken up for implementation by Panchayats at village level; (ii) be responsible for the identification or selection of persons as beneficiaries under the poverty alleviation and other programmes.

The PESA Act considers 'gram' as spatial expression of a self-managing community in accordance with its traditions and customs. The 'Gram Sabha' is only a legally structured expression of 'gram samaj' (village community). Logically, therefore, the core activity of the Gram Sabha should be preparing and implementing the plan, programme and strategy, drawing primarily on its traditional system of resource mobilisation and utilisation in the Panchayat. Any externally sponsored activities should be ancillary to its core activity. Section 4(e)(ii) betrays a misconception that tribal people are not competent to exercise their freedom. It speaks of the 'responsibility' of the Gram Sabha (not the right of the Gram Sabha) for identification and selection of persons as 'beneficiaries' (not active participants) in poverty alleviation and other programmes. The question arises whether the approach in the central act is in consonance with the ideal that state legislatures are to enact their respective laws in accordance with 'customary laws, social and religious practices and traditional management.'

Moreover, the Gram Sabha cannot in isolation make much dent on national planning policy. Interlinkages of tribal organisations of different levels and networking not only among the organisations of different tribes but also involving organised forums of peoples of largely comparable socio-economic category would be necessary.

Section 4(f) empowers the Gram Sabha to issue certification of utilisation of funds for the plans, programmes and projects implemented by the Panchayat in its area. The act presupposes that there are no other agencies/organisations of the government, who work in the Panchayats or if there are, they are not accountable. This lacuna coupled with the unwillingness of states to devolve funds to Panchayats has limited the role of Gram Sabha in its development. As such, most developmental departments continue to carry out their projects/programmes without even consultation with the Gram Sabha. For instance, in some states there are Joint Forest Management Committees[2] functioning autonomously of the Panchayats. These and similar other institutions operating within the jurisdiction of a village should submit themselves to the planning, monitoring and scanning functions of the Gram Sabha. And the central act itself should be clear on this matter. While the Bhuria Committee report gives credence to the role of traditional Panchayats of the tribal peoples, the Act supposed to be based on the report does not make any provision to recognise the role of traditional Panchayats.

Concluding Remarks

The foregoing analysis makes it clear that the PESA is one of the progressive legislations for tribal welfare, providing for self- governance and recognising the traditional rights of tribal communities over natural resources. Recognising the importance of the Fifth Schedule Areas in nine states, the Act provides the Gram Sabha with powers of social audit and prevention of land alienation.

The provisions of the Act are far-reaching in their implications, but there are several problems with regard to their implementation. While the tribal communities remain ignorant of its enabling provisions, the state governments have become quite uncomfortable with the mere existence of the Act, and have been attempting to dilute its spirit.

This Act made it mandatory for the states having Scheduled Areas to make specific provisions for providing a wide range of powers to the tribes for their development. The Act recognises traditional customary rights over local natural resources. It accepts the validity of customary law, social and religious practices of community resources. It emphasises the role of Gram Sabhas.

The PESA empowered villages to protect community resources, control social sector functionaries, own minor forest produce, manage water bodies, give recommendations for mining leases, be consulted for land acquisition, identify beneficiaries for poverty alleviation and other government programmes and have a decisive say in all development projects in the villages (Das, 2005).

Section 4(M) of PESA authorises the Gram Sabha to act in all areas where the tribes face threat to their survival and welfare because of their continued exploitation. The PESA creates legal space for direct community action, and therefore, PESA directly confers ownership to the Gram Sabha on minor forest produce (MFP) which has been a support for their survival. But it has been observed that this right has been neglected or violated rather than adhered to. The commercial value of MFP has been appreciated resulting in the nationalisation of MFP and thereby optimising the state's revenue. PESA aims at ensuring significant protection against any arbitrary, discriminatory, and motivated action of the state relating to land acquisition and resettlement and rehabilitation (R and R) in tribal regions.

The non- implementation of PESA comes from the nexus of bureaucrats and politicians who would lose authority in tribal areas. Forest department officials have long viewed the resource rich tribal regions as source of revenue. They often collude with timber mafias for petty gains. They fail to realise that forests are the only source of sustenance for tribes. In the vast tribal areas of Andhra, MP and Odisha, the tribes are primarily dependent on the collection and selling of the non-timber forest produce (NTFP).

Economic liberalisation has brought the corporate giants into the region hunting for minerals for their mega size industrial exploits. Industry is wreaking havoc with the living conditions of the tribes under the liberalisation regime. Their acts force the helpless tribes to leave the land they have known to be their own since ages. Compensation and rehabilitation plans are hardly ever implemented with honesty and dignity.

It has been remarked that 'PESA is the single most important instrument for dealing with the economic and emotional alienation of the tribal people, which lies at the root of the growing menace of Naxalism. Its effective implementation would generate a deep sense of effective participation among tribal people in the conduct of their own affairs'.

Notwithstanding plethora of legislative and protective measures, provisions of PESA, the socio-economic conditions of tribes in India are more deplorable as these acts are not implemented practically.

Further, it has been demonstrated that distressed migration of male members in tribal pockets of India, inter alia, results in increase in female-headed households; feminisation of poverty; impact on reproduction and population growth in sending areas; no formal entitlements to land or ownership; dependent on irregular and insufficient remittances; loss of social and other support networks; not enough labour to work the land and limited political participation (Tripathy, 2005).

It has also been observed that non-recognition of tribes over resources and restrictions on their use, alienation of tribes from the means of production, denial of due entitlement of labour, distressed payment of wages, and misappropriation of funds, have kept the tribal labour in the web of misery and starvation. In tribal dominated states in India, the life support system of the local tribes has been snatched away by non-tribes and state institutions. As a result, tribal movement originated in fierce struggle of their rights (Tripathy, 2000).

Policy Implications

In the above backdrop, we can forward the following policy measures:

1. An appropriate development strategy calls for a reorientation of economic policy where priority to the protection of existing livelihood, generation of usual employment, production for people's needs, and ecologically sustainable harnessing and use of natural resources are ensured. The local population must be empowered to control the natural resources and decide their utilisation and replenishment to ensure fulfilment of basic needs. Such an approach will safeguard the cultural values and ensure biodiversity, allowing space for participation of women and marginalised peoples in all decision-making process of the village community.
2. It is necessary to change the attitudes of the socially powerful towards full acceptance of grassroots participation in planning and management of local level development. A major area of training for Panchayat members is awareness and capacity-building for mobilisation and sustainable management of social, physical and financial resources in order to improve the livelihoods of the rural poor.
3. Committed to a people-oriented and ecologically sound economic policy requires the development of a people's democracy based on people's control over resources. This should be inbuilt in the local community following the basic principle that the first claim on the use of resources should be the satisfaction of basic needs and the protection of livelihood. Investment in social forestry, reclamation of agricultural land, provision of

free and compulsory education, health services and guaranteed employment or source of employment with multiple livelihood options, equitable sharing of resources with utmost priority for tribes, immediate implementation of PESA, in the Fifth Scheduled Areas, will certainly ameliorate the situation of the marginalised section and minimise the unrest in tribal areas.

Notes

1. Gram Sabha was to be comprised of all adults over 18 years of age and residing within the boundaries of the village Panchayat.
2. The Joint Forest Management Committee (JFMC) is responsible for protection and regeneration of their adjacent forest and are entitled for usufruct sharing from the forest protected by them.

References

Bardhan, Pranab and Dilip Mookherjee (2002), 'Relative Capture of Local and Central Governments: An Essay in the Political Economy of Decentralisation', *Working Paper Series*, Center for International and Development Economics Research, pp. 99–109, http://repositories.cdlib.org/c

Das, Achyut (2005), *Governance in Tribal Areas: Myths and Realities*, Agragamee, Rayagada, Orissa.

Oates, Wallace (1972), *Fiscal Federalism*, Harcourt Brace, New York.

Rao, M.G. (2001), 'Fiscal Decentralisation in Indian Federalism', *Working Paper 98*, ISEC, Bangalore.

Ratho, Sujata (2007), 'Tribal Welfare through Panchayats: The Experience of PESA in Orissa', *RGICS Working Paper No. 55*, Rajiv Gandhi Institute for Contemporary Studies, New Delhi.

Saxena, N.C. (2003), 'Issues in Panchayats', http://www.panchayats.org/downloads/panchayats%20nc%20sax.pdf

Sen, Amartya (1999), *Development as Freedom*, Oxford University Press, Oxford.

Tiebout, C. (1961), *An Economic Theory of Fiscal Decentralisation in Public Finance: Needs, Sources and Utilisation*, Princeton University Press, New Jersey.

Todaro, Michael P. (1994), *Economic Development in the Third World*, Longman, London.

Tripathy, S.N. (2000), *Glimpses on Tribal Development*, Discovery Publishing House, New Delhi.

—— (2005), *Female Headed Households in India*, Sonali Publishing House, New Delhi.

World Bank (2000), *Overview of Rural Decentralisation in India*, Vol. I, Washington, D.C.

11

Impact of Decentralised Governance on the Implementation of MGNREGS in Scheduled Areas of Odisha

An Overview

Nilakantha Panigrahi

The planned efforts for the development of backward communities particularly for the tribal people have their foundation in pre-Independent India. The Scheduled District Act of 1874 gave a special status to the tribal dominated areas and has restricted the implementation of general rules and regulations in tribal areas. Understanding the backwardness of these areas, the Indian Education Commission during 1882 had suggested making preferential treatments for the tribal children in the schools located in tribal regions. In a later period while considering the backwardness and tribal concentration, the Government of India Act of 1935 for the first time created partial and fully excluded areas. The Cripps Mission of 1942, the Cabinet Mission of 1946, and the Government of India Act 1947 had enormous influence on the formulation of special policies for the tribals. However, the Constituent Assembly framed two-way strategies for tribal development: providing protection from exploitation and simultaneously assisting them through economic activities. In this regard Thakkar Bappa and Jaipal Singh, two Indian proponents of tribal interests had enormous influence to prepare the draft of the Constitution. However, Gandhiji was of the view that the true foundation of the civil revolt will be possible through networking of rural organisations (i.e. Panchayats) functioning in the villages which will help in restructuring the government and economic activities. This philosophy of Panchayati Raj Institutions was highly neglected in the post-Independent period. As a part of the Directive Principles of State Policy, Panchayati Raj Institutions were treated more with concessional approaches in which the 'State was taking steps to organise village panchayats and endowed them with such powers and authorities as may be necessary to enable them to function as units of self-government'. The Panchayati Raj Institutions (PRIs) from time to time have been revived with the recommendations of the Balawantrai Mehta

Committee (1952); Ashok Mehta Committee (1977); CAARD Commission (1985); Singhui Committee (1986); Sarkaria Commission (1988); Thungon Committee (1985); Sixty-Fourth Amendment Bill (1989), and lastly by Seventy-Third Constitutional Amendment Act (1992). However, the major setback came to PRIs during the period of 1960–80 due to irregular elections, and less flow of financial resources to these organisations (Mathew, 1994). This has substantially affected the growth of Panchayati Raj Institutions of the State. After five decades the nation rightly felt the need of a revolutionary Act popularly called as Panchayat Extension to the Scheduled Area, Act 1996 (PESA Act). The basic premise behind this Act is to decentralise and entrust the financial and administrative powers with the PRIs in Scheduled Areas of the country and thereby to bring the tribal communities to the level of the non-tribal.

The powers given under PESA Act 1996 are as follows: Ownership of minor forest produce; approval of development plans; selection of beneficiaries under various programmes; consultation on land acquisition; manage minor water bodies, control mineral leases, regulate/prohibit the sale of intoxicants; prevent alienation of land and restore unlawfully alienated land of STs, manage village markets; control moneylending to STs; and control institutions and functionaries in all social sector. In addition, as per this Act the Gram Sabha in Scheduled Area has been given the power for the enforcement of the regulation or restriction of the sale and consumption of any intoxicants; the ownership of minor forest produces; prevention of alienation of land and restoration of any unlawful land of a ST; control over moneylending to the STs; control over all local market; safe guard the cultural identity, community resources and resolve the disputes.

The National Advisory Council (NAC) subsequently recommended for amendment of the PESA Act, 1996 with respect to the definitions of key terms used in the Act for greater clarity; constitution of Gram Sabha at the hamlet level and power to constitute committees; mandating 'prior informed consent' as pre-requisite for land acquisition and licensing for minor minerals; reinforcing the need to align Central and State laws in conformity with PESA; enabling the State government to make rules; enabling the Centre to issue directions and Provision for grievance redress under the Act.

Objectives

The paper First, attempts to provide a brief profile of the regional geography of tribal population and the regions covered under PESA in the State of Odisha. Second, it critically analyses the operational status of the extent of decentralisation of power and programmes to the PRIs in practice. Third, the paper reviews the impact of such decentralisation on the implementation of Mahatma Gandhi National Rural Employment Guarantee Scheme (MGNREGS) in Scheduled Areas of the State of Odisha. Finally, the paper concludes that the globalisation processes enthusiastically adopted by the state has partially affected the decentralisation processes, as a result, the State is yet to establish inclusive processes of development to the desired level which is really a concern for the development of tribal population and tribal dominated regions of Odisha even after the adoption of PESA.

The present paper is based on both secondary and primary data collected by the author while working at NKC Centre for Development Studies (ICSSR Institute), Bhubaneswar. The findings of the research project 'Impact of MGNREGA on the livelihood improvement of Tribal households: A study in KBK region of Odisha', supported by ICSSR, New Delhi, 2012–13 is taken into account during the analysis. The details of the universe covered in the study can be viewed from Table 1.

Table 1

Details of Study Universe

District	*CD Block/ Panchayat Samitis*	*Gram Panchayat–1*	*Villages*	*Gram Panchayat--2*	*Villages*
1	*2*	*3*	*4*	*5*	*6*
Kalahandi	Madanpur-Rampur	Barabandha	Barabandha Dudukaranja Dumeri	Muding	Chitalpada Ghodapokhari Muding
Malkangiri	Mathili	Salim	Nuagada Salim Talapadar	Udulibeda	Badaliguda BayaPujariguda Pedaguda
Nabarangpur	Papadahandi	Dengaguda	Biriguda Dengaguda Khutuguda	Mokia	Bamini Mokia Skadaguda
Subarnapur	BirMaharajpur	Bahalpadar	Bahalpadar Gudguda Saradhapalli	DurjanTaila	DurjanTaila Masinapalli Sagjury

Sources: 'Impact of MGNREGA on the livelihood improvement of Tribal households: A study in KBK region of Odisha', supported by ICSSR, New Delhi, 2014; NKC Centre for Development Studies, Bhubaneswar.

The details of the study universe are given in above table. All the study Panchayat Samitis/CD Blocks, Gram Panchayats, villages are located in interior pockets of the concerned districts and are characterised by various socio-economic indicators. The backwardness of the people and area is reflected in the proportion of BPL households, share of ST population, rainfall, irrigation coverage, population density, rural-urban proportion, consumption of chemical fertilisers, cropping pattern, net sown area, literacy level, particularly of women, wage rates paid, in agriculture and non-agriculture etc.

Tribal Communities in Odisha: A Regional Geography

The scheduled tribe communities of Odisha contribute substantially to the demographic structure and social fabric of the state. There are 62 tribal communities, with a total population of 8.14 million (Census of India, 2001a, b), who belong to Austro-Asiatic, Dravidian and Indo-Aryan language families. Out of them, 12 tribal communities have been identified as backward and presently known as Particularly Vulnerable Tribal Groups. Almost 44.21 per cent of the total land area in Odisha has been constitutionally declared as Scheduled Area.

Except for the coastal belt, most of the districts of the State are either partially or fully declared as Scheduled Area. The present Scheduled Area of the state includes six districts that are fully and five districts that are partially within it. The districts of Mayurbhanj and Sundargarh are the full scheduled districts, while Keonjhar is the partially scheduled district in the northern zone of the state. Similarly, Koraput (undivided) is a full scheduled district, while Kandhamal and Kalahandi are partial scheduled districts in the southern zone of the state. Out of 314 Community Development Blocks of Odisha, 118 (37.3%) blocks are covered under the Tribal Sub-Plan (TSP) of the state. The tribal population of Odisha constitutes 22.08 per cent of the total State population (Census of India, 2001a, b). The major tribes in the northern zone of the state, based on their numerical strength, are, *Santhal, Munda, Ho, Juanga, Bhuyan, Bathudi, Kharia, Kolha, KolLahara, Kisan, Oraon, Gond, Lodha* and *Mirdha.* The major tribal communities of southern zone include *Khond, Koya, Gadaba, Paraja, Omanatya, Pentia, Saora, Bonda, Didayi* and *Shabar.* There are 15 tribal groups distributed in different parts of Odisha each having more than one lakh population. The tribal communities like *Santhal, Gond, Munda, Ho, Birhor, Bhumija, Kharia, Lodha, Oraons* and *Kissan* in the northern zone of the state cut across the state boundaries and are also found in the neighbouring states of Jharkhand, Chhattisgarh, and West Bengal. Similarly, *Koya, Khond, Saora, Shabara, Paraja* and *Gadaba* tribal communities of the southern zone are also found in Andhra Pradesh and Chhattisgarh.

The tribal economies are still primitive from the point of view of resource utilisation, technology adoption and diversification of cropping pattern. A study of the tribal economy requires an understanding of the concept of community, common property, meaning of land and the role of non-tribals, particularly scheduled caste groups, such as *Panas* and *Damos* who significantly influence the tribal economy. Land is the pivotal property and tribal people retain strong emotional attachment to it even though they do not enjoy legal right over land. Apart from land-based resources, Minor Forest Produces (MFPs) and/or Non-Timber Forest Produces (NTFPs) play a vital role in their economic life, sustenance and labour processes. The Roy Burman Committee (1982) pointed out the commercial viability of MFPs starting from family level to the national level. The Task Force on Development of Tribal Areas (1983) of the Planning Commission since then has also highlighted the importance of forest resources and the role of tribal communities for its management. More specifically, in Mayurbhanj, Keonjhar and Sundargarh districts the tribal communities namely *Santhal, Munda, Ho, Bhuiyans* and *Oraons* of northern zone are more or less exposed to the mining and industrial operations. Quite a sizeable segment of them have been migrating from their native to different urban and industrial pockets of Odisha and Jharkhand in search of wage labour. A look into the level of literacy among these tribal communities also reflects a distinct variation between these two zones. As per the 2001 Census, the literacy rate among the Kissan was 50.19 per cent, while it was 50.88, 39.69, 54.20, 40.43 and 46.96 per cent among *Bhuyan, Munda, Oraon, Santhal* and *Gond* of the northern zone respectively. The level of literacy among the major tribal communities of Southern zone is much less, which was reported to the extent of 11.73, 12.62,

14.69, 17.96, 21.21, 31.87 and 41.13 per cent among *Koya, Didayi, Bondo, Paraja, Gadaba, Kondh* and *Saora* of the southern zone respectively (ibid.). The impact of these development processes has been quite varied on different tribal communities and the penetration of exogenous forces has generated differential impact on the tribal communities. Therefore, there is a need to understand the overall framework of development intervention in these regions.

Incidence of Poverty in Odisha: Differences across NSS Regions

A brief profile of the NSS region in terms of sharing of the geographical areas, tribal population and population density is given in Table 2. The data reflect that both the northern and southern regions share around 74.20 per cent of the state geographical area, but 52.16 per cent of the state population. In such a situation when a poverty ratio of 48.01 per cent for the year 1999–2000 for rural Odisha was reported, the State earned the dubious distinction of being the poorest state in India ahead of Bihar (43.33%). When the headcount ratio (HCR) for the three NSS regions of Odisha was worked out, there were predictably some strong responses to it. The HCR for the coastal region of rural Odisha, at 31.74 per cent was regarded as an achievement even though this was expected. But, at the other extreme, the HCR for the Southern NSS region of rural Odisha, at a staggering of 87.05 per cent, attracted a great deal of attention of academics and led to significant development interventions in terms of funds flow (Haan and Dubey, 2003).

Table 2

Some Features of NSS Regions

NSS Region	*Districts (undivided)*	*Share (%) in State's Area*	*Share (%) in State's Population*	*Population Density (persons per sq. km)*
'Northern' (Northern Plateau plus Central Table Land)	Mayurbhanj Keonjhar Sundergarh Sambalpur Dhenkanal Balangir	42.18	34.69	194
'Southern' (Eastern Ghats)	Kalahandi Kandhamal Koraput	32.02	17.47	129
'Coastal' (Coastal Plains)	Cuttack Puri Balasore Ganjam	25.8	47.84	438

Note: The data presented above are for the 13 districts prior to their division in 1992.

Source: Government of Odisha, Statistical Abstract of Odisha, 2002, Directorate of Economics and Statistics, Odisha, Bhubaneswar; Census of India, 2001, Series 2, Final Population Tables, Paper 1 of 2001, Directorate of Census Operations, Odisha.

Are North and South Odisha Comparable in terms of Tribal Population?

It can be argued that large differences in the density and extent of concentration of tribal population between the northern and southern regions lead to the observed differences in the extent of aggregate/chronic poverty between these regions.

Table 3

Density and Concentration of Tribal Population

Region	*ST Population as per cent of Total Population*	*Per cent share of ST Population in Total ST Population of the State*
Northern	35.22	53.66
Southern	34.67	34.90

Source: Census of India 2001a, Series–1, Part-II B(iii), Primary Census Abstract: Scheduled Tribe Population.

On the contrary, as can be seen from Table 3, while the density of tribal population is very nearly the same in the north and south NSS regions, there is much greater concentration of tribal population in the north as compared to the southern region. In fact, the northern region has more than a proportionate share of the state's tribal population (53.66%) relative to the share of tribals in the state's total population (34.69%). For the state as a whole, we have an indirect estimate of the incidence of chronic poverty. Radhakrishna et al. (2004) estimated the incidence of chronic poverty and stated it at 24.4 per cent for rural Odisha during 1999–2000, (the second highest after Bihar at 25.3%). This meant that a little more than 50 per cent of the poor were chronically poor in rural Odisha. Since such indirect estimates are not available at the level of NSS regions, attempt made through indirect method to obtain estimates of the incidence of chronic poverty for the three NSS regions of Odisha. Elsewhere, it has been found using inter-state data for 1999–2000 that the incidence of chronic poverty (rural) and poverty gap (rural), are very strongly correlated (r = 0.97) (Padhi and Mishra, 2005).

Thus, in 1993–94, the incidence of chronic poverty in the north and coastal NSS regions were comparable (about 19%), whereas in the south it was as high as 34.08 per cent. The same regional pattern obtains in respect of poverty gap and the per cent chronically poor among the poor (Table 3). On the whole, there is enough ground to probe into the superior performance of the northern NSS region on the poverty front particularly with respect to the tribal population.

Table 4

Indirect Estimates of Incidence and Relative Extent of Chronic Poverty and Poverty Gap, 1993–94

Region	*Incidence of Chronic Poverty ('Very Poor' as per cent of rural population)*	*Poverty Gap*	*Chronically Poor as per cent of All Poor*
Northern	18.99	10.41	41.60
Southern	34.08	18.78	49.38
Coastal	19.03	10.21	41.95

Source: (i) Government of India (1997), *Sarvekshana*, Vol. XXI, No. 2, 73rd Issue, October–December (NSS 50th Round, 1993–94), Ministry of Statistics, Planning and Programme Implementation, Department of Statistics, New Delhi.

Thus, the higher incidence of aggregate/chronic poverty in the southern region cannot be explained in terms of a higher density and/or concentration of tribal population. This perhaps means that economic conditions of the tribal people vary from context to context. This needs to be studied to examine the efficacy of existing policies and programmes, and for drawing out implications for policy reforms and interventions. In the present case, it may be quite useful to study the northern region to identify the factors which can explain its relative success in poverty reduction.

Status of PRIs in Odisha

Odisha is one of the few States in the post-independent period to take up the Panchayati Raj as its main fulcrum of rural administration. Odisha Gram Panchayat Act was enacted in the year 1948. Subsequently in the year 1961, three-tier systems of Panchayati Raj Institutions (PRIs) were introduced in Odisha. With respect to the number of Panchayat Samitis, there were 214 numbers in 1961 which increased to 304 in 1963, 307 in 1966–67 and 314 in 1983–84 which is continuing upwards now. There were 13 number of Zilla Parishad as up to 1991–92 which increased to 30 in 2000–02.

Over the last 50 years Panchayati Raj Institutions have emerged as one of the powerful institution in bringing about rapid and sustainable development and socio-economic transformation in rural Odisha. It has an integrated prospective towards improving the quality of lives of rural people and ensuring equity and effective peoples' participation.73rd amendment of the Constitution has conferred constitutional status to PRIs. The Provisions of Panchayats (Extension to Scheduled Areas) Act aims at empowering PRIs in Scheduled Areas for economic development and social justice. In the year 2002, election to 3-tier of PRIs held in conformity with 73rd Amendment and PESA thereby empowered tribal people. The Government has the obligation to bring out Panchayati Raj Institutions as institution of Self-Government as per 73rd Amendment of the Constitution of India 1992. 73rd Amendment marks a new era in the federal set-up of the country and provides constitutional status to the PRIs. The prime objectives of the 3-tier Panchayati Raj System are to eradicate poverty, uplift standard of living of people in the rural areas, and bring about a healthy society by creating awareness for hygiene, sanitation and eradication of illiteracy. The state has established a State Election Commissioner to conduct the election of PRIs. The 73rd Amendment of the Constitution mandates Government to endow the Panchayati Raj Institutions with such powers and authority as may be necessary to enable them to function as institutions of self-Government. It also provides that powers and responsibility shall be devolved upon PRIs subject to such conditions as may be specified therein, with respect to the preparation and implementation of plans for economic development, social justice as may be entrusted to them including those 25 subjects listed in the 11th Schedule. In respect of 21 subjects, functionaries have been brought under the control of PRIs. The State has handed nine subjects in respect of which funds have been transferred to PRIs. At present around 1,00,862 elected representatives of 30 Zilla Parishads, 314 Panchayat Samities and 6,234 Gram Panchayats are getting the opportunity to participate in the governance of PRIs. Panchayats at village level are expected to perform certain obligatory functions to provide basic services to all the people living in the area. Gram

Panchayats in Odisha have been empowered to levy taxes and manage community assets created out of different poverty eradication and area development schemes. They as constitutional bodies represent the model of community participation and social empowerment. Basic services among others include primary education, primary health, safe drinking water, sanitation and street lighting, environment protection, common property resources (CPR) management.

Frequency of Representation in PRIs

The 73rd Amendment of the Constitution of India has empowered Gram Sabha at village level, Panchayat Samiti at block level and Zilla Parishad at district level. During 2002 in Odisha there were 5,261 number of Gram Panchayats with 93,781elected representatives, 314 number of Intermediary Tiers, i.e. Panchayat Samitis with 6,541 elected representatives and 30 number of Zilla Parishads having 884 number of elected representatives (State Election Commission, Odisha, 2002). As regards participation of women in Panchayati Raj bodies Odisha has introduced 33 per cent reservation for them and the achievements with regard to the participation of women have become more spectacular when it is seen against the backdrop of a low literacy level of women in the State (Mathew, 1994).

An attempt has been made to know the status of both male and female candidates elected unopposed for different posts of PRIs during the year 2002. Of the total of 87,543 Ward members elected, around 38,150 (43.57%) have been nominated unopposed in the State, while it is 3.88 per cent in case of Sarpanch and 5.44 per cent in case of Panchayat Samiti members. The data when compared with few coastal districts and Scheduled districts in absolute numbers, it reflect that the unopposed elected candidates for the post of Ward members are 1,020 in case of Jagatsingpur, 791 in case of Balasore, 1008 in case of Khurda and 984 in case of Puri district, was much less than the Scheduled districts of Koraput (1,818) and Sundargarh (1,703). Similarly, the women members who have been elected unopposed were 378, 347, 304, 320 in the districts of Jagatsingpur, Khurda, Balasore and Puri respectively, while in Scheduled districts their share was 671, 914, 485, 504 and 718 in the districts of Koraput, Mayurbhanja, Nawarangpur, Rayagada and Sundargarh respectively. This at one level indicates that in comparison to many coastal districts where the development indices are much higher, the villagers in Scheduled districts have shown their higher degree of village unity and unanimously elected their Ward members. As regards women contestants for the post of Ward members, in coastal districts their participation is much above the line of women reservation of 30 per cent. In case of Scheduled districts their share is less than 30 per cent of target reservation. However, it is 21.17, 26.53, 23.14, 27.87, and 28.49 per cent in Koraput, Malkangiri, Nawarangpur, Rayagada and Sundargarh respectively. This indicates that in spite of the reservation, tribal women are yet to come forward to participate in the decentralised processes of administration through PRIs. Similarly, for the post of Sarpanch the data reflect that a total of 19, 11, 18 and 24 numbers of Sarpanchs have been unopposedly elected in tribal districts of Koraput, Malkangiri, Rayagada, and Gajapati respectively. This also partly justifies that the villagers have usual faith and unanimity in accepting their leaders. Similar is the situation in tribal districts while the people elected their Panchayat Samiti members unopposed, both in case of male and female candidates. In case of contest for the post of Panchayat Samiti members and Sarpanchs, tribal women have just fought as per their reservation requirements.

MGNREGA: Basic Features

- Provision of 100 days of unskilled wage employment to a rural family in a financial year with equal wage for men and women;
- Ban on contractors and labour displacing machines;
- Ensuring Participatory planning and identification of works through Palli Sabha;
- Making payment of wage on weekly basis but not later than 15 days;
- Unemployment allowance to job seekers if work is not provided to job seeker within 15 days of application;
- Provision of social audit by Palli/Gram Sabha;
- Involvement of Panchayati Raj Institutions (PRIs) in planning and execution of MGNREGS works.

Even though the Act has had a positive impact on the lives of the millions of people across the country, the draft report of the Comptroller and Auditor General of India and many other studies have found a number of implementation problems resulting in low result of the Act. There are still confusions among the people with respect to the registration for work under the Act; irregular maintenance of the job card; lack of transparency in the maintenance of the muster roll; submission of work application; and payment of maintenance allowance; lack of adequate staffs in the implementation of the Act; poor awareness among people; non-creation of productive assets and their poor maintenance.

Significance of MGNREGA in Odishan Context

Odisha has the dubious distinction of being the poorest state in the country. In 2004–05, the incidence of rural poverty was as high as about 47 per cent. On top of it, the intensity of rural poverty has also been very high: some 25.2 per cent of poor are reckoned to be 'Very Poor'. In other words, about half of the poor population belongs to the 'Very Poor' category. Within Odisha, it is noteworthy that there are significant regional variations in the incidence of poverty: while in the coastal region, it was 27.4 per cent, in the southern and northern NSS regions, it was as high as 72.7 per cent and 59.1 per cent respectively in 2004–05, the three regions contributing 27.1 per cent, 28.9 per cent and 44 per cent respectively to the total poor in the state (Panda, 2004: 229; Padhi et al., 2009; Padhi and Panigrahi, 2011). Apart from the regional variation and concentration of poverty in the state, there is significant variations across and concentration of poverty within ethnic/caste groups. Thus, among ST, SC and OBC social groups, in 2004–05, incidence of poverty was 75.8 per cent, 49.9 per cent and 37.1 per cent respectively, contributing 41.5 per cent, 18.7 per cent and 31.1 per cent of the total poor in the state, respectively. As against this, for the category of 'Others' (mainly belonging to upper and middle castes), the incidence of poverty was only 23.5 per cent, contributing only 8.7 per cent to all poor of the state (Panda, 2004: 228). Second, partly reflecting a low productivity agriculture and low level of organisation and bargaining power among agricultural labour, agricultural wages have been much below the statutory minimum, and indeed the lowest among the major states of India. A third area of serious concern is the high rate of open unemployment that has emerged rather recently. Thus, according to 'current daily status' criterion (which roughly measures the extent of seasonal unemployment in rural areas), in 2004–05, the rate of rural unemployment was a high of 10.2 per cent of the labour force (the fourth highest among 16 major states). This translates into about 3.3 million currently unemployed persons (Padhi, 2009: 104–105). Finally, the extent of seasonal distress migration is known to be very significant, particularly from districts where agriculture is drought-prone and absorption of labour in agriculture and rural non-farm activities is quite inadequate. For all the above reasons, one would expect that MGNREGA, as a demand-driven, guaranteed public employment programme, would generate a high level of demand for work under the MGNREGA provisions in a state like Odisha.

Need of Regional Level Analysis of MGNREGA and the Role of PRIs

There is no doubt that MGNREGA is the first tangible commitment to the poor that they can expect to earn a living wage, without loss of dignity and demand this as a right. The guarantee of 100 days of employment per household at minimum wages is possibly the most important feature of the Act. Even though the Act has had a positive impact on the lives of the millions of people across the poorest districts in the country, the draft report of the Comptroller and Auditor General of India and many other studies have found a number of implementation problems resulting in low result. Therefore, there is a need to address the issues which have become hurdles for its success. An attempt has been made in the following to analyse the key issues. The MGNREGA objective can be fulfilled only if States implement it by ensuring conformity to processes prescribed under the Act with respect to registration, design, distribution and maintenance of job cards, maintaining transparency in muster rolls, inappropriate wage rates, work application process and unemployment allowance, adequacy of staff, awareness generation, creation of productive assets and their maintenance. Secondly, the role of PRIs as per the Act in the implementation is quite important. In order to make their participation more effective, a study of regional variation need to be quite relevant to improve the implementation status of MGNREGA in the state.

Study Findings

Planning of MGNREGS

Planning is one of the most critical inputs for the successful implementation of MGNREGA. Understanding its importance the Act has well recognised and spelt out processes and methods of planning to be made, so as to provide employment within 15 days. This has been codified for accomplishment at various levels of

Gram/Palli Sabha, Gram Panchayat (GP) and block level Panchayat Samitis. Many studies on the functioning of MGNREGA have suggested that there is a top-down approach followed during the planning in MGNREGS, which talks of the poor or lack of awareness on the part of the villagers on various aspects of the scheme (Shankar and Shah, 2008; Chhabra et al., 2009; Padhi et al., 2010; Mehta, 2009). The present study tried to find out the type of planning measures undertaken at village and GP level. The data were collected with the help of a structured interview schedule, elicited information from Panchayat Executive Officer and the GP Sarapanch and also through focus group discussions organised among the villagers.

A look into the data reflects that out of eight GPs, in five (62.5%) the Gram Sabha meeting was organised during the month of October 2013. The registers of the concerned villages show that except the GPs of Nabarangpur and Kalahandi districts, people's participation and signature in Gram Sabha registers are quite high. The common development programmes discussed in the Gram Sabha meetings include MGNREGS, BRGF, Health, Sanitation, Forest Right Committee, housing programmes like IAY and Mo-Kudia. Resolutions were passed in all Gram Sabha meetings. Other issues discussed include delay in wage payment under MGNREGS works and the selection of beneficiaries for different schemes. Diagram 1 gives details of roles performed by different PRIs in the study universe.

Diagram 1

Roles performed by different PRIs in the Implementation of MGNREGS

District Panchayat	Prepared a list of all the existing employment and development oriented programmes in the district and other centrally and state sponsored programmes that aim at providing additional employment and development of infrastructure in rural areas. Approved the estimates against the funds available, employment to be generated under them and the total underemployment existing at the district level after receiving the plans from the block level.
Block Panchayat	Prepared a list at the block level of existing and required infrastructure. Estimated the total resources available and the employment that will be generated through the resources. Estimated the total employment generated. Prepared a plan after receiving village level plans.
Village Panchayat	Listed the existing infrastructure at the village level and identify the missing infrastructure Discussed the resources required to construct the missing infrastructure. Discussed the employment generated by creating the missing infrastructure.

Source: Primary Survey, 2013.

The responses were collected from the MGNREGS participant households in study villages. When we asked about the participation of the beneficiaries during last 12 months period, around 60.33 to 68.3 per cent households positively responded participating in the Gram Sabha or Palli Sabha meetings. Lowest response in this regard was reported in Malkangiri district (60.83%)

due to the fact that the beneficiaries in this district do not show their interest much due to Naxal pressure. With respect to their participation in the Gram Sabhas, a total of 37.47 per cent respondents opined that they have shared their views on various development issues discussed in the meeting which ranges from 39.72 per cent in case of Malkangiri to 51.76 per cent in case of Subarnapur district, in which the MGNREGS were also discussed in the Gram Sabha meetings in all the villages. The responses vary from 82.35 per cent in case of Subarnapur district to 68.34 per cent in case of Malkangiri district, the lowest one. The above responses substantiate the fact of the in-depth participation of respondents in the planning process at Gram Sabha level in each study universe. The inter-district variations on different indicators of planning process reflect a wide gap between Malkangiri (Lowest) and Subarnapur district (Highest responses). People's involvement in planning possess at Gram Sabha level is insignificant in Malkangiri; followed by Kalahandi (75.6%) and Nabarangpur (79.06%) district (Table 5). This is largely influenced by the involvement of concerned officers in the process, geographical inaccessibility and awareness of the villagers on various programmes.

Table 5

Planning Process under MGNREGS and the Role of Gram Sabha

(% of MGNREGS participants)

Descriptions	*Districts and Responses*				*Total (N–475)*
	Kalahandi (N–120)	*Malkangiri (N = 120)*	*Nabarangpur (N–120)*	*Subarnapur (N–115)*	
Agreed that Gram Sabha convened in the last 12 months and attended at least one meeting	82 (68.33)	73 (60.83)	86 (71.66)	85 (73.91)	326 (68.63)
Respondents spoke in the GS meetings	38 (46.34)	29 (39.72)	44 (51.76)	44 (51.76)	178 (37.47)
Agreed that GS conducted exclusively for MGNREGS	0.00	0.00	0.00	0.00	0.00
Agreed that MGNREGS related issues were discussed in GS	42 (67.74)	21 (42)	36 (52.94)	49 (70)	148 (59.2)

Source: Primary survey, 2013 (Figures in the bracket are percentage to the total).

It was commonly understood by the households that due to illiteracy, shyness and dominance of few tribals and non-tribals in the village meetings, effective participation of the tribals in Gram Sabha is not taking place. This was visible in Malkangiri district (39.72%), Nabarangpur district (45.34%) and Kalahandi district (46.34%). The participants told that MGNREGS was specifically discussed in the Gram Sabha meeting. So far as the participatory planning is concerned the study shows that little less than 50 per cent participants got an opportunity to discuss any issue relating to MGNREGS in Gram Sabhas. In other words more than 50 per cent beneficiaries did not participate in Gram Sabha which is of big concern.

The study also collected the responses of the non-beneficiaries about the planning processes made at Gram Sabha and GP level. Almost 97.50 per cent (117 out of 120) households viewed that Gram Sabhas were held in their villages, while of them 84.83 per cent (84 nos. of households) attended the Gram Sabha meetings. The lowest participation in Gram Sabha was observed in Malkangiri district to the extent of 50 per cent, followed by Nabarangpur (73.33%) and Kalahandi (76.66%). Around 51.51per cent expressed their unwillingness to attend the meeting due to the fact that decisions in the Gram Sabha are predecided and motivated in favour of the PRI members and influential people of the village. Of the 84 households who had participated in the Gram Sabha meeting, only 38 (45.23%) had spoken in the meeting and 75 (89.28%) viewed that MGNREGS issues were discussed in the Gram Sabha meetings.

Data with respect to the programme planning made for MGNREGS were also collected from Panchayat Samiti Office in all sample blocks. In all the blocks except Malkangiri district (where the research team did not get cooperation during data collection), the block officers viewed that the details of proposals to be implemented under MGNREGS were prepared at Gram Sabha and Gram Panchayat offices. Compilations of the programmes are made at Panchayat Samiti to estimate the total physical and financial requirements of the blocks for onward submission.

Extent and Level of Awareness on MGNREGA

Mahatma Gandhi National Rural Employment Guarantee Act (MGNREGA) ensures community participation at various stages of the implementation of MGNREGS. A few of these stages are planning, implementation, monitoring and social audit. In addition, it also ensures minimum days of employment and minimum wages for payment to the households. On this premise the study attempted to find out the extent and level of awareness of both the MGNREGS participant and non-participant households. This is one of the most important indicators which influence the whole processes of implementation made by different stakeholders.

The study adopted 27 awareness indicators to assess the awareness level of MGNREGS participant and non-participant households. These indicators include knowledge about the provision of wages, job card, unemployment allowances, time line, entitlement, social audit, facilities at work sites, work process, role of certain institutional mechanisms engaged in implementation and monitoring were collected from the beneficiary households shows that there is a wide variations in the awareness levels of the households across the districts. Among the participant households one finds around 51.85 per cent households in Malkangiri district who have awareness score of less than 10, while such households are quite less to the extent of 33.33 per cent in case of Kalahandi district and 37.03 per cent in case of Subarnapur district. In case of Nabarangpur district around 37.03 per cent households have highest level of awareness within the score range for 22 to 27 indicators. Thus, Nabarangpur district has highest level of awareness, while, Malkangiri district has lowest level of awareness on MGNREGA (Table 6 and 7).

Table 6

Awareness Correlates across Study Districts of the Participant Households

District	*Participants Households*		
	Householdwise Total Awareness Score within 10	*Householdwise Total Awareness Score within 11 to 21*	*Householdwise Total Awareness Score within 22 to 27*
Kalahandi	9 (33.33)	13 (48.14)	5 (18.57)
Malkangiri	14 (51.85)	10 (37.03)	3 (11.11)
Nabarangpur	11 (40.74)	6 (22.22)	10 (37.03)
Subarnapur	10 (37.03)	11 (40.74)	6 (22.22)

Source: Primary Survey, 2013 (Figures in the bracket are per cent to the total).

Table 7

Awareness Correlates across Study Districts of the Non-Participant Households

District	*Non-Participant Households (In %)*		
	Household wise Total Awareness Score within 10	*Household wise Total Awareness Score within 11 to 20*	*Household wise Total Awareness Score within 21 to 27*
Kalahandi	66.66	18.51	14.81
Malkangiri	81.48	14.81	3.70
Nabarangpur	70.37	18.51	11.11
Subarnapur	74.07	18.51	7.40

Source: Primary Survey, 2013.

Management of MGNREGS Job Card

Job card is a legal document of special importance. It is issued by the Gram Panchayat to each registered household. Within a fortnight of submission of application, Gram Panchayat has to issue the job card in the presence of the local people. Job card is the medium of maintaining transparency in the whole process of implementation of MGNREGA. The cost of the photograph of the eligible members pasted on the job card and on the opening of job card is treated as the programme cost. A copy of the job card is maintained at Gram Panchayat office. The study shows that all the households individually possesses job card. Around 98.74 per cent households use the job card to get employment under MGNREGA. On an average, a job card has one male and one female member in each family. Around 26.63 per cent of the members listed in the job card at GP level possess pass book either in bank and/or post office in their names. In order to get the job card from the local Gram Panchayat office around 92.63 per cent households have not paid any form of speed money, while 7.35 per cent households told that they have paid some money to get their job cards. In Kalahandi and Subarnapur districts none of the households have paid a single rupee to get their job cards. In case of Malkangiri district around 28.33 per cent households have paid some money to the panchayat members to get their job cards. With respect to the possession of job cards by the households the data reflect that all respondents in Kalahandi, Nabarangpur and Subarnapur could show their job cards kept in their houses, while in Malkangiri district around 20.50 per cent households could not produce their job cards to the research team.

Facilities and Safeguards at Work Sites

As per MGNREGA, Gram Panchayats are mandated with the responsibility to provide worksite facilities like medical aid (first-aid), drinking water, shade for shelter and the provision of crèche if there are more than five children below the age of six years by the wage earners. The services of women may be provisioned at worksite if there are children below six years of age with the workers. Keeping this in mind, the study tried to explore the status of worksite facilities provided by the GPs in the sites of different study villages. With respect to the provision of first-aid, around 61.47 per cent respondents agreed that it was available regularly during the work, while 27.58 per cent viewed that first-aid was not available. In Subarnapur district first-aid services were available only in case of 20 per cent, while 54.78 per cent respondents denied on the availability of this service. In case of Malkangiri district a highest of 95.83 per cent respondents agreed of its availability. Around 11 per cent viewed that availability of first-aid services in the worksite was not regular. Similarly, with respect to the availability of drinking water at the worksite, around 80.84 per cent respondents viewed that drinking water was always provided by the Gram Panchayats, while 18.32 per cent commented on its non-availability in the worksite. The status of availability of drinking water in Kalahandi and Nabarangpur was quite satisfactory, while it was very poor in case of Malkangiri district. As regards the crèche, around 71.37 per cent denied the fact of its availability, though in 58.50 per cent cases the respondents agreed that there was a need of having crèche for the children in the worksite. In Subarnapur and Malkangiri districts not a single respondent spoke about having a crèche, though there was a need of crèche for the kids.

With respect to the availability of shade and floor sheet for workers at the sites, around 46.32 per cent respondents agreed that during the summer such sheds were available to take shelter, while 14.74 per cent respondents said that such sheds were not regularly available, while 38.95 per cent fully denied on the availability of any sheds in the worksite. In case of Malkangiri, only 3.33 per cent respondents agreed of having sheds. Visits by the members of the Panchayati Raj Institutions, Block Development Officials and Programme Coordinator were quite regular to the worksites. Thus, in terms of providing worksite facilities, Malkangiri district has poor service delivery, while the districts like Kalahandi and Nabarangpur have better worksite facilities.

Maintenance of Transparency

In order to find out the level of transparency in the management of MGNREGS, the study tried to trace the responses with respect to certain indicators like verification of indicators, entry of certain data in the job card, entry of fake names in the job card, attendance of the beneficiaries etc. where Gram Panchayat functionaries are suppose to play a very crucial role.

With respect to the verification of entries made in the job card with respect to the number the data reflect that around 88.63 per cent respondents viewed that no verifications have been made, while only 5.05 per cent households does this verification by themselves. While going through the job cards one finds various forms of irregularities. In case of 13.26 per cent job cards, entries were not made for some years, while equal numbers (13.26%) found with incomplete entries. The respondents admitted the fact of fake information in 9.05 per cent of job cards, while in case of 32.84 per cent of job cards, entries were found over written. One gross violation in the job card was observed of not putting the signature of the beneficiaries which was observed in case of 78.74 per cent job cards. All these indicators of transparency in the job cards were very seriously observed in case of Malkangiri and Subarnapur districts. Comparatively, job cards were found maintained better in case of Kalahandi and Nabarangpur districts. However, signature column in the job cards was observed blank in many job cards of all four study districts (Table 8) With respect to the entry of names of members, other than family in the job cards, the study found such cases only in case of 1.68 per cent, while in Subarnapur and Kalahandi districts not a single respondent pointed out any wrong entry of other names in the job cards. Realising the incompleteness of the job cards the PRI members at Gram Panchayat level justified that they do not have time to look into these aspects, since they are fully engaged in increasing development activities decided by the government. It was rightly observed that the PRI members at Gram Panchayat and Panchayat Samiti levels suffer from attitudinal problem and systemic callousness which could have been reduced through training and skill transfer as a part of the implementation of the progressive Act like MGNREGA.

Table 8

Irregularities in the MGNREGS Job Card of the Beneficiary Households

Irregularities	*Responses/Districts*				*G. Total (N=475)*
	Kalahandi (N=120)	*Malkangiri (N=120)*	*Nabarangpur (N=120)*	*Subarnapur (N=115)*	
Entries were not made in few years	1 (0.83)	15 (12.50)	2 (1.67)	45 (39.13)	63 (13.26)
Some entries are incomplete	1 (0.83)	15 (12.50)	2 (1.67)	45 (39.13)	63 (13.26)
Fake information entered in the card	1 (0.83)	33 (27.50)	0 (0.00)	9 (7.83)	43 (9.05)
Some entries overwritten	42 (35)	40 (33.33)	45 (37.50)	29 (25.22)	156 (32.84)
Some signature column is blank or partly blank	75 (62.50)	114 (95)	89 (74.17)	96 (83.48)	374 (78.74)
Entries made during last few days anticipating the survey	27 (22.50)	25 (20.83)	10 (8.33)	18 (15.65)	80 (16.84)

Source: Primary Survey, 2013 (Figures in the bracket are % to the total).

Work, Wages and Working Conditions

Around 30.11 per cent of the workers said that the supervisors had marked attendance in an official Muster Roll. However, intra-district variations are observed. The attendance is taken also in the note book (66.52%). Such practice was observed in case of Kalahandi (70%), Nabarangpur (73.33%) and Malkangiri (63.48%). Almost 83.37 per cent respondents said that attendance is taken once a day. Around 88 per cent respondents said that they have signed in the muster roll only after the work is completed, while 10.74per cent of the total said that they have not signed the muster roll (Table 9).

Table 9

Proportion of Responses by the MGNREGS Participants on Work and Working Conditions at Worksite

Description of Items	*Districts/Responses*				*G. Total (N–478)*
	Kalahandi (N–120)	*Malkangiri (N–120)*	*Nabarangpur (N–120)*	*Subarnapur (N–115)*	
Attendance marked in the Muster Roll	36 (30)	28 (23.33)	32 (26.67)	47 (40.87)	143 (30.11)
Attendance marked in the Note Book	84 (70)	76 (63.33)	88 (73.33)	68 (59.13)	316 (66.52)
Attendance marked daily	108 (90)	85 (70.83)	107 (89.17)	96 (83.48)	396 (83.37)
Signed on the Muster Roll after the work is completed	62 (51.67)	54 (45)	65 (54.17)	43 (37.39)	221 (47.16)
Average number of days work recorded accurately	11.34	13.06	10	11.42	11.45
Find names who did not work	00	7 (5.83)	1 (0.83)	00	8 (1.68)
Find names of dead persons	00	00	00	00	00
Machines were used at the worksites	00	00	00	00	00
Contractor were involved in the work	00	00	00	00	00
Beneficiaries were explained how wage is calculated	00	00	00	00	00
Separate pay slip provided to each labourer	80 (66.67)	117 (97.50)	94 (78.33)	87 (75.65)	378 (79.58)

Source: Primary Survey, 2013 (Figures in the bracket are per cent to total).

With respect to the average number of days worked by the beneficiaries under MGNREGS it was reported to the tune of 11 days in case of Kalahandi, 13 days in case of Malkangiri, 10 days in case of Nabarangpur and 11 days in case of Subarnapur district. Only 1.68 per cent respondents said that bogus names of the persons who have not worked but have been reported in the job cards, while not a single name of the deceased person have been reported entered in the job card. The study did not find a single case where machines have worked and/or contractors were engaged in undertaking the work under MGNREGS. However, during the group discussions in villages of Kalahandi and Malkangiriit which were shared by the villagers was that the work was undertaken actively by one or two persons, none officially identified by the PRI members and village leaders.

Assets created under the MGNREGS are related to agriculture, construction or renovation of water bodies (ponds, tanks, check dams, field channels), construction of roads and other land improvement works. In all the districts the study found that digging of earthwork for road construction, check dam construction, field channels are the common infrastructure provided under MGNREGA. This tunes to the extent of 92.50 and 95.65 per cent in case of Nabarangpur and Subarnapur district respectively, while it is 85.83 and 80.83 per cent in Kalahandi and Malkangiri districts respectively. The villagers opined that repairing/renovation works were undertaken on preference than on making new infrastructures.

Payment of Wages

Payment of wages is one of the end goals of MGNREGA which aims to ensure employment and raise the income level of the villagers. Keeping this in mind the study tried to find out various dimensions of wage payment system like time gap in payment, place of payment, payment of pay slip, status of payment, modes of payment etc. Around 37.47 per cent beneficiaries have been paid their wages within 15 days of work completion, which is 60 per cent in case of Subarnapur, and 69.17 per cent in case of Kalahandi. Around 22.53 per cent households have been paid within 16 to 30 days of work completion which is 37.50 per cent in case of Nabarangpur, while 73.33 per cent respondents of Malkangiri district viewed that their wages are paid within 31 to 90 days. This is followed by 34.17 per cent in case of Nabarangpur district. Similarly, 25.83 per cent respondents viewed that payment in their cases took above 91 days.

With respect to the wage payment to the beneficiaries, the study found that none of the beneficiaries were paid in the form of cash in hand at the worksite or GP office. Around 60.10 per cent beneficiaries have been paid through post office and bank account, which is 23.33 per cent in case of Malkangiri district which is the lowest; and 77.39 per cent in case of Subarnapur, the highest. Similarly, 76.67 per cent households were paid through cash; in case of Malkangiri district, which was only 5.83 per cent in case of Kalahandi, and 54.17 per cent beneficiary households in Nabarangpur district since they had not opened their bank account. The beneficiaries viewed that payment through bank is most suitable to release the cash easily and also in short time when compared with the time taken by the post office and/or payment made by hand.

Payment of pay slips to the beneficiaries by the authorities was enquired in the field. While 19.78 per cent beneficiaries were not handed over any pay slip, 79.58 per cent beneficiaries were provided with separate pay slips. In Kalahandi district, 31.67 per cent beneficiaries were not provided with any pay slip, followed by 21.66 per cent in case of Nabarangpur district and 24.35 per cent in case of Subarnapur district. On the day of the study, around 31.36 (149 households) per cent beneficiaries were not paid wages for their last work. It was 42.60 per cent in case of Subarnapur, 7.50 per cent in case of Nabarangpur, 55 per cent in case of Malkangiri district and 80.83 per cent households in case of Kalahandi district. The delay as observed is basically due to the time consuming processes to prepare the bills and to deposit the amount in the bank. In none of the study districts the beneficiaries have reported of receiving money towards sharpening of the tools. The provision of payment towards sharpening of the tools for digging earth during the works under the Act is not known to the beneficiaries, nor has any of the persons engaged in implementing the programme informed the beneficiaries or paid them as per the Act.

Delay in Wage Payments

The delay in the payment of wages to the beneficiaries under the programme was calculated. The responses when analysed show that around 73.50 per cent beneficiaries have received their payment within 15 days of the completion of the work in case of Kalahandi, followed by 71.88 per cent in case of Malkangiri district, 65.71 per cent in case of Subarnapur district and 23 per cent in case of Nabarangpur district which is as per the provision of the Act. A serious problem raised in the inordinate delays in wage payment, which was reported to the extent of as much as 72.46 mean days in case of Malkangiri district was the highest, followed by 32.59 mean days in case of Nabarangpur district, 18.58 mean days in case of Subarnapur district and 17.68 mean days in Kalahandi district the lowest one (Table 10). Such delays particularly in Malkangiri district questions the efficiency of payment through the banks which otherwise aims to minimise the time gap for wage payment in appropriate means of payment. The study of Padhi et al. (2010) with respect to the management of NREGA and challenges in Odisha found out such delays to the extent of 26.1 mean days in Nuapada, 24.7 mean days in Ganjam, 18.5 mean days in Sundargarh and 14.1 mean days in case of Dhenkanal district. Since then, in spite of so many reforms made in the implementation of MGNREGA on various aspects of its implementation, still one finds very little improvement in case of Malkangiri and Nabarangpur districts with respect to the payment of wages. Delay in the payment is directly linked to poor planning and implementation of MGNREGS.

Table 10

Extent or Delay in Wage Payments under MGNREGS in Study Districts

District	*No of Days (Mean) of Delays Since Completion of Work*		
	Maximum	*Minimum*	*Mean*
Kalahandi	60	6	17.68
Malkangiri	180	30	72.46
Nabarangpur	180	8o	32.59
Subarnapur	60	7	18.58

Source: Primary Survey, 2013.

Participation in Social Audit under MGNREGS

Participation of the villagers in various stages of planning and implementation of MGNREGS is one of the objectives of the Act. The final stage of participation of the villagers in the process is reflected through social audit of MGNREGS. The study tried to find out the participation of the villagers in the social audit process adopted by the government functionaries to account the implementation of work under MGNREGS. The responses of the villagers in this regard are not giving a very encouraging picture. The study in total observed that only 14.10 per cent households have participated in social audit process, while other households expressed their ignorance in this regard. A district wise look into the process shows that Malkanagiri district has the lowest level of participation by the villagers in the social auditing process to the extent of 6.66 per cent, followed by Nabarangapur district (7.82%), while Kalahandi and Subarnapur district reflects an extent of 21.61 and 20 per cent respectively (Table 11). In all the districts the villagers viewed that they have never came across such a process in their village where the government authorities have asked them to do the social auditing of the activities carried out under MGNREGS.

Table 11

Participation of Households in Social Audit of MGNREGS

District	*Total HH*	*Participation*			
		Yes	*%*	*No*	*%*
Kalahandi	120	26	21.66	94	78.33
Malkanagiri	120	8	6.66	112	93.33
Nabarangpur	120	24	20	96	80
Subarnapur	115	9	7.82	106	92.17
Grand Total	475	67	14.10	408	85.89

Source: Primary Survey, 2013.

Note: HH-Households.

MGNREGS making Development Inclusive

The end objective of MGNREGA is to make people an inclusive component in the development process. Considering the limitations of the development programmes during 10th Five-Year Plan, the 11th and 12th Five-Year Plans emphasised the development programme as inclusive by nature. The present study wanted to know whether MGNREGS has made the development programmes inclusive involving people and the areas into it. Keeping this in mind the study tried to understand the perception of both beneficiaries and non-beneficiaries on MGNREGS and its impact on the life and living of the households. Around 46.52 per cent beneficiaries opined that MGNREGS is very important in the life and living of the people, while 46.52 per cent households responded saying that MGNREGS is somewhat important to human living. MGNREGS has brought a change in the lifestyle of the beneficiaries, while 98.73 per cent beneficiary households viewed that MGNREGA has not only reduced hunger, but also helped to avoid hunger of the villagers. Around 95.99 per cent households felt that the programme has helped people not to adopt migration as the solutions; while 80.42 per cent viewed that such a programme has also helped to meet the expenses of the treatment of illness of family members and

65.89 per cent viewed that the program has helped people to pay back their debt; 96.63 per cent opined that MGNREGS have helped to create income generating assets in their villagers. Due to MGNREGA there is a hike and standardisation of wage rates in the region (58.94%).

Major Findings and Policy Implications

Lack of Awareness

One of the most important obstacles in the successful implementation of MGNREGS is lack of awareness on the part of majority members of PRIs on the right-based philosophy of the Act. Though most of the villagers are aware of 100 days of wage work, minimum wages, piece wage rate, and provision of work within 5 kms, but a sizeable 59 per cent beneficiaries do not know the fact that MGNREGS is an Act.

Worksite Facilities

With respect to the provision of first-aid by the Gram Panchayat, around 61.47 per cent respondents agreed that it was available regularly during the work, while 27.58 per cent said that first-aid was not available. In Subarnapur district, first-aid services were available only in case of 20 per cent, while 54.78 per cent respondents denied on the availability of this service. As regards the provision of crèche, around 71.37 per cent denied the fact of its availability, though in 58.50 per cent cases the respondents agreed that there was a need of having crèche for the children in the worksite. In Subarnapur and Malkangiri districts, not a single respondent told about having crèche though there was a need of crèche. With respect to the availability of sheds and floor sheets for workers at the sites, around 46.32 per cent respondents agreed that during the summer such sheds were available to take shelter, while 14.74 per cent respondents said that such sheds were not regularly available, while 38.95 per cent fully denied on the availability of any sheds in the worksite. In case of Malkangiri only 3.33 per cent respondents agreed of having sheds. In terms of providing worksite facilities by the Gram Panchayats, Malkangiri district has poor service delivery, while the districts like Kalahandi and Nabarangpur have better worksite facilities provided under MGNREGS.

Role of Gram Sabha

The role of Gram Sabha in the entire process is hardly known to many belonging to both participant and non-participant households. Further, most of the respondents were unaware of the provision of job application and the provision of unemployment allowances to be paid to the job seekers, in case employment is not provided within 15 days of application. Only 1.68 per cent respondents said about the listing of bogus names of persons in the job cards, while not a single name of the deceased person has been reported entered in the job card. This reflects the quality listing made by Gram Panchayats. The study did not find a single case where machines were used and/or contractors were engaged in undertaking the work under MGNREGS. However, during the group discussions, it was reported by few villages of Kalahandi and Malkangiri that the work was undertaken actively by one or two persons, none officially identified by the PRI members and village leaders. Gram Panchayats have paid wages only to 37.47 per cent beneficiaries within 15 days of work completion, which is 60 per cent in case of Subarnapur, and 69.17 per cent in case of Kalahandi. Around 22.53 per cent households have been paid within 16 to 30 days of work completion which is 37.50 per cent in case of Nabarangpur. Around 73.33 per cent respondents of Malkangiri district said that their wages are paid within 31 to 90 days. This speaks that decentralisation of power enjoyed by the Gram Panchayats is a dependent one and GPs function as a post office just to deliver the package programmes decided by the upper bodies without looking into its qualitative dimensions.

Payment of Wages

Around 60.10 per cent beneficiaries have been paid through post office and nationalised bank accounts, which is 23.33 per cent the lowest in case of Malkangiri district, followed by 77.39 per cent the highest in case of Subarnapur. Similarly, 76.67 per cent households were paid through cash in Malkangiri, which is only 5.83 per cent in case of Kalahandi, while around 54.17 per cent in Nabarangpur district paid their remuneration on hand. This justifies that the transparent processes with respect to the payment of wages are yet to be established in few districts which is one of the objectives of decentralisation. A serious problem raised is the inordinate delays in wage payment, which was reported to the extent of 72.46 mean days in case of Malkangiri district the highest, followed by 32.59 mean days in case of Nabarangpur district, 18.58 mean days in case of Subarnapur district and 17.68 mean days in Kalahandi district. Such delays particularly in Malkangiri district questions the efficiency of payment through the banks which otherwise aims to minimise the time gap for wage payment by fair means of payment. On an average a Scheduled Tribe household has generated a total of 34 number of person days out of MGNREGS. However, one finds inter-district variations in terms of man-days creation out of MGNREGS. Around 51.16 per cent households had 25 days of employment during the year 2011--12, while only 1.47 per cent households have got 100 days of employment. Inter-district variations in the duration of employment in MGNREGA reflect that a highest of 3.53 per cent households have got 100 plus days of employment during 2011–12 in Kalahandi district, while it is 2.54 per cent in case of Malkanagiri district, 1.28 per cent in Nabarangpur district, but not a single tribal household has received 100 plus person-days of employment out of MGNREGS in Subarnapur district.

Women Participation

The study found an average number of 31 person-days of employment for a male against 39 days for a female. With respect to the duration of participation in MGNREGS by men and women workers, the data reflect that women almost share little less than half of the work force, but have less participation in MGNREGS in the districts of Malkanagiri, Nabarangpur and Subarnapur while in Kalahandi district the women have better participation. When one also looks at the duration of participation, women have more days of participation than males. In the districts of Malkangiri, Nabarangapur and Subarnapur not a single woman has benefitted 100 days of employment out of MGNREGS. Looking at the prevailing inequalities of wage payment to the men and women in agriculture, MGNREGS has positively impacted in ensuring equal wages in each study district. This has resulted in a higher wages for women leading to significant improvement in terms of women's earning opportunities and increased contribution of women to the household income.

Policy Implications

Institutional capacities of Gram Sabha, Gram Panchayat, Panchayat Samiti and district level institutions need to be improved and strengthened in terms of skilled man power and computerisation to implement MGNREGS. Awareness movement on the rights provided under MGNREGA may be transferred to practice by the members at various levels. PRIs and its overall functioning in tribal areas need to be strengthened by way of skill transfer to the PRI members and improvement in the infrastructure base since PRIs play key roles in the successful implementation of the MGNREGA. The developmental needs of the villages and people should be focused in place of political and bureaucratic focus which will make the processes of decentralisation and transparency more realistic. Wage payment under MGNREGA should have less dependent decentralisation processes so as to meet the ultimate goal of providing timely benefits to tribal wage earners. Processes for the payment of unemployment allowance should be kept in place and activated. PRIs at various levels should encourage this. The financial disbursement processes should be less attached with bureaucratic complicacies and political impositions. Quality supervision of various works under MGNREGS by different functionaries of district and Panchayat Samitis may be ensured. For this number of staff at various levels may be placed. Payments through banks should be made compulsory. Delay in payment through these institutions should be minimised. Payment of wages through cash should not be adopted as an alternative to bank and post office. Muster Roll (MR) should be maintained regularly and need to be available at work sites. Filling of MR should be made on spot. This will not only make the decentralisation transparent, but also empower the villagers. Provision of disclosure and social audit under MGNREGA should be proactive. Grievance redressal mechanisms should be placed at various levels of PRIs in the line of Ombudsman. This can reduce human lapses and improve quality of implementation of MGNREGS. Maintenance of records and registers should be update and ICT infrastructure at GP level should be ensured so as to maintain the records and ensure quality governance. Data bank at GP office should be developed and strengthened. The dependent data bank system should be stopped. MIS at GP level through computerisation should be ensured and maintained effectively. The scope of involvement of civil societies in various stages of MGNREGS should be widened.

References

Ambastha, P., P. Vijaya Shankar and Mihir Shah (2008), Two Years of NREGA: The Road Ahead, *Economic and Political Weekly*, Vol. 43, No. 8.

Behera, N.K. and N. Panigrahi (2006), *Tribals and the Indian Constitution*, Rawat Publications, Jaipur.

Chhabra, S., R.L. Raina and G.L. Sharma (2009), 'Management of MGNREGS: A Study of Six Districts', presented in the National Seminar on 'MGNREGA: Issues and Challenges', organised by NKC Centre for Development Studies, Bhubaneswar and Lal Bahadur Shastri Institute of Management, New Delhi.

Census of India (2001a), Series–1, Part-II B(iii), Primary Census Abstract: Scheduled Tribe Population.

—— (2001b), Series–2, Final Population Tables, Paper 1 of 2001, Directorate of Census Operations, Odisha.

Government of Odisha, Statistical Abstract of Odisha (1997), 'The Aged in India: A Socio-Economic Profile', *Sarvekshana*, Vol. XXI, No. 2, 73rd Issue, October–December (NSS 50th Round, 1993–94), Ministry of Statistics, Planning and Programme Implementation, Department of Statistics, New Delhi.

—— (2002a), Directorate of Economics and Statistics, Odisha, Bhubaneswar.

—— (2002b), Website of the Department of Panchayati Raj.

—— (2002c), 'Chronic Poverty in India: Incidence, Causes and Policies', *World Development*, Vol. 31, No. 3, pp. 491–511.

—— (2002–03), *Annual Report on the Administration of Scheduled Areas in Odisha for 2002–03*, ST and SC Development Department.

—— (2004), *Human Development Report–2004*.

—— (2006), 'Economic Survey, 2006–07', Directorate of Economics and Statistics, P&C Department.

Government of India (2012), 'MGNREGA Operational Guidelines, 2012', MoRD, Department of Rural Development, MGNREGA–1 Division, Krishi Bhawan, New Delhi, September 20.

—— (2013), *Report of the Task Group on Social Audit*, Office of the Comptroller and Auditor General of India.

Haan, Arjan de and Amaresh Dubey (2003), 'Poverty in Odisha Divergent Trends: With Some Thoughts on Measurement Issues', Mimeo, paper presented at the Workshop on 'Monitoring of Poverty in Odisha', Nabakrushna Choudhury Centre for Development Studies, Bhubaneswar, 26–27 February.

Mathew, G. (1994), *Panchayati Raj: From Legislation to Movement*, Concept Publishing House: New Delhi.

Mehta, G.S. (2009), 'NEGP in UP: Changes in Condition and Creation of Employment, Income and Wage Rates', presented in the National Seminar on 'MGNREGA: Issues and Challenges', organised by NKC Centre for Development Studies, Bhubaneswar and Lal Bahadur Shastri Institute of Management, New Delhi.

MGNREGA (2012), 'Report to the People', MoRD, Department of Rural development, (MGNREGA–1 Division), Krishi Bhawan, New Delhi, 2 February.

Padhi, S. and A.K. Mishra (2005), Chronic Poverty across Indian States: Some Correlates and Determinants, (Mimeo), Paper presented in the consultation workshop on 'Chronic Poverty in Odisha: Sustainable Livelihood, Development Policies and Governance', August 25, NCDS: Bhubaneswar.

Padhi, S. and N. Panigrahi (2011), 'Tribal Movements and Livelihood: Recent Development in Odisha', *Working Paper No. 51*, Chronic Poverty Research Centre (CRPC), Indian Institute of Public Administration (IIPA), New Delhi (With Prof. S.P. Padhi).

Padhi, S., N. Panigrahi and A. Mishra (2009), 'Tribal Population and Chronic Poverty in Odisha: The North-South Divide', *Working Paper No. 27*, Chronic Poverty Research Centre (CRPC), Indian Institute of Public Administration (IIPA), New Delhi (With Prof. S.P. Padhi and A.K. Mishra).

Padhi, S.P., S. Meher and N. Panigrahi (2010), 'MGNREGA: Issues and Challenges in Odisha', presented in the National Seminar on 'MGNREGA: Issues and Challenges', organised by NKC Centre for Development Studies, Bhubaneswar and Lal Bahadur Shastri Institute of Management, New Delhi.

Panda, M. (2004), 'Poverty in Odisha: A Disaggregated Analysis (2003)', Draft, Indira Gandhi Institute of Development and Research, Mumbai.

Panigrahi, N. (2007), *Role of Indigenous Institutions in Tribal Livelihood: An Empirical Study in a Tribal Dominated District of Odisha*, Report submitted to SRTT-ISEC, Bangalore.

—— (2014), 'Impact of MGNREGA on the Livelihood Improvement of Tribal Households: A Study in KBK Region of Odisha', supported by ICSSR, New Delhi and NKC Centre for Development Studies, Bhubaneswar.

Radhakrishna, R., K. Hanumantha Rao, C. Ravi and B. Sambi Reddy (2004), Chronic Poverty and Malnutrition in 1990s, *Economic and Political Weekly*, Vol. 39, No. 28.

Radhakrishna, R. (1990), 'Chronic Poverty and Malnutrition', *Economic and Political Weekly*, Vol. 39, No. 28, July 10.

Shah, M. (2007), 'Employment Guarantee, Civil Society and Indian Democracy', *Economic and Political Weekly*, Vol. 42, No. 45, November 17.

State Election Commission (2002), Profile of PRI Members in Odisha, (Mimeo), State Election Commission, Government of Odisha: Bhubaneswar.

12

Pattern of Local Governance for Tribes in Maharashtra

Analysis of Strategies and Policies for Inclusive Development

S.T. Shirsath

The rationale behind the inclusive development is hidden in the abject poverty and increasing exploitation of tribals who according to Nehru, maintain artistic tradition and zest for life and are extremely disciplined. They are more democratic than others in India. Tribals try to enjoy life. They are more civilised than urban people (Guha, 2008). The demand for statehood in Bihar, Madhya Pradesh, Assam, Manipur, and Himachal Pradesh leading to Jharkhand, Chhattisgarh, Nagaland, Manipur and Uttaranchal was to protect their land customs and to end their exploitation. Over a period of sixty years after Independence, tribals live in primitive darkness without schools, hospitals, roads, electricity, with their land seized by others and their forests closed to them by the State. The dispute over land and forest were at the root of Naxal movement in sixties, initially in West Bengal and thereafter spreading to number of states including Maharashtra. Economic liberalisation has improved the lives of many million Indians, but there are some Indians who have been adversely affected by freeing of market and opening of economy to outsiders. Among those who have suffered trans-economic liberalisation, the tribals of Orissa (Odisha) are perhaps the foremost. Three thousand acres of land use for Alumina project there, was cultivated by tribals. Overall result in India was marked by sharp inequality by 1991 (Guha, 2008). In a nutshell the rationale behind the new programme is to attack the inequality in the field of tribal areas and bring them to the main stream by creating confidence among them about protection of their rights over land, forests etc.

It is appropriate to review such kind of development process in the context of excluded tribes in India. Tribals in India have a significant degree of cultural and ethnic diversity. They differ in their socio-economic levels and behavioural patterns. Moreover, tribal situation in the country poses particular problems of development, not encountered in other areas (Singh, 1999). Development is a very complicated task and needs more careful attention than has been paid to it so far (Kulkarni, 1980). Mostly, such tribal communities live in rural and wild area. So, local self-government in rural areas [Panchayati Raj Institutions (PRIs)] played an important role in the tribal development. Panchayat is a nomenclature associated with rural life in India from time immemorial. However, since 1992, following the 73rd constitutional amendment, Panchayats have acquired a new meaning as 'institutions of local self-government' with the specific task to prepare and implement 'plans for economic development and social justice' (Oommen, 2004). This Amendment was undertaken to ensure Panchayati Raj system with certain revolutionary and progressive measures (Samal, 2007).

Excluding the operation of Part IX of the Indian Constitution the 'Fifth Scheduled Areas', the Parliament had withdrawn the legislative power of the State legislatures and the special powers conferred on the governors to make regulations for the scheduled areas on the Panchayati Raj set-up. Taking into consideration the special conditions that exist in the scheduled areas, the parliament reserved to itself the power to make a separate legislation with necessary modifications for the scheduled areas (Samal, 2007). In the last decade, Government of India became more aware about tribal development and especially tribal's participation in Local Governance and their Social and Economic development. The PESA endeavours to enhance tribal representation in local governance and further increased the effort to uplift them socio-economically (Chauhan, 2003).

The present research undertaking makes an attempt to search how tribes in India are excluded from the development process; evaluate efforts and pattern of inclusive development by the Government of India for tribal betterment and focus on the problems of tribals especially illiteracy, economic backwardness and poverty in the light of development process.

Methodology

This study is based on both the primary and secondary data collected from various sources. The secondary data, used to study the theorisation and policy study purpose were collected from various organisations viz., Government departments, voluntary agencies and statistics, research publications, reports of individuals and institutions. This study was conducted at the Fifth Scheduled Area of Maharashtra State. Primary data were collected from multistage sampling in ten districts from fifth scheduled areas of constitution i.e. twenty blocks from ten selected districts and two village Panchayats from every block in all forty village Panchayats were selected for the study purpose. The final list of respondents included 480 samples. Among them 40 were Sarpanchas (Chairman of village Panchayat), 40 were member of village Panchayats and 400 were tribal villagers (Ten from each village Panchayat area). Using structured interview schedule developed and standardised by the researcher, the data were collected during 2008–2011. Both qualitative and quantitative data were used to undertake the study with the help of narration, observation, tables and percentages. Content analysis of the responses was also done.

Tribes in India

Scheduled Tribes (STs)

The Constitution of India does not define the word 'tribe', rather, it only mentions about identifying a group of communities as Scheduled Tribes. The term 'Scheduled Tribes' first appeared in the Constitution in the Article 366(25) as '... such tribes or tribal communities or parts of or groups within such tribes or tribal communities as are deemed under Article 342 to be STs for the purposes of the constitution'. Article 342 prescribes procedure to be followed in the matter of specification of scheduled tribes. Accordingly, President of India has the authority to specify the tribes. Even the Parliament has power to include or exclude a tribe from the list of STs (Constitution of India).

Majumdar's (1958) definition of a tribe is still relevant in the anthropological understanding of a tribe. As per their definition a tribe is: a relatively isolated or semi-isolated community living mainly in forest, hill or hill clad settings; an autonomous cultural system; economically self-sufficient by exploiting natural resources in a primitive or crude mode, involving a low level of technology and distributed within a well demarcated territory, distinct world-view or belief system, folklore, deities and its own dialect.

Tribal Demography of India

Tribals in India constitute 8.2 per cent of the total population (2001 census); and they have distinct cultures, customary practices, dialects and economic pursuits in different ecological settings. The areas inhabited by the tribals constitute a significant part of the underdeveloped areas of the country. The prominent tribal areas constitute about 15 per cent of the total geographical area of the country. The Government of India's list of Scheduled Tribes (STs) included 212 tribes in 1950, 458 in 1990 (MoPR, 2009) which rose to 533 by 2009 (tribal.gov.in). Now, the number of tribes included in the list of STs contributes a notable section of total population of the Indian society. However, they are away from the mainstream of the society.

Excluded Tribes in India

Tribal Economy

Historically, the tribal economy was based on subsistence agriculture and/or hunting and gathering forest produce. However, since the tribal people treated land as a common resource, they rarely had land titles, and thus, lost their lands to outsiders when exploitation of forest resources began. This ensured that a majority ended up as small and marginal landholders. It is fairly well documented that the well-being of social groups in India differs a lot. Recent researches have tried to quantify the disparities in level of living of various population groups. As a population group, STs are at the bottom on the range of development indicators including consumption and poverty (Dubey, 2009). More than half of the rural tribal population is found to be below poverty line as per the latest survey available with the Ministry of Rural Development (tribal.gov.in).

As per the Planning Commission of India, the incidence of poverty among STs is a critical issue for the country (Table 1). As compared to other groups of community, ratio of below poverty line is quite higher among STs.

Table 1

Percentage of Population below Poverty Line in India 2004–05

Level	*Rural %*				*Urban %*			
	ST	*SC*	*OBC*	*Other*	*ST*	*SC*	*OBC*	*Other*
India	47.20	36.80	26.70	16.10	33.30	39.90	31.40	16

Source: Planning Commission of India SC = Scheduled Castes, ST = Scheduled Tribes, OBC = Other backward classes

Another survey conducted by NCAER (National Council of Applied Economic Research, India), gives more clear picture of spoiled tribal economy (Shariff et al., 2005). The survey shows that there is a higher incidence of poverty in the STs population (Table 2).

Table 2

Levels on Income and Material Well-being

Element		*Scheduled Tribe*	*All Average*
Household income (₹)		19,557	25,653
Per capita income (₹)		3,786	4,846
Work participation rate	Male	51.6	51.9
	Female	27.7	18.4
Source of income:	Agriculture + allied	55.6	55
	Salaried	14.8	16.5
	Agricultural wage	11.7	7.9
	Others	17.9	20.6
Households reporting land holdings %		69	63.4

Source: NCAER–HDI Survey, 2005.

The Head Count Poverty ratios are considerably higher among STs, 51 per cent as compared to all-India average 39 per cent. More than half of the ST population is reported to be below poverty line. The survey also provides distribution of household income for various caste categories for rural areas. The household income of STs is ₹ 19,557 and the per capita income is ₹ 3,786, which is much lower than that of the national average. This brings to fore the lack of access to asset and other types of employment and wage stability for the STs as compared to general population. The data suggest that the share of income from agriculture and agricultural wage is relatively higher than salaried and other. The work participation rate of STs, especially of females is higher than that of national average, whereas in the case of males there is no variation.

The tribal economy is structured around two key elements; land and forest. This is operationalised in three different ways; by gathering of minor forest produce, by shifting agriculture, and by settled agriculture. Traditionally, barter was an effective mechanism to share resources, especially related to the minor forest products. With increased exposure to non-tribal customs, this has changed dramatically. For example, the level of awareness among tribals concerning the use of money and the value of their products is generally poor. As a result, they are often victimised by unscrupulous traders, who buy tribal produce at low prices. This leaves the tribals economically vulnerable and open to exploitative labour practices. Moreover, encroachment by non-tribals into tribal lands in search of timber and other resources has pushed tribals deeper into the remote areas, thus further marginalising them (Shankar, 2005).

Micro Observations

The field-based study observed some crucial facts about tribal education, family income, incidence of poverty and starvation. The study has cited various reasons behind the exclusion of tribes from the mainstream.

Table 3

Educational Status

Education	*Primary*	*High School*	*Graduate*	*Postgraduate*	*Illiterate*	*Total*
Villagers	82 (20.5%)	62 (15.5%)	25 (6.25%)	08 (2%)	223 (55.75%)	400 (100%)
Sarpanch and members of village Panchayat	14 (17.5%)	36 (45%)	06 (7.5%)	02 (2.5%)	22 (27.5%)	80 (100%)
Total	96 (20%)	98 (20.41%)	31 (6.45%)	10 (2.08%)	243 (50.62%)	480 (100%)

Tribes, being disproportionately poor, most heavily suffer the ills of an inequitable and ineffective education system in India (Table 3). The ratio of illiteracy is more than 50 per cent among tribes. This proportion is less in politically active tribals but pursuing higher education is an exception. Primary education is as good as illiteracy because quality of primary and secondary education is very poor. The dropout rate is the major drawback of this education system. Tribals are so ignorant due to the lack of education and hence they are too far from the jobs and modern resources of income. Government is trying for their education but the efforts are falling short as there is very meagre response from tribes. Some years ago the educational condition of tribes was worse than mentioned above but efforts done by government have slightly been improving their condition.

Table 4

Annual Income

Income Group	*Below 25,000/-*	*25,000/- to 50,000/-*	*50,000/- to 1 lakh*	*Above 1 lakh*	*Total*
Villagers	212 (53%)	169 (42.25%)	11 (2.75%)	08 (2%)	400 (100%)
Sarpanch and members of village Panchayat	16 (20%)	39 (48.75%)	15 (18.75%)	10 (12.5%)	80 (100%)
Total	228 (47.5%)	208 (43.33%)	26 (5.41%)	18 (3.75%)	480 (100%)

Poverty among tribals is on a large scale (Table 4). More than 53 per cent of tribal communities' annual family income is less than ₹ 25,000. This proportion is a bit lower in politically active tribals. But the income of 95 per cent tribal villagers is less than ₹ 50,000. This ratio sheds light on the poverty of tribal communities. Only 3.75 per cent of tribals get the annual income of more than one lakh rupees. There is a little improvement in politically active tribals.

The following factors are responsible for the poverty in tribal communities:

- Dependency on conventional production resources;
- Undeveloped farming and negligible participation in jobs;
- Unawareness of detachment from the other world and
- Unavailing of government scheme.

Besides poverty, unemployment and low standards of living were a matter of concern.

Table 5

Starvation

Starvation	*Frequent Starvation*	*Sometime Starvation*	*Never Starvation*	*Total*
Villagers	190 (47.5%)	158 (39.5%)	52 (13%)	400 (100%)
Sarpanch and members of village Panchayat	16 (20%)	51 (63.75%)	17 (21.25%)	80 (100%)
Total	206 (42.91%)	209(43.54%)	69 (14.37%)	480 (100%)

Tribes mainly suffer from hunger and malnutrition. Our study shows that only 13 per cent of tribals and 21.25 per cent of tribal leaders think that hunger and starvation are not their problems. Around 47.5 per cent of tribal villagers and 20 per cent of tribal leaders think that they have to face starvation frequently (Table 5). Naturally, there is disparity in getting nutritious food between rural tribals and tribal leaders. Tribals starvation is a grave issue mainly because of their dependency on traditional foodstuffs, natural vulnerability and isolation from the outside world. Some improvements have taken place because of governmental efforts. However, comprehensive efforts are needed to further uplift the tribals.

In a nutshell, tribals situation about education, income, starvation is a matter of concern. Government is making efforts but efforts in large scale are needed in this matter. Out of this, government's inclusive pattern for tribal development came forward. There are innumerable constraints responsible for lower pace of tribal development process than desired (tribal.gov.in). Some of them are;

(a) *Destruction of forests:* The forests are not only the source of livelihood for tribals but there is an intricate relationship between tribals and forests in forest ecosystems. The depleting forest resources are threatening imminent food security for a good portion of the tribal population.

(b) *Lack of awareness:* There is a lack of awareness among tribal population about various developmental programmes launched by the Government of India and states. This lack of awareness results in tribal exploitation.

(c) *Nonuse of Tribal Rights and Concessions:* The tribals have been given numerous rights and concessions under various statutes of Central as well as State Governments. But unfortunately, they are deprived of the benefits due to their ignorance and the apathy of enforcing agencies.

Inclusive Pattern for Tribal Development

Reforms in Local Governance

Governance is the medium of development and tribal development is a mandatory object of Indian governance (Pati and Jena, 1989). The Constitution of India also mentioned the way of tribal development. In this regard, the local self-government has been a carrier of developmental work in India for a long time. From the pre-Vedic and Vedic period to the formation of Indian Republic, the important and role of local governance was so elementary in the process of development (Chauhan, 2003). After Independence, village panchayats came to be established more systematically with defined powers and functions through the Constitution of India.

It is in times of grave economic crises that the attention of a nation's leadership turned to administrative reforms. The first Administrative Reform Commission (ARC) was set-up in 1966 in India ,with a view of comprehensive examination of India's public administration under the chairmanship of Morarji Desai (later Hanumanthaiya). Actually, first ARC did not pay sufficient attention to tribal development and also to the implementation of recommendations by the government (Maheshwri, 2004). However, the 73rd Constitutional Amendment (1992) made provision of SCs, STs and women's reservation and began a new era of local governance for tribal development. Some of the important features of the Panchayat amendment include:

- The role is assigned to the Gram Sabha.
- Three-tier structure across the country.
- Direct elections at all levels.
- Reservation for SCs and STs, one-third of the total seats to women.
- Identifying 29 subjects in the XI Schedule of the Constitution and
- Setting up of a State Finance Commission and Election Commission (Oommen, 2004).

Tribal Representation in Panchayati Raj

In essence, the 73rd Constitutional Amendment is a key aspect of reforming process in the local governance. It has also increased tribals' participation in the three-tire system of local governance (Table 6). Presently, Scheduled Tribes hold position as a member in the District Panchayat (1,711), Middle Panchayat (11,548) and Gram Panchayat (3,20,482). Here, more than one-third are tribal women (MoPR, 2009). Comparative representation of tribals with total number of seats is near about 8 per cent to 10 per cent, which is only because of reservation policy.

Table 6

Representations in Panchayati Raj of India

Gram Panchayat (2,33,622)				*Panchayat Samiti (6,094)*				*Zilla Parishad (545)*			
Category			*Total No.*	*Category*			*Total No.*	*Category*			*Total No.*
Gen.	*SC*	*ST*		*Gen.*	*SC*	*ST*		*Gen.*	*SC*	*ST*	
18,64,207	5,06,329	3,20,482	2,691,018	1,13,646	33,304	11,548	1,58,498	11,228	2,711	1,711	15,650

Source: State of Panchayats Report, Government of India, 2009.

This political participation can empower STs, not only politically but also socially and economically, in deciding policies and plans for themselves, which will also help them to be aware about their own problems.

Panchayats Extension to the Scheduled Areas (PESA) Act 1996 as an Inclusive Pattern for Tribal Development

PESA's Implementation: The Ministry of Rural Development, Government of India constituted a committee of selected members of Parliament and experts to make recommendations on the salient features of the law for extending provisions of Part XI of the Constitution to the Scheduled Areas. In December 1996, the Parliament passed the Provisions of the Panchayats (Extension to the Scheduled Areas) Act, (PESA), and subsequently, the President's assent was accorded on 24 December 1996 to make it a part of the Constitution, recognising the tribal's right to self-rule (MoPR, 2009).

PESA act is a Central legislation that extends the constitutional provisions of Panchayati Raj to Fifth Schedule Areas, subject to certain exceptions and modifications. Nine states, namely, Andhra Pradesh, Chhattisgarh, Gujarat, Himachal Pradesh, Jharkhand, Madhya Pradesh, Maharashtra, Orissa (Odisha) and Rajasthan have Fifth Schedule Areas (FACP, 2008). For the purpose of effective implementation and Tribal's participation, a review meeting of the PESA states on implementation of the PESA Act, 1996 was held on 13 November 2007 in New Delhi. An action plan for implementation of PESA in letter and spirit was agreed to by the states in the review Meeting (MoPR, 2008).

Features of PESA Act: Salient features of the Extension Act may be discussed under following heads. A village in scheduled areas '... shall ordinarily consist of a habitation or a group of habitations or a hamlet or a group of hamlets comprising a community and managing its affairs in accordance with traditions and customs'. Every village shall have a gram sabha consisting of persons whose names are included in the electoral rolls for the panchayats at the village level. PESA takes cognizance of the fact that political empowerment is the beginning of economic development. It, hence, reserves a minimum of 50 per cent of the seats for the members of the tribal communities and also all posts of chairpersons in the Scheduled Areas, even where the population of tribals have been reduced to minority status. The chairpersons' post at all levels of the panchayats shall be reserved for STs. In case some ST communities have no representation at intermediate or district level panchayats, the state government shall nominate such underrepresented STs but such nomination should not exceed one-tenth of the total elected members of the panchayats. Every legislation on the panchayats in fifth scheduled area shall be in conformity with the customary law, social and religious practices and traditional management practice of he community resources. PESA, unlike the IX Schedule, empowers the gram sabha and not the Gram Panchayat to approve plans, programmes and projects and to issue utilisation certificates, select beneficiaries for poverty alleviation and other programmes. In a very significant move, the PESA makes a consultation with the gram sabha mandatory. before any acquisition of land in the village or before resettlement and rehabilitation of the Project Affected Persons in the village. The gram sabha has been vested with the command over natural resources in the village including the minor minerals, water bodies and the minor forest produce. No mining lease can be granted without the prior recommendation of the gram sabha. PESA also empowers the gram sabha to have control over village markets, all plan and Tribal Sub-Plan resources, and control moneylending in the village (MoPR, 2009; Pal, 2000). As per provisions of the 'PESA' Act, all of the nine state have taken necessary action. Government of Maharashtra has made the necessary amendments to the Maharashtra Zilla Parishads and Panchayat Samitis Act, 1961 and Bombay Village Panchayats Act, 1958 (MoPR, 2008). The Maharashtra State tries to protect tribal tradition and it provides tribals more facilities and income sources; and assures about tribal welfare through local political participation and implementation of various schemes.

Limitations of PESA: The objects of the PESA Act are partially fulfilled. This Act gives powers to the Tribal Panchayat, but it needs more clear and transparent provisions. The PESA Act is one of inclusive pattern for tribal development. But goals cannot be achieved because of limitations in the implementation by government and governmental institutions. Besides, the lack of awareness in the tribal community is a major hurdle in the performance of the PESA. In this connection, this study has observed the following facts by way of its findings of field work: The reducing rate of poverty, illiteracy, hunger and malnutrition is not notable. The rate of child mortality, women illness, crimes against tribes are very high than among non-tribes despite of the efforts undertaken by PESA. More than 95 per cent of tribal villagers know nothing about PESA Act and its provisions. They are also ignorant about special status of their village Panchyats. More than 65 per cent of tribal people prefer Traditional Panchayat (*Jat* Panchayat) over village Panchayat. Out of total members of local self-institutions, 60 per cent of representatives are already active members or their relatives in traditional panchayats. PESA made 50 per cent of reservation in Panchayat Institutions which belongs to Fifth Schedule of Indian Constitution but more than 50 per cent of tribals do not know about such reservation policy. It is found that even tribal leaders representing their people have little knowledge of the reservation policy at panchayat level. More than 50 per cent of tribes are not satisfied about the performance of PESA as an inclusive pattern for tribal development. They want transparency and more autonomy in village panchayats. Approximately, 10 per cent of village panchayats are working without individual office. The office of village panchayats runs in the house of Sarpanch or Gram Sevak (Rural Development Officer).

Reforms by the Second ARC

The second Administrative Reform Commission was set-up under the chairmanship of Veerappa Moily on 31 August 2005. The Commission made as many recommendations on various aspects of administration including reforms in the various areas. A part of such document is directly related to Fifth Schedule area. The eight recommendations out of total 256 under the document of 'Local Governance' are related to tribal development and working of tribal panchayats (Moily, 2006). These recommendations and action taken by the government may create ideal model of local governance for tribal development. The recommendations made by ARC have been accepted by government up to some extent. Government is positively thinking for the upliftment of the STs through the help of PESA Act. Government has given certain parameters to the state legislatives for handy implementation of PESA Act. Government will provide adequate funds by Finance Ministry for the betterment of STs. Government is willing for uniformity in local governance of Scheduled Area through PESA Act. In nine states the Act has been implemented. Government has clearly determined the authority of Gram Sabha and Panchayat for empowerment of STs.

Result of Tribal Development Efforts

The results of these recommendations have been highlighted by scholars (Shankar, 2005). Improvement of bargaining capacity of agro-forest based products, resulting in getting fair prices; reduced cost of crop production, due to the use of botanical pesticides, traditional soil and land management practices, organic manure, biological pest control, and the use of disease resistant, drought- and pest-resistant traditional seed varieties; reduced expenditure on allopathic medicine for human and animal health due to revival of the use of herbal medicines and support to local healers; extra income for women due to value-adding and processing techniques of the raw forest and agriculture products. For example, leaf plate making, turmeric powder production etc.; less money spent on buying seeds due to the conservation programmes of traditional seed varieties at institutional, community and farmer level; Increased production from agro-forest and livestock based activities, resulting in more food for consumption, more income generating activities, and less need to migrate elsewhere in search of paid work; increased opportunities for women to save money. Women's village groups have created revolving funds which provide small loans for income generating activities, such as vegetable cultivation, small shops, agro-forestry based processing units, and duck and chicken raising activities; the revival of local food customs, herbal medicines, and the preparation of supplementary nutritional foods for vulnerable groups is contributing to the improvement of health, nutritional status, and has lowered the rate of mother and child mortality; the formation of grain banks which meet emergency consumption needs and supply of food grains to the needy.

Conclusion

Now it is accepted, that routine system and procedure of government is not useful for tribal development and to achieve goals. Since last six decades Government of India has made some different efforts. However, desired results have not been seen yet. Lack of awareness among STs and administrative problems in the implementation of PESA Act are the prominent hurdles in the developmental process. If we work on the limitations, this Act might prove as a milestone in the inclusive development of excluded tribes.

We should admit that Indian tribals are still not in the mainstream of development. But, Indian government has implemented the pattern of all-inclusive development for tribals with the help of 73rd Amendment, PESA Act and by doing continuous administrative reforms. Guarantee of representation in PRIs through reservations and efforts towards sustainable economic development are nucleus of the pattern. As a result of this, unawakened tribes are becoming vigilant. Their income is growing along with their increasing representation in local governance. Ratio of their problems like illiteracy, unemployment, poverty and starvation is decreasing while their living standard is elevating. However, government's efficient and participatory efforts should be accelerated to specify development with the participation of local tribes.

References

Chauhan, Abha (2003), *A Decade of Women's Empowerment through Local Government in India*, Institute of Social Science, South Asia Partnership, Canada, pp. 2–6.

Dubey, Amaresh (2009), 'Poverty and Under-nutrition among Scheduled Tribes in India: A Disaggregated Analysis', Fourth Annual International Conference on Public Policy and Management, Indian Institute of Management, Bangalore (IIMB), pp. 9–12.

Fifteenth Anniversary Charter on Panchayati Raj (FACP) (2008), 'Inclusive Growth through Inclusive Governance', Government of India, p. 14.

Guha, Ramachandra (2008), *India After Gandhi*, Oxford, London, pp. 261–80.

Hasnain, Nadeem (2009), *Tribal India*, Palaka Prakashan, Delhi, p. 344.

Kulkarni, S.D. (1980), 'Problems of Tribal Development in Maharashtra', *Economic and Political Weekly*, Vol. 15, No. 38, p. 1598.

Kumar, Arun (2009) 'Tribal Women in Local Governance: A Study of Andhra Pradesh in India', Research Paper, p. 1.

Majumdar, D.N. (1958), Races and Cultures of India, Asia Publisher House: Bombay.

Maheshwri, S.R. (2004), *Administrative Reforms in India: Past, Present and Future Prospects*, Centre for Policy Research, New Delhi, p. 243.

MoPR (2008), *Annual Report*, Government of India, New Delhi, pp. 30–31.

—— (2009), *State of Panchayats Report*, Government of India, New Delhi, p. 20, chapter–4c, 29, 1–8, annexure 27(1).

Moily, Veerappa (2006), *Report of Second Administrative Reform Commission*, Government of India, New Delhi, pp. 1–67.

NACDOR (2006), *Millennium Development Goals and Dalits*, Status Report, National Conference of Dalit Organisations, Delhi, p. 39.

Oommen, M.A. (2004), *Deepening Decentralised Governance in Rural India*, Centre for Socio-economic and Environmental Studies, Kochi, Kerala, India, December, pp. 1–3.

Pal, Mahi (2000), 'Panchayats in Fifth Scheduled Areas', *Economic and Political Weekly*, Vol. 35, No. 19, p. 1603.

Pati, R.N. and B. Jena (1989), *Tribal Development in India*, Ashish Publishing House, New Delhi, pp. 11–12.

Samal, Avinash (2007), 'Institutional Reforms for Decentralised Governance and the Politics of Control and Management of Local Natural Resources: A Study in the Scheduled Areas of India', Research Paper, p. 5.

Shankar, K.J.N Gowtham (2005), 'Strengthening Tribal Economies through Endogenous Development', *COMPAS Magazine*, pp. 2–15.

Shariff, Abusaleh, Prabir K. Ghosh and Abhilasha Sharma (2005), 'Relative Socio-economic and Human Development Profile of Scheduled Tribes in India', in H.C. Sim, S. Appanah and N. Hooda (eds), *Forests for Poverty Reduction*, Food and Agriculture Organisation of the UN, Bangkok, pp. 83–98.

Singh, Awadhesh (1999), *Tribal Participation in Rural Development Programmes in Uttar Pradesh: Dynamics of Public Administration*, Department of Public Administration, University of Lucknow, p. 104.

Singh, S.K. (2000), *Panchayats in Scheduled Areas: Status of Panchayati Raj in States and Union Territories*, Concept Publishing Company, New Delhi, p. 27.

e-references

http://arc.gov.in/

http://darpg.nic.in/arpg-website/6threport-localgov.pdf

http://tribal.nic.in/index3.asp?subsublinkid=303&langid=1

http://www.tribal.gov.in/

13

A Decade of Change through Dalit Leadership

Narratives from the Kuthambakkam Village Panchayat, Tamil Nadu

Ramkumar G.

India is the biggest democracy country in the world. While, the Constitution of India guarantees equal rights and opportunities to all the citizens before law, certain section of the people still continue to face discrimination. They are facing discrimination since ancient times in the name of Caste system. The one of the excluded in this category is Scheduled Caste (Dalits), have been excluded socially, politically, economically and in all the spheres of life (Singh, 2012).

Therefore, government had taken many initiatives to uplift the Dalit people and passed several acts to remove the caste discrimination, before and after the independence of India (Thorat, 2009). In that path, one such milestone in the independent India was the institutional reform of local governance. This reform gave democratic space for the Dalit to participate in the political and decision-making process at the village level. Though, the concept of local governance[1] existed since long time, there was no participation of marginalised community.

Thus, the local governance had many critics among Indian national leaders in India during the independence. Gandhi believed in the gram swaraj (village self-governance), whereas Dr Ambedkar opposed it based on his own experience. Nehru found it preferable to adopt centralised institution machinery (Manor, 2010: 63). However, the panchayat raj was incorporated in directive principle of state policy of the Indian Constitution.

The panchayat, which existed before the institutional reform, has failed because of many reasons such as irregular election, lack of participation of the downtrodden people and weaker section, lack of power and financial resources (Goel and Rajneesh, 2009). To fill this gap, it was necessary to conduct regular periodical election, reservation of the weaker section and provide financial assistance on regular basis (Goel and Rajneesh, 2009: 22).

Therefore, for the inclusion of this excluded group in the democratic process, the Parliament passed 73rd Amendment of Indian constitution in 1992 to stipulate the devolution of power at the grassroots. The amendment ensures the participation of marginalised people – Scheduled Caste (SC), Scheduled Tribe (ST), women and Other Backward Class (OBC) – through providing reservations (Tanabe, 2007: 559). Moreover, decentralised governance enables them to plan and utilise government schemes for their development.

The main features of the 73rd Amendment are provision for 'Gram Sabha' which consist of all the adult members who registered as electoral member in every village. Women have been given reservation for not less than one-third of total seats at all the levels and the reservation in total seats. The post of chairman is also reserved for scheduled caste (SC) and scheduled tribe (ST) with respect to proportion of their population and reservation for backward classes (Mathew, 2003).

Though, it ensures the participation of Dalit people, still discrimination practices continue at the village level. The elected dalit representatives are facing different kinds of discrimination. They were exploited mentally, physically etc. (Mathew and Nayak, 1996). These kinds of practices are not exceptions to Tamil Nadu. The elected dalit representative faced discrimination, are exploited and sometimes gruesomely killed by the village upper caste in Tamil Nadu (Palanithurai, 2013; Dorairaj, 2013).

For instance, a dalit panchayat president of Nakkalamuthanpatti village panchayat in Tamil Nadu expresses his fear that 'My hands are tied; I have not been allowed to discharge my democratic duties. A couple of ward members belonging to the dominant caste hurled verbal abuses at me. I left the village as I faced an imminent threat of my life' (Dorairaj, 2013). Also the caste Hindus have forced dalit aspirants to keep off the polls, or fielded proxy candidates, or 'auctioned' the PRI posts to the highest bidder (Viswanathan, 2012).

Devakumar (2007: 47–48) wrote on the murder of the dalit elected president in Melvalavu in Madurai district. The election got cancelled in 1996 as nominated dalit candidates withdrew their nomination. Then, Murugesan, a dalit candidate won as president in the third polling 1977. In the same year, he was murdered by chopping off his head. Therefore, dalit faced problems like murder of their candidates. In some village panchayats in Tamil Nadu, dalits elected as presidents are being used as a puppet candidates and are controlled by upper caste members. If the elected dalit members claim their rights, they are attacked physically.

In the face of all these struggles, few elected dalit representatives have fought against the discrimination and have succeeded in their roles and have brought changes in the village through their leadership skills (Vishwanathan, 2001). Some of them have started getting acceptance among the non-dalit people and some even have been reelected.

One such village panchayat is Kuthambakkam village panchayat, which is situated in Poonammallee block, Tamil Nadu. This village faced lots of problems such as, illicit arrack (liquor) brewing, unemployment, poor education and sanitation, etc. before the implementation of 73rd Amendment. Soon after the implementation, Elango Rangasamy, an educated dalit candidate became the village president and brought changes in the village which resulted as model village for many other villages. He has initiated many new measures for the good governance in the panchayat by involving women in panchayat activities, more participatory gram sabha etc.

Therefore, this paper deals with the problems faced by the dalit community in the village panchayat and changes that happened through dalit leadership. This leads to form objectives of this paper as:

- To know the different kinds of problems faced by the dalit community in Kuthambakkam village panchayat.
- To understand the changes that happened in the village panchayat and the role of dalit leadership.

Methodology

This paper adopted qualitative research approach as it focused on to understand the nature of dalit leadership and the changes which happened after the implementation of 73rd Amendment. The data and information about this phenomenon was collected through in-depth interviews (18), group discussion (2), observation etc. The unstructured interview was conducted with people between the age group of 30 years and above and the group discussion organised with women SHGs (Self Help Groups) members in the Kuthambakkam village panchayat. The observation has taken place through attending the panchayat meeting and staying in the village during the fieldwork.

The literature has explained the discrimination, struggles faced by dalit elected representatives in village panchayat. On the other hand, not much literature disseminating the knowledge on change made by dalit leaders in village panchayat was available. Thus, this paper would add knowledge in this direction.

Table 1

Geographical and Population Details of the Kuthambakkam Panchayat

Name of the Hamlet	*Caste of People Living*	*Families*	*Male*	*Female*	*Total*
Kuthambakkam	Idayar, Aasari, Amattan, Naidu, Muthaliyar	283	589	576	1165
Kuthambakkam South	Dalit (Paraiyar community)	353	842	810	1652
Kuthambakkam North	Dalit (Paraiyar community)	188	473	437	910
Ukkottai	Vanniyar and Dalit	76	150	143	293
Irulappalayam	Vanniyar	132	300	289	589
Kannadapalayam	Vanniyar, BC and MBC migrated people	43	180	172	352
Samathuvapuram	Iyar, Idayar, Naidu, Chettiyar, Achari, ST, Dalit	100	220	210	430
Total		1175	2754	2637	5391

Note: The above information was obtained from the village panchayat office in Kuthambakkam village on August 2013.

Kuthambakkam village panchayat is an agriculture-based village, situated in Poonamallee Block, Thiruvallur district, Tamil Nadu (which is 30 km away from Chennai). This village panchayat has seven hamlets, which is divided based on caste except Samathuvapuram (Table 1). This village panchayat has a population of 5,391, in which around fifty per cent population is from dalit[2] community.

Social Status of Dalits: Before 1994

Dalit people in Kuthambakkam village panchayat lived in poor social, economic condition before the implementation of 73rd Amendment. They lived with many other problems like poor education, illicit arrack etc.

Caste Practices: Like many other villages in India, caste discrimination including untouchability was practised in Kuthambakkam village panchayat. Geographically, these village hamlets are segregated on the basis of different castes. Dalit people were not allowed to enter the streets where the village upper caste people live. Particularly, two streets namely *Periya theru* (Periya street) and *Pappan theru* (Pappan street). Similarly, they were not allowed in the temples which are Kuthambakkam hamlet. However, this situation has started changing in late seventies and early eighties.

There were many reasons such as dalit movements, change in occupation for the change in the caste practices. In the late seventies, dalit movement had started in this region (Poonamallee). It questioned the untouchability practices and all kinds of discrimination practices that happened in this region and others. Adding to that dalit people have changed their occupation to produce illicit arrack from agriculture labour. Even though, dalit people's social condition remained poor.

Infrastructure and Basic Amenities: Dalit people live in two hamlets namely, Kuthmbakkam North and Kuthambakkam south (Table 1). They were deprived of good infrastructure facilities and basic amenities in the panchayat till 1996. Almost all of them were living in huts with weaved palm leaf roofs and mud walls. Also, two or three families stayed in one hut with no privacy. Especially, Kuthambakkam North hamlet is congested and geographically a small place. During rainy days the streets would get flooded with rainwater, and the people in North hamlet had to go to nearby panchayat for their shelter, till the rain-water was drained out.

Alongwith poor housing, dalit people were also deprived of other infrastructure facilities such as water, road, electricity, drainage etc. The inside roads and inter-hamlets laid by gravel was fully damaged. No proper roads were marked and the sides of the road was surrounded by bushes. People struggled to go on the road during rainy seasons as it was muddy. Similarly, the dalit hamlet did not have proper drinking water facilities. They had to get water from the well nearby.

Livelihood: The primary occupation of the Kuthambakkam village panchayat is agriculture. There was no other employment opportunity available in that village panchayat. Majority of dalit people were landless and wage labourers in the village panchayat. Muthaliyar community people were holding the majority of the land. Therefore, people from North and South hamlet worked in their land. As one 64-year old participant said, 'all the children would go to cattle rearing and elders goes and work in Muthaliyar's and Naidu's people land. We didn't have any land to do agriculture'.

However, dalit people who had small pieces of land have cultivated in their land. Though, it was much later. Some of them took land on lease and cultivated. However, this scene has started changing since late eighties. Many factors, such as shifting from agriculture to illicit arrack, industrialisation etc. are involved in the change. Majority of the dalit people were involved in the job of making and selling the illicit liquor. This had both positive and negative impact.

The positive aspect of the illicit arrack among dalit people was that it gave them a good income. Therefore, it had spread in the whole dalit hamlets. And they stopped going for agriculture work. This resulted in decrease on the dependence of Muthaliyar and Naidu community. Also, some of dalit people's economic level started increasing. Furthermore, this created nuisance to dalit people as well as the village.

Due to illicit arrack, fights among the people have increased. There was a similar situation in North hamlet as well. 'During the night time, there would be some shouting or problems always, whereas in Kuthambakkam, it would so silent' told by the participant from Kuthambakkam South. Because of the illicit arrack, this village panchayat became *karumpulli gramam* (Black Dot village) in the police records. Therefore, the life of dalit people was so miserable with no peace. However, people who were bribed came out. Thus, it was difficult to eradicate illicit arrack from this village. The production of illicit arrack affected education of the children very much.

Education Status: Dalit people were deprived of education due to various reasons such as poor socio-economic condition, lack of awareness of education, illicit arrack etc. One primary school was there in Kuthambakkam Hamlet (where Muthaliyar and Naidu community people live) since 1906. After that if they had to study, they had to go out of the village to pursue higher education. Later, one primary school has started in Kuthambakkam South hamlet in 1962.

Due to poverty, children from dalit community went for work as a *padi aal*[3] to Muthaliyar's and Naidu's house. Even the children who were sent to school, mostly failed in either primary or middle school and they would quit their education after that. On the other hand, very few of the children pursued higher studies (Graduation and above), despite their poor economic condition.

One such person, namely Elango shared, 'I was wearing good uniform but boys and girls were coming with torn trousers and skirts and they eat lunch for many days. I used to share my lunch with them. Also, we had to walk for 7 to 8 km every day in the eroded and unrepaired roads. This made us to remove the trousers and slippers every day to cross the water ponds in the midst of the roads.'

Moreover, illicit arrack was one of the other important things affecting education of dalit children in eighties and early nineties. The illicit arrack has increased the fights among families, which affected children's education. Then, the dropout students went to work of assisting in making illicit arrack and got money. Following that many of their friends stopped going to school and went to make illicit arrack. Thus, the education of the dalit children was greatly affected due to the illicit arrack. Even the panchayat which was there before the implementation of 73rd Amendment, has not done much for the development of dalit people.

Local Government before 1996: After the independence, Tamil Nadu government implemented panchayat in 1950s, as Tamil Nadu Panchayat Raj Act. However, the panchayat was not decentralised fully in terms of functions, finance etc. The seats like president, vice president and all the posts in Kuthambakkam village panchayat were occupied by the Muthaliyar and Naidu community people, because of their social and economic status. The posts of Village administrative officer and village assistant were also occupied by the same community people.

Later, in 1986, a candidate from dalit community had become a ward member in this panchayat. During that period, Elumalai muthaliyar, the then Kuthambakkam village president has done something in dalit hamlet in terms of gravel road, building for school in South hamlet, well for drinking water etc. In spite of all these activities the social and economic condition of the dalit people remained poor.

This was the situation of dalit people, while implementing the decentralised local governance in Tamil Nadu. Dalit people continued to struggle with many problems such as poverty, health issues, illicit arrack, low education status, infrastructure etc.

Social Change: Post-Decentralisation

After the enactment of 73rd Amendment of the Constitution of India, election for the decentralised local government was conducted in Tamil Nadu during 1996. Kuthambakkam village panchayat was one among them. The pinnacle was that the president post of Kuthambakkam village panchayat was reserved for Scheduled Caste candidate. Mr Elango was the first dalit panchayat president of that village panchayat. This political structure subsequently brought change in the lives of the dalits of the locality which can be seen in many aspects of the village such as infrastructure, education etc.

Infrastructural Change: The Panchayat in Kuthambakkam village has carried out many activities in order to improve the infrastructure facilities of dalit people as they were the most downtrodden. As mentioned in the above section (social status of dalit), majority of the people were living in huts, with broken roads, and no drainage facilities. But, after the implementation of decentralised panchayat, the panchayat had constructed concrete houses for dalit people through different central and state government schemes like Indira Awas Yojana (IAY) and Kalaignar group housing scheme. This made them dream of having a pucca house on their own. As a result of proper implementation of these schemes and programmes, Kuthambakkam turned into a hut-less hamlets.

In all these housing programmes, Samathuvapuram[4] is a unique one in many ways. This scheme, Periyar Ninaivu Samathuvapuram, was launched by Tamil Nadu government in the year 1997–98. It was implemented in Kuthambakkam village panchayat in 2000. Though, it was implemented all over

Tamil Nadu, the way it was constructed in Kuthambakkam village remained exceptional.

Materials like lime, laterite soil, cement and sand were used to construct good houses for people. Then, compressed mud block[5] made locally have been used to construct the houses which is made locally. Similarly, wood has been used to make doors and windows for the houses, whereas iron plates were used in other panchayats. The most unique thing in Samathuvapuram is 'twin house model' in which one wall will be common for two houses. In this, one house was given to Dalit family and the adjacent for other caste families such as, Idayar, Iyar, Naikkar, Chettiyar, Achari etc.

Many personalities such as Sahip Singh Varma and Vengaya Naidu had visited Samathuvapuram and stayed for a day. Also, often students from different educational institutions around India and other countries visit this place since it has become a model village for caste harmony. This scheme made many dalit families to live along with other caste group people equally.

Apart from housing facilities, all the streets of Kuthambakkam village panchayat have good concrete cement road. No only this, improvements continued for water, electricity, drain and sanitation, graveyard for all the hamlets and other infrastructure facilities. Eventually, dalit people's life has started changing. As one participant from dalit community said that, 'one could not say that this is dalit colony'.

Unlike many other village panchayats, this panchayat has not stopped only with infrastructure. It has done much more in education, governance, women empowerment and annihilation of illicit arrack from the village etc.

Change in Education: Illiteracy was high among dalits compared to many other castes in Kuthambakkam village panchayat. Panchayat took several initiatives to improve the education status of the village in terms of infrastructure as well as other facilities like computer, TV, fans, etc. Though, the fund for education in village panchayat is limited.

Adding to that, Elango, village president (1996–2006), formed a Trust, namely, Trust for Village Self Governance (TVSG) to help the activities of the panchayat. Through this trust, he has helped the student's in terms of bags, books, uniform and paying for their school/college fees. Most importantly, he has worked to eradicate the illicit arrack, one of the reason for student's dropouts from village. He went to every household and created the awareness on importance of education. Later, other members from the panchayat also supported for that cause.

Annihilation of Illicit Arrack: There was a period in Kuthambakkam village panchayat history, where majority of dalit families were involved in production and distribution of illicit liquor. As a result, they have faced lot of problems and also could not lead a normal life. The trigger for eradication of illicit liquor to this village came in the form of implementation of Panchayat raj institutions. Elango went and spoke to the families involved in that business. Even though, Elango (former president) got opposition and threat from section of this population, he took many initiatives[6] and eradicated the production of illicit arrack.

Decentralised Local Governance: Kuthambakkam village panchayat has taken many efforts in bringing changes among the lives of the people from marginalised communities. The role of Elango, the first two terms (1996–2006) panchayat president, was the crucial one when all the changes have happened.

Elango: The Change Maker of the Panchayat

Elango was the first on in the village who went out for higher education. His family's education and economic background was not every appreciable but he had the thrust to change the condition of his family and community. He mentioned that, 'I was born in a middle class family among the downtrodden of this village (south hamlet). I was the only boy who got the chance to go to Chennai and pursue my higher education. I witnessed poverty in my own eyes. Dalit women used to come and get some food from my mother.'

He was shocked to visualise the condition of Chennai since the village he hailed from had very less infrastructure and development. Though the distance between the two locations is just 40 kilometres, the difference in social and economic condition was vast. In order to bring change, he started organising people with the help of his friends. He started small activities such as tuition centres for dalit children and created awareness on effects of illicit liquor.

After his higher education, in 1983, he joined the Central Electro Chemical Research Laboratory as an assistant scientist. He was working with Kundrakudi Adigalar in order to make Kundrakudi as a model village. Also he was inspired by Adigalar work. Elango shared, 'After seeing my involvement and dedication, one day Adigalar told 'when you show such interest on this village, why could not you try to do something for your village'. I told that I wanted to work for science and technology and along with that I could do something to my village. But, he quoted, 'there are plenty of Elango who will take care of science and technology, but Elango are not available for working in their villages. Even one Elango can make a big change and it will become the opening. This had penetrated in my mind.'[7]

Those words made him quit that job and start working for his village. Subsequently, the panchayat election came in the year of 1996 and he contested and won the election. His previous experience came in handy while deciding activities or vision for his village. He was the village president for consecutively two terms (1996–2006).

Initiatives and innovative: His first task after winning the election was to prepare the development plan for the village panchayat. He understood the main objective of panchayat, as he mentioned' 'The social and economic development of the marginalised communities is one of the main focuses of the village panchayat.' The negotiation took place at various junctures with the ward members from other caste groups. The activities were selected from each ward based on the needs of the people and priorities were allocated to those activities based on the importance.

The finalised development plan was then discussed in the grama sabha and approval was obtained. The panchayat council meetings and grama sabha meetings were the approval bodies of this village panchayat. Many initiatives and innovative methods were implemented to improve the dalit people hamlets, in terms of housing, health, employment, eradication of illicit arrack and education.

The innovation methods were introduced at various levels. In housing, the panchayat brought innovation in areas such as cost-effective design, use of different bricks, quality materials and providing livelihood to local people. Samathuvapuram scheme is implemented in this village panchayat to reduce caste differences and bring harmony. The land allocated to Samathuvapuram scheme was encroached by some powerful localities. The village panchayat, then, intervened and got back the land.

Similarly, the schemes such as IAY and Group House did not have sufficient budget allocation to construct a quality house. Therefore, president helped them either financially or materially to complete the houses. Likewise, panchayat constructed drainage channel with waste materials, since the money allocated was less.

The president found innovative ways to reduce the cost of construction and get contribution from various stakeholders. He received donations from outsiders for completing the work. The labour part was contributed by the local people. The panchayat also found cost-effective models for street lights and renovation of ponds. The innovations and inventiveness of this sort saved lots of village panchayat budget and used them for important needs.

Trust for Village Self-Governance: Mr Elango formed a NGO called Trust for village Self-Governance (TVSG) in the year of 2002 to support the panchayat activities. He mobilised additional funds required for the developmental activities of the panchayat through this NGO. He also provided livelihood opportunities through various activities such as burner making, first-aid kit preparation, and small handlooms. More than thirty women are working in those units. TVSG also works for taking education to children of Kuthambakkam village by organising spoken English, computer literacy, evening tuition etc.

Adding to education, Elango has created panchayat academy to disseminate the knowledge to other panchayat leaders who are willing to bring change in their village level. He provides training for panchayat representatives from other villages. Apart from these activities, he is also forming SHGs for women empowerment.

Transparency, Accountability and Responsibility: The good governance consists of characteristics such as transparency, accountability and responsibility. These factors are important in the changes that happened in this village. The works of this panchayat were carried out in a more transparent manner. Similarly, the panchayat was more accountable to the people. And the representatives, especially the president took responsibility in improving the condition of the hamlets and made it as a model village panchayat.

Grama sabha played an important role in disseminating the information to the people. The beneficiaries were selected in grama sabha, contracts were finalised in grama sabha and final decisions on all the actions were taken based on the opinion of the people.

Gopal, a residence of south hamlet told that 'Elango often visited our hamlet to check the needs of the people, cleanliness of the streets and garbage, road facility, water distribution and cleanliness of the water tanks. He gave money to poor and elderly.' Similarly, Mani, a resident of south hamlet told that, 'People used to fight to get ration from the ration shop. President used to come to ration shop and sit there. Then, no one will fight. They get things quietly and go home. Even, if any one from his family comes to get ration, they has to stand in the line.'

Many changes have taken place in Kuthambakkam village panchayat under the Mr Elango's charismatic and dynamic leadership. However, his leadership got changed in the third term (2006), as it was reserved for general woman. Now, there is no any, new initiatives taking place in Kuthambakkam village panchayat. This resulted in diminishing of people's participation in grama sabha's.

Conclusion

The 73rd Amendment of the Indian Constitution is an important milestone in the institutional reform in India. This gives the opportunity for marginalised community to take part in the political and decision-making process at the village level for their empowerment. Kuthambakkam is an example for that. Through the dalit leadership, many changes in terms of social, economic and political have taken place in the village. However, will the changes happen in the other village panchayat is a big question. There are several factors which involved in the changes such as, assertiveness of Dalit community, Charismatic leadership and more than fifty per cent of the population being Dalit.

Notes

1. Local governance in the village panchayat level is called as Panchayat Raj.
2. Here, Dalit refers to the Paraiyar community people in Kuthambakkam village panchayat.
3. Padi aal means sending the children to work to get some goods as a wage for his/her work in which padi is an instrument to measure the goods like paddy, millets, etc.
4. This scheme is a Tamil Nadu government scheme, which aimed at spatial equality. Samthuvapuram means the place of equality. The information has been accessed from http://tnrd.gov.in/schemes/st_samathuvapuram.html on January 2014.
5 It is a kind of brick comparatively huge, strong and cost effective.
6. The initiatives are door to door campaign about the ill effects of the illicit arrack, organising awareness programmes, inviting the police (commissioner) and creating awareness among the people about the punishments and rehabilitation measures, which also includes creating alternate employments for the people who are involved in making the illicit arrack.
7. It has been taken from the document shared by Mr Elango.

References

Devakumar, J. (2007), 'Caste Clashes and Dalits Rights Violations in Tamil Nadu', *Social Scientist*, Vol. 35, No. 11, pp. 39–54.

Dorairaj, S. (2013), 'Disempowered Dalits', *Frontline*, Vol. 30, No. 7, pp. 35–37.

Goel, S.L. and S. Rajneesh (2009), *Panchayati Raj in India: Theory and Practice*, Deep and Deep Publications, New Delhi.

Manor, J. (2010), 'Local Governance', in Niraja Gopal Jayal and Pratap Bhanu Mehta (eds), *The Oxford Companion to Politics in India*, Oxford University Press, New Delhi, pp. 61–79.

Mathew, George (2003), 'Panchayati Raj Institutions and Human Rights in India', *Economic and Political Weekly*, Vol. 38, No. 2, pp. 155–62.

Mathew, George and Ramesh C. Nayak (1996), 'Panchayats at Work: What It Means for the Oppressed?', *Economic and Political Weekly*, Vol. 31, No. 27, pp. 1765–71.

Palanithurai, G. (2013), *Dalits and Dalit Representatives in Rural Local Governance: Voices from the Field*, Concept Publishing Company, New Delhi.

Singh, Karunakar (2012), 'Panchayati Raj Institutions and Social Inclusion of Dalits', *Social Action*, Vol. 62, No. 3, pp. 74–86.

Tanabe, A. (2007), 'Toward Vernacular Democracy: Moral Society and Post-postcolonial Transformation in Rural Orissa, India', *American Ethnologist*, Vol. 34, No. 3, pp. 558–74.

Thorat, Sukhadeo (2009), *Dalits in India: Search for Common Destiny*, Sage Publications, New Delhi.

Vishwanathan, S. (2012), 'Constitutionally Empowered Act', *The Hindu*, June 18.

Part IV

Gender Issues and Empowerment of Women through PRIs

14

Decentralisation and Women's Development in India[1]

An Institutional Perspective

V. Rama Krishna

The idea of local self-government had existed in India even in ancient times. Even if we accept its beginning as an organisational concept with the Ripon's resolution it is more than a century and two decades old. In its tumultuous career it has seen many ups and downs. In spite of a formal inauguration by the Prime Minister Jawaharlal Nehru in 1959, after the Balvant Rai Mehta committee recommendation in 1957, these institutions could not take proper roots in the country. Some of the scholars even declared that Panchayati Raj Institutions (PRIs) were like failed God. The Janata Government appointed the Ashok Mehta committee to rejuvenate the PRIs. But the 73rd and 74th Amendment, which were passed in 1992 and came into force in April 1994, have virtually revolutionised the idea of local self-government – both rural and urban – by bestowing constitutional status on them. These amendments were passed in the light of the experience of the Local-Self Governing Institutions in India. They have made a sincere attempt to overcome the limitations faced by these institutions. The paper discusses PRIs for the rural areas, created after a great and prolonged struggle, have given rural dwellers their self-governance structures and a fair degree of empowerment. Further, it elaborates about the participatory involvement of citizens and accountability of local self-governance structures which are almost totally absent. Finally, the paper made an attempt to comprehend the revolutionary changes brought about by the 73rd Amendment, where it suffers from some serious limitations and offers a charter for more formally recognised structures that could be organised on a wider scale.

Nature of Federalism in India

The Indian Constitution declares that India shall be a Union of States. However, India is not a true federal state with states coming together to form the Union. The Parliament may by law establish new states on such terms and conditions as it thinks fit (Article 2). Also Parliament may, by law, increase or diminish the area of any state, or alter the boundaries or the name of any state, or separate or unite two or more states or parts of States or unite any territory to a part of any State (Article 3). The only check on this absolute power of Parliament is that any Bill for altering a state must be referred to the legislature of the state(s) affected, for expressing its views within a specified period (Article 3). The views of the state legislature are not binding on the Parliament. In effect, the states are administrative territories to be altered at the will of the Parliament, and theoretically all states could be united into a single state.

However, in reality, the Parliament has acted with great restraint and circumspection when it came to formation of new states or altering existing states. In India's vast, complex and plural polity with enormous linguistic diversity, formation of states is an intensely political, and often, a highly contentious issue. Most of today's states have been formed as part of the linguistic reorganisation of states between 1953 and 1956. In addition, the North-Eastern region saw the formation of six new States. The merger of Sikkim and conversion of some Union territories into states accounted for the other new States. Altogether, there are now 25 states in India, each State having its own political executive, Legislature and permanent bureaucracy. In addition, there are seven Union territories directly governed by the Union government. There have been demands from time to time for a fresh reorganisation of States, but on account of the complexity and contentious nature of the effort, no government or political party seriously pursued it. Recently, there are efforts to carve out three new States from the three large states of Uttar Pradesh, Bihar and Madhya Pradesh. There is also a proposal to confer statehood on the Union territory of Delhi, the national capital.

Decentralisation in India

A vast country like India cannot be run only through two-tiers of government as discussed above. States in India are as large as independent countries of Europe. In terms of population, Uttar Pradesh is bigger than Russia, Maharashtra is about as big as Germany. Many of these States are internally very diverse in terms of dialects or local languages spoken, in terms of eating habits and cultures. So, federal power sharing in India needs another tier of government, below that of the State governments. This is the rationale for decentralisation of power. The basic idea behind decentralisation is that there are a large number of problems and issues which are best settled at the local level. People have better knowledge of problems in their localities. They also have better ideas on where to spend money and how to manage things more efficiently. Besides, at the local level it is possible for the people to directly participate in decision-making. This helps to inculcate a habit of democratic participation. Local government is the best way to realise one important principle of democracy, namely local self-government.

Similarly, local government bodies exist for urban areas as well. Municipalities are set up in towns. Big cities are constituted into municipal corporations. Both municipalities and municipal corporations are controlled by elected bodies consisting of people's representatives. Municipal chairperson is the political head of the municipality. In a municipal corporation such an officer is called the mayor.

The beginning of the idea of decentralisation in India as an organisational concept can be traced to Ripon's Resolution in 1882 which aimed at involving the 'intelligent class' of public-spirited men in the management of rural areas under the British rule. In the years to come district boards and taluka boards were set up with nominated members to look after health, roads and education. But this effort did not succeed in making villages as basic unit of local self-government. A resolution of 1918 restated that the objective of self-government is to train people in the management of their own local affairs. The District Board Act of 1922 led to the reconstitution of the Boards. They were entrusted with the responsibilities of road maintenance, tree planting, hospitals, schools and drainage etc. Panchayat Act of 1920 was conceived as local courts and was completely judicial in character. As there was hardly any devolution of finances and responsibilities, its role as the local unit of administration, development and rural upliftment remained non-functional.

Among the Indian leaders, Mahatma Gandhi made a very strong plea for village republics. Article 40 under the Directive Principles of State Policy included in the part IV of the constitution, advised the government to take steps to organise village panchayats and endow them with such powers and authority which would enable them to function as units of self-government. State governments were supposed to enact appropriate legislation for this purpose. The Indian planners and policy makers launched a multipurpose Community Development Programme (CDPs) with the objective of improving the conditions of the rural masses. This programme aimed at training and sending development personnel Block Development Officers (BDO), Extension Officers and Village Level Workers (VLWs) into villages. This group of officers was supposed to act as agents of change. They were expected to galvanise rural masses by encouragement, demonstration and offer of material assistance. The CDPs failed to achieve the desired objectives. The Planning Commission requested a committee under the chairmanship of Balvant Rai Mehta to develop the ideas for a system of democratic decentralisation which would anchor the rural developmental efforts. The Balvant Rai Mehta Committee Report came up with a number of recommendations that were incorporated in the panchayat legislation of the various states in the following years. This committee recommended democratic decentralisation with a provision of a three-tier structure (village-block-district).

It also recommended for transfer of resources and responsibilities and channelisation of funds for various developmental programmes through the three-tier system. This report generated opportunity for launching block planning in states like Andhra Pradesh and Tamil Nadu and district planning in others like Maharashtra and Gujarat. In the 1960s, Panchayati Raj Institutions (PRIs) were portrayed as a God that failed. One of the main reasons of failure was the sabotage by state politicians who were not enthusiastic about devolving powers to the district level or below. They were apprehensive that PRIs with real powers may pose a threat to their power and influence. Towards the end of the 1960s when Indira Gandhi was donning a progressive garb and wished to implement land reforms, it was argued that PRIs could not be involved as they were dominated by the upper caste and landed elements.

The 1960s also witnessed the advent of the Green Revolution that necessitated centralised planning and came in conflict with the ideals of decentralisation on which PRIs were based. Since rural areas in many parts of the country were still under the hands of feudal landed interest, government sponsored inputs for ushering the Green Revolution could have been monopolised by them. Both central and state government had started bypassing and thus undermining the authority and significance of the PRIs during this period. Central government created its own administrative machinery for implementing many of Indira Government programmes such as Small Farmers' Development Agency, Drought Prone Area Programme, Integrated Rural Development Programme and National Rural Employment Programme, aiming at economic justice. The lack of resources, absence of coordination, dependence on district development staff, lack of delegation of effective authority, domination by the higher castes and better off sections of society had rendered the PRIs ineffective and purposeless as institutions of decentralisation and development. By the middle of 1970s governments both at the centre and in the states had become indifferent to the PRIs. They had become defunct; elections to these institutions were not being held and at most of the places the sitting councils were either dissolved or suspended (Narayan, 2004).

Local Self-Government and Women Empowerment

With the 73rd and 74th Constitutional Amendments in 1992, we completed the federal puzzle in our country, creating units of local self-government at the rural and urban levels. While there are still enormous challenges in implementing the legal provisions with regard to rural decentralisation, tremendous energy is being expended within many state governments to solidify this process. Issues such as untying of funds, streamlining of programmes, capacity building and training of gram panchayat members are among the hottest potatoes being tossed around in state legislatures. So, in this journey towards a healthy federalist governmental arrangement, the patient instrumentalism of policy-makers seems to be working fairly well. While there are gaps in intergovernmental institutions that can oversee and regulate the interchanges, given the magnitude of the local government initiative in the last decade to expand the base of the third level, it seems that enough is going well. As George Mathew says: 'the panchayats districts and below are now treated as the third stratum of governance. ...' Today in India if there is a strong centre it is not by virtue of its powers over other units but because the lower units – states, districts, blocks, villages – are powerful. This is exactly the opposite of what India started with. Thus, one can say that strong regional and state level political parties have strengthened India's democracy and federal character (Mathew, 2000).

The lopsided approach can be traced even to the drafting of the two seminal pieces of legislation that have given rural and urban local governments their current positions – the 73rd and 74th Constitutional Amendments respectively – and perhaps explains the difference in attitude that people in government have towards these two forms of local government even today. The 73rd Amendment was the culmination of over four decades of struggle and intense debate by a range of players: three generations of Gandhians, advocates of rural self-government, and champions of three-tier federalism. This saw numerous initiatives for promoting Panchayati Raj Institutions as well as two national committees separated by two decades – the Balwantrai Mehta committee in 1957, and the Asoka Mehta committee in 1977. Associated with this energy – possibly because of it – there is also a great deal of documentary evidence on the evolution of rural decentralisation in India. The mid-1980s saw the crystallising of some of this energy: for example, one of the recommendations of the National Commission on Urbanisation (NCU) was to suggest that Article 40 of the directive principles of state policy – requiring states to organise panchayats as units of local self-government in rural areas – be expanded to include urban areas as well.

And without citizen participation, federalism is like a batsman without a partner at the crease: decentralisation of what is called the '3 Fs' – funds, functions and functionaries – needs to be accompanied by accountability as well. This accountability ought to be directly to citizens, rather than to some other level of government. One form of such accountability is to provide formal opportunity for citizens to participate in local governance (Hosp, 2003). Citizen engagement is one of the critical success factors for federalism in a young democracy such as India's local governments act as a political kindergarten to educate the citizen (Jean Drèze and Amartya Sen, 2002). In the absence of this, the urban voter is not only disconnected from government, but also illiterate about the politics of change. So today, when we are often confronted with a cynical citizenry, it begs the question: what comes first, the indifference or the disempowerment?

According to Riker (1975) federalism is an outcome of rational bargain among various constituents. The bargain may be for political or economic gains. In the political bargain, the constituents give up political autonomy for security from external threat. The economic bargain is to enable a common market and to ensure optimal provision of public services by reaping economies of scale and catering to diverse preferences. However, while striking the bargain, the constituents try to preserve their valued identity and seek special status. Motivation for special status may be purely for expanding economic opportunities and securing freedom from exploitation by larger and more powerful members of the federation. The objective may be purely political – of enhancing freedom and representation to constituents or to maximise political power and influence. It may also be cultural or religious – of preserving group identities. It may simply be a means of accommodating diverse group interests within a unified framework.

Polly Datta's (2007) article notes that though it was an early starter in decentralisation programmes, West Bengal seems to have failed to keep pace with the resurgence of Panchayati Raj Institutions (PRIs) in India during the 1990s and is now lagging behind other states. The Mukarji and Bandyopadhyay Committee found in their evaluation report in 1993 that the PRIs of West Bengal were suffering from conceptual and programmatic constraints. Inability of the state to perceive the PRIs as self-government institutions was denoted as a conceptual constraint which, the Committee felt, eventually led to a programmatic constraint. His article demonstrates that the conceptual limitation originally identified by the 1993 Committee appears to be legitimised in the very conceptualisation of the 'feasibility frontier' offered by the Left Front Government of West Bengal.

Citizen Participation

From a constitutional standpoint, there has always been a bias towards the rural voter, whether it is the directive principles of state policy or the 73rd Constitutional Amendment. While the voter was a central figure in the 73rd Amendment, in the 74th Amendment on urban decentralisation, there is no mention of the phrase 'a body consisting of persons registered in the electoral rolls'. Even in Article 243S, which discusses the ward committee(s), the amendment is still engaged with institutional arrangements rather than recognising the centrality of the registered voter, as in the case of rural decentralisation.[2] These constitutional amendments have percolated down to state laws for rural and urban decentralisation that mirror these biases (URL: EPW).

The structure above solves many problems of urban governance described in the earlier sections of this document, as detailed below: It will give formal voice to every voter to participate in issues of local governance, removing the lopsided treatment of the rural and urban voters that has prevailed since the 73rd and 74th Constitutional Amendments were passed. The evidence suggests that gram sabha meetings 'seem to be a forum used by some of the most disadvantaged groups in the village – landless, illiterates and scheduled castes/tribes. This suggests that these groups find the gram sabha useful and that gram sabha meetings may play some role in moving policy in a direction favoured by these groups'. The same could be true of urban area sabhas as well, possibly solving an issue of elite capture in urban planning and public expenditure. The study finds correlation between levels of awareness of the gram sabha and levels of participation. This higher awareness also has another possible effect: how it changes the mental attitude, from emasculation to empowerment. Irrespective of whether a voter participates or not, she now has the knowledge of the opportunity to participate. This needs to be measured as well, in terms of what voters begin to feel about being 'empowered', irrespective of their actual participation. The gram sabha findings also observed that participation from women is lower in rural areas. If anything, the hypothesis could be that not only will the sabha concept work well in urban areas and generate socially equitable outcomes, but that these sabhas could also be a more significant presence in local governance issues than in rural areas, and possibly more successfully address universal participation issues across caste, economic status and gender.

Inverted Pyramid: Marginal Role of Stakeholders (Women)

In the ultimate analysis, all power in democracy is vested in the people, who are the true sovereigns. This presupposes that any power transferred to any representative government should be only to the extent that people cannot directly manage on a day-to-day basis for reasons of convenience. In any case, such power should be exercised as close to the people as possible. Only such powers a local government cannot, for reasons of convenience and coordination, exercise locally should be transferred to a larger tier of local government or a State, and only those that cannot be exercised by the State must be transferred to the Union. Unless power is really transferred to people, Indian democracy will continue to be illusory, and people will have no role or participation in governance. Only when power is vested in stakeholders and local government can people understand the true meaning of vote, and use it as a precision tool to judge their representatives. Only then will sensitive, sensible and effective leadership emerge from the grassroots to build a truly democratic, strong India capable of fulfilling its potential in a substantial measure.

Neglected Local Self-Governance

In all our debate on federalism over the past 50 years, the most neglected aspect is local self-governance. There cannot be true federalism without the local people having near-complete control over their destinies through their elected governments or empowered stake-holders' groups over all matters of day-to-day concern to them. The locally elected governments at all levels, viz., village, town, city, sub-district or district must be completely autonomous and must be recognised as tiers of self-governance on par with the Union and the States. They must have their own local legislatures to deal with subjects under their jurisdiction and their own elected executives. The local bureaucracy must be totally responsible to the local elected governments alone. Just as the Union-State relations are highly skewed, local self-governance has been either non-existent, or where it exists, has been severely eroded by States.

The much-talked-about 73rd and 74th Amendments to the Constitution of India are but very hesitant initial steps in the direction of true democratisation of our polity. These amendments, with the new 11 and 12 Schedules in the Constitution, now make constitution and periodic election of local governments mandatory. They also prevent dismissal of local governments en masse on political grounds whenever a new party ascends to power in the States. The Constitution also provides for appointment of a State Election Commission in each State as an independent institution to conduct and monitor elections to local governments. A State Finance Commission is appointed in every state to recommend to the State government the distribution of resources between the State and local governments (Narayan, 2004).

These provisions, incorporated in 1992, are long overdue and salutary. However, several States have shown little inclination to implement these provisions in true democratic spirit. Elections have not been held for local bodies for years despite the constitutional prescription. Their reluctance to constitute local governments is predictable, given the culture of centralisation in the country, and unwillingness to share power with local tiers of government. Eventually, all States have to fall in line and conform to the constitutional directives. However, the real lacunae in local self-governance stem from the inadequate and feeble provisions even in the 73rd and 74th Amendments. The 11th Schedule lists 29 subjects that may be entrusted to the Panchayats (rural local governments) by the State Legislature, at its absolute discretion. Similarly, 12th Schedule lists 18 subjects for urban local governments. As we have seen, the 7th Schedule which contains List-II pertaining to States guarantees that the State has full legislative and executive powers except in respect of emergency powers etc. However, the extent of powers of local governments even in respect of subjects listed in the 11th and 12th Schedules is entirely dependent on the State Legislature, and they have no independent powers. Again, predictably few States are willing to part with real control of these subjects. In effect, the local governments have titular role in governance and all effective power vests in States.

As of now, the State Finance Commissions, even where appointed, could not make much headway. Except in one or two States, there is no serious effort to devolve adequate resources to the local governments. Most crucially, the local bureaucracy is appointed and controlled by the State governments. Thus, neither authority nor resources are available at the local level.

Conclusion

All successful plural democracies followed this route of true federalism and local self-governance. The examples of the United States, Germany, and Australia, among others, demonstrate the need for people's empowerment and decentralised governance. From the foregoing, major reforms are critical for the future of Indian democracy.

A review of Union-State relations and far-reaching governance reforms leading to transfer of more subjects to the States, vesting the Union with certain special powers for preserving the unity and integrity of the nation; the institution of elected Governors in States with a fixed tenure of office; repeal of Article 356 with suitable alternative powers to the Union to defend the Constitution; transfer of effective control of All-India Services to States; and elimination of discretion in all matters of fiscal devolution are critical for successful federalism and effective governance. Equally importantly genuine local governments with an inviolable and clearly defined legislative and executive jurisdiction, effective control of local bureaucracy and adequate and non-discretionary fiscal devolution, and direct empowerment of stakeholders over local institutions and public services – these are among the major initiatives needed to correct the serious distortions and imbalances in our plural democracy. Our state structure today has become an obstacle to such empowerment of people, and creation of a true democracy in which freedom is enlarged, self-governance is real and meaningful, empowerment is genuine, rule of law is possible, and above all self-correcting mechanisms for governance are available.

India stands at the inflection point of two critical trends: the increasing importance of local governments, and a critical mass of urbanisation. Both these have significant implications for governance outcomes on a range of important quality-of-life issues for citizens. Citizen participation is not just a moral argument; it is a strong accountability mechanism for local governments. While rural participation is imbedded in the Constitution, citizen involvement in rural areas is still very indirect. This needs to be urgently corrected.

Notes

1. Directive principles of state policy: Article 40, which states 'Organisation of village panchayats. The state shall take steps to organize village panchayats and endow them with such powers and authority as may be necessary to enable them to function as units of self-government.' Article 243b of the 73rd amendment which states "Gram Sabha' means a body consisting of persons registered in the electoral rolls relating to a village comprised within the area of panchayat at the village level'.
2. Article 243S which states '(ii) the legislature of a state may, by law, make provision with respect to (a) the composition and the territorial area of a wards committee; (b) the manner in which the seats in a wards committee shall be filled'.

References

Datta, Polly (2007), 'Devolution of Financial Power to Local Self-Governments: The "Feasibility Frontier" in West Bengal', *South Asia Research*, Vol. 27, No. 1, pp. 105–24.

Drèze, Jean and Amartya Sen (2002), *India: Development and Participation*, Oxford University Press: Delhi.

EPW. http://www.janaagraha.org/core/epw_ramesh_ramanathan-fdcp.pdf (accessed on 30 July 2009).

Hosp, Gerald (2003), 'Fiscal Federalism for Emerging Economies: Lessons from Switzerland?', *Publius: The Journal of Federalism*, Vol. 31, No. 1, pp. 1–21.

Mathew, George (2000), 'Democracy at Work: Evolving Federalism through Political Representation in Socio-Cultural Pluralism', monograph presented at the Conference on 'Cooperative Federalism, Globalisation and Democracy', Brasilia, 9–11 May.

Narayan, Jayaprakash (2004), Loksatta Study in Andhra Pradesh, available on their web site: www.loksatta.org. Also confirmed by Janaagraha in a sample study of two polling booths in Bangalore during the 2004 elections, pp. 1–8.

Riker, William (1975), 'Federalism', in Fred I. Greenstein and Nelson W. Polsby (eds), *Handbook of Political Science*, Vol. 5, Addison-Wesley, Reading, MA.

15

Empowerment of Women through Participation in Local Government in Maharashtra

Ruby Ojha

Participation of disadvantaged segments of the population in the process of development ensures their well-being. Mainstreaming women through their active involvement in the formulation and implementation of policies is acknowledged as a precondition for achieving equitable development of the society in any developing country. This process of the advancement of women is possible only when women's equal participation in political life is encouraged at all levels. This is required not only for simple justice or democracy but as a necessary condition for women's interests to be taken care of.

Throughout the world, the power relations that shape social, political, economic and cultural life prevent women from participating fully in all areas of their lives, whether it is in the home, or in the public arena. While women's dedicated efforts to challenge the status quo have allowed more women to reach positions of power in recent years, but they continue to be underrepresented in all areas of decision-making. They still face significant barriers to their full and equal participation in the structures and institutions which govern their lives.

Empowerment is a process, though the result of the process may also be termed empowerment. But more specifically, the outcome of empowerment should manifest itself as distribution of power between individuals, genders, groups, classes, castes, races, ethnic groups or nations. Empowerment means the transformation of structures of subordination, through radical changes in law, property rights, control over women's labour and bodies, and the institutions that reinforce and perpetuate male domination (Batliwala, 1993).

One of the strategies to empower women and to overcome barriers preventing her equal participation in decision-making process is to allow her to obtain political power. Politics still continues to be a male bastion where self-made women are the exceptions rather than the rule. There can be no true democracy, no true people's participation in governance and development without equal participation of women and men.

Objective

Objective of the paper is to find whether encouraging women in local self-government through reservation has played a proactive role in empowering them as decision-makers and by their very presence demanding their rights.

Methodology

The paper will take an account of available literature on the subject i.e. published books, reports, research works, journals and newspapers including field studies. It will also review the experience of the authors of field-based study in a few talukas of Maharashtra in the form of case studies.

Local Government

73rd and 74th Amendment of the Indian Constitution, 1993, in a three-tier panchayat system constituted in every state, ensures reservation of seats for Scheduled Castes (SCs) and Scheduled Tribes (STs), in proportion to their total population in a panchayat area, and one-third of these seats for women in the directly elected seats of members in all panchayats. The offices of Chairpersons in the panchayats at all levels are reserved for the SCs/STs and women as the State legislature may decide, provided that not less than one-third of the Chairpersons' positions are reserved for women.

This reservation has opened a new chapter in the history of democratic decentralisation in India. It has helped in devolving power and giving opportunities to the disadvantaged people and women at the grassroots level to express their voice in the decision-making process. The 73rd and 74th constitutional amendments also revitalised the local government in rural and urban areas by granting special representation to women so that they have their share of power and responsibility too.

As a result, more than a million elected women representatives are present today in the institutions of local governance in rural and urban India. Thus, the social and economic opportunities available to these women, particularly to those belonging to socially disadvantaged groups such as SCs and STs, is an extraordinary phenomenon which is there in spite of otherwise terribly poor human development indicators of Indian women. Reservation has created an opportunity to take the feminist discourse ahead to enhance the qualities of women and to attain the benefits of feminist leadership in local governance.

Scope of Elected Women's Participation in Maharashtra

Maharashtra is situated between the latitude of 150°33′ S to 220°07′ N and approximately from longitude 720°21′ W to 810°20′ E. Spread over an area of about 308,000 square km, Maharashtra is the third largest state in India. The population of the state is recorded 11,23,72,972 in 2011 Census. In terms of population Maharashtra is the second largest State in the country with about 9.29 per cent of the country's population. Male population is 5,83,61,397 and female population consist of 5,40,11,575. The sex ratio is against the women as per 1,000 male there are 946 female.

The three tiers of panchayat system are spread across the state of Maharashtra and the e-panchayat services are made available for the employees/users and citizens across the state. The deployment envisages coverage of 34 Zilha Parishads, 351 Panchayat Samities and 28,006 Gram Panchayats to bridge the digital divide and further socio-economic opportunities for its citizens. Maharashtra cabinet has increased the women's quota from 33 per cent as per the 73rd and 74th Amendment to 50 per cent seats in local self-government bodies. The State Election Commission is implementing the Kranti Jyoti scheme to make women representatives competent to handle governance.

Even before the 73rd and 74th Amendment, which made 33 per cent reservation for women mandatory in the country, women in Karnataka, Andhra Pradesh and Maharashtra had been contesting elections and participating in panchayats. The oldest known all-women panchayat that held office was in Nimbut village in Pune district of Maharashtra (1963–68). Three states – Orissa, West Bengal and Maharashtra – conducted elections with 33 per cent reservation for women immediately after the 73rd Amendment. Bihar was the first state to offer 50 per cent reservation for women in panchayats in 2005, following which Uttarakhand, Himachal Pradesh, Madhya Pradesh and Rajasthan also announced 50 per cent reservation to be implemented in the panchayat election in early-2010. Kerala also announced 50 per cent reservation for women in panchayats and other local bodies.

Reservation for women in Maharashtra has provided an opportunity to change the face of political leadership. This has also given many women a greater understanding of the working of politics. The social horizons of the members have also widened. This is a welcome change to have understanding and tolerance towards the members of other religions, particularly in a country like India where there is diversity of religions and castes. Women have gained a sense of empowerment by asserting control over resources, offices and most of all by challenging men. They have got a sense of satisfaction and wish fulfilment.

The extent of women participation in local governments in Maharashtra is given in Table 1.

The table suggests that in last eight years, percentage of Gram Panchayat Women Members has increased from 33.33 per cent to 49.90 per cent. This indicates full implementation of 50 per cent reservation for women policy of the government. While the mandatory provisions of the Constitution regarding elections and reservations are adhered to in all the States, the devolution of powers and resources to Panchayats from the States has been highly uneven across States. As per the Panchayat Devolution Index (Alok, 2013) which is prepared using 26 indicators drawn from Framework, Functions, Finances, Functionaries, Capacity Building and Accountability, Maharashtra is holding the number one position in 2012–13.

Table 1

Evidence of Women Participation in Local Government in Maharashtra

Particulars	*Statistics*	
	2006	*2013*
Total no. of Districts	33	34
Total no. of Zilha Parishad Members (District Office)	1951	1955
Total no. of Zilha Parishad Women Members	658	661
Chairmen of Zilha Parishad	33	33
Women Chairperson of Zilha Parishad	11	15
Total no. of Panchayat Samiti (Block Office)	349	351
Total no. of Gram Panchayats	28,553	28,006
Total no. of Gram Panchayat Members	2,32,644	2,03,203
Total no. of Gram Panchayat Women Members	77,548	1,01,466
Percentage of Gram Panchayat Women Members	(33.33)	(49.9%)
Chairmen of Gram Panchayat	28,553	32,463
Women Chairperson of Gram Panchayat	9,487	12,773

Source: 1. http://www.wedo.org/wp-content/uploads/women-local-self-governance-in-indian-context.doc
2. http://ruralnic.in/sites/downloads/IRDR/10.%20Panchayati%20Raj%20Institution%20PRI.xls

Case Studies

1. *Grampanchayat in Sangamner Taluka of Ahmednagar District in Maharashtra* finds that due to reservation for women in local governments under the provisions of 73rd Constitutional Amendment Act, a new set of women representatives have come into gram panchayat. Reservation has created a space for women's needs within the structural framework of politics and legitimised women issues. But this affirmative action of reservation has not been successful in ensuring 'Proper and effective representation' of women in Panchayats.

In order to assess the effectiveness of political empowerment and level of Political participation of rural women, a micro study was carried out at Sangamner Block of Ahmednagar District of Maharashtra (Benke, 2011). Here the number of total Villages was 171, total Gram Panchayats were 141, total Mahila Sarpanches Reserve–30 Open-25 Total-55, total Mahila Ward Members 455 and total Mahila Vice-Sarpanches were 21.

Out of 141 Gram Panchayats in Sangamner Block, total 38 Gram Panchayats were selected for survey. 15 Mahila Sarpanches, six women Vice-Sarpanches, and 123 women ward members were interviewed. Their response regarding their participation and performance at the grassroot bodies was found to be both positive and negative. On the positive side it has been noticed that due to reservation of seats many women were elected to local bodies. Reservation has created a space for women's needs within the structural framework of politics and legitimised women's issues. The women also feel happy and energetic by being placed at the mainstream of the society and given opportunity to share power with men. Reservation has also led to the recognition of the identity of women and their presence in the public life. This is a remarkable change. It is also noticed that there is an upsurge of women's power at the grassroot bodies. Women have started asserting themselves, leading to a new kind of social revolution in the society. Some of the women representatives are slowly and steadily gaining confidence and trying to perceive their roles by familiarising themselves with Panchayat rules and regulation. The important aspect of the study was that the women who reluctantly entered into politics showed great maturity in outlook, enthusiasm, increased political consciousness and perception of their role and responsibility.

After becoming panchayat members they became important members of their families. They got high self-esteen which enhanced their capacity to work. Political participation has also created better understanding between the members of the different religious groups as the members of Panchayat Raj Institutions belong to different religions.

On the negative side, the constitutional provisions have not materialised into reality. It has been noticed that the elected women representatives are treated 'as puppets' in the local bodies. The majority of them stay as silent audience in the events of the Gram Panchayat meetings and seldom take part in the deliberations. They hardly express their own views relating to identifying beneficiaries, assigning contracts, locating development projects, budget preparation, planning etc. Just sitting and listening to the deliberations in meetings has been their style of involvement. The reasons that distress the route of women empowerment and participation are identified as lack of awareness, experience, knowledge, skill, leadership quality, low level of education, lack of exposure, influence of family, caste, social outlook, patriarchy etc. Illiteracy has become a major obstacle in the path of playing active role in the functioning of local bodies. Husbands and family members do not want their women representatives to interact with government officials and others in the matter of taking decisions. The caste factor is one more check in the route of women's participation. Higher caste people are found hesitant to honour the low caste elected women representatives and to obey decisions taken by them. Thus, women panchayat members are confronting innumerable complications, nuisance and disgrace at the hands of traditional power holders.

It is observed that many factors are affecting the process of participation and level of performance of women in the grassroots bodies. These factors may be categorised as of two types: (i) Internal factor, and (ii) External factors. The internal factors which offer the process of women empowerment and participation are identified as: lack of awareness, experience, knowledge, skill, leadership quality, low level of education, lack of exposure etc. It is noticed that women representatives are not aware of their functions, duties and responsibilities. In fact, they do not know what role they have to play in the functioning of local government. Lack of education or low level of education has become a major obstacle in the path of playing active role in the functioning of Panchayats. The elected members are unable to understand the basic of working of Gram Panchayats. As a result they provide an ineffective leadership. Due to lack of exposure and experience, women members in several cases are dependent on their husbands in the matter of decision-making. In many cases they do rely upon the traditional power holders. The external factors which affect the process of participation and empowerment of women are: influence of family, caste, social outlook, patriarchy etc. The dominated Indian society does not perceive women as capable or worthy of leadership.

2. *A study by Gadpale, Smita (2014), Exploring Challenges and Issues Faced by Women Councilors in Urban Local Bodies in Thane District, Maharashtra* also shares mixed findings. As per the officials' opinion very high number of women candidates, about 90 per cent, act as puppets the in hand of their family members. In short, very few are working independently. The officials said that generally women councilors are inexperienced with no or minimal educational qualification, lack confidence and enthusiasm and show less interest in the functioning of municipal bodies than their male counterparts. At the same time, officials also stated that there are lots of expectations from Women Councillors as they only can bring change in the form of non-corrupt, clean and participative governance.

According to other municipal officers the number of such women councillors is increasing who are taking interest in ward level activities as well as municipal functioning. The ward officers shared that most of the women councillors are like active male councilors and know very well about the work they are supposed to do. Most of the times they do not have much technical knowledge about works/schemes but they are more concerned about how to implement the schemes fully and on time. They are also concerned about the welfare of the citizen.

The secretary of Thane Municipal Corporation shared that women's reservation in local bodies is a powerful instrument to bring change in municipal governance and empowering women councillors. He said that women councillors are raising meaningful questions in the meetings in respect of issues mainly related to basic services – water supply, electricity, road construction, small repairs in wards, sanitation, collection of garbage, health services to women and children, education to children, issues pertaining to women and children. However, they hesitate to raise question with respect of an incidents of corruption and unauthorised construction. In such situations they mostly follow their political party's stand and never express their opinion.

Municipal officials expressed the need of regular training for women councillors, as there was no provision made for their training on regular basis by Thane Municipal Corporation. Whatever training has been conducted, that was organised by All India Institute of Local Self-government.

In Interview with Women Councillors, the study found that most of them are in the process of learning and understanding the municipal functioning. They have accepted the fact that their learning period is longer than that of any male councilor. This is because they are facing challenges in accessing all types of information, lack of experience and confidence. Besides, family responsibilities, time pressure, always burdened with 'no stigma on her character' they also face pressures from within the political parties. Very few are able to work independently or get supportive environment in the family.

It was noticed that those women councilors who are having their second term, are able to work independently. However, their entry in electoral politics is still tough as the first preference goes to existing ruling politicians and family members of politicians.

Women councillors have agreed that there is a constraint in attending complete session of discussions on municipal budget in the corporation as meetings get extended to late night. Travel in the night was also found unsafe for them. But they are comfortable with raising issues at ward level which are mainly related to basic services like collection of garbage, water supply, petty repairs, anganwadi, municipal schools and another thrust area to get more benefits from government schemes for women and children in their ward. Women councillor have shared that they are not directly involved in processing the tenders and dealing with contractors. Very few have knowledge about tendering process and contracts/agreements. Most of them expressed that they can balance both family affairs and politics because of family support only. Family support plays key role in their political career. Women councillors work with determination and focus on strengthening their constituencies, so that party recognises their work and considers their name for next election. Money and muscle powers are strong challenges before them and these resources are totally controlled by the male politicians.

Most women councillors expressed the need of support in the form of formal training and guidance from senior colleagues. They were not satisfied with the current training programmes organised by the state government training institution. Difficulties were faced in understanding the administrative and legal language which is complicated.

In interview with Political Party officials it was found that reservation for women in municipal bodies is not in their priority agenda. Some political party representatives of Thane city expressed that party officials are always providing opportunities to capable candidates irrespective of gender. Still it has been observed that only few women councillors have been able to get entry into critical, higher positions in municipal committees like standing committee, transportation committees and planning committee. Around 50 per cent reservation for women in ULBs is definitely putting challenge in front of all the political parties.

For women councillors (WCs), being a woman becomes very challenging and the challenges and issues faced by them are multidimensional. This research study identified few areas in which the WCs faced problems, obstacles and challenges.

Family 'Responsibilities' and 'Support'

Majority of women councillors made the statement that their first priority is family and then politics. Few of them said that they always try to maintain the balance between family responsibilities and their work as councillor. Majority of the respondents agreed that they are burdened with family responsibilities. Few of them were having guilt feelings because due to their work as women councillors they have missed important occasions or were unable to satisfy the needs of the family. For them being 'Councillor' is temporary but relationship with family is lifetime and this affected their growth and spread in politics, adversely.

Barring a few exceptions to the rule, very few respondents enjoyed real family support. They never thought about developing their career in politics at the cost of their families.

Support from Municipal Administration

Majority respondents were giving negative response to the question about whether municipal support is available to them in terms of access to information. Every respondent was of the opinion that municipal administration is gender biased. They were supporting their opinion with several illustrations.

Support from Party Members and Colleagues including Male Councillors

All the respondents expressed the need of support from the senior members as well as male colleagues within their party. The party support encourages them to perform well. Many respondents shared that in many matters especially involving financial decisions e.g. huge infrastructure schemes, floating tenders, identifying contractors, they were not consulted.

Majority of the respondents stated that there is tough competition between male and women councillors in every party. Support from male colleagues was mainly depending upon the subject of support. Few male colleagues provide support in accessing the information, understanding technical aspects. But there is limitation to such support.

Respondents expressed the need of separate training within the political party. Further, they added that one training workshop organised for new councillors by government training institution is not enough. Also quality of training should be improved.

Every respondent expressed the challenge of understanding the political tactics, strategies applied in municipal business and 'politics' within the political party. Respondents found it very difficult to face internal conflict within the party. Most of the time, they did not understand these political conflicts and tactics. So they tried to avoid it. But sometime their work and status also got affected by such practices. Majority respondents expressed that they wanted to be a part of clean politics.

Few respondents have freely shared the fact that they have experienced higher degree of controls because of being a woman. The women councillors can participate in general body meeting. They can raise questions and take part in debates but only on subjects related to their wards. On many occasions, they eagerly wanted to put their opinions in meetings, but they were stopped by their senior male colleagues.

Lack of Experience and Knowledge

The respondents holding second term mentioned that first terms of councillorship was the learning period to understand the municipal system as well as political dynamics within the party. In the first term they had experienced few embarrassing situations while interacting with municipal officials, participating in meetings and discussion and also in some public events due to lack of knowledge. They shared their difficulties in understanding mainly the technical part of schemes of water supply, sewerage, gutter lines, tendering process, dealings with the contractors, understanding municipal budget, and municipal laws, rules and regulations. Due to these difficulties they were unable to contribute in discussions and meetings. Now they are in better position in the second term. They have opined that procedures are simple but municipal officials make them difficult.

They have shared that these factors affected their self-confidence. At the same time they knew that for effective participation in the municipal business they have to take tremendous efforts and need to invest considerable time.

Time and Place of Meetings

Majority respondents did not find timing and place of meetings suitable for them. Their convenience is not considered while deciding the time for the meetings. As a result, they fail to attend the meeting and get familiar with key decisions or proposals discussed in these meetings. Many respondents shared that they find it very difficult to attend to a problem communicated in the late night meetings. For that they depend on male colleagues/activists in the party. This creates another set of obligations for them.

Interference from Family Members

It was observed during the course of interviewing the respondents that while performing their functions or taking any decision, particularly where financial element is involved, they have consulted their family members. In case of few respondents all civil works in the ward is taken care of by their husbands or sons.

Control of Resources

Majority respondents replied that they have limited participation in utilisation of councillor's fund, implementation of any schemes, preparing and utilising ward budget, proposal submissions to municipal budget, tenders, contracts etc. Access to these resources is controlled by male politicians. It was observed that the respondent to faced this challenge.

On the question of what does reservation for women councilors mean to them? they said politics is dominated by male politicians. Only because of reservation women are seen in good numbers. Since they are now involved in the process of decision-making, their status in the society and family has improved in general. Women councillors can raise issues and questions pertaining to women's development and protection which are not raised by men politicians and are able to make financial provisions through municipal budget for the same. Women reservation would ensure equal opportunity to them to participate in governance and resource allocation. Women can bring qualitative changes in the local politics by less corruption practices and transparency in Municipal governance.

Women reservation at local level is not enough. It should be provided at state assembly as well as in the parliament. It would support women councilors having aspiration to participate in the state/national politics.

A Few Other Observations

Usha Pillare, Panch, Chikhali gram panchayat in Gadchiroli Maharashtra. Usha Pillare, a ward member of the Chikhali panchayat belongs to the OBC community. She is a committed panch, who was elected because of the encouragement of the parisar sangh (women's federation), with which AAAS works. She was elected unopposed. She has the full the support of her husband in her work but is not a proxy panch member. She has used the knowledge provided by Aalochana (NGO) about the women's component of the panchayat's nidhi (funds), to disseminate information and to ensure appropriate utilisation of the money. She raised the issue in the panchayat and also informed the federation, which in turn brought up the matter in the mahila gram sabhas. Usha is aware of the financial matters of the panchayat and of her rights is able to take confrontations and opposition. Along with the cluster federation, she successfully approached the local MLA to sanction the construction of a meeting hall. Since the formation of a mahila sabha is compulsory in the state, she has always tried to inform all SHG members in the federation about the sabha and attendance has been high at sabha meetings. Usha knows that there are huge challenges ahead and hopes that she will be able to meet them and motivate others to participate effectively in decentralised governance.

The concept of political participation is closely associated with the concept of empowerment. A mutually supportive functioning of the two can certainly redirect and influence a process which has largely failed to tap the energy, knowledge and ability of women so far. The inadequate representation of women in decision-making bodies has been a historical reality in our society.

If numbers are indicative of progress, Maharashtra does not seem to fare badly in respect of women's representation in panchayats. The 50 per cent reservation has been largely successful in this State. Reservation appears to have given women an opportunity to prove their capabilities in governance. The confidence they have inspired in their constituency has encouraged more women to enter the political arena. The commendable part is that women have contested general category seats and won, says Sunil Chavan, Officer-in-Charge of Panchayati Raj. The elected women make sure funds are used properly and that their villages and districts actually benefit from their leadership, says Chavan. He says an interesting aspect of having women leaders is that they give a lot of importance to women's literacy and care of the girl child. The literacy rate among women has improved significantly. This, in turn, has increased awareness and independence among women.

By and large, reservation has been beneficial for women in Maharashtra, says Mariam Dhawale of the All India Democratic Women's Association. Not only should it be extended but the percentage should be raised.

Dhawale, who has worked extensively in the field, says that instances of women office-bearers being used as proxies by men are bound to occur in a largely patriarchal society. In many cases, upper-caste men refuse to accept or take directions from a lower-caste woman leader. Yet in the 20 years since it was first introduced, the explosive reactions have decreased. In fact, you hardly hear of any violent or disrespectful incident towards elected women members nowadays, says Dhawale.

Raseela Dhodi, a member of the gram panchayat and an ex-sarpanch of Dongari village of Thallassery taluk in Thane district's tribal belt, says it is we women who understand the basic needs of the village. We are the ones who know the problems relating to water, health of women and children, facilities in schools, ration cards, roads, and so on. When a woman is the sarpanch, more often than not, these problems are addressed. When a male is elected, he is invariably involved only in politics and fails to look at real problems. Dhodi says that her village has had both male and female sarpanches in recent times and that the village has begun to realise that women are more effective.

For Suman Patil, a member of the panchayat samiti from Bokadvira village in Uran taluk in Raigad district, it has been a long journey to leadership. She came to the village 20 years ago as a daughter-in-law. She says 'I could hardly go out of the house, and sitting next to a man who is not your husband was unthinkable'. It took some time, but eventually she decided to contest the elections.

'In the beginning I found it very difficult to address men. Then I thought, what is there to be afraid of? People have voted for me, they have confidence in me, so I should prove that I am capable of helping them. I used to stand at the site of road works through the day to make sure the work was completed. The men used to laugh, but then they got used to it.'

Bokadvira sarpanch, Hemlatha Patil says SHGs in rural areas and the setting up of cottage industries have also played a role in making women in villages independent.

Vibhuti Patel, an economist was part of a gender audit of the budget. She says, 'We have repeatedly seen that elected women leaders look into issues such as construction of schools, area development, immunisation, garbage collection, marriages – anything that affects the family and daily life. In most cases, there was no corruption and funds were used wisely and not diverted to irrelevant activities.'

In spite of the positive stories, there are still many areas that are extremely backward, says Hemlatha Patil. In Marathwada, many of the women sarpanches have no role in decision-making. 'They attend the meetings but do not even sit. When we went to those areas, we realised how poor, illiterate and unaware they were. Furthermore, caste continues to play an ugly role in politics.'

Even before reservation for women was enforced in 1993, Maharashtra had initiated a 30 per cent quota for women in municipal councils. It was among the first few States to have an all-women panchayat body. There are many such in existence today. Seemingly, the State is among the progressive ones, yet there are areas untouched by this progress.

Conclusions

The aforesaid discussion shows that women in Maharashtra have shown their adaptability to roles in governance and decision-making. All the cases mentioned in the paper also show that women's performance often far outshines that of men as their concerns remain close to the ground realities and survival issues. The evidences of women's participation, involvement, role and performance in decision-making vary from place to pace. The policy for reservation of women is a beginning which has the potential to start the process of empowerment of women but this is not the answer to gender inequality. Reservations do not automatically lead to the enhanced participation of women in developmental activities. Several issues, including women's knowledge and training, family support, perception of political parties towards them etc. need to be addressed. Reservations have definitely made women more visible and the process of their gradual political integration has begun but so far they have generally been unable to secure a strong presence to push gender interests.

Though the large number of women-related legislations are in place, it is seen that these laws are not satisfactorily implemented. A major reason for this is the lack of adequate knowledge and awareness regarding these special legislations. Also, there is absence of gender sensitivity on part of the functionaries at the all levels such as law enforcement, police, prosecution, medical profession, education etc. Although the Constitution guaranteed the equal rights for women, the reality is that they are not seen as equal. The case studies reveal that patriarchal society enforces rules and laws in such way that has detrimental effect on self-confidence of women, limit their access on resources and information, restrict their freedom of movement in the public place and thus keep them in a lower status than men.

As quantity itself is a quality the introduction of direct election to the reserved seats at local levels is undoubtedly a breakthrough. In no other way could these women in large numbers have moved into these institutions and participated in them. Though improvements are clearly visible but still there is a gender imbalance that prevents elected women members to influence decisions. Low literacy levels, absence of education and limited or no exposure lead to a lack of confidence. As a result, women at local levels are unable to comprehend the true spirit of political decentralisation and recognise the opportunities that it provides.

Policy Recommendations

Due to socio-political and religious bindings, elected women are not able to live up to the expectation. To ensure a meaningful participation of the elected women members as an essential step to empower them, the following policy suggestions may be taken into consideration: There should be unbiased distribution of work among the men and women members so that participation of women members is ensured in all type of functions. Opportunities for education, health care and employment should be expanded and there should be motivational programmes to create greater awareness about improving the status of women. Specific programmes should be undertaken by the government and non-government organisations to create realisation about the benefits of women's full participation in decision-making in their empowerment. Women should be given various opportunities and support for leadership training in order to take up political and leadership positions. There is urgent need to undertake research on women's participation in politics, their voting behaviour, consciousness and participation in the political parties. Finally, measures to increase the quantity of women representatives need to be accompanied by measures to improve the quality of participation.

References

Alok, V.N. (2013), 'Strengthening of Panchayats in India: Comparing Devolution across States, Empirical Assessment 2012–13', sponsored by Ministry of Panchayati Raj, Government of India, The Indian Institute of Public Administration, New Delhi.

Batliwala, Srilata (1993), 'Defining Women's Empowerment: A Conceptual Framework', www.genderatwork.org/updir/batliwala-empowerment-framework.htm, retrieved on 10 May 2005.

Benke, Suvarna Ashok (2011), 'Women in Panchayat Raj Institutions: A Case Study in Maharashtra', *Online International Interdisciplinary Research Journal* (Bi-Monthly), Vol. I, No. II, November-December.

Census of India (2011), Office of the Registrar General and Census Commissioner, Government of India, New Delhi.

From Reservation to Participation, Capacity Building of Elected Women Representatives and Functionaries of Panchayati Raj Institutions, http://pib.nic.in/release/release.asp?relid=50131

Gadpale, Smita (2014), 'Exploring Challenges and Issues Faced by Women Councilors in Urban Local Bodies in Thane District, Maharashtra', Dissertation (unpublished), submitted in Partial Fulfillment of the Requirements for Degree of Master of Arts in Social Exclusion and Inclusive Policy, under the guidance of Professor Vibhuti Patel, Centre for Study of Social Exclusion and Inclusive Policy, S.N.D.T. Women's University, Mumbai.

Ghoge, Ketaki (2014), 'Maharashtra: Parties Not Putting Women Politicians in Poll Position', *Hindustan Times* (Mumbai), September 6.

Khan, Mostafizur Rahman and Ara Fardaus (2006), 'Women, Participation and Empowerment in Local Government: Bangladesh Union Parishad Perspective', *Asian Affairs*, Vol. 29, No. 1, January-March, pp. 73–92.

Ministry of Panchayati Raj, Government of India, http://lgdirectory.gov.in/rptconsolidateforrurallb.do, accessed on 6 September 2013.

Thakkar, Usha (2005), *Democratisation in Progress: Women and Local Politics in Urban India*, Tulika Books, New Delhi.

16

Dalit Women in Power Politics

A Study of Gram Panchayats in Telangana

S. Satyam

Panchayats (traditionally panchayat is an institution in which decisions regarding social issues in the village are taken by five wise men of the village) are not new to India. Some of the studies viewed that the participation of people in the election of panchayats is high but high voter turnout was not indicative of an overwhelming interest in the process of democracy of local government. The influential factors of decision-making in the election are social solidarity, avoidance of tension within the village, bribery, fear of exclusion from below poverty line lists and often simply the thrill of participating in the festival of elections.

Though the concept of Panchayat Raj is well known to rural people and active participation of government officials and elected members has enhanced general interest in the gram panchayat politics in recent years, effectiveness and efficiency much to be improved. Functional and institutional issues like financially viable, involvement in micro level planning, functions, powers and resources, regular elections of gram panchayats at regular intervals, allocation of funds and strengthening gram sabhas are yet to be strengthened. Still social inequality was visible in the contexts of periodical village assemblies, regular elections and in terms of sufficient representations of weaker sections of society like SCs and STs and women.

In a democracy, power is legitimated through popular electoral mandates, and leadership is based on the popular will. In the context of democracy in India, such mandate has been continuously enshrining and new factors like caste and social mobility has emerged as very important factors. In political terms, periodic elections and rule of law are and of themselves proving much better instruments in changing the reality of the citizens, especially with respect to gender inclusivity. In the current system, people serve the political leadership. Based on the existing literature, political leadership is connected with ethical and cultural character, the traits and ethical-cultural character of the followers with whom the leader interacts.

Leadership of women in Panchayati Raj Institutions (PRIs) has brought in some positive changes, although political affairs like factional disputes continuing in dominating village politics were hindering women leadership. In such scenarios, some committees have expressed the need to restrict the hold of political parties in PRIs and on the contrary, the Santhanam committee explicitly recommended that there should be no legal provision prohibiting political parties from influencing panchayati raj elections. These committees suggested that political parties should be inhibited from nominating candidates for panchayats and allotting party symbols for different candidates in the panchayat elections. The Siddiq Ali and Santhanam committees recommended that political parties should not be recognised for the purpose of panchayat elections. Possibilities such as disallowing political parties from participating in elections and in the operation of panchayati raj bodies, applying pressure for unanimous elections, promoting consensus in the working of PRIs and making panchayats as politics-free zones, have been suggested in various seminars and conferences. In contrast, the study by B.S. Bhargava emphasised that successful functioning of Panchayati Raj system depends to a great extent on the role of political parties and the nature of politics generated in the system.

As regards to Women's Empowerment as a major social change issue, women's entry into the local political bodies at village level panchayats through the 33 per cent reservation system which was provided by the Constitutional (73rd Amendment) Act, 1992 was largely discussed and brought grassroot level observations based on the empirical investigations.

The 73rd Constitutional Amendment Act has been hailed as a revolutionary step towards decentralisation of power and governance. The amendment provides for the village assembly i.e. the Gram Sabha (GS). It also ensures uniformity in terms of tenure. Administrative units and all states are obliged to conduct periodic elections by an autonomous body. The Amendment gives constitutional status to village, block and district level bodies under the Indian Constitution. Moreover, the Gram Sabha (GS), as a basic democratic unit of India, has given due importance and strengthened its institutional process by providing compulsory and regular direct elections to five-year terms for all members at all levels, one-third of all seats are reserved for women, reservations for SCs and STs proportional to their populations and chairpersons (Sarpanches) of the panchayats are among others.

Further, the Act also constituted institutionally a three-tier system of Panchayati Raj for all States having population of over 20 lakh, regular elections (every five years), and appointment of State Finance Commission to make recommendations as regards the financial powers of the panchayats and constitution of District Planning Committees to prepare development plans for the district as whole. As per the Constitution (73rd Amendment) Act, the PRIs have been endowed with such powers and authority as may be necessary to function as institutions of self-government and contains provisions of devolution of powers and responsibilities upon panchayats at the appropriate level with reference to the preparation of plans for economic development and social justice; and the implementation of such schemes for economic development and social justice as may be entrusted to them.

Background of the Study

The significance of the amendment is that it provided reservation of seats for women, SCs and STs at all levels including the village, intermediate (mandal, taluka/block) and district panchayats (Manikyamba, 1989). As a result, a common system of governance that aims for actual people's participation has been introduced in all the states of the country. In short, an attempt has been made to realise Mahatma Gandhi's concept of Gram Swaraj through the Panchayati Raj Act. Consequent upon the enactment of the Act, almost all the States/UTs, except Jammu and Kashmir, National Capital Territory of Delhi and Uttaranchal (now Uttarakhand) have enacted their legislation. As a result, according to the report of the Ministry of Rural Development (2013), 2,32,278 panchayats at village level; 6,022 panchayats at intermediate level and 535 panchayats at district level have been constituted in the country. The report has also argued that these panchayats are being manned by about 29.2 lakh elected representatives of panchayats at all levels.

But, recent literature (e.g. Crook and Manor, 1998; Jha, 1999; Mathew, 2000; Oommen, 1997; Vyasulu, 2000; World Bank, 2000 and Smitha, 2007) on these institutions have argued, the ambiguity surrounding the concept of 'self-government' and power to local people, especially in decision-making power that still rests with the State governments have prevented most states from devolving any substantive power to the panchayats. Such findings are consistent with a wider literature on the problems most commonly associated with decentralisation in India.

Review of literature has concluded that women's political career especially at grassroot politics, depends upon cooperation and support of family members and collaboration between husband and wife. It is clear that without support of husband, women cannot enter into politics and it is essential for women. Further, women mostly depends husband's good rapport with the people and his association with political party at the time of elections.

In Telangana, Self-Help Groups (SHGs) were involved vigorously in gram panchayat politics and SHGs supporting women brought into mainstream political process. In addition, there is strong synergy between SHGs and PRIs, SHGs as collective citizens are used by local government for local government for implementation of politically strong democratic weapon and in democratic system they have emerged as prominent factors in acquiring elected power. Some studies highlighted the state responsibilities in strengthening of function of panchayati raj through trainings, power and financial allocation and devolutions.

The 73rd Constitutional Amendment Act 1993 has given priority for the reservation of seats for members of Scheduled Castes, Scheduled Tribes and women both at the membership and functionary level. This effort was meant to create conditions favourable to democratic decentralisation through wider participation. In general, the emergence of panchayati raj has brought visible changes in Srirampur and Chittapoor villages in the form of roads, health facilities, drinking water etc. but there are several problems still continuing at grassroot politics in India in general and in the study villages specified in particular. In this research we found out some of the problems faced by gram panchayats. The smooth functioning of the panchayats is being disturbed by hurdles like inadequate financial resources (to maintain proper facilities of Gram Panchayats), misuse of welfare funds, domination of bureaucracy over elected panchayat leaders, as most of the elected members have no literacy.

Regarding women leadership, constitutional provisions, government policies, social action plans and awareness of rural women together have provided women with necessary skills to enjoy equal opportunities. The Panchayati Raj has provided a common forum for social, economic, political and legal advancement of rural women. Now women are more than nominal members in the panchayat bodies and this is an epoch-making step in the women's empowerment and political participation.

Methodology

In India with complex and rigid social, political and cultural settings, in majority cases women's entry into politics or exercising their power is determined by personal settings. Personal determination and dedication towards political move is still matter of familial equations. Formal leadership power, in my opinion, varies by caste, class, culture and religious matters but women's leadership quality still relied upon family along with above structure. In such circumstances, leadership of dalit women at grassroot is to be understood with the basic research questions of how their leadership qualities were considered. What are the determining factors that stimulated them to emerge as leaders? How are they treated by specific society in specific social system? For these research questions, women leadership was studied in PRIs with special reference to the district of Nizamabad of Telangana.

Objectives

This study's main objective is to understand the development of political consciousness, especially among dalit women leaders; secondly, to clarify the challenges confronting women leaders within these two villages and thirdly, to understand the popular perceptions of the capabilities of women leaders. The study explores women's capabilities and performances in using resources effectively and lobbying for development projects. It also examines the degree of awareness of the members of gram panchayat about their powers and duties.

Sample Size and Area of the Study

Since this study intended to grasp factual information in a systematic manner, it selected two villages namely, Srirampoor and Chittapoor gram panchayats of Balkonda mandal of Nizamabad district in Telangana. The unit of study is only at gram panchayats, especially elected ward members and sarpanches. Both qualitative and quantitative methods have been used for collection of data. As regards to sample strategy, a survey was adopted covering 40 elected members.

Sources of Study

The present study is partly based on empirical research; it compares leadership qualities of male and female members at the level of gram panchayat in two villages. But, dalit women were given much attention to interpret the issues concerning the study objectives. It may be noted that the village of Srirampoor was newly created as a separate gram panchayat in 1996. Before that, it was a small hamlet under Chittapoor. When it formed an independent village, women were elected as Panchayat leaders called as Sarpanch. Prior to that, village had only male Sarpanches.

The data has been collected from two villages. Including village sarpanches and all gram panchayat ward members, 40 respondents have been interviewed. For this study, an intensive questionnaire and face-to-face interviews were used. This was useful in gaining proper information about the functioning of village sarpanches and general political participation. Analysis of general perceptions of sarpanches and ward members and selected people has been presented. The data has been collected primarily from elected gram panchayat leaders, such as ward members and Sarpanches. As secondary sources, textbooks, articles, NGO reports, field research work, central and State government's occasional papers have been used.

Analysis and Findings

The paper is devoted to an analysis of the general perceptions and opinions on dalit women leaders. It also aims at analysing the functioning of women leaders in their villages, with regard to development programmes taken up by women sarpanch and ward members. Initially it begins with understanding social structure and extends to examine the functioning of women leaders in their villages, with regard to development programmes taken up by women sarpanch and ward members.

Social Structure

These villages comprise of different caste groups such as *Munnuru Kapu, Gundla, Tenugu, Mala, Madiga, Chindula, Mere, Vyshya, Chaakali, Patkari, Aarre, Kammari, Kummari, Ousali (gold smith) Mangali, Gouds, Chenchula, Vaddera, Reddies, Brahmanas, Golla and Muslims.* This village consists of caste organisations, women groups, farmers' organisations, youth associations and others like educational development committee, mothers committee, water users committee, watershed committee and forest development committees. These developmental committees are working under grama panchayat offices of selected villages.

Caste-wise Representation and Political Participation

Caste and religion are dominant factors in Indian public life (Narang, 1987). The elections for panchayats, municipalities, assemblies and even parliament prove that the caste influence is fairly strong. In fact, the Panchayati Raj system has strengthened the caste system.

Table 1

Distribution of Gram Panchayat: Caste-wise

Caste	Name of the Villages								
	Srirampoor			Chittapoor			Total		
	Women	Men	Total	Women	Men	Total	Women	Men	Total
SCs	5 (71.47%)	5 (50%)	10 (58.82%)	0 (0.00%)	2 (11.76%)	2 (8.69%)	5 (38.46%)	7 (25.92%)	12 (30%)
BCs	2 (28.51%)	5 (40%)	6 (35.29%)	6 (100%)	15 (88.23%)	21 (91.30%)	8 (61.53%)	19 (70.37%)	27 (67%)
Others	0 (0.00%)	10 (100%)	1 (5.88%)	0 (0.00%)	0 (0.00%)	0 (0.00%)	0 (0.00%)	1 (3.70%)	1 (2.5%)

Source: Filed study.

The caste distribution of respondents (Table 1) shows that 67.5 per cent members belong to backward castes while 30 per cent are scheduled castes and remaining 2.5 per cent members are from other castes. According to the data, women's participation including two villages only comes to 32.5 per cent while male percentage is 67.5 per cent. Comparatively speaking, women's participation percentage is higher in Srirampur village than Chittapoor.

The purpose of this section is to understand the political background of leaders at grassroots level. Their affiliation with political parties is significant in this context. The gram panchayat leader's membership for a political party is an indication of the leader's ideological commitment on the one hand and political parties' role in that village on the other. Respondents were distributed according to their political party affiliation (Table 6); 65 per cent of the overwhelming majority belongs to Congress party and 20 per cent of the respondents are supporting the Telugu Desam Party. And very recently the Telangana Rashtra Samiti (a regional party) has also acquired a few panchayat leaders (12.5%) and the remaining one person (2.5%) belongs to Bharatiya Janata Party. Among women respondents, a very high percentage of women panchayat leaders are supporting the Congress party (84.62%) and a very small percentage belong to TDP, (15.30%). But there is no women participation in BJP, and TRS parties.

It is obvious that all panchayat leaders are supporting the political parties. In all the political parties, the main intention is to increase the participation of Backward classes, Scheduled castes, Tribes and women communities in panchayat raj institutions. It is clear that panchayats are accepting the involvement of political parties into panchayat raj system; political parties are providing the financial and public support to panchayat level leaders during panchayat elections. The above analysis shows that majority of the panchayat leaders belongs to scheduled caste and other depressed classes in panchayat bodies. Another significant thing is that the panchayat system is also encouraging the young and educated women into the decision-making process.

Women in Panchayats

In order to know the perception of respondents on the functioning of women leaders, we asked the question 'have women leaders brought visible changes in village development?' The opinions expressed by respondents are classified into three categories; (1) Yes, women leaders have brought about visible changes in some areas (it includes drinking water facility, village roads development, sanitation, loans, health facilities, educational facilities, library, village electrification, irrigation and agricultural development etc). (2) No. Women leaders can't bring visible changes in their respective villages and (3) No response.

According to our data, majority of the respondents (60%) feel that women leaders brought visible changes. According to the respondents, woman sarpanch brought many welfare schemes such as Deepam; through this scheme nearly 40 gas cylinders were sanctioned to scheduled castes and backward castes of DWCRA group women. And she also sanctioned four sewing machines under DRDA (District Rural Development Agency) for backward caste's women, four autos for unemployed youth. Moreover, the woman sarpanch built a drinking water tank with capacity of 75,000 litres and pucca house loans for poor people under Ambedkar Awas Yojana scheme. Woman sarpanch also built a new Gram Panchayat Office, school building and school compound wall under Jawahar Rojgar Yojana and Tenth Finance Commission's fund. Thus, she has tried to get medical facilities for her village.

Nearly 30 per cent of the leaders have disagreed with the view that women leadership is effective. In their view, women leadership has not brought any visible changes. Respondents claimed that new developments were possible because of male effort. Women leaders have depended upon their husbands. Around 20 per cent of the people were indifferent.

A comparative analysis between two villages regarding women leadership shows that in Srirampur, overwhelming majority of 70 per cent felt that women leadership is effective and people of village considered them as capable persons in village development. But in Chittapoor village, respondents (52.17%) have given least importance to women leaders. A general observation can be made that the respondents here considered women leaders as ineffective for village development as well as for women's welfare.

In response to the question, 'Do you think that the strength of women leaders in the village panchayat is satisfactory?', as many as, 47.5 per cent of the respondents gave positive replies (Table 2). Only 10 per cent of them did not answer either way. Some variations, however, are evident in the responses given by women leaders that there is no adequate representation of women. Women respondents thought that state and central governments have to take responsibilities to improve women's strength numerically. And they also stated that reservation system has not been properly functioning. These perceptions indicate that state and central governments have to implement effective provisions for women's representation in all panchayat bodies.

Table 2

Perceptions on the Strength of Women Leaders in Village Panchayats

Response	*Name of the Villages*								
	Srirampoor			*Chittapoor*			*Total*		
	Women	*Men*	*Total*	*Women*	*Men*	*Total*	*Women*	*Men*	*Total*
Yes	3 (42.85%)	6 (60%)	9 (52.94%)	2 (33.33%)	8 (47.05%)	10 (43.47%)	5 (38.46%)	14 (51.85%)	19 (47.5%)
No	4 (57.14%)	4 (40%)	8 (47.05%)	4 (46.67%)	5 (29.41%)	9 (39.13%)	8 (61.53%)	9 (33.33%)	17 (42.5%)
No response	0 (0.0%)	0 (0.0%)	0 (0.0%)	0 (0.0%)	4 (23.52%)	4 (17.39%)	0 (0.00%)	4 (14.81%)	4 (10%)
Total	7 (100%)	10 (100%)	17 (100%)	6 (100%)	17 (100%)	23 (100%)	13 (100%)	27 (100%)	40 (100%)

Source: Field study.

We tried to find out the reasons for inadequate representation of women in village panchayats. For this purpose, only women respondents were interviewed. In their opinion, women's families were not allowing entry into politics because of conservative social values. Another reason for inadequate representation was because of traditional headmen. Every caste community is represented by one person, who is aged, economically and socially influential. Of the total population of the village, this group comprises nearly five to six headmen for each village. These traditional leaders do not accept women leadership. So, traditional people's attitudes have to be changed regarding women's participation in politics. Women's own diffidence has to be overcome. According to present data, women's education level is up to 10th standard only. Compared to men, women's educational status is very poor. But it can be overcome through effective special provisions for women in rural India.

Moreover, other social constraints also hinder women's empowerment in gram panchayats. In India, village politics is dominated by the traditional landed and upper caste people. This leadership has not been giving opportunities to any of the marginalised sections such as Scheduled castes, Tribes and women. So, rural traditional leadership is the main social obstacle to women empowerment in rural politics. It indicates that only people's attitude and government policies can change women's status in grassroot politics.

In response to the question 'In your experience, what are the obstacles women faced as Panchayat leaders?' (This question was asked only to women respondents); data is given in Table 3, all of the respondents agreed traditional headmen and panchayat officers like village secretary and mandal level officials have neglected women leadership (nearly 60%). These women leaders felt very bad regarding their responsibilities. Even though, women actively participate at grassroot politics, still they face problems from the village headmen and officials.

Table 3

Views on Obstacles that Women Face as Panchayat Leaders (Women Leaders only)

Statements	*Name of the Villages*		
	Srirampoor	*Chittapoor*	*Total*
Problems from village people	4 (57.3%)	0 (0.00%)	4 (30.76%)
Obstacles from officials	2 (28.5%)	0 (0.00%)	2 (15.38%)
From both sides	1 (14.2%)	6 (100%)	7 (53.84%)
No response	0 (0.00%)	0 (0.00%)	0 (0.00%)
Total	7 (100%)	6 (100%)	13 (100%)

Source: Field study.

In our research, we found that women's leadership and their capacity are being praised by the people of the two villages and especially by women. In our observations and conversation with elected members of gram panchayat, women's unity and cooperation together strengthened their confidence in grassroot politics. Cheema Neeraja (original name was changed) one of my respondents, said that 'I got immense support from my DWCRA members during panchayat elections and won MPTC with their support'. We can understand, through this statement, that only with women support she got tremendous majority in elections. There we can say that men and women both equally accepted women leadership for their future development directions.

Even though the Panchayati Raj system brought about visible changes in the condition of villages, especially that of women, still there exist institutional, social and psychological obstacles. Some general orientations and social norms impose restraints on women participation and performance. Consequently, women tend to remain in peripheral roles even when they have special provisions in village politics. Some women are still deteriorating themselves in their grade due to lack of education and awareness. Some women feel that they are only meant for household work. One respondent said, 'If we took active participation in politics in Panchayat Raj our family will be broken.' Some active members of gram panchayat said that their views were neglected by male members and officials. They were not even allowed to express village problems. Women leaders are still hesitating to attend gram panchayat meetings and sit in front of aged and politically experienced persons.

Economically sound and aged traditional village leaders literally reject the concept of women's entrance into grassroot politics. According to their opinion women should not come out from home and women do not know how to handle village problems. Besides, village headman system is dominating over elected panchayat leaders irrespective of gender. According to the headmen of the village women should not come into public sphere, they should not hold any office chair. But in recent political scenario in villages, the traditional and headmen leadership was neglected by political parties because political parties want their strength in quality and quantity.

Political parties such as Indian National Congress, Telangana Rashtra Samithi, Baratiya Janata Party and other democratic organisations' regional political parties were trying to get women and new young people's membership. Especially, women and political parties are getting confidence, cooperation and support during elections by working together. One woman respondent said 'we have got support from political parties in the form of money and muscle power; otherwise we would have been dominated by other landlords and economically sound people'. For instance, respondents were distributed according to their political party affiliation (see following picture); 65 per cent of the overwhelming majority belongs to Congress party and about 32 per cent of the respondents are supporting the Telangana Rashtra Samiti, and remaining belongs to Bharatiya Janata Party. Among women respondents, a very high percentage of women panchayat leaders are supporting the Congress party (54.62%) and remaining belong to TRS, (40.28%) and BJP, (6.18%) parties.

However, women leaders desired changes in the form of psychological and institutional transformation in village panchayats. Vijayalaxmi, who was the first woman sarpanch of Srirampur village, said 'While I was working as a sarpanch, I had faced obstacles from panchayat officials, they didn't even consider my applications, which were only for the sake of village people. Often I used to bring my husband to mandal revenue office because without my husband they used to neglect me'. This sort of attitude has to be changed. Another institutional change has to be made for better functioning of gram panchayat in that economical independence and more financial assistance has to be provided. Otherwise development of village would be deteriorated. One woman said 'Whenever gram panchayat meeting was conducted, we used to have argument with each other for funds distribution for our ward's development'. It seems lack of financial resources result to conflicts among panchayat leaders.

Here are some suggestions that need focus for the better involvement of women in Panchayati Raj Institutions such as requirement of attitudinal change in both men and women. There is a feeling that women are meant only for household activities and bearing children,0 needs to be replaced by a feeling of equal partnership of women and men. To inculcate this, they should be imparted education for bringing about social and political awareness among both. There should be increased emphasis on ensuring the participation of women in the meetings of panchayats at all the levels, especially at gram sabha level. This is needed to promote and enhance their leadership qualities and self-confidence. It will help them to perform better in the panchayats and ensure their participation in the meetings. Attendance of all women must be made compulsory from Gram Panchayat to Zilla Parishad for effective participation and participation in decision-making process. The Gram Sabha is basic unit of effective democratic system which needs to be strengthened through active participation, regular functioning with proper provisions. The proper provisions in conducting gram sabha are sensitisation, awareness, information and participation. These important issues are lacking, based on the present study, is highly missing. Therefore, effective leadership from women community will appear at the grassroot, especially gram panchayats and in Gram Sabhas soon with proper socio-political and democratic provisions.

Conclusion

Since women constitute one-third of the panchayat representatives and also since, at least one-third of the gram sabha members in the meeting are to be women, it is important that they emerge as new leaders to take up the challenging role in tribal politics. Reservation of seats for women, especially for tribal women is essential for some more years, but efforts are required to ensure that women's political participation go beyond it which will help to foster new image of women who can come into politics themselves and perform independently. In the final analysis of the review, women leaders have exhibited their determination to occupy the public space, though there are hurdles in the process of empowering women. In order, to overcome the hurdles there is a need to make the 'empowerment process', viable and sustainable for the elected women representatives.

It is necessary that women come out of this domination and subordination for which they need to be educated and trained. Though these two are not sufficient conditions in themselves, their dearth prevents women from taking important decisions. Besides lack of awareness, education and training, the respondents also expressed their opinions regarding other problems. Lack of financial or economic resources was considered as the most important one. Interference by government officials and their non-cooperative attitude, groupism, besides family problems and traditional values, were other problems.

References

Agarwal, Deepti (2001), 'Empowerment of Rural Women in India', *Social Welfare*, Vol. 48, New Delhi, July.

Andhra Pradesh Panchayati Raj (Reservation of seats of ward members and offices of sarpanches of Gram Panchayats) Rules, 1995, G.O.MS.NO. 285, Panchayati Raj and Rural Development (Election-III) Department, 20 May.

Austin, Granville (1976), *The Indian Constitution: Cornerstone of a Nation*, Oxford University Press, Bombay.

Basu, Aparna and Bharati Ray (2003), *Women's Struggle: A History of the All India Women Conference, 1927–2002*, 2nd edition, Manohar, Delhi.

Basu, Aparna (1976), 'Role of Women in the Freedom Movement', in B.R. Nanda (ed.), *Indian Women from Purdah to Modernity*, Vikas, Delhi.

—— (1996), *Mridula Sarabhai: Rebel with a Cause*, Oxford University Press, Delhi.

—— (2008), 'Women's Struggle for the Vote', *Indian Historical Review*, Vol. 35, No. 1.

Chattopadhyaya, Kamaladevi (1983), *Indian Women's Battle for Freedom*, Abhinav Publications, New Delhi.

Coonrod, John and Supriya Banavalikar (2003), 'Visiting the Women and Panchayati Raj Campaign', August, http://www.thp.org/india/trip803

Crook, Richard and James Manor (1998), *Democracy and Decentralization in South Asia and West Africa: Participation, Accountability and Performance,* Cambridge University Press: Cambridge.

Desai, Vasant (1990), *Panchayati Raj: Power to the People*, Himalaya Publishing House, Bombay.

Devasia, Leelamma (2001), 'Rural Women's Empowerment: A Grassroot Level Experiment', *Social Welfare*, Vol. 48, No. 4, July.

Devi, Jagrani (2003), 'Women Leadership in Panchayati Raj', August, http://www.pucl.org/topics/gender/2003/panchayats.htm

Dey, S.K. (1961), *Panchayati Raj in India*, Asia Publishing House, Bombay.

Dhillon, Gurmeet (1980), 'Rural Women in Decision-making Action', *Kurukshetra*, Vol. 26, No. 9, February.

District's Documents of Zilla Panchayati Raj Office, Nizamabad, 2003.

Documentation on Panchayati Raj: Summaries of Major Reports (1991), Centre for Panchayati Raj, NIRD, Hyderabad.

Dubeshi, P.R. (1990), 'Decentralisation and Rural Development', *Kurukshetra*, Vol. 29, March.

Dwaraki, S. Narayanswamy and B.R. Palanithurai (1997), *Major Issues in New Panchayati Raj System*, Kanishka Publications, New Delhi.

Forbes, Geraldine (1998), *Women in Modern India*, Cambridge University Press, Cambridge.

Gangrade, K.D. (1974), *Emerging Pattern of Leadership*, Rachana Publications, Delhi.

Ghosh, Dilip (1997), 'Grassroots Women Leaders: Who are They? A Study in a West Bengal District', *Journal of Rural Development*, Vol. 16, No. 2, Hyderabad.

Government of Andhra Pradesh (2003), Nizamabad District Profile, September, http://nizamabad.nic.in/code/profile

Gurumoorthy, T.R. (2000), 'Self-Help Groups Empower Rural Women', *Kurukshetra*, Vol. 48, No. 5, February.

Ijlal, S.M. and Anis Zaid (1988), *Politics, Power and Leadership in Rural India*, Commonwealth Publishers, New Delhi.

India, Panchayati Report (2001), *Four Decades of Decentralised Governance in Rural India*, Vol. II, NIRD, Hyderabad.

Inter-Parliamentary Union (1999), Participation of Women in Political Life: An Assessment of Developments in National Parliaments, Political Parties, Governments and the Inter-Parliamentary Union, five years after the Fourth World Conference on Women, Geneva, http://www.ipu.org/pdf/publications/womenplus5_en.pdf, viewed on 12 November 2012.

Janabha (2001), Gram Panchayat Office: Chittapoor, Mandal: Balkonda, District: Nisamabad, A.P.

Jhas, S.N. (1999), 'Introduction' in S.N. Jha and P.C. Mathur (eds.), *Decentralisation and Local Politics; Readings in Indian Government and Politics,* Sage Publication: London.

Joshi, H.G. (2010), *Dynamics of Women Leadership*, Ace Books India, New Delhi.

Kaul, Shashi and Shradha Sahni (2009), 'Participation of Women in Panchayati Raj Institutions', *Studies on Home and Community Science*, Vol. 3, No. 1, pp. 29–38.

Krishna, Sudhir (1997), 'Women and Panchayati Raj: The Law, Programmes and Practices', *Journal of Rural Development*, Vol. 16, No. 4, Hyderabad.

Madan, N.L. (1989), *Indian Political System: Socio-Economic Dimensions*, Ajantha Publishers, Delhi.

Mandal, Jyotirmay (2003), *Women and Reservation in India*, Kalpz Publications, Delhi.

Manikyamba, P. (1989), *Women in Panchayati Raj Structures*, Gain Publishing House, New Delhi.

—— (2003), 'The Numbers Dilemma: Success Stories and Manipulative Mechanism', *South Asian Journal of Socio-political Studies*, Vol. 3.

Mathew, George (2000), *Status of Panchayati Raj in the States and Union Territories of India*, Concept Publishing Company, New Delhi.

Mehta, S.R. (1972), *Emerging Pattern of Rural Leadership*, Wiley Eastern Private Limited, New Delhi.

Menon, Madhava N.R. (1995), 'Democratisation of the Polity and Restructuring of the Judicial System at the Grassroots', *Kurukshetra*, Vol. XLIV, December.

Menon, Nivedita (1995), *Gender and Politics in India*, National Publishing House, New Delhi.

Ministry of Panchayati Raj, Government of India (2013), Rashtriya Gram Swaraj Yojana. http://www.panchayat.gov.in/documents/10198/595743/USQ%201863.pdf, viewed on 10 December 2013.

Mishra, Anil Dutt (2002), *Panchayati Raj: Gandhian Perspective*, Mittal Publications, New Delhi.

Mishra, S.N., Lokesh Kumar and Chaitali Pal (1996), *New Panchayati Raj in Action*, Mittal Publications, New Delhi.

Mishra, Shweta (1997), 'Women and 73rd Constitutional Amendment Act: A Critical Appraisal', *Social Action*, Vol. 47, January–March.

Mohanty, Bidyut (2003), 'Women's Presence in Panchayats (Village Councils) in India: A New Challenge to Patriarchy', paper presented at International Conference on Women and Politics in Asia, Halmstad, Sweden, 6–7 June.

Narang, R.H. (1987), A Comparative Study of the Soio-Economic and Home Factors Affecting the Academic Achievement of Boys and Girls (10 and 11 Years) in the Rural and Urban Areas, Buch, M.B. (ed.) *Fourth Survey of Research in Education*, Vol. 1, NCERT: New Delhi.

Oommen, T.K. (1997), Popular Participation in Promoting Development: The Class of India (Mimeo), Jawaharlal Nehru University: New Delhi.

Panda, Snehalata (1996), 'Emerging Pattern of Leadership among Rural Women in Orissa', *Indian Journal of Public Administration*, Vol. 42, No. 3–4.

Parida, Dayanidhi (2010), 'Women and Panchayat Raj: A Study', *Orissa Review*, February-March, pp. 22–23.

Ruth, J. Alsop, Anirudh Krishna and Disa Sjoblom (1999), *Inclusion and Local Elected Governments: The Panchayati Raj System in India*, World Bank, Washington, D.C., www.siteresources.world bank.org, accessed on 2 February 2011.

Sapru, R.K. (2010), *Public Policy: Art and Craft of Policy Analysis*, PHI Learning Private Limited, New Delhi.

Shah, B.L. (1980), *Panchayati Raj: The Role of Panchayati Raj in Independent Rural Development*, Cosmo Publications, New Delhi.

Singh, J.L. and G.P. Pandy (1998), *50 Years of Panchayati Raj and Rural Development*, Manak Publications, Delhi.

Smitha, K.C. (2007), 'Socio-economic Determinants of Women Leadership at the Grassroots', *Working Paper No. 186*, Institute for Social and Economic Change, New Delhi.

Spio, K. (1997), 'The Role of Women in the Rural Society', *Journal of Rural Development*, Vol. 16, No. 3, New Delhi.

Vyasulu, Poornima and Vinod Vyasulu (1999), Women in Panchayati Raj Gram Roots Democracy, *Economy and Political Weekly*, Vol. 34, No. 52.

World Bank (2000). Overview of Rural Decentralization in India, Vol. 11, Washington D.C.

17

Women's Empowerment through Panchayati Raj Institutions

A Sociological Study of Odisha

Gadadhara Mohapatra

The rural development strategy in India has undergone a paradigm shift from 'philanthropy' to 'welfare' and at present from 'welfare' to 'rights-based approach' towards poverty alleviation. India is a welfare state with inclusive growth as planned strategy of rural development. The participation and representation of people in the planning process is important as ownership and leadership of delivery process at grassroots level (GoO, 2013–14: 1). Literally 'Panchayat' means assembly (*Yat*) of five (*Panch*) persons who are generally wise and elders chosen and accepted by the village community. Prior to independence, these assemblies were present in Indian villages and used to settle disputes between individuals and villages. The term 'panchayat' is relatively new, having originated during the British Administration. 'Raj' literally means governance or government. Thus, Panchayati Raj is the government at village panchayats which can be treated as decentralised form of Government where panchayats are responsible for their own affairs like planning, developments, social justice etc. (GoO, 2013–14: 7).

The term 'empowerment' is essentially an enabling process to make people capable of taking decisions concerning their development and changing their lives for the better. The Panchayati Raj Institutions (PRIs), through 73rd Constitutional Amendment, have been designed to empower the people at three appropriate levels. The Amendment provided institutional mechanism and was meant to rekindle the flame of self-governance. The basic objective of the democratic decentralisation through reactivation of the Panchayati Raj system was to realise Gandhiji's concept of 'Gram Swaraj' (Aslam, 2007: 79). The most important aspects of the widening democratic decentralisation has been the reservation of seats for the women and dalits. Extending reservation to women in PRIs has certainly led to the increased participation of women in panchayats as voters, candidates, and elected members of PRIs taking part in decision-making, planning implementation and evaluation (Mathur, 2006: 130).

Participation of women in panchayat dates back to 1963–68, when there was an all women panchayat in Nimbut village in Pune district of Maharashtra. However, in recent years, participation of women in panchayats is mandated for all panchayats throughout the country. However, this formal position has not necessarily led to substantivise participation. While reservation has resolved some of the problems, the constraints which stem from traditional village institutions and familial and socio-cultural forces still remain. Protagonists of reservation argue that the male dominated political system has so far refused to provide space to women and that reservations can create the space to enable women to exert pressure on the system to bring their issues on the political agenda (Sharma, 1998: 36; Mathur, 2006: 130).

There is evidence to show that in many areas women attempt to address the more vital needs of women. As such, they work on schemes for bringing piped water into the village, inspect development works and nutrition centres under the Integrated Child Development Services (ICDS) and pay particular attention to children's education. They also take the initiative in a variety of family and matrimonial matters, from abusive or alcoholic husbands to settling land disputes (CWDS, 1999: 137 quoted in UNDP, 2003; Mathur, 2008: 85). However, certain constraints which stem from traditional village institutions and familial and socio-cultural forces still remain (Mathur, 2008: 84). Social constraints feature (a) patriarchal ordering of society that leads to tokenism and surrogate representation; (b) illiteracy which deprives women participation in decision-making; and (c) low caste position combines the oppression of caste and patriarchy (UNDP, 2003: 42; Mathur, 2008: 86).

It is in this context, the paper attempts to study the women's participation in panchayats, the empowerment aspects and emerging patterns of women leadership among the dalit and tribal groups in the state of Odisha.

Defining Women's Empowerment

In this section, an attempt has been made to conceptualise women's empowerment by exploring the literature from gender and/or women studies.

Empowerment refers broadly to the expansion of freedom of choice and action to shape one's life. It implies control over resources and decisions. For poor people, that freedom is severely curtailed by their voicelessness and powerlessness in relation particularly to the state and markets. There are important gender inequalities, including within the household. The World Bank adopted an institutional definition of empowerment in the context of poverty reduction and defines empowerment as the process of assets and capabilities of poor people to participate in, negotiate with, influence, control and hold accountable institutions that affect their lives (World Bank, 2002: xviii). The UNICEF women's equality and empowerment framework emphasises women's access, awareness of causes of inequality, capacity to direct one's own interests, and taking control and action to overcome obstacles to reducing structural inequality (UNICEF, 2001). The United Nations Development Programme's Gender Empowerment Measure focuses on inequalities in economic and political participation and decision-making power and power over economic resources (UNDP, 1995). The definition used by the International Fund for

Agricultural Development includes both access to productive resources and the capacity to participate in decisions that affect the least privileged (Popular Coalition to Eradicate Hunger and Poverty, 1995).

Empowerment is the most frequently used term in the development discourse in contemporary times. In the World Summit for Social Development held at Copenhagen in March 1995, empowerment featured prominently as an objective. The Draft Declaration of the Third Preparatory Committee adopted by the heads of states and governments asserted that 'the most productive policies and investments are those which empower people to maximise their capacities, resources and opportunities'. It also emphasises that the main objective of development is to empower people, particularly women, to strengthen their capacities. This is to be achieved through the full participation of people in the formulation, implementation and evaluation of decisions determining the functioning and well-being of society (Burra et al., 2005: 44–45). The Indian government's country paper for the Copenhagen Summit included a section on 'Empowering the People – Models of Mobilisation'. This paper saw the empowerment of people in enabling them to help themselves and removing social, economic, cultural and psychological barriers, which would transform them from being passive recipients of government programmes to being active participants and managers of their own affairs (GoI, 1995 cited in Burra et al., 2005). In the fourth World Conference on Women convened at Beijing, China, the resolution was adopted to promulgate a set of principles concerning the equality of men and women. More importantly, the declaration emphasises to intensify efforts to ensure equal enjoyment of all human rights and fundamental freedoms for all women and girls who face multiple barriers to their empowerment and advancement because of such factors as their race, age, language, ethnicity, culture, religion or disability, or because they are indigenous people.

There exists a wide range of studies on women's empowerment within the field of gender and development studies. In an extensive exploration of the term empowerment, Kabeer (1999, 2001) focuses on three dimensions that define the capacity to exercise strategic life choices: access to resources, agency and outcomes. Amartya Sen (1985, 1999) has written extensively on the importance of substantive freedoms and the individual freedom to choose and achieve different outcomes. Mayoux (1995) has classified three dimensions of empowerment: Power to, Power with and Power within. Power to: refers to the power of individuals first to survive, gain control over labour, their body, their family resources and also including freedom from violence and fertility and decision-making process within their household. Power with: refers women collectives are able to negotiate their gender, caste, class and other initiative in institutions of the market such as labour market, commodity market, financial market, the state government offices and Gram Panchayats. And Power within: refers to the desired power from individual and collective both involving three dimensions such as self-awareness, confidence and assertiveness. According to Andre Beteille (1999), much of the literature on empowerment is context driven and is about radical social transformation, oppressed-oppressor relationship, redistribution of power and social change. The critical question to him is linked with the nature of social transformation and its measurability. Empowerment could be invoked in the context of human rights, basic needs, economic security, capacity building, skill formation, condition of dignified social existence. Implicit in the idea of empowerment is a certain theory of social change from hierarchical to an egalitarian and democratic type of society.

The most distinctive feature of the term 'empowerment' is that it contains within it the word power. Empowerment is therefore, concerned with power, and particularly with changing the power relations between individuals and groups in society. Women's empowerment is thus the process, and the outcome of the process, by which women gain greater control over material and intellectual resources, and challenge the ideology of patriarchy and gender-based discrimination of women in all the institutions and structures of society (Batliwala, 2013: 43).

Pandit Jawaharlal Nehru stated that 'You can tell the condition of a nation by looking at the status of its women' and Eleanor Roosevelt defined as 'A woman is like a tea bag: you cannot tell how strong she is until you put her in hot water (Eleanor cited in Ayres, 1996: 199). The concept of gender equality is enshrined in the Indian Constitution in its Preamble, Fundamental Rights, Fundamental Duties and Directive Principles. The constitution not only grants equality to women, but also empowers the State to adopt measures of positive discrimination in favour of women. India has also ratified various international conventions and human rights instruments committing to secure equal rights of women. Key among them is the ratification of the Convention on Elimination of All Forms of Discrimination against Women (CEDAW) in 1993. The women's movement and a widespread network of non-Government organisations which have strong grassroots presence and deep insight into women's concerns have contributed in inspiring initiatives for the empowerment of women. However, there exists a wide gap between the goals enunciated in the constitution, legislation, policies, plans, programmes and related mechanisms on the one hand, and the situational reality of the status of women in India, on the other (Amutha and Rajkumar, 2007).

The next section deals with the interconnectedness between decentralisation and the Panchayati Raj system in India.

Decentralisation and Panchayati Raj Institutions

Decentralisation has emerged as the key element in the present discourse of improving governance. It has become a very fashionable term and all countries, whatever their mode of government, are vying with each other in experimenting with decentralisation (Manor, 1999 cited in Mathur, 2006: 124; 2008: 72). In Gandhi's dream, India was seen as a slightly decentralised polity, with its villages having extensive political and economic autonomy. The dominant concept was of village republics and village self-sufficiency – gram swaraj (village self-rule). A web of interdependent political and economic networks through the creation of a self-reliant village economy and local self-government was regarded as the most effective way of meeting the basic needs of people. Gandhi elaborated that each village must be a complete republic, independent of its neighbours for its vital needs and yet interdependent for many others in which dependence is a necessity. In this structure composed of innumerable villages, there will be ever widening but ascending circles. He emphasised that life will not be a pyramid, with the apex sustained by the bottom. But it will be an oceanic circle whose centre will be the individual, always ready to perish for the village (Ghosh, 2005; Mathur, 2006, 2008).

Gandhiji's ideas about decentralisation and panchayats effectively meant self-rule of the village community, leaving minimal functions to the governments of the provinces and the Centre. He conceptualised organising the Indian polity based on communitarian principles where power does not flow from the top to bottom, but travels from the village communities to the districts, and then upwards to the provinces and the Center (Bandhopadhyay, 2003: 3986; Mathur, 2006: 125). While the concern for national unity formed the background of the debates in the Constituent Assembly, the discussions were also marked by issues of social and economic exploitation of the depressed classes. B.R. Ambedkar, who represented the depressed classes, strongly argued that empowering village institutions would perpetuate the dominance of the upper castes who would continue to exploit the lower castes and the poor people. He applauded the fact that the draft constitution had 'discarded the village', which he damned as nothing 'but a sink of localism, den of ignorance and narrow-mindedness' (Mathur, 2006: 125). Gandhi's panchayat offered entirely a new pattern of structuring the Indian economy and polity; however it could not fit into the framework of the representative system of parliamentary government strategy of economic development. The constitution considered the individual and the not the village as the basic unit of the political system. The Constitution of India that was adopted was federal parliamentary in nature with a pronounced bias towards centralisation. As a concession to the advocates of the panchayat system, the Constitution included the *Directive Principles of State Policy* which states that: 'The State shall take steps to organise village panchayats and endow them with such powers and authority as may be necessary to enable them to function as units of self-government.' The panchayat system was not accepted as an alternative form of political and economic organisation but the government was encouraged to organise panchayats within the proposed federal parliamentary structure (Mathur, 2006: 125).

The next section provides an overview of the evolution of panchayat system, the three-tier structure of panchayats, the panchayat election and the women's participation in panchayats, the empowerment aspects and emerging patterns of women leadership among the dalit and tribal groups in the State of Odisha.

Panchayati Raj in Odisha: An Overview

Odisha became a separate province in 1936. It is one of the few states in the post-independent period to take up the Panchayati Raj as its main point of rural administration. The Odisha Gram Panchayat Act, 1948 is the first legislation prescribing constitution, power and functions of Gram Panchayats in the State of Odisha. During the Chief Ministership of Nabakrushna Choudhury, a further attempt was made through constitution of Anchal Sasan and creation of Anchal Fund under the Orissa Estate Abolition Act of 1951. The Anchal Sasan Act (1955) was intended to accord full power to Anchal, a local authority which was at the higher level than the Gram Panchayat. But, the Anchal Sasan Act was not implemented which prevented Odisha's pioneering role in the democratic decentralisation process much earlier to the Balwant Rai Mehta Committee Report (Xaxa, 2013: 117). The fate of Gram Panchayat during 1950s and early 1960s was under the mercy of several departments like Board of Revenue Department, Department of Agriculture and Community Development and then moved to the Political and Services Department. In December 1959, it was placed under the Department of Planning and Coordination with a Secretary to head the department (Xaxa, 2013: 117). The B.R. Mehta Committee recommendations were given effect in the year 1961 and the three-tier system of PRIs was introduced in Odisha. Both Panchayat Samiti and Zilla Parishad Acts were enacted. In July 1962, a new Department of Community Development and Panchayati Raj was created. The Panchayats, Samiti, Parishads and former District Boards came under its purview. Thus, the three-tier Panchayati Raj System introduced in Odisha took few years to get established. In 1967, Odisha came under Swatantra-Jana Congress coalition government. As a part of poll promise, the State Legislature abolished the Parishad in 1968 and a two-tier system was in operation. This enhanced the role and responsibility of the Panchayat Samities. Odisha, who introduced legislation on grassroot democratic bodies ahead of many states in India, could not retain its tempo. The Five-Year Plan was dormant and there was visible stagnation. It remained relegated for two decades including the second generation PR bodies recommended by Balwant Rai Mehta Committee (Xaxa, 2013: 117).

In 1990, Odisha under Biju Patnaik acted ahead of the Central Government's initiative 27 years ago, when he was Chief Minister of Odisha, he could create a pro-active government for democratic decentralisation. He had also introduced the concept of Panchayat industry and award to Samiti for visible industrial development. His short tenure prevented Panchayat System to get his dynamic vision and wisdom being translated into action. In the year 1991, three landmark legislations were enacted to facilitate devolution of power to the PR bodies to bring about rural development through people's participation and cooperation. The elections for PR bodies were held in 1992. A new social, revolution in rural Odisha ushered and one-third seats were reserved for women in all the tiers of PR bodies (Xaxa, 2013: 18).

However, in its present form, it came into existence in 1994. Gram Panchayats are treated as the unit for formulation of developmental programmes, Panchayat Samitis emerged as an important institution for implementing different developmental programmes like poverty alleviation programmes and social security schemes etc. and Zilla Parishads function as supervisory body. In order to avoid overlapping and duplication of work in the field, Zilla Parishad is to prepare a Master Plan for the district as a whole undertaking all the aspects of integrated development (GoO, 2013–14: 7). Before 73rd Constitutional Amendment came into force, Government of Odisha had adopted some of the important provisions such as reservation for women, SCs, STs, in its existing Panchayati Raj Acts. Subsequently, the Odisha Panchayati Raj Acts were further amended for full conformity with the Constitutional amendment.

Elections to the Gram Panchayats and Panchayat Samitis in Odisha were held before the 73rd Amendment came into force. Accordingly, Odisha became the first state to introduce one-third reservation for women in panchayats. The State conducted elections to PRIs during 10th to 15 January 1997 and implemented 33 per cent reservation of seats for women in Panchayati Raj Institutions (PRIs) at a time when the centre was still deliberating on the issue. The percentage of elected women representatives is slightly higher than 35 per cent against a reservation percentage of 33 per cent under the provisions of Panchayat legislations. In Zilla Parishads, 14 women have been elected against unreserved posts, whereas in Panchayat Samitis there are 133 women. In Gram Panchayats there are 2,652 women against unreserved posts. The reservation is rotated at the time of Panchayat elections that is, every five years. In Odisha, the two-child norm is in force. No special safeguards are available against the removal of women Sarpanch and they are treated at par with male Sarpanch.

In 2011, the Government of Odisha has made 50 per cent reservation for women in PRIs to achieve gender equality in the representation in panchyat raj bodies. The state legislature unanimously gave its confirmation to the Orissa Panchayat Laws (Amendment) Bill, 2011 by amending the Odisha Gram Panchayat Act, 1964, Orissa Panchayat Samiti Act and the Orissa Zilla Parishad Act enhancing the quota for women from the existing 33 per cent to 50 per cent (*The Economic Times*, 8 April 2011). By amending the Panchayat laws, the Bill also provided reservation of the seats and office of the Chairpersons for two terms as it was felt that the operation of single term did not attract more candidates. The experience of first term would be useful in the second term for the women to prove themselves as the true representatives of women as well as the entire community. It was implemented in the PR elections in February-March 2012. This was being done in view of the efficiency, abilities and success shown by women in various spheres and in order to empower the women in the decision-making process at local self-government (Xaxa, 2013: 121). The Odisha Panchayati Raj Department and the United Nations Entity for Gender Equality and Empowerment of Women (UN Women) have signed an agreement for promoting women's political leadership and empowering the elected representatives in the local government. At present the programme is being implemented in six states, i.e. Andhra Pradesh, Bihar, Karnataka, Madhya Pradesh, Odisha, and Rajasthan. The main objectives of the programme are capacity building of the elected women representatives at the Gram Sabha level, research and policy advocacy to address the legal and political issues pertaining to local self-governance and evolution of a centre of excellence. Reservations for SCs and STs in Panchayats are made in accordance with their percentage in the population. SCs representation is 16.36 per cent and STs representation is 26.71 per cent.

Extension of Panchayats to the Scheduled Tribe Areas (PESA)

Odisha also falls under the purview of the Panchayat Extension to the Scheduled Areas (PESA) Act. The state has districts, which either fall partially or completely under this act. Fully scheduled area includes Mayurbhanj, Sundargarh and Koraput district, whereas PESA implemented in some parts in the eight districts of Raigada, Keonjhar, Sambalpur, Boudh, Ganjam, Kalahandi, Bolangir and Balasore district in Odisha.

Panchayati Raj Department, Odisha

The Panchayati Raj Department carried out its activities through 30 Sections at Government level, and 30 Zilla Parishads, 314 Panchayat Samitis (PS), 6,232 Gram Panchayats (GP) at the field level. Zilla Parishads and District Rural Development Agencies (DRDA) at district level, Panchayat Samitis at Block level and Gram Panchayats at village level are the existing structures through which Panchayati Raj Department activities are being carried out in rural Odisha. Besides, there is State Institute for Rural Development (SIRD) established in 1964 at Bhubaneswar for training and capacity building of PRIs elected representatives and field functionaries at the State Headquarter level. Likewise, there are three Extension Training Centres (EXTCs) at Bhubaneswar, Bhawanipatna (Kalahandi) and Keonjhar for imparting such training at regional level (GoO, 2013–14: 8).

In order to support the rural artisan and producers in facilitating marketing of their products, the Panchayati Raj Department constituted an autonomous body at the state level called 'Odisha Rural Development and marketing Society' (ORMAS) in 1991, under Societies Registration Act-1860. The counterpart of ORMAS at district level is known as District Supply and marketing Societies (DSMSs) which plays an active role as a catalyst for providing all kinds of training, capacity building and marketing support to rural artisans and producers.

The Panchayati Raj Department, Government of Odisha is committed to strengthen PRIs as 'Institutions of Self-Government'. Out of 29 enlisted subjects of 11 departments were transferred to Panchayati Raj Institutions in the line of 73rd Constitutional Amendment (1992). District Level Officers, Block Level Officers and Village Level functionaries of 11 departments have been made accountable to Zilla Parishad, Panchayat Samitis and Gram Panchayats respectively for implementation of the subjects or schemes transferred to PRIS.

Odisha had taken the lead in providing reservation in favour of SCs, STs, and Women in three-tier PRIs even before the 73rd Constitutional Amendment. A distinguishing feature of the Panchayati Raj system in Odisha is that either the Chairperson or Vice-Chairperson of all the three tiers of PRIs is a woman (GoO, 2013–14: 9).

The basic function of the Panchayati Raj Department is to realise the objectives of alleviating rural poverty and providing improved quality of life for the rural population especially people living below the poverty line (GoO, 2013–14: 9). While the Ministry of Rural Development, Government of India implements various schemes and programmes including the wage-employment schemes, self-employment schemes, and rural housing schemes, matters relating to devolution of powers to PRIs, decentralised planning, Finance Commission grants, and the Backward Region Grant Fund (BRGF) are dealt with by Ministry of Panchayati Raj, Government of India (MoPR, 2012: 21).

Under the legislation as it stands amended, Panchayats at all the three levels have been entrusted with duties and functions with regard to 21 out of 29 matters listed in the Eleventh Schedule of the Constitution (Table 1).

Table 1

Devolution Index

S.No.	*Name of the Department*	*Activities Devolved*
1	Agriculture	Kharif and rabi programme, soil conservation, horticulture, and watershed activities.
2	Food, Supplies, and Consumer Welfare	Public distribution system.
3	Health and Family Welfare	Healthcare including hospitals, Primary Health Centres (PHCs), dispensaries, and Maternal and Child Health (MCH) centres.
4	Women and Child Development	Socio-economic development of women, integrated child development, welfare of disabled, adoption of children, and welfare of the aged.
5	Water Resources	Minor irrigation, water management.
6	School and Mass Education	Expansion and development of educational facilities, establishing and maintaining hostels and other welfare literacy campaign (TLC)measures, adult and non-formal education, and the total literary campaign (TLC)
7	Fisheries and Animal Resources Development	Development of livestock, veterinary services, feeding and fodder, dairy development, inland fisheries, marine fisheries, marketing processing infrastructure and welfare measures.
8	Cooperation	Agricultural credit and risk management.
9	Panchayati Raj	Regeneration of minor forest produce species, training, MFP collection, processing and marketing charges, rural housing including Indira Awas Yojna, rural water supply, roads, culverts and bridges, waterways, non-conventional energy, poverty alleviation programmes, wage employment programmes, and markets and fairs.
10	SC and ST Development	Eradication of untouchability, curbing atrocities against SCs/STs, educational and economic development.

Source: MoPR, GoI Report, 2012: 21–22.

There has been devolution not only of functions but also of functionaries. District and block level officers and village level functionaries of the 11 departments are accountable to the Zilla Parishad, Panchayat Samiti, and Gram Panchayat respectively for implementing the schemes transferred to PRIs, although they continue as employees of the respective departments.

Three-Tier Structure of PRIs

Odisha has 30 districts, 58 sub-divisions, 316 tehsils, 1,863 revenue circles, 314 blocks, and 51,061 villages, which have been grouped into 6,234 gram panchayats. Out of these, there are 12 tribal districts, 18 tribal blocks, and 1,902 tribal gram panchayats, which come under the purview of the PESA Act. PRIs at the district, block, and village level are the Zilla Panchayats, Panchayat Samitis, and gram panchayats respectively. Table 2 gives the breakup of elected representatives (ERs) at the various levels.

Table 2

Social Breakup of Panchayati Raj Institutions (PRIs): Elected Representatives (ERs)

Level	*Total ERs*	*SC*	*ST*	*Women*
District	854	139	219	296
Block	6,227	1,025	1,074	2,188
Village	93,781	15,746	25,453	33,602

Source: MoPR, 2012.

Palli Sabhas

Odisha also has Gram Sabhas and Ward Sabhas at the village and ward levels respectively. There are 87,542 ward members in the state. Voters from a revenue village constitute the Palli Sabha and ward members preside over its meetings. One-tenth of the members present must be women (MoPR, 2012). At least two weeks' time is given for holding a Palli Sabha. The Gram Panchayat convenes the meetings once a year in February. The Gram Sabha fixes the place of the Palli Sabha if there are many wards in a revenue village. The Palli Sabha takes all the important decisions like selection of beneficiaries and preparing schemes, as well as selection of the village labour leader.

There are support functionaries at all the three levels in the form of seven Standing Committees (SCs) for the planning, finance, anti-poverty programmes, agriculture, animal husbandry, soil conservation, horticulture, watershed development and fisheries. The support functionaries also look into the public works, irrigation, electricity, drinking water supply and rural sanitation. The functionaries also look into the matters of health and social welfare including women and child development, public distribution system, welfare of weaker sections, forest, fuel and fodder. It also gives attention to the promotion of handicrafts, cottage industry, khadi and village industries, and rural housing and finally in promoting education, sports and culture. Apart from the SCs, there are also government functionaries who are support staff and assist the Panchayats in carrying out their functions at each level (Table 3).

Table 3

PRI Support Functionaries in Odisha

Gram Panchayat	*Panchayat Samiti*	*Zilla Parishad*
SC members	SC members	Collector
Gram Sachiv (Panchayat Secretary)	Junior Engineer/Addl. JE	Project Director, DRDA
Panchayat Executive Officer	Gram Panchayat Extension Officer	SC members
Rojgar Sewak (NREGS)	Programme Officer (NREGS)	Zilla Parishad CEO
ASHAs (under NRHM)	BDO	
AWWs (ICDS)		

Source: Panchayati Raj Department, Government of Odisha website.

Odisha Panchayat Elections, 2012

Odisha conducted its panchayat elections in the month of February 2012, which was spread over five phases. Over 2.4 crore voters elected 1,00,841 leaders as sarpanches, block samiti nominees, ward members, and zilla parishad members. These leaders consist of 87,528 ward members and 6,228 sarpanches at the panchayat level, 6,231 nominees at the panchayat samiti level and 854 at the zilla parishad (ZP) level. Again for the first time, Maoists took part in the panchayat elections in two tribal dominated districts in western Odisha and won unopposed. Interestingly, earlier they had given a call to boycott the elections in eight districts, including Malkangiri, Kandhamal, Koraput, Nuapada and Nayagargh. But in these instances they put up candidates and ensured that no one else contested in those seats. Thus, in the recent elections Maoists have won in 30 blocks. About 25,000 members and 32 sarpanches have been elected unopposed in those blocks. This phenomenon is a major concern not only to the State but also to the Central Government, since this has serious implications for the use of development funds which are at the disposal of the panchayats of the backward districts under various schemes like the MGNREGS, Backward Region Development Fund etc. (Mohanty, 2012). Another interesting feature of the recent poll is that the Jhodia community of Koraput District boycotted the polls on the demand that they should be declared as a Scheduled Tribe. Since they are currently listed as OBC, their land is easily taken over by the upper castes. Hence, in Kashipur Block, nobody had filed nomination and no election was held in three zones of the tribal block. The villagers also boycotted the panchayat election in other districts such as Balasore and Mayurbhanj to demand access to basic services. Another notable feature of this election was that out of a total of 3,989 candidates who were elected unopposed in Ganjam district as many as 2,115 were women. Among them there were 2,014 ward members, 49 sarpanches, 51 nominees and just one zilla parishad member (Mohanty, 2012).

Empowerment of Women in Panchayati Raj System in Odisha

Review of empirical studies on empowerment of women in Panchayati Raj system in Odisha, by Snehalata Panda (1996), Bidyut Mohanty (2002), Sachidananda Satpathy (2002), Dayanidhi Parida (2010) reveals that due to strong caste feelings women belonging to upper caste have not come forward to represent the Panchayat which provided an opportunity to the women from the labour and lower caste to emerge as a potential force in village politics. It is found that, due to illiteracy and poor socio-economic status, the women leaders could not assert their influence on the decision-making process. Though reservation has made women able to participate in the electoral process of the local self-governance system in a large way, women leadership has come under immense pressure due to the criminalising Panchayat elections including harassment and murder. Due to social tradition of male superiority, women leaders are not getting any chances to defend their voice before elderly male persons. They are feeling shy while talking in a meeting. Women leadership faced tremendous pressure in their normal functioning as power-hungry male members did not accept them at par. The percentage of women at various levels of political activities increased dramatically, but it is found that women were still not able to exercise their power, in many cases they were just rubber stamps either in the hands of their family; members or in the hands of their senior party members (Xaxa, 2013: 119).

The system of Panchayati Raj, which was initiated mainly for people's participation in political and economic processes, somehow has not been successful in ensuring women's participation. Though women have significant contribution to politics, their representation to political institutions like Lok Sabha, Rajya Sabha is very insignificant. Parida and Nayak's (2009) writing on *Empowerment of Women in India* with specific reference to Odisha, explored that subordination of women in society acts as a structural constraint to their participation in political activities. This constraint operates more or less for all classes and communities of women (Parida and Nayak, 2009: 214–15). It is often seen that husbands and family members influence the women representatives in taking decisions. In most cases the women representatives are ignored and they are invariably influenced by male family members. Another fact is that women members depend considerably on their menfolk for decision-making. The relatives of women representatives are sometimes taking active part in their official activities. Thus, reservation under Panchayati Raj for women is at present in the transitional phase and women are not adequately empowered in practice to play an effective role because of social, economic and political factors. Although women's participation in PRIs is very high in absolute sense, yet analysis in relative terms shows that the participation in decision-making is very low. Women have waited for centuries without striving hard to achieve their rightful position and status. They should strive seriously to unshackle themselves from these restrictive chains. They should, therefore, transform as 'women vote bank' and 'pressure group' and exert sufficient pressure on the political heavyweights to gain their rightful share. Only when women succeed in getting larger political decision-making power, can they use it to formulate necessary enactments and safeguard to eliminate gender bias, which would therefore pave way for securing economic power as well. Therefore, gaining of political power is a prerequisite without which other societal injustices can never be rectified (Parida and Nayak, 2009: 215).

Conclusion

From the above analysis of women's participation in panchayats, we can conclude that though reservation has enhanced women's participation in the electoral process of the local self-governance system in a large way, women leadership has come under immense pressure due to the criminalisation of Panchayat elections. The Maoist control of panchayats in Malkangiri and Koraput districts of Odisha is a negative development noticed in the last panchayat election held in 2012. The main concern is that the Maoists are controlling the development funds like MGNREGA, Backward Grant Fund that accrues from the devolution package. It is found that, due to illiteracy and poor socio-economic status, the women leaders could not assert their influence on the decision-making process. It is suggested that increased participation of women in the Panchayat meetings at all the levels may help them to promote and enhance their leadership qualities. Attitudinal change in both men and women are required to encourage rural women to enter into politics. Education can certainly play an important role in bringing social and political awareness among people.

References

Amutha K. and V. Nirmal Raj Kumar (2007), Women Empowernment: Issues and Challenges, in V.S. Ganesmurthy (ed.), *India: Economic Empowerment,* New Century Publications: New Delhi.

Aslam, M. (2007), *Panchayati Raj in India,* National Book Trust India: New Delhi.

Ayres, Alex (1996), *The Wit and Wisdom of Eleanor Roosevelt: An A-Z Compendium of Quotations, Paperback,* Penguin Books: Plume.

Bandhopadhya, D. (2003), 'Twelfth Finance Commission and Panchayat Finance', *Economic and Political Weekly,* Vol. 38, No. 23, June 7, pp. 2242–43.

Batliwala, Srilata (2013), *Engaging with Empowerment: An Intellectual and Experiential Journey,* Women Unlimited an associate of Kali for Women, New Delhi.

Beteille, Andre (1999), 'Empowerment', *Economic and Political Weekly,* Vol. 34, No. 10–11, pp. 589–97.

Burra, Neera et al. (eds) (2005), *Micro-Credit, Poverty and Empowerment: Linking the Triad,* Sage Publications, New Delhi.

Centre for Women's Development Studies (CWDS) (1999), *From Oppression to Assertion: A Study of Panchayats and Women in Madhya Pradesh, Rajasthan and Uttar Pradesh,* CWDS, New Delhi.

Ford Foundation (1959), *India's Food Crisis and Steps to Meet It,* Government of India, New Delhi.

Ghosh, B.D. (2005), *Decentralization and Poverty Reduction Kerala and West Bengal,* Institute of Social Sciences: New Delhi.

Ghosh, Buddhadeb (2000), 'Panchayati Raj: Evolution of the Concept', *Occasional Paper Series No. 25,* Institute of Social Sciences, New Delhi.

Government of India (1978a), *Report of the Committee on Panchayati Raj Institutions,* New Delhi (Chairman: Ashok Mehta).

—— (1978b), Five Year Plan 1978–83, New Delhi.

—— (1982), *Report of the Working Group on District Planning,* Planning Commission, New Delhi (Chairman: C.H.H. Rao).

—— (1985), *Report of the Committee to Review Existing Arrangements for Rural Development and Poverty Alleviation Programmes,* Ministry of Rural Development, New Delhi.

Government of Odisha (GoO) (2013), Budget Outcome 2013–14, Panchayati Raj Department, available at: http://orissapanchayat.gov.in

Kabeer, Naila (1999), Resources, Agency, Achievements: Reflection on the Measurement of Women's Empowerment, *Development and Change,* Vol. 30, pp. 435–464.

—— (2001), 'Discussing Women's Empowerment: Theory and Practice', *SIDA Studies No. 3,* Stockholm.

—— (2001), 'Discussing Women's Empowerment: Theory and Practice' SIDA Studies No. 3, Sen, Amartya (1985, 'Well-being, Agency and Freedom. The Dewey Lectures 1984'. *The Journal of Philosophy,* 82(4), pp. 169–221.

Manor, James (1999), *The Political Economy of Democratic Decentralization,* World Bank: Washington DC.

Mathur, Kuldeep (2006), 'Empowering Local Government: Decentralisation and Governance', in Amitabh Kundu (editor chief) and Muchkund Dubey et al. (eds), *India Social Development Report 2006,* Council for Social Development, Oxford University Press, New Delhi.

—— (2006), 'Empowering Local Government: Decentralisation and Governance', in *India Social Development Report*, Council for Social Development, Oxford Press: New Delhi.

—— (2008), *From Government to Governance: A Brief Survey of the Indian Experience*, National Book Trust of India: New Delhi.

—— (2013), *Oxford India Short Introductions: Panchayati Raj*, Oxford University Press, New Delhi.

Mayoux, Linda (1995), 'From Vicious Circle to Virtuous Circles? Gender and Micro-enterprise Development', *Occasional Paper*, United Nations Research Institute for Social Development, United Nations Development Programme, p. 82.

Ministry of Panchayati Raj (MoPR) (2012), *Capacity Assessment and Capacity Development Strategy (CA-CDS) Report for Strengthening Panchayati Raj Institutions in Odisha*, Government of India.

Mohanty, Vidyut (2002), Women and Political Empowerment, Institute of Social Sciences: New Delhi.

—— (2008), *From Government to Governance: A Brief Survey of the Indian Experience*, National Book Trust, New Delhi.(2012), 'Odisha: Panchayat Election Results and their Meaning for the Assembly Pool', *Mainstream*, Vol. L, No. 30, July 14.

Panda, Snehalata (1996), Emerging Pattern of Leadership among Rural Women in Orissa, *Indian Journal of Public Administration*, Vol. 42, No. 3–4.

Parida, Dayanidhi (2010), Women and Panchayati Raj: A Study, *Orissa Review*, February–March, 2010.

Parida, Subhas C. and Sasmita Nayak (2009), *Empowerment of Women in India*, Northern Book Centre, New Delhi.

Popular Coalition to Eradicate Hunger and Poverty (1995), Empowerment of the Poor, Discussion Paper 1, Conference on Hunger and Poverty, Brussels, 20–21 November.

Satpathy, Sachidananda (2009), Women's Empowerment and Panchayati Raj: A Case Study from Orissa, unpublished M. Phil Dissertation.

Sen, Amartya (1992), *Inequality Reexamined*, Clarendon Press, Oxford.

—— (1999), *Development as Freedom*, Knopf: New York.

Sharma, Kumud (1998), 'Transformative Politics: Dimensions of Women's Participation in Panchayati Raj', *Indian Journal of Gender Studies*, Vol. 5, No. 1.

United Nations Development Programme (UNDP) (1995), Human Development Report 1995: Gender and Human Development, Oxford University Press: Oxford.

—— (2003), 'Decentralisation in India: Challenges and Opportunities', *Discussion Papers Series 1*, Human Resource Development Centre, New Delhi.

UNICEF (2001), 'The Women's Equality and Empowerment Framework', New York, available at: http://www.unicef.org/programme/gpp/policy/empower.html.

World Bank (2002), *Empowerment and Poverty Reduction: A Sourcebook*, Washington, D.C., USA.

Xaxa, Johani (2013), 'Empowerment of Women in Panchayati Raj System: A Study of Odisha', *Odisha Review*, February-March, pp. 116–22.

18

Representation, Inclusion and Empowerment of Women through Panchayati Raj Institutions

Bihar Perspective

Anuja

The position of women in politics and socio-economic activities has always been miserable. Although women constitute half of the population, their participation in all spheres of life has been negligible since ages.

Political participation means, in nutshell, the involvement of those affected by decisions in the decision-making process. The involvement may include a right to elect representatives, to vote on an issue, to campaign and canvass, to decide matters, etc. Political participation is voluntary involvement of individual(s) in political action. Contesting in elections is the highest level of political participation. It has been found that women's participation in politics worldwide has been of a very low degree. In short, women's participation as political actors has improved but their grip over power structure, at least at the party level, has not been impressive (Verma and Yadav, 1996).

Panchayati Raj Institutions (PRIs) are the vehicles of political empowerment of people at the grassroots level for shaping their own destiny. A vast majority of people are living at the grassroots level in the rural and remote areas without any touch of modernity. A large section of such deprived people belong to scheduled castes, scheduled tribes and other Backward castes as also women in general at the grassroot level.

The three-tier Panchayat Institutions in Bihar consist of a Gram Panchayat at the lowest level, Panchayat Samiti at the Block level and Zila Parishad of the District level. The chairman of the Gram Panchayat is called Mukhiya, the chairperson of the Panchayat Samiti is called Pramukh and the chairperson of the Zila Parishad is called Adhyaksha.

Bihar, after 73rd Amendment of the constitution, enacted Bihar Panchayati Raj Act, 1993 making provisions regarding reservation for the Scheduled Castes, the Scheduled Tribes, Women and Backward class of citizens.

The 73rd and 74th Constitutional Amendments have accorded Indian women a scope for political representation. Despite such provisions, most of them face constraints in pursuing a political career due to various personal, social and institutional reasons. They are generally asked to contest because the seat is reserved for a woman candidate. In reality, they receive little support in exercising their mandate, which demotivates them to participate politically. The sustainability and legitimacy of the local governance structures depends on the capacities of the women, but one finds that women are unable to play an active role in governance and get confined to taking part in only the electoral processes. Gendered identities and practices limit their capacities to articulate and act upon their claims and concerns.

The Constitution says that reservations for women must be not less than 33 per cent. Which means it can be more. Usually, Bihar is spoken of as a very feudal, traditional, socially backward backwater. But the credit must go to Bihar for being the very first State to have legislated that reservation for women will go up to 50 per cent. In the last elections, 55 per cent of the candidates elected to the panchayats were women. Not only had the percentage increased but the actual number of women elected was larger than the reserved quota in a state like Bihar. So, it is not surprising that the example set by Bihar has now been picked up by Chhattisgarh, Madhya Pradesh, Rajasthan and Himachal Pradesh. All these states have raised their reservation quota to 50 per cent. Sikkim has raised it to 40 per cent.

During the last five years Bihar has witnessed a fairly new kind of political empowerment among the deprived sections of the society. The change was noticeable on the political front during this election where 54.44 per cent women for the first time casted their vote more than men. This extraordinary social revolution has taken place in conservative Bihar, in the most tradition-bound rural state.

Despite the remarkable effort made by the Govt. of Bihar for reserving 50 per cent seats for women in Panchayati Raj, their socio- economic and political empowerment/development continues to be major concerns. It will be very interesting to explore the linkages between women's increased representation, with a guaranteed reservation of 50 per cent seats in panchayats in relation to their actual participation. Off and on various questions do crop up in mind: Have women made an impact on these local political institutions of panchayats and on their overall empowerment in the given social and political contexts? How effective have been this reservation policy in PR for women? Does the entry of women into politics affect the communities' attitudinal response towards them? Could elected women representatives get empowered in real of terms of social, economic and political sphere? Did this reservation benefit every section of women? Does this mobilise women to take social action?

Today, India can honestly boast that there are more elected women representatives in India alone than in the rest of the world put together. This revolution is without precedent in history and without parallel in the world, and yet remains a completely silent revolution, largely because the male population has either been acquiescent or wholeheartedly accepted this process. Therefore, this empowerment of women reflects a deep sense of social justice in the processes of social engineering going on in contemporary India, and it also reflects the very deep democratic spirit that prevails in our social, political and economic ethos.

It is for sure that without the system of reservation, women would have had little role to play in grassroots politics in India. Surveys show that 95 per cent of women representatives claimed they could never have come to acquire positions in panchayats, if there were no reserved seats (Centre for Women's Development Studies Reports, 1999). Reservation has at least succeeded in bringing the womenfolk of rural India into the political forum, and elected women could now imagine standing against a man in future. Women members of panchayats are gradually learning to adjust to the new political conditions. The political knowledge of women is increasing and gradually a sense of confidence is getting instilled in them, as they are now aware of the problems being faced by their locality. By all accounts, as each election round passes, it is clear that women have certainly made their presence felt in the power struggles once dominated by men. There are many instances where women have been self-motivated to fight an election. In several instances, the Gram Sabha has persuaded women with leadership potential to stand for election, and this has a far-reaching impact on the empowerment of women.

But even so, there are many instances of illiterate women being elected and holding office and women acting as proxies for their husbands, of discrimination by male members of the panchayat against women holding office, of misuse of the no-confidence and right-to-recall provisions and of the two-child norm in some states to get rid of women representatives.

Given the present scenario, political representation in numbers alone cannot be a sufficient mechanism for women to exercise their agency. Years of discrimination have incapacitated them to articulate the priorities of their constituency and influence the decision-making. They need skills, knowledge and information to express their concerns and influence the decision-making processes as per their concerns.

Various studies have been conducted on Panchayati Raj as a whole and women in PRIs in particular. Hence, it is necessary to mention about the literature which has provided with the conceptual frame of reference for the research, which also facilitated an understanding of the status of research problem area and indicated insightful clues to the research approach method. Therefore, available relevant studies have been reviewed.

Nirmala Buch (2006) in her newly edited book, which is a collaborative study of CWDS *From Oppression to Assertion: A Study of Panchayats and Women in MP, Rajasthan and UP* reveals women representation in Panchayati Raj like: the experience of women, their representation, participation, impact and perceptions depend substantially on the local socio-political context. She selected these states which are low on indicators of social development and gender because this will help in giving an idea to see what women's critical mass of one-third in number entering these grassroots democratic structures have achieved despite the socio-political and economic odds stacked against them.

She also mentioned in her writings that if women make even small, positive beginnings here, these would be important to see what the state and civil society could do to support them. Another interesting work carried out by J. Devika and B.V. Thampi (2008) on 'Gendering Governance or Governing Women? Politics, Patriarchy, and Democratic Decentralisation in Kerala State, India' has been referred in this proposal, which basically expresses women in formal political institutions and local governance, women at the interface of politics and development, and women in oppositional civil social struggles that unfold outside the formal spaces of politics in Kerala. The major context of this work is certainly the institutionalisation of political decentralisation in Kerala in the mid-1990s, and of localised planning through the People's Planning Campaign which not only promised 33 per cent reservation of seats for women in local bodies, but later, they were also promised a share in budgetary resources through the institutionalisation of the Women's Component Plan in local bodies. The results of the experiment are mixed. The numbers of women who have entered the local bodies have exceeded thirty-three per cent of the total number of seats. Nupur Tiwari (2009) is with the Ministry of Panchayati Raj and Development of the North Eastern Region in her article 'Rethinking the Rotation Term of Reservation in Panchayats' says that women need to be empowered in this realm to facilitate their real empowerment. To promote women's empowerment there is an immense need to extend the rotation term of reserved positions for women. In this way, this would allow women in Panchayats the time and space to negotiate their own power relationships within them. If they are given 10 to 15 years of continued opportunity, it can encourage and nurture their desire to be assertive and independent. Without a longer term, true empowerment of women representatives will be a more difficult proposition.

Report on the 'Study on EWRs in Panchayati Raj Institutions' Ministry of Panchayati Raj, GOI, provides useful insights in this regard. The political and social empowerment of women in our panchayats is one of the most significant achievements of India in the last decade. For, at a stroke as it were, over a million women in rural India have been liberated from the kitchen and the courtyard and brought into positions of authority and responsibility in their village communities. Even at the block and district levels, they have assumed office and learned to not only contest elections (and win them) but also to exercise power in the larger interests of the public good. There are still formidable problems to be overcome. Many women are hesitant and tentative in rising to the occasion. Often, the men of the village do not accord them the respect and regard that is their due. Officials take advantage of their inexperience and poor education. Effective devolution is so uneven and inadequate that oftentimes even the most able women are crippled for want of the rightful allocation of functions, finances and functionaries without which effective Panchayati Raj is rendered impossible.

As far as women are concerned, there is no dearth of researches on women in Panchayati Raj Institutions (PRIs). The above stated literatures show that some of the hurdles are gender-specific and some are generic in nature and related to the larger issue of the empowerment of the panchayats. What emerges clearly is that the more effectively the panchayats are endowed with powers and authority, the more effective is the role of women in panchayats.

Bihar is one of the states which scores among the lowest across all human development indicators in terms of health, Below Poverty Line families, literacy, per capita income, etc. Bihar is spoken of as a very feudal, traditional, socially backward state. It is also a State known for its deeply ingrained caste and gender divisions. The selection of this area is because the indicators of women's education, literacy, health and economic participation are very low. Many social evils and practices like: domestic violence, dowry, gender discrimination at all stages are affecting women badly. Thus, through this study it will be revealed that after becoming leaders in local politics what impact women have on day-to-day working and on their empowerment in the political and social milieu. The reservation for women in panchayats have provided a possibility for demolishing traditional gender, caste, class roles and hierarchy bias but it is a long and difficult process to demolish patriarchal structure manifested in the household and the state overnight.

Empowerment of women is becoming an increasingly popular term in human rights and development discourses. It enables to challenge the skewed distribution of power relations in a society. Although women constitute half of the population, they are subjugated unequal in socio-economic and political status. Indian democracy has entered the next century but a large mass of women are kept out of political arena still. Empowerment also demands political inclusion of decision-making and changes in the existing power relations. Political inclusion of women is only possible through effective representation as voters and participation in PRIs election. Therefore, empowerment and political inclusion through representation are essentially related. The 73rd Amendment Act is a major step towards political empowerment of women through PRIs. This has resulted in the entry of large number of women into decision-making bodies in the rural areas, who were otherwise home makers. But equality and rights for women have always been claimed as crucial components in state policy. When we take an example of Bihar state, the status of women is lower in terms of all development indicators such as education, health, justice and of course, governance. But since 2006, the state took an important step in the realm of PRIs in Bihar which introduced 50 per cent reservation for women and became the first state to do so. This to some extent enhanced their status within families and society as well. They obtained new recognition and respect and the feeling of emancipation was realised. The paper is an attempt to highlight through secondary sources that whether representation and inclusion in the political field are the most important factors for empowerment of women. It also tries to explore the reasons for this through theoretical assumptions and explain whether such representation leads on to empowerment of women as a collective group.

It is argued that women need to be 'empowered' in the realm of political decision-making so as to facilitate their 'real' empowerment. About one million women entered panchayats after 73rd Constitutional Amendment Act. It is a known fact that 40 per cent of the elected women represented the marginalised sections and about 70 per cent women representatives were illiterate and most of them had no previous political experience. Therefore, it was but natural that there was a widespread apprehension that women will be manipulated by men. However, in spite of several instances of such manipulation and capitulation by women, the presence of such a large number of women in panchayats has indeed had a deep impact on gender equity. There are a huge number of panchayats working in different circumstances, the extent of empowerment of women vary from region to region and panchayats work under different legal frameworks – as States have the discretion to define the scope and ambit of Panchayati Raj – every spectrum of political behaviour, ranging from abject subordination of women to remarkable instances of social and political assertiveness can be seen in the functioning of panchayats (Tiwari, 2012).

A recent survey, commissioned by the Ministry of Panchayati Raj and executed by the Nielsen Company–ORG Marg under the guidance of an academic advisory committee, provides many new insights into social and political empowerment of women in the new Panchayati Raj Institutions (PRIs). This is the largest-ever survey on any aspect of panchayat functioning, covering Gram Panchayats in 23 states, with a total sample size of over 20,000, including Elected Women Representatives (EWRs), Elected Male Representatives (EMRs), ex-EWRs, official functionaries and members of the community. Nearly three-fourths of the EWRs in the sample belonged to the Scheduled Caste, Scheduled Tribe and OBC categories, and were evenly divided above and below the poverty line. The majority of the elected representatives had contested only one election (87%) and hence the proportion of first timers in politics was also high (86%). Around 14 per cent were re-elected more than once at the Gram Panchayat level. Further analysis showed that the majority of ex-women representatives could not get re-elected because the seat from where they were elected was de-reserved in the next round. While no gender discrimination in the panchayat is reported by 60 per cent of elected women representatives, acceptability in panchayat meetings and enabling them to raise issues freely was mentioned by 94 per cent. A supportive professional environment evidently motivates elected women representatives to perform better, as 60–64 per cent reported an increase in their interaction with line departments and parallel bodies (Tiwari, 2012).

Now majority of women representatives are no more proxy of their male relative patrons. Around 58 per cent of women representatives are now taking their own decisions to contest elections. This is a big achievement. Nearly 15 per cent of women Pradhans are able to win elections second time. Women belonging to younger age groups of 21–35 years have shown better performance compared to the women belonging to the age group of 35 years and above. Women members of active committees at village level were found to be more successful at panchayat level. Again quoting the Report, dalits were also benefited by the whole process. Reservation has inspired and prompted them to contest elections. There can be no greater evidence for the fact that not only has Panchayati Raj attracted women to politics in large numbers, but also that this wish to contest for elections seems to be most keenly felt among the women belonging to the SCs and STs (Tiwari, 2012).

In conclusion, it can be said that to some extent representation and inclusion in Panchayati Raj Institutions have empowered women in Bihar. Mahatma Gandhi has said, 'Perfect democracy is based on individual freedom', embarking on this thought must be realised the significance of gender equality. Effective governance can only be attained through equal participation and leadership. The last 15 years of Panchayati Raj in this country has seen women grow stronger in terms of their participation in politics. Several states like Andhra Pradesh, Bihar, Chhattisgarh, Himachal Pradesh, Jharkhand, Kerala, Karnataka, Madhya Pradesh, Maharashtra, Odisha, Rajasthan, Tripura, Uttarakhand, West Bengal and Assam have already passed legislations in favour of 50 per cent reservation for women. The reservation for women in the elected representatives to panchayat has affected an increase in the number of elected women representatives after 1993. As per the latest available statistics, Elected Women Representatives (EWRs) are 36.75 per cent of the total elected representatives in the Panchayati Raj Institutions.

The political and social empowerment of women in our panchayats is one of the most significant achievements of India in the last decade. For, at a stroke as it were, over a million women in rural India have been liberated from the boundaries of kitchen and courtyard and brought into positions of authority and responsibility in the village communities. Even at the block and district levels, they have assumed offices and learned to not only contest elections but also to exercise power in the larger interests of people. Indeed, the proportion of women getting elected tends to be significantly higher than the reserved quota, with women from the scheduled castes and scheduled tribes often securing higher proportion of seats and chairpersonships than the women of forward classes. As we can see through the latest report on Panchayats in India that women representation in Bihar (54%) has been found highest among other states. Therefore, it is important to mention that due to the reservation, women became a category of political citizens and they are having decision-making powers in the patriarchal structure households.

References

Buch, Nirmala (2006), 'From Oppression to Assertion: A Study of Panchayats in MP, Rajasthan and UP', collaborative study of CWDS.

Centre for Women's Development Studies Report (1999).

Devika, J. and B.V. Thampi (2008), 'Gendering Governance or Governing Women? Politics, Patriarchy, and Democratic Decentralisation in Kerala State, India', Research Report.

Tiwari, Nupur (2009), 'Rethinking the Rotation Term of Reservation in Panchayats', *Economic and Political Weekly*, Vol. 44, No. 5, January.

—— (2012), 'Women and Panchayati Raj', *Yojana*, Vol. 56, June, pp. 36–40.

Verma, Ravindra Kumar and Gyanendra Kumar Yadav (1996), 'Women in Bihar Politics', *Economic and Political Weekly*, Vol. 31, No. 15, April.

Part V

State Specific Experiences in Structure and Functions in PRIs

19

Status of Devolution of the Funds, Functions and Functionaries in United Andhra Pradesh

Task Unfinished?

M. Gopinath Reddy

It is also often argued that decentralisation is a more effective and an efficient framework for delivering pro-poor programmes. The perceived benefits of decentralisation range from stimulation of economic growth and alleviation of rural poverty to strengthening civil society and reducing the responsibilities of the centre (Manor, 1999). It was observed that project costs are four times higher in centralised systems when compared to decentralised systems. Besides, asset maintenance is much better in the decentralised systems (Bardhan, 1996). Decentralisation with its potential benefits coupled with the declining legitimacy of centralised systems has attracted support from a diverse range of ideological schools. While decentralised systems are found to be superior in terms of intra-regional targeting efficiency, their delivery systems target better in low poverty regions and not as well as high poverty regions (Bardhan and Mookherjee, 2000).

This paper dwells on the present status of rural local bodies (panchayati raj institutions) in the state of Andhra Pradesh in the aftermath of 73rd Constitution Amendment. The focus of the paper would be on the devolution of the functions and functionaries and the funds (3 Fs) in the state. The paper also looks at the status of the State Finance Commission (SFCs) and the recommendations made by the SFC and the extent of acceptance of the recommendations by the Andhra Pradesh Government. It is now two decades since 73rd and 74th Constitutional Amendment Acts were passed and it is good time to take stock of the progress of the decentralisation experience and what it had achieved and where it did not take off and the reasons. The paper also looks at status of the District Planning Committees (DPC) in the state as these institutions have important links with the devolution of the functions, functionaries and funds and the planning aspects to be under taken by the DPC.

The issues raised in Vision 2020 document on local bodies are also addressed in the paper. Keeping in view the main objectives of the 73rd Constitutional Amendment Act, the Andhra Pradesh government passed the Andhra Pradesh Panchayat Raj Act 1994. The main features of the Andhra Pradesh Act are the following: it is aimed at promoting participatory democracy; it seeks to ensure regular elections to the Panchayati Raj Institutions (PRIs) for a period of 5 years and prevent scandalous suppression of the local bodies; it aims to create institutions of self-government at the panchayat level by endowing them with the needed powers, authority and finances. It provides for revenue raising powers for the panchayats; it specifically mandates the creation of an independent State Finance Commission (SFC) for the purpose of ensuring financial transfers to the Panchayati Raj bodies; and lastly, it seeks to promote bottom-up planning process.

Vision 2020 of Andhra Pradesh Government and Role of Local Bodies

The Government of Andhra Pradesh articulates its commitment to strengthening local bodies in its Vision 2020 document in the following words: 'By 2020, the AP government will be an enabler of market-based development by providing a growth conducive, deregulated policy environment. Decentralised decision-making will be the norm local bodies encouraged and empowered to participate in administration. Andhra Pradesh government will remain transparent, effective and responsive to the people, primarily by maintaining close contact with them and involving them in governance. In order to achieve this vision AP government feels that decentralisation is an essential part of the programme to make government institutions more efficient and responsive. The state is, therefore, determined to strengthen its administration through responsible management by PRIs and community organisations. To this end, it will enable local management by devolving administrative and economic powers and responsibilities. To successfully implement this framework, change in administrative system will be carefully managed. According to the Vision 2020 document, local empowerment is already emphasised in the 73rd and 74th Constitutional Amendments. Accordingly, the state will devolve the administration of government services to the appropriate PRIs. It will also provide gram panchayats control over local services such as sanitation and primary schools and mandals and zilla parishads control over 'shared' services, such as secondary schools and colleges. Directly involving people in the management of services they use is another important initiative required. The people can play a major role in managing education, health and infrastructure services through Community-Based Organisation (CBOs) such as school committees, or development of women and children in rural areas (DWCRA) (Government of India, 1999).

Status of Devolution of Funds, Functions and Functionaries: Andhra Pradesh Versus Few Major States

It is realised that, decentralisation to rural local governments is meaningful only when the panchayats have adequate untied funds to provide public services assigned to them. Assignment of adequate and appropriate revenue sources to rural local governments is extremely important in the Indian context. The inability to assign potent revenue sources has led to local governments carrying on unfunded mandates and this has resulted in poor service delivery. Inadequate assignments combined with low levels of effort by the rural local governments have led to high levels of transfer dependence and low fiscal autonomy (Rao and Rao, 2004).

Article 243G of the Constitution empowers panchayats to function as institutions of self-government for the purposes of preparing plans and implementing schemes for economic development and social justice in their respective areas for various matters, including those listed in the 11th Schedule which is merely illustrative and indicative.[1] Unlike the division of powers and functions enumerated in the Union List and State List, no clear demarcation exists between the state and panchayats. It is for the State legislature to make laws regarding the devolution of powers and functions to the panchayats. Almost all states and union territories claim that they have transferred responsibilities in varying degrees to the panchayats, by enacting laws in conformity with the Constitution Amendment Act (CAA). However, the functional domain of panchayats pertains only to traditional civic functions in several states.

Another challenge before the state government has been the allocation of activities to the appropriate tier of the panchayat system. Traditionally, the lowest-level panchayat - the village panchayat - has been the most active in almost all states. Generally, the village panchayats carry out major functions, including core functions, whereas intermediate and district panchayats in most states are allotted supervisory functions or act mainly as executing agents for the state government (Jha, 2004).

When the authority and power in respect of certain activity is transferred from the state to the panchayats, the latter should have the prerogative of making 'decisions', in respect of planning and implementation of such activity. In the sphere of devolution of responsibilities to lower levels of governance, some important principles should be kept in view. In the first place, the principle of 'subsidiarity' needs to be given adequate attention. The principle of subsidiarity postulates that any function which can be performed by a lower tier, should be handled by that tier alone and not by any higher tier of PRI. Second, the state government should not unilaterally withdraw responsibilities and power already granted to the panchayat without adequate justification and prior consultation with the latter. Third, responsibilities, authorities and powers granted to the panchayats should be extremely specific, clear and simple in order to be comprehended by the panchayats. Lastly, whenever, functions and responsibilities are transferred to the panchayats, it should be ensured that the necessary funds, functionaries and freedom in decision-making also accompany such transfer (Government of India, 2001).

Keeping above the framework in mind of the Constitutional Amendment Act, the status of devolution of Functions, Funds and Functionaries has been analysed across major states of India.

Table 1

Transfer of Subjects and Its Coverage under Activity Mapping in Few Major States of India

State	*Transfer of Subjects through Legislation*	*Subjects Covered under Activity Mapping*
Andhra Pradesh[2]	17 Subjects	9 Subjects
Karnataka	29 Subjects	29 Subjects
Kerala	26 Subjects	26 Subjects
Bihar	25 Subjects	25 Subjects
Madhya Pradesh	23 Subjects	23 Subjects

Source: The Ministry of Panchayat Raj, Government of India (2006).

Devolution Index for Major States

Further, a recent survey by the Indian Institute of Public Administration (IIPA, 2010) has updated Devolution Index regularly done by National Council for Applied Economic Research (NCEAR) for the years 2006–07, 2007–08 and 2008–09. IIPA's survey constructs an index[3] for all the 23 States including Andhra Pradesh.[4] The four dimensional sub-indices and the composite devolution index for important states is presented below:

Table 2

Devolution Index (D) and Sub-indices

Rank	*States/UTs*	*D1*	*D2*	*D3*	*D4*	*D*
1	Kerala	92.59	80.76	69.62	61.25	74.73
2	Karnataka	90.74	77.95	56.11	64.08	69.45
3	Tamil Nadu	89.63	77.11	58.76	49.58	67.06
4	West Bengal	96.30	70.90	61.56	46.25	66.51
5	Maharashtra	73.52	65.52	62.78	44.17	61.49
6	Madhya Pradesh	74.44	63.52	53.50	54.17	59.78
7	Gujarat	54.44	59.78	51.56	44.58	53.07
8	Andhra Pradesh	70.74	45.01	53.77	35.83	50.10
National Average		69.37	47.76	36.65	37.40	45.04

Source: I.I.P.A.Survey (Alok and Chaubey, 2010).

It is clear from Table 2, that Kerala is ranked first with Index value close to 75 followed by Karnataka (69.5), Tamil Nadu (68.9), West Bengal (66.5). The value of Maharashtra and Madhya Pradesh were lower around 60 whereas Gujarat and Andhra Pradesh values are above 50.

Status of Local Finances: Andhra Pradesh Experience

The *general fund* budget or untied resources for the three tiers of local government is derived from two sources: transfers from the state and local revenues. Transfers from the centre have generally been low, sparking demands to the Finance Commission to revise these transfers, with little result (Reddy and Sreedevi, 2004). This reluctance to increase the level of transfers to local governments is partially attributed to the poor revenue-raising of local bodies in

AP, which in practice result in their bodies being under-funded. In recent years, partly because of fiscal constraints at the state level, Centrally Sponsored Schemes (CSSs) have come to dominate planned expenditures even in what are traditionally state services such as education, health, water and sanitation (in 2002/03, 58 per cent of the planned spending on elementary education came from the centre). CSSs are also an important source of funding for items that fall within the domain of PRIs (World Bank, 2006: 67).

Dependence on fiscal transfers could reduce fiscal autonomy and if the transfers are conditional and purpose specific, it could reduce the autonomy of local governments to allocate resources according to their own priorities.

It is a general perception that panchayats are financially and technically ill-equipped to perform even the core functions, much less the welfare functions and other economic functions related to agriculture and industries. Hence, many of the core functions that traditionally belonged to panchayats – drinking water, rural roads, street lighting, sanitation, primary health, and so forth – have not been transferred fully in some states; they are being performed by the line departments of the state Government or the parallel parastatals. As a result, the per capita total expenditure of panchayats remains abysmally low in all states except Andhra Pradesh, Chhattisgarh, Goa, Gujarat, Karnataka, Kerala, Maharashtra, and Tamil Nadu.

The power of panchayats to impose taxes was considered imperative to enshrine in the Constitution under article 243H, to impart certainty, continuity, and strength to panchayats.

Devolution of taxes to panchayats can easily be linked with the activities assigned to them, which vary from state to state. From various lists including the list of the 11th Schedule, certain basic functions could be said to be in the exclusive domain of panchayats. Even these essential services require huge funds. To this end, the devolution of taxes to the three tiers of the panchayats needs to be linked to the activity mapping for the devolution of functions and functionaries.

Table 3

Own Revenue of Panchayats (all tiers) as Per cent of Respective State Own Revenue of Selected States (₹ Crores)

State	*Sum of Own Revenues (2005–08)*	*States Own Revenue (2005–08)*	*Own Revenue of Panchayats as % of State Own Revenue*
Andhra Pradesh	415.4	30,057	1.38
Gujarat	111.5	22,986.6	0.49
Karnataka	198.0	26,419.8	0.75
Kerala	292.7	12,824.4	2.28
Madhya Pradesh	56.4	13,070.3	0.43
Maharashtra	582.3	50,523.1	1.15
Tamil Nadu	258.5	30,014.6	0.86
All States	2,610.6	3,13,749.3	0.83

Source: Devolution to Panchayats in India: Empirical Assessment 2011–12 (MoPR & IIPA 2011–12)

It is clear from the above data (Table 3) that proceeds from internal sources (own revenues) constitute a very insignificant share to the panchayat pool, when seen against the background of states' own revenue sources during 2005–2008. Kerala stands first with 2.28 per cent followed by AP (1.38%), Maharashtra (1.15%), whereas panchayats' share for all states stands at 0.83 per cent. In other words, panchayats rely more on fiscal transfers from the state governments in the form of shared taxes and grants.

In addition, analysis suggests that tax collection remains low because of both design and implementation issues. Although Gram Panchayats (GPs) have the power to levy taxes on some items, the lack of rules prescribing the maximum and minimum tax rates means there are no incentives for GPs to raise taxes and risk losing voters' support (Sarumathy, nd), and thus prefer to lobby for increased transfers. Additionally, low income levels in villages result in low tax revenue collection, so GPs income is meagre (Reddy and Sreedevi, 2004). This same situation is generated at the Mandal Parishad (MP) and Zilla Parishad (ZP) levels, with the additional constraint that the numbers of items for which the MPs and ZPs can levy taxes is limited.

In practice, therefore, internal revenue mobilisation at the Panchayat level is weak, and panchayats are largely dependent on transfers from the state and central government and have limited discretion regarding expenditure in Andhra Pradesh.

In Andhra Pradesh, as compared to other Southern Indian States, the Gram Panchayats' income is very meagre. District-wise classification of gram panchayats as per income reveals that this dismal picture is more glaring. Out of 21,809 Gram panchayats in AP, a total of 13,455 (61.7%) GPs have annual income of between ₹ 40,000 and 1,000,000; 13.7 per cent of GPs have income between ₹ 1,00,000 and ₹ 2,00,000; 6.2 per cent have between ₹ 2,00,000 and ₹ 3,00,000; 5.8 per cent have between ₹ 3,00,000 and ₹ 4,00,000; 3.7 per cent have between ₹ 4,00,000 and below ₹ 5,00,000; 4.3 per cent have between ₹ 5,00,000 and below 10,00,000 and 1.3 per cent of GPs have ₹ 10,00,000 and below ₹ 15,00,000 and lastly 1.7 per cent of GPs have above ₹ 15,00,000. The income of the GPs mentioned in the table includes income from all sources. One can imagine with such meagre sources of income for a majority of the panchayats, what kind of developmental needs of the people can be meaningfully addressed. The income is not sufficient even to attend core functions of the panchayats, leave alone large array of functions mentioned in the 11th Schedule of the CAA. In contrast to AP village panchayat resources, in the state of Tamil Nadu, the picture is better with as many as 7,400 GPs out of 12,618 panchayats have income between ₹ 1 lakh and 5 lakh and as many as 3,180 village panchayats have income between ₹ 5,00,000 and ₹ 10,00,000. A substantial of them (nearly 1,500 village panchayats) have income between ₹ 10 lakh or 25 lakh (See Table 4). In the State of Karnataka, the Government has developed a detailed range of activity mapping with the responsibility of implementing wide ranging development schemes. As a result, the average budget for a Gram Panchayat in Karnataka has increased to ₹ 35 lakh. The state government has transferred 435 plan, 230 non-plan in about 26 development sectors to the panchayats (Babu and Sivanna, 2008).

Table 4

District-wise Classification of Gram Panchayats as Per Income in Andhra Pradesh

Name of the District	*Total Gram Panchayats*	*Upto 40,000*	*Above 40,000 below 1,00,000*	*Above 1,00,000 below 2,00,000*	*Above 2,00,000 below 3,00,000*	*Above 3,00,000 below 4,00,000*	*Above 4,00,000 below 5,00,000*	*Above 5,00,000 below 10,00,000*	*Above 10,00,000 below 15,00,000*	*Above 15,00,000*
Srikakulam	1,101	786	162	23	19	20	21	57	5	8
Vizianagaram	928	451	276	126	26	22	7	15	0	5
Visakhapatnam	944	215	88	126	220	170	71	14	22	18
East Godavari	1,012	174	176	131	129	133	112	85	35	37
West Godavari	887	50	105	251	153	91	59	103	46	29
Krishna	972	38	165	239	114	97	74	179	25	41
Guntur	1,022	71	129	260	203	173	94	68	11	13
Prakasam	1,043	428	364	147	35	11	10	12	8	28
Nellore	961	383	371	133	24	11	10	16	7	6
Kadapa	808	345	79	208	76	56	15	11	11	7
Kurnool	898	379	306	77	42	32	13	20	11	18
Ananthapur	1,001	717	195	18	20	10	8	24	4	5
Chittoor	1,380	760	367	125	42	21	11	29	10	15
Karimnagar	1,194	446	269	153	116	74	90	26	8	12
Adilabad	866	701	33	29	28	42	17	12	4	0
Khammam	770	172	157	184	108	59	40	36	5	9
Warangal	1,014	88	255	249	120	100	52	96	18	36
Mahabubnagar	1,348	1,181	80	62	1	1	2	6	2	13
Medak	1,059	631	284	73	17	11	5	10	6	22
Ranga Reddy	705	213	65	86	60	78	75	60	38	30
Nalgonda	1,178	487	440	123	46	21	8	33	5	15
Nizamabad	718	124	249	168	71	51	15	28	8	4
Total	21,809	8,840	4,615	2,991	1,670	1,284	809	940	289	371

Source: Commissioner of Panchayati Raj, Govt. of AP.

Establishment of SFCs and the Status of its Reports

As already mentioned above, panchayats rely more on fiscal transfers from the state governments in the form of shared taxes and grants. State taxes are shared according to the recommendations of the State Finance Commission (SFC). Constitution of the SFC at a regular interval of five years is a mandatory requirement for states. Besides tax sharing, the SFC is assigned the task of reviewing the financial position of panchayats and making recommendations on the assignment of various taxes, duties, tools, fees, and grants-in-aid to be given to panchayats from the consolidates fund of the states (Alok, 2008).

The First State Finance Commission in AP was constituted in 1995, which recommended that 39.24 per cent of the States revenue (both tax and non-tax) should be devolved to Local Bodies at the ratio of 70 per cent to PRIs and 30 per cent to ULBs, respectively. This report recommended that provisions related to percentage of devolution may be incorporated in the Andhra Pradesh Panchayati Raj Act. The SFC recommended categorisation of panchayats as advanced, ordinary, backward and tribal with weightage to be suggested by the Planning Department to measure the rate of development.

(a) A Panchayat classified as backward gets 1.66 times the amount given to an 'ordinary' Panchayat.
(b) A tribal Panchayat gets 2.66 times the amount given to ordinary Panchayat
(c) An 'advanced Panchayat gets 0.66 times state amount given to an ordinary Panchayat

It is ascertained that the recommendations of the First SFC regarding sharing of taxes, Duties, Fees and Grants to PRIs were not accepted. However, in compliance with the recommendations of the first SFC, the second State Finance Commission (SFC) was set up on 1998. Its recommendations were as follows:

The Second SFC recommended a total additional devolution of ₹ 1,793.94 crore, which amounted to 10.39 per cent of the total tax and non-tax revenues of the State, including the share of Central taxes. Of this amount, 6.76 per cent was recommended to go to Rural Bodies and 3.63 per cent to Urban Bodies. Regarding the vertical sharing formula between the three levels of panchayats, the second SFC recommended that Gram Panchayats be given 50 per cent, Mandal Parishads 30 per cent and Zilla Parishads 20 per cent.

Grants to Panchayats

The recommendations of Second SFC regarding grants to PRIs are as follows: The Eleventh Finance Commission grant of ₹ 152.05 crore for providing Civic Amenities to Gram Panchayats and Municipal Bodies, Data Bank, Maintenance of Accounts etc. might be distributed as per the formula of the SFC. Construction of office building for 177 Mandals that did not have office buildings might be taken up and completed in a period of 3 years by allocating ₹ 12 crore per annum. Provision ought to be made of ₹ 2.41 and ₹ 2.07 crore respectively per annum as grants for providing toilet and drinking water facilities in schools. An amount of ₹ 6.50 crore ought to be provided per annum for special repairs to school buildings of PRIs. ₹ 4.88 crore ought to be provided per annum for maintenance of office buildings of Mandal Parishads, Zilla Parishads and other buildings. A grant equivalent to 5 per cent of salary ought to be provided to meet the additional expenditure due to pay and DA revision.

The Second SFC recommended that the revenue foregone by the Panchayati Raj Institutions due to abolition of land cess should be given to them as compensation and distributed on population basis. It recommended on the following distribution for transfer of ₹ 200 crore to PRIs on account of different State revenues.

Table 5

The Recommendations of Second SFC Regarding Grants to PRIs

Name of the Local Body	*₹ in Crores*
Zilla Parishad	40
Mandal Parishad	25
Zilla Parishad	135

There is no information as to whether these recommendations were accepted. According to the figures available on the transfer of funds to Panchayats, it does not seem as if they have been accepted.

Constitution of Third SFC

As per the G.O. Ms. No. 13 (P.R and R.D Dept, 16 January 2003) Government of AP has constituted the Third State Finance Commission under the Chairmanship of D.L. Narayana with a condition that the Commission shall make its report available by 15 July 2004 covering a period of five (5) years commencing from 1 April 2005. The Commission could not submit their report for want of information from PRIs and Municipal Bodies and requested the Govt. for extension of one year period beyond 15 July 2004, but the Government have rejected the request of the Commission. As per the G.O. Ms. No: 322 (P.R and R.D Dept, 8 October 2003), the Government have reconstituted the Third State Finance Commission under the Chairmanship of B. Satyanarayana with a period of 3 years from the date of commencement of the Commission i.e. up to 28 December 2007. The term of the reconstituted Commission has been extended up to 31 January 2008 as per the G.O. Ms. No: 390 (P.R. and R.D. Dept, 23 December 2009).

The functions of the Commission, among other things, are to suggest the ways and means and the resources to augment the financial position of Local Bodies namely Gram Panchayats, Mandal Praja Parishads, Zilla Praja Parishads, Municipal Councils, Notified Areas and Municipal Corporations in the State.

The report of the Third State Finance Commission covers Rural Local Bodies coming under the Panchayat Raj Department and Urban Local Bodies coming under the Municipal Administration Department. The recommendations of the Third State Finance Commission have to be examined by a Committee constituted on this and to suggest on various measures to improve the financial position of Local Bodies keeping in view the ways and means of the Government.

As per the G.O. Rt. No. 379 (P.R and R.D Dept dated: 10 March 2008), the Government is hereby constituted a Committee with the following Members to examine the report of the Third State Finance Commission and suggest to the Government the various steps to be taken on the recommendations of the Commission.

Minister (PR) – Chairman; Minister (RD) – Member; Minister (Home) – Member; Minister (Revenue) – Member; Minister (Law) – Member; Prl. Secretary(RD) – Member; Minister (MA and UD) – Member; Minister (Finance) – Member; Prl. Secretary (Finance) – Member; Prl. Secretary(RD) – Member; Prl. Secretary (MA and UD) – Member; Spl. C.S. (PR) – Member-Convener.

The above Committee is requested to examine the report of the Third State Finance Commission in detail and suggest various steps to be taken by the Government on the recommendations of the Commission within 3 months. The latest information is that Committee Report is not made public as the Committee constituted for the purpose is seized of the matter.

Table 6

Summary of the SFC Recommendations and the Extent of Their Acceptance/Rejection in Andhra Pradesh

SFC	*Recommendations Made*	*Recommendations Rejected*	*Recommendations Accepted with Modifications*	*Recommendations Accepted*
I SFC	84	24 (28.5)	5 (5.9)	55 (65.4)
II SFC	82	36 (43.9)	4 (4.8)	42 (51.2)
III SFC	Report submitted on 29th January. Considerable delay in passing ATR (In 2014 it was done).			
IV SFC	Not yet constituted in Telangana and recently constituted in AP			

Source: Andhra Pradesh Government.

AP Government Memorandum to the Fourteenth Finance Commission: Some Issues Concerning Local Bodies Finances

Following the 73rd and 74th amendments to the Constitution, the Central Finance Commissions have been emphasising the need to provide an impetus to the decentralisation process in both rural and urban areas and the need for supporting them through a predictable and buoyant source of revenue, substantially higher than the present levels, in addition to their own revenues and other flows from the state and central governments (Report of the Thirteenth Finance Commission). Despite this imperative, the Finance Commission transfers to local bodies have remained by the large ad hoc and not linked to the divisible pool of central taxes. The Thirteenth Finance Commission examined this issue in detail and came to the conclusion that providing assistance to local bodies directly from the divisible pool of central taxes over and above the share of state governments was not consistent with the Constitutional provisions. Recognising the need to allow the local bodies to benefit from the buoyancy of central taxes, the Commission recommended that local bodies be transferred a percentage of divisible pool of central taxes after converting this share into grant-in-aid under Article 275. Accordingly, the Commission recommended basic grant equivalent to 1.50 per cent of the divisible pool of central taxes in each year of the award period. In addition, the Commission recommended performance grant equivalent to 0.50 per cent of the previous year's divisible pool in 2011–12 and 1 per cent thereafter. The Government feels that this is a pathbreaking recommendation which enabled the local bodies to share the buoyancy of central taxes even though the transfers are in the nature of grants. The Government earnestly appeals to FFC to carry forward this initiative forward in the interest of empowering the local bodies and promoting democratic decentralisation. These grants may be distributed between the rural and urban local bodies in proportion to their share in total population.

District Planning Committees (DPCs) and its Implementation

One of the key objectives of the Panchayati Raj is to ensure that the process of planning for development in the country as a whole follows a bottom-up approach and commences at the grassroots level. The core approach is that the village panchayat plans prepared with people's participation are joined by plans prepared by the Intermediate and District Panchayats and then these are consolidated by the District Planning Committees (DPCs) along with Municipal plans into the draft district development plans, in accordance with Article 273 2D of the Constitution. The State Annual Plan is an integration of all the Draft District Development Plans.

Andhra Pradesh Government, despite its proposed commitment to strengthen planning process could not bring the Act of District Planning Committee 2005 until 2006 (Act No. 40 of 2005).

After the notification of DPCs the process of elections to DPC has been completed. Some observations are made below on the working of DPC (Reddy, 2010).

1. In all the districts DPC have been constituted in the month of the September by completing the formalities of nominations of the members to the DPC (G.O. Ms. No. 418 dated: 6 September 2007) besides elected members.
2. However, in the thirteen Backward Region Grant Fund (BRGF) districts DPCs have conducted their meetings quite hurriedly in view of the deadlines for submission of proposals to get BRGF funds. In the process the comprehensive plans required to be prepared at the level of village, intermediate and districts, as required by the Act have not been undertaken thus negating the spirit of bottom-up planning.
3. Since the rest of the districts are not BRGF districts, no meetings have been conducted yet.

Conclusion

AP remains one of the 'decentralisation deficit' states in the country. Although on devolution index its value is 50 but it is lagging behind all the South Indian States. Further, this is not encouraging when one observes field level situation. Genuine devolution of 3 Fs has still not taken place. Most of the recommendations of the first and second SFC were not accepted by the government. The present status of the Third Finance Commission recommendations is not yet clear. Although DPC have been constituted, their functioning as agents for the preparation of comprehensive districts plans may be said to be poor and lack luster. The functions enshrined in the XI Schedule of the constitution are not fully entrusted to PRIs to plan and implement schemes at the grassroots level. The Government of Andhra Pradesh is of the considered view that local bodies should be considered as a third tier for the purpose of devolution from the divisible pool of central taxes. As indicated above, the local bodies are suffering from huge resource constraints. Keeping in view the imperative of promoting inclusive and participatory growth, local bodies may be recommended grants equivalent to 4 per cent of the divisible pool of central taxes.

Notes

1. The 11th Schedule lists 29 functions (Core functions: Drinking Water; Roads, culverts, bridges, ferries, waterways, and other means of communication; Rural electrification, including distribution of electricity; Health and sanitation, including hospitals, primary health centres, and dispensaries; Maintenance of community assets. Welfare functions: Rural housing; Non-conventional energy sources; Poverty alleviation programme; Education, including primary and secondary schools; Technical training and vocational education; Adult and informal education; Libraries; Cultural activities; Family welfare; Woman and child development; Social welfare, including welfare of the handicapped and mentally retarded; Welfare of the weaker sections, and in particular, of the Scheduled Castes and Scheduled Tribes; Public distribution system. Agriculture and allied functions: Agriculture, including agricultural extension; Land improvement, implementation of land reforms, land consolidation, and soil conservation; Minor irrigation, water management, and watershed development; Animal husbandry, dairying, and poultry; Fisheries; Social forestry and farm forestry; Minor forestry and farm forestry; Minor forest produce; Fuel and fodder; Markets and fairs. Industries: Small-scale industries, including food processing industries; Khadi, village, cottage industries) that PRIs are mandated to have control and communerative resources need to be allocated to discharge these functions.
2. Latest Position: A Task Force constituted under the special Chief Secretary for Activity Mapping has prepared detailed formulations. Draft Government orders incorporating activity mapping in accordance with the recommendations of the committee are under the considerations of a Group of Ministers for finalization. After the completion of these discussions departments have been directed to finalize the Government orders for issue.
3. The index covered parameters such as functions, (D2) finances (D3) and functionaries (D4) besides using 'framework' (D1) as the fourth dimension to the existing 3F structure. The 'framework' dimension looked at four mandatory provisions, viz., (a) establishing the State Election Commission (SFCs), holding regular panchayat elections, establishing State Finance Commissions (SFCs) at regular intervals and setting up District Planning Committees (DPC) (V.N. Alok and P.K. Chaubey).
4. Although Devolution Index was developed for later years (2011–12 and 2012–13), AP was not considered as there were no elections held to PRIs and urban local bodies after the expiry of their term in the year 2011. As a result, AP also lost to the extent of ' 3,000 crores.

References

Alok, V.N. and P.K. Chaubey (2010), *Panchayats in India: Measuring Devolution by States*, Macmillan, New Delhi.

Alok, V.N. (2008), 'Role of State Finance Commissions in Fiscal Decentralisation in India', in M.A. Oommen (ed.), *Fiscal Decentralisation to Local Governments in India*, Cambridge Scholars Publishing, Newcastle upon Tune.

Babu, Devendra M. and N. Sivanna (2008), 'Finances of Rural Local Governments in Karnataka: Structure, Pattern and Policy Implications', paper presented at the conference on 'Issues Before the Finance Commission: Empowering the Panchayati Raj Institutions', 22–23 December.

Babu, Devendra M. (1998), 'Status and Working of Decentralised Bodies in Andhra Pradesh: An Analysis', paper presented at one day seminar, organised by Institution for Social and Economic Change, Bangalore.

Bardhan, Pranab and Dilip Mookherjee (2000), 'Capture and Governance at Local and National Levels', *American Economic Review*, Vol. 90, No. 2, pp. 135–39.

Bardhan, Pranab (1996), 'Decentralised Development', *Indian Economic Review*, Vol. XXXI, No. 2, pp. 139–56.

Government of India (1999), *Mid-Term Appraisal of the Ninth Five Year Plan*, Planning Commission, New Delhi.

—— (2001), *Report of the Working Group on Decentralised Planning and Panchayati Raj Institutions for the Tenth Five-year Plan*, Ministry of Rural Development, New Delhi.

—— (2007), *Second Administrative Reforms Commission*, Sixth Report, Local Governance, October.

IIPA (2010), Report of the Technical Committee of the Ministry of Panchayati Raj to Prepare Draft Joint Memorandum on Behalf of Panchayats to the 13th Finance Commission, Indian Institution of Public Administration, New Delhi (Chairman: V. Ramachandran).

Jha, Shikha (2004), 'Panchayats: Functions, Responsibilities, and Resources', paper presented at the National Institute of Rural Development, Hyderabad, India, January 23.

Manor, J. (1999), *The Political Economy of Democratic Decentralisation*, Directions in Development Series, World Bank, Washington, D.C.

Rao, Govind and Vasanth Rao (2004), 'Expanding the Resource Base of Panchayats: Augmenting Own Revenues', *Economic and Political Weekly*, January 26.

Reddy, M. Gopinath (2010), 'Decentralised Planning Process in Andhra Pradesh: A Late Starter', *Indian Journal of Public Administration*, New Delhi, October-December.

Reddy, M. Gopinath and N. Sreedevi (2004), 'Local Finances in Andhra Pradesh: A Situation Analysis', *Indian Journal of Public Administration*, Vol. L, No. 3, July-September, pp. 829–39.

Sarumathy, M. (2001), 'Andhra Pradesh', in R.C. Choudhury and S.P. Jain (eds), *Patterns of Decentralised Governance in Rural India*, Vol. 1, National Institute of Rural Development, Hyderabad, India, pp. 25–63.

World Bank (2006), 'India: Inclusive Growth and Service Delivery: Building on India's Success', *Development Policy Review*, Report No. 34580-IN, June 15.

20

Accountability of Mukhiyas

Strengthening of Panchayats in Bihar

Smita Agarwal

Decentralisation can best be understood as a political process in the sense of the devolution of resources, tasks and decision-making power to democratically elected lower-level authorities, which are largely or wholly independent of central government (World Bank, 2004). It is rational to argue that decentralisation facilitates time-specific and location-specific knowledge to implement policies that influence people's welfare. Decentralisation in political, fiscal, and economic systems affects development outcomes in a number of ways. First, decentralised provision of social and physical infrastructures should correspond with the diverse demand conditions in different regions and match their resource endowments better than central provision. Even with regard to the provision of quasi-public goods, identification of target groups of beneficiaries is easier and implementation of policies more effective when undertaken by decentralised governmental units (Ostrom et al., 1993). Second, the decentralised governmental units function within a large nationwide unified market free from impediments to the movement of factors and products, it can provide a congenial environment for the efficient functioning of the market economy. Thus, drawing on the decentralisation theorem introduced by Oates (1972), in an ideal decentralised system, existing resources will be allocated to yield the maximum possible output (locating on the production possibility frontiers) and the competitive environment including intergovernmental competition will be conducive for technological progress (shift in the frontier). Further, decentralisation may increase the probability of empowering local elites in capturing larger share of public resources at the cost of the poor (Dreze, and Sen, 1996).

Armed with philosophy of decentralisation along with political environment of India, the Government of India passed a series of constitutional reforms in 1993, to democratise and empower local administrative institutions beyond the two tiers of the Centre and the States in the third tier of local governance that has been divided into three layers of district, sub-district and village levels in terms of the 73rd and 74th Constitutional Amendment Act for rural and urban areas respectively. With coalition government at the centre comprised of different regional parties ruling at state who are mostly the partners of the coalition, the case study of Indian experience of decentralisation provides an important context of understanding the ways in which decentralisation can influence overall socio-economic welfare. The experiences of different States with respect to decentralisation vary a lot. Though the literature on federalism explains the economic gains from decentralised decision-making and related issues (Rao and Singh, 2003, 2006), there are very few empirical studies examining the causal relationship between decentralisation and development outcomes. Much of the demonstrated gains are in the nature of assertions or qualitative statements. This study, attempts to analyse the impact of decentralisation in India that tends to create its own system of patron-client relationship. Thus, it dissolves the issue of participation and accountability which was the central concern of decentralisation. This is the result of way decentralisation process occurred without adequate fiscal decentralisation that creates such complexity. In order to show this phenomena, case study of a panchayat in Bihar would be discussed.

73rd Amendment Act and its Working

Institutions of local governance (Panchayati Raj) have existed in India since 1882. However, prior to the 1990s, these institutions were largely ineffective. In response to various Committee reports, and political demand, the Union government passed the 73rd Amendment of the Indian Constitution with the stated aim of 'revolutionising democratic participation and local development planning'. The amendment mandated that every Indian state institute Panchayati Raj Institutions (now on, PRIs) within one year, and defined several mandatory and discretionary items to be devolved to PRIs. Broadly speaking, political decentralisation was made mandatory, but the extent of administrative and fiscal decentralisation was left to individual state's discretion. To summarise the main features of this Act:

Institutions

Introduction of a three-tiered Panchayat structure, with the constitution of a local participatory forum at the village level called the Gram Sabha. Panchayats shall have a uniform five-year term and elections to constitute new bodies shall be completed before the expiry of the term. In the event of dissolution, elections will be compulsorily held within six months.

Representation

In all PRIs, seats shall be reserved for Scheduled Castes and Scheduled Tribes in proportion to their population and one-third of the total number of seats will be reserved for women.

Policy Decentralisation

The 73rd Amendment, in the XI Schedule, created a list of 29 different areas of rural local government. States were asked to use their discretion in conferring both fiscal and administrative autonomy, and delegating functions and responsibility to PRIs.

Implementation

A close look at researches carried on after 73rd Amendment Act says that the extent of political decentralisation has been relatively uniform across states. In terms of mandated political representation for women and disadvantaged minorities, it has significantly increased their presence in local elected bodies. Recent evidence by Chattopadhyay and Duflo (2001) suggests that this has affected policy outcomes. Women and men favour different public goods, and hence increasing female representation in PRIs has altered the mix of public good provided. However, evidence on how mandated political representation in PRIs has affected participation of various groups is limited. Most studies (Buch, 2005; Panda, 1996; Athreya and Rajeshwari, 1998) consist of village or Panchayat case-studies, and concentrate on the effects of mandated political representation and the participation of these groups in the Gram Sabha and Panchayat meetings. These note that while reservation allows women to legally participate in local elections, accounts of intimidation and acrimony from high-caste, better educated males are not rare. In some cases female candidates openly represent their husbands or other powerful village male even to the extent that they actively attend panchayat meetings. Some authors have attempted to assess the effectiveness of female representatives to participate in meetings and in accomplishing development goals (Gowda et al., 1996; Mayaram and Pal, 1996). Similar to Chattopadhyay and Duflo (2001) these authors conclude that while female members are able to secure developmental benefits for villagers in some cases, in others where their initial power base is weak, they face considerable problems.

The extent of fiscal and administrative decentralisation has exhibited significant inter-state variation that has affected local accountability which was the key feature of decentralisation process. As far as administrative decentralisation is concerned majority of 29 subjects are in concurrence with state government responsibilities that has caused ambiguity in the delineation of functions to panchayats. The large body of rules and regulations incorporated in the state conformity acts have given state government significant power over panchayats. Moreover, there is no clear demarcation of functions between the three tiers of the panchayats. This has created uncertain situation and has hindered accountability. In certain cases when roles are defined functions are not matched with corresponding funds and functionaries transfers leading to non-existence of powers for panchayats (Mukarji and Duatta, 1996). More often than not, state bureaucracies keep control over key decisions involving resource allocation. In most cases, they are under the jurisdiction of senior bureaucrats with locally elected panchayat members having little control

Unclear demarcation of administrative functions has also affected the extent to which fiscal devolution has taken place. Fiscal decentralisation or autonomy of a State is given by the extent to which it is able to finance its public expenditure from the revenue sources assigned to it. Thus, one measure of decentralisation will be the share of a state's own revenue in its expenditures. However, as the statutory transfers are mandated in the Constitution and given on the basis of recommendation by the Finance Commission, an independent

Constitutional body. In case of local bodies despite the prevalence of constitutional body, state legislators have not devolved adequate fiscal autonomy to panchayats who remain heavily dependent on transfers from central and state government (Jha, 2000). The majority of these are in the form of tied grants that are given to local elected authorities. There is little discretion in resource allocation decisions as they have been given limited taxation and revenue collecting powers. Moreover, the lack of adequate bureaucratic structures at the local level implies that they are unable to efficiently mobilise their own resources. Comprehensive central planning is the negation of federalism; and planning even in a mixed economy framework has significantly contributed to the concentration of economic power with the Centre. In the event, the potential benefits of decentralisation have not been realised (Rao, Shand and Kalirajan, 1998).

Thus, the above discussion of working of panchayats show that local accountability has been eroded. There is high participation in local elections, but low attendance in meetings of the locally elected bodies. Evidence from interview-based case studies suggest that people perceive panchayats to be ineffective, of limited importance in local development planning and without adequate power or financial resources to implement essential projects (Alsop et al., 2000). It is often suggested that village panchayats are seen mainly as beneficiary selection committees over which individual villagers exert little power and which are not accountable to villagers. In addition, since Gram Panchayats are multivillage institutions, resolution of competing village demands is difficult. Researches even suggest that the village of the Panchayat head is favoured in resource allocation (Chattopadhyay and Duflo, 2001). As a result, panchayat heads are able to create their own patronage system. The targeted policy of central government which percolates downward gives an upper hand for head of panchayats not to allow any free discussion. So it benefits the supporters of heads. Had panchayats the autonomy to decide their programmes, many programmes that do not suit a panchayat would not be discussed and funds therein could be diverted to other programmes. As a result it would have lessened the grip of panchayat heads. The central concern is to discuss this process and suggest some way forward so that panchayats can truly become agents of self-government.

Field Observation: A Case Study of Bihar

Bihar had a twisted history of decentralisation. Due to political rivalries and centripetal tendencies, panchayats saw decline from 1970s till 1990s. After the implementation of 73rd Amendment Act, elections did take place but panchayats could not function due to legal complications of state's own Sanchayat Act that tended to challenge certain policies of weaker section. Finally, the cloud was lifted in 2000 that led to formal functioning of panchayats. In 2006, with new state government, new ideas were implemented. As a result Bihar became the first state to implement 50 per cent of reserved seats for women. Following this historic step, a research was initiated to understand the implications of this reservation for women. While research was taking place regarding women empowerment, interactions with the public that was also part of research to countercheck what elected women representatives were saying, brought forward certain observations. This unveiled the limited fiscal decentralisation and brought forward complicated system of accountability. Around 200 people of Ramdhiri-2 Panchayat of Mathiani Block of Begusarai district of Bihar were interviewed. They were asked questions on the following: Whom do they approach in times of problems? Do they attend Gram Sabha meetings? How are they informed about the meetings? If they don't attend why do they not attend the meetings

The field work findings suggested that at the village level, there is a very high level of dependence over the mukhiyas. This study shows that Mukhiya is integral not only to village politics but also to its social fabric. Right from getting ration and employment cards and government assistance to their personal problems like domestic and finances for marriage of daughter to taking sick people to hospital etc.; the mukhiya is expected to take care for all their problems. So the work of mukhiyas increases manifold thus making it imperative for other family members to help the mukhiya. Mukhiya for the village was not only a source of authority, and an intermediary to the government but much beyond that. He/she is seen as an arbitrator, a judge, a patron and a dependable person in the village, but above all that the villagers think it to be their duty to help them in such crisis because they had voted for them. Vote is seen as a mechanism to ascertain that the person who becomes the representative would serve them in these situations. So the performance of a mukhiya is not judged in the village (as some scholars judge them to be) based only on the formal governmental work and development parameters. His/her behaviour and nature is judged by the way he/she involves or takes part in the problems of common villagers. This expectation creates an unsaid pressure of being everywhere.

For example, there was an accident in a distant village in one of the panchayats (Ramdhiri–2 Panchayat of Mathiani Block in Begusarai). The mukhiya was informed through a telephone call and was expected to be there. The lady mukhiya discussed the matter with her husband and it was decided that the husband will drive his motorcycle (the only vehicle they had at home) to look for some jeep or car to carry the victim to the nearest hospital, which was around 15 km from the village. The overall process was expected to take around 2–2.5 hrs. By this time the lady mukhiya, though very concerned, could not do anything because even if she wanted to be at the spot of accident she had to walk 6 kms and by that time the victim would be on the way to hospital. So, the process was followed but by the evening the report came that the victim could not survive due to intense bleeding. So the body was brought back to the village and the husband of the mukhiya came back home to take the mukhiya to the victim's home for condolence. He informed that the accident victim was a poor person so all the expenditure from hiring a jeep to hospital and medicines had to be paid from their pocket and now that the person had died they also needed to help with the funeral and post-funeral rites that are more expensive. 'So', he claimed 'it is not just about physical exhaustion, but also monetary support that they expect in all these'. When asked if this money was in the form of loan, he said, 'Loan! Yes, theoretically speaking it is a loan, but I know the fact that his family can never pay the money and it does not look good if I ask them for it.

These are sensitive situations and if I ask for money back, it would be wrong on our part. Morality issues as you know.' This was just one of many such instances in the daily life of the villagers where the presence of the mukhiya or his/her representative was thought to be pertinent. One who could afford such involvement and help was considered to be generous and able, those who could not had to pay the price in next elections. The idea of representation for the common villagers is that of getting benefitted from his/her presence. There are multiple factors that add to their 'dependability'. Their powers and authority places them above ward commissioners in popularity and their proximity makes them more approachable than to the MLA. They being 'one among them' make them more accessible than the BDO.

Approachability is such a crucial factor that it sets a village mukhiya apart from other representatives, even from the urban local governance. Further, the schemes and benefits that poor villagers get from the panchayats and other rural level schemes are more lucrative than in municipalities. In Mathiani block of Begusarai, there was a village which was earlier a part of one of the panchayats in the block. But the villagers complained that in the recent delimitation drive to redraw the municipal boundary, due the influence of local MLA, the village was included in the municipality to support the prospects of his candidates at municipal level. The villagers were very unhappy with this and wanted to get back to the panchayats. One dominant reason was that they did not get the kind of help they used to get earlier. They felt highly discriminated as there were no proper schemes to support them in the urban governance system. They cited a recent example of post-flood situation. They claimed that every year after floods, government sent special funds and packages to panchayats to revive villages affected by floods and so they used to get good benefits. But this year even though the level of devastation was much higher, they had not received anything even after two months had lapsed. The village adjacent to theirs had got packages from government as it fell under panchayat system. The local representative said that they had no direction from the government and shall only help once they get necessary funds from government. The villagers felt very helpless in the situation. In Mathiani block the recent state elections led to redrawing of constituency; consequently one part of panchayat has been merged with the town. Earlier they could get lot of benefits through Panchayats which has stopped, making life difficult.

The Gram Sabha meetings are one of the important aspects of any panchayats in Bihar where the plans and programmes are decided. The decision over the needs of the panchayat and the framework to get things done is linked. It is other than the elections themselves, the only other form of direct participation of common villagers in decision-making about their future and development of the panchayat at large. So the participation in these meetings is taken very seriously by the government also. It is mandatory to video graph all such meetings and submit the CDs to the BDO along with the list of panchayat development activities decided upon. The attendance is also marked. All these data highlighted in the tables were cross checked with the official attendance submitted to the government, and also took a close look of the CDs of such meetings. The gram sabha meetings in Bihar are held 4 times in a year, all on days of a holiday to ensure maximum participation i.e. on 26th January (Republic Day), 1 May (Labour Day), 15 August (Independence Day) and 2 October (Gandhi Jayanti). Some of the meetings in different villages were attended especially on the 2nd October meetings in the panchayats of Mathiani block. The timing of meetings of different panchayats varies and is on discretion of the mukhiyas; so it was possible to attend different meetings at different panchayats, but not all. So it will be helpful to talk a little about the personal experience of the meetings before getting to the tables and drawing conclusions from there.

The preparations for the meetings start much in advance. One can see some paddle rickshaws carrying loudspeakers on each announcing the date and timings of the meetings. Another mode that is used is '*dhol*' (the traditional drum), where a person travels in various wards, beats the drum and spreads information about the meetings. But the mukhiya also takes special care in getting the people to the venue. He/she telephones the local ward members and in some places, a day or two before the day a small meeting is arranged, which is not attended by all the ward members. In the meeting one can sense the presence of loyalists as there is not much questions or comments. It is a session when the mukhiyas announces his/her agenda of the day and guides the loyal ward commissioners to mobilise the villagers. On the day of the meeting, people start gathering much in advance. The panchayat office being often too small or non- existent, the school playground or other open space is used for the sabha. The mukhiya is the central protagonist in the whole play. He/she channelises and mobilises and on the day is the central performer. He/she suggests some schemes and programmes to be filled with the present budget and a priority list of things to do is set up. There is a strong set of loyalists backing the mukhiya and regular clapping can be heard whenever any new thing is offered as an idea. Those opposed are booed and silenced. If there are aged and seniors speaking, the mukhiya counts the practical problems and hurdles. At the end the predetermined list of the schemes by mukhiya is placed to vote and the aggressive loyalists get it passed. In the case of woman mukhiyas, one can see the active role of their husbands in arguing and making a case for the plans, as if everything was prediscussed and well planned. Sometimes, one gets the feeling that the sabha is fixed, where a hegemon in the form of mukhiya is getting his/her ideas legitimised. In some cases, the gram sabha looks anything but democratic. It is not surprising that there is so high disillusionment with the proceedings among the villagers who then concentrate on getting their personal issues like BPL cards and others sorted out, rather than talking about development plans for the panchayat.

An important factor also needs to be highlighted here. The programmes are predecided by the state or central government. This is because gram sabhas do not have autonomy to raise funds, so they are dependent on funds that come from above. So money that would go into development work and priorities are predecided. Mukhiyas only have the autonomy to choose beneficiaries or decide where common infrastructure would be built. Here mukhiya uses his/her discretionary power and doles out benefits to his loyalists or '*tolas*' he/she knows that support him/her. So it is evident that there are structural constraints that reduce the autonomy on mukhiyas to allocate funds to the programmes or plans. This can be seen in Bihar which has abysmal performance in terms of devolution of finances to panchayats.[1]

The idea of participation among the common villagers is based on three factors: (a) attendance in gram sabha; (b) confidence in their participation (and lack of confidence and the reasons for it); and (c) general demands (whether individual based or based on development of panchayat). In general, the participation across all panchayats – be it male headed or woman headed-is extremely low. On an average, it is only 19.32 per cent in case of Mathiani block. Large number of men and women do not attend the meetings. However, there is one important fact revealed by the table that whenever there is a woman headed panchayat, the participation of women in the gram sabha meetings go up – in Mathiani it is 21 per cent compared to 15.8 per cent in male headed. However, the percentage attendance in all the panchayats is similar in all within 20 per cent. It thus reflects that women feel more confident and willing to participate in gram sabhas when the mukhiya is a woman. This partly helps in fulfilling one of the aims of reservations that was perceived as bringing women into politics, further bringing the other non-participative women also outside their homes that can make politics more inclusive.[2]

There are very strong reasons for disillusionment from the meetings, which is reflected in the responses of those who do not attend the meetings regularly or do not attend it at all. About 17.06 per cent do not get the information about the meetings. This may be due to various factors including the mode of communication and willingness of mukhiyas on the matter. Mukhiyas generally want their supporters to be present for the meeting and a kind of 'whip' is launched for the same. Though speakers on rickshaw and 'dhol' is used in some panchayats, in most of them no special care is taken about it. The loyalists get phone calls from the mukhiyas. The overall system is full of loopholes and no special care is taken to mend it. A healthy quorum is ensured by filling the space with supporters to show good attendance in videos of the gram sabha, which as mentioned earlier, is compulsory. What is worrying in the whole process is the high degree of disinterest generated among masses due to the way gram sabha is conducted. There is a general disenchantment about the value of their participation in gram sabhas. Whereas the Act wanted to use gram sabha as instrument of direct democracy which was central concern of decentralisation process in India. This is across all panchayats. An average of 22 per cent believes that mukhiyas come with a set agenda and the gram sabha is simply used to legitimise their wishes. There is no recognition or respect to dissenting voices.

The common villagers are dependent on the mukhiyas for other benefits that no one cares to strongly oppose him/her and above that they have loyal supporters who get things in their favour. There are a high percentage of those who cite corruption at the level of mukhiyas in distribution of schemes and benefits that disdains them from attending such meetings. They complain of a high degree of nepotism whereby relatives, friends and other loyalists only seem to benefit from the schemes. This also is a general phenomenon across all panchayats – whether male headed or female headed. About 50 per cent of those not regular or not attending at all, claim this as a major reason. The tables reflect that the presence of woman mukhiyas in any way does not change the situation. It is further interesting, that only 4.7 per cent (of overall average) of respondents cite reasons of not being free or engaged in other work. This shows that some of the villagers have time and information of the gram sabha to be held but many among consciously avoid the meetings. This is because their interests are not taken care in these meetings.

Since gram sabhas are meant to fulfil everyone's interest but when some are left out they decide to opt out of it. So it is seen that panchayats have definitely bridged the distance between ruler and ruled through gram sabhas that has the sole authority for passing any programmes to be implemented but some groups are left behind. This is in sharp contrast to functioning of legislatures and Parliament where there is no direct involvement of the people for whom policies are made. Mukhiyas have to take care of the public for non-official work also; nonetheless it has failed to devolve decision-making to the people. Mukhiyas have come to occupy another tier in the functioning of the government.

Based on the observations generated by these readings, one also needs to revisit the existing literature[3] on role of middlemen in Indian politics which had discussed about the role of middle men in getting development work done in rural India. These studies were done prior to passing of 73rd Amendment Act. It is clearly reflected that the mukhiyas have taken up the central role in development process in the villages. It shows more prominently that the role of 'fixers' has declined and the mukhiya themselves have taken up this role. They nurture their panchayats; have full control of development activities and above all, give healthy returns to loyalists in the form of government schemes and other benefits that flow from the top. What it has led to is a distinct kind of phenomenon in local politics. Although in Bihar, the panchayat elections are not contested on party lines, as in many other states, the mukhiyas are often lured by the parties to work for them. Many mukhiyas get co-opted in the party system with local posts. They in turn use their mobilisation and power at local level to garner votes for these parties in elections. Though this aspect is not much related to the present work but it does point at manoeuvring tactics of both male and woman leaders for their positions higher up. Many representatives claim to stand for re-elections. Further, many also expressed interest in contesting elections at higher levels.

Thus, we see that due to limited autonomy panchayats have become implementing agency of the centre and state. If more financial and administrative autonomy is given to panchayats, then need-specific programmes can be devised. So mukhiyas continue to assert that their hands are tied because of limited autonomy and they can have only limited discussions on the availability of programmes. Once they have autonomy, the siphoning off funds would be limited as panchayats have high approachability which has already been discussed earlier. As a result discussions will be more open. Since it is people's money which would be collected and used, so their participation would be more and accountability can be increased.

Conclusion

Thus, we see that panchayats despite being a decentralised organisation have not been able to fulfil its aim of participation and accountability. This arises from the fact that panchayats are not independent in terms of finances. In order to bridge this anomaly, panchayats need to have tax raising capacity. This requires political will as panchayats are state subjects. State elites see panchayats as voter constituents, so giving them freedom would pose greater challenge to the leadership. Since panchayats have 29 subjects it requires autonomy.

Notes

1. 'Strengthening of Panchayats in India: Comparing Devolution across States, Empirical Assessment 2012–13', http://www.panchayat.gov.in/documents/10198/378720/devolution_report_2013-14_f_.pdf
2. Anne Phillips, *The Politics of Presence*, New York: Oxford University Press, 1995, p. 4.
3. G. Ram Reddy and G. Haragopal, 'The Pyraveekar: "The Fixer" in Rural India', *Asian Survey*, Vol. 25, No. 11, November 1985; James Manor, 'Small-Time Political Fixers in India's States: "Towel Over Armpit"', *Asian Survey*, Vol. 40, No. 25, September-October 2000; Subrata K. Mitra, 'Room to Manoeuvre in the Middle: Local Elites, Political Action, and the State in India', *World Politics*, Vol. 43, No. 3, April 1991.

References

Alsop, R., A. Krishna and D. Sjoblom (2000), 'Are Gram Panchayats Inclusive?', South Asia Social Development Unit (SASSD), unpublished.

Athreya, V.B. and K.S. Rajeswari (1998), *Women's Participation in Panchayat Raj: A Case Study from Tamil Nadu,* M.S. Swaminathan Research Foundation: Chennai.

Brown, C.C. and W.E. Oates (1987), 'Assistance to the Poor in a Federal System', *Journal of Public Economics*, Vol. 32, pp. 307–30.

Buch, Nirmala (2005), Women and Panchayats: Opportunities, Challenges and Supports, in L.C. Jain (ed) *Decentralization and Local Governance,* Orient Longman: Hyderabad.

Dreze, J. and A.K. Sen (1996), *India: Economic Development and Social Opportunity*, Oxford University Press, Delhi.

Chattopadhyay, R. and Esther Duflo (2001), 'Women's Leadership and Policy Decisions: Evidence from a Nationwide Randomised Experiment in India', Mimeo, MIT.

Gowda, S.G., M.S. Dhadave and M.V.S. Gowda (1996), 'Developmental Role of Women Members of Panchayati Raj Institutions: A Study in Karnataka', *Journal of Rural Development*, Vol. 15, No. 2, pp. 249–59.

Jha, S. (2000), 'Fiscal Decentralisation and Rural Local Government: Panchayati Raj Institutions in India', unpublished.

Kalirajan, K. and K. Otsuka (2010), 'Decentralisation in India: Outcome and Opportunities', Working Paper ASARC 2010/14.

Manor, James (2000), 'Small-Time Political Fixers in India's States: "Towel Over Armpit"', *Asian Survey*, Vol. 40, No. 25, pp. 816–35.

—— (2010), 'Local Governance', in Niraja Gopal Jayal and Pratap Bhanu Mehta (eds), *Oxford Companion to Politics in India*, Oxford University Press, New Delhi.

Mathew, George (1994), *Panchayati Raj: From Legislation to Movement*, Concept Publishing House, New Delhi.

—— (2002), *Status of Panchayats in India*, Institute of Social Sciences, New Delhi.

Mathew, George and B.S. Baviskar (2009), *Inclusion and Exclusion in Local Governance: Field Studies from Rural India*, Sage Publications, New Delhi.

Mayaram, Shail and Pritam Pal (1996), *The Politics of Women's Reservation: Women Panchayat Representatives in Rajasthan Prformance, Problems and Potential*, Working Paper 074, Institute for Development Studies: Jaipur.

Mitra, Subrata K. (1991), 'Room to Manoeuvre in the Middle: Local Elites, Political Action, and the State in India', *World Politics*, Vol. 43, No. 3, pp. 390–413.

Mukarji, N. and A. Datta (1996), 'New Perspectives of Local Government', ISS Occasional Paper Series No. 20, Institute of Social Sciences, New Delhi.

Oates, W.E. (1972), *Fiscal Federalism*, Harcourt Brace Jovanovich, New York.

Ostrom, E., L. Schroeder and S. Wynne (1993), *Institutional Incentives and Sustainable Development: Infrastructure Policies in Perspective*, Westview Press, Oxford.

Panda, Snehalata (1996), Emerging Pattern of Leadership among Rural Women in Orissa, *Indian Journal of Public Administration*, Vol. 42, No. 3–4.

Pauly, M.V. (1973), 'Income Redistribution as a Local Public Good', *Journal of Public Economics*, Vol. 2, pp. 35–58.

Phillips, Anne (1995), *The Politics of Presence*, Oxford University Press, New York.

Prudhomme, R. (1995), 'The Dangers of Decentralisation', *World Bank Research Observer*, Vol. 10, No. 2, pp. 201–20.

Rao, C.H.H. (2005), *Essays on Development, Regional Disparities and Centre-State Financial Relations in India*, Academic Foundation, New Delhi.

Rao, M.G. and A. Das-Gupta (1995), 'Intergovernmental Transfers and Poverty Alleviation', *Government and Policy*, Vol. 13, pp. 1–3.

Rao, M.G. and N. Singh (2003), How to think about Local Government Reform in India, in *Economic Reform and Liberalisation in India Essays in Honour of Richard T. Shand*, ed. by K.P. Kalirajan Cheltenaham, Edward Elgar: UK.

—— (2006), 'The Political Economy of India's Fiscal Federal System and its Reform', *Publius: The Journal of Federalism*, p. 14.

Roa, M.G., R. Shand and K.P. Kalirajan (1998), Convergent of Income in Indian States: A Divergent View. IIPF Conference Cordoba, Argentina.

Reddy, G. Ram and G. Haragopal (1985), 'The Pyraveekar: "The Fixer" in Rural India', *Asian Survey*, Vol. 25, No. 11, pp. 1148–62.

Sivaramakrishnan, K.C. (2000), *Power to the People? The Politics and Progress of Decentralisation*, Konark Publishers, New Delhi.

World Bank (2004), Fiscal Decentralisation to Rural Governments in India, Oxford University Press: New Delhi.

Reports

http://finance.bih.nic.in/documents/reports/achievement-report-2013.pdf

'Strengthening of Panchayats in India: Comparing Devolution across States, Empirical Assessment 2012–13', http://www.panchayat.gov.in/documents/10198/378720/devolution_report_2013-14_f_.pdf

The State of the Panchayats: A Mid-term Review Appraisal, Report of the Ministry of Panchayati Raj, Government of India, 22 November 2006.

21

Rhetoric of Participatory Development

An Analysis of Functioning of PRIs in Goa

Alaknanda Shringare

Panchayats were in operation in Goa since liberation with limited powers. In the year 1962, first Panchayat election was held. Passing of 73rd Amendment Act forced the Government of Goa to pass Goa Panchayati Raj Act in 1994. 73rd Amendment Act provided for devolution of powers, functions and finances to Panchayats which would enable them to act as units of participatory development. As the decision over transfer of powers and functions to these institutions of local self-governments was left to the State government what have been widely noticed is the reluctance on part of state legislators to devolve more powers and functions to PRIs in Goa. Out of 29 subjects only 18 subjects are devolved to Panchayats and 6 are devolved to Zilla Panchayats.

While there are plenty of research works available on functioning of panchayats in other states, in Goa there are very few research works in this area. The works of Tanaji Halarnkar (1990), Aureliano Fernandes (1999, 2008), Seema Salgaonkar (2006) and Seema Fernandes (2013) analysed the functions, finances, elections of Panchayats. Seema Salgaonkar's work mainly deals with women participation and functioning of panchayats in Goa. The present paper tries to critically analyse PRIs as agencies of participatory development. The paper argues, lack of will on part of elected representatives proved participatory development rhetorical in Goan village panchayats.

Participatory Development and PRIs

Amartya Sen defines development as a process of expanding the real freedoms that people enjoy. Participation can be seen as achieving development by using freedom. In such a framework, Haragopal (2003) views participation is not necessarily formal but substantive in the sense that it not only includes people's involvement in the collective decision-making process in the development but also their assertion to alter the direction of development by making the system more accountable. Participation can also be seen to have intrinsic value for the quality of life (Dreze and Sen, 2006) As observed by Dreze and Sen (2006), being able to do something through political action for oneself and others is one of the elementary freedoms that people have reason to value.

Local democracy represents one means of participation in the larger democratic system, which is relatively accessible to the disadvantaged, and can be potentially a stepping stone towards other forms of democratic participation (Dreze and Sen, 2006), For Dreze and Sen (2006), local democracy can be used as a potential force to bring social change, social equity and public accountability. While examining the benefits of decentralised democracy, Peter deSouza (2013) observed that democratic decentralisation enables to break the hold of rural elites over resource use and distribution by giving greater say to hitherto disadvantaged groups, as well as it makes possible deeper involvement of marginalised groups, in the planning, implementation and monitoring of those developmental processes that have an impact on rural areas.

Over two decades of Panchayati Raj experience produced mixed experiences in India. There are more challenges than achievements to talk about. No doubt PRI is slowly evolving itself but at a very slow pace. They are evolving more as decentralised institutions rather than participatory institutions. Decentralisation is not necessarily conducive to participatory development or planning. Representative element is gaining significance over participatory element in most PRIs. The essence of decentralised planning is to bring planning process close to the people where people can plan their own development.

Participatory development became the buzz word in the new process of governance, which stressed more on decentralised planning. Participation of people in the plan process as well as implementation and evaluation of the same are considered essential for the success of plans. Participation of people is viewed as the precondition for the accomplishment of development programmes. However, the questions like what is development and how much of participation are the questions mostly debated from various perspectives. In recent years, development has taken a human face in the form of Human Development; however, it has yet to transform itself into reality in India. No doubt participatory development has been stressed in plan process, especially through a decentralised governance, yet there are obstacles when it comes to appreciating plans initiated by people or giving their opinion a due share in the decisions related to development. It also indicates the gap in government's perception of development and peoples' perception of development.

Participatory development ensured through PRIs is a novel step towards bridging these gaps between different views of development. It is an attempt to involve people in the process of development and also to plan development according to their needs and demands. However, reluctance on the part of authorities to devolve more power to people is proving to be a hindrance in realising the goal of PRIs.

If new governance process demands participation of people, the perceived developmental demands of neoliberal world are creating obstacles to it. The pressure on land and resources are immense. The recent developments in Goa also point towards similar trends. The issue of SEZs, Regional Plan 2011, Mopa

Greenfield airport, mega housing projects created an environment of distrust between the people and elected representatives. Gram Sabhas became more active and participation of people increased in the meetings of the gram sabha. Increased participation of people in gram sabha meetings is not an expression of success of PRIs but more a reflection of distrust between people and elected representatives. People started demanding more powers to the gram sabha which was systematically denied.

Local Self-Government in Goa

Goa had a unique history of local self-government in the form of Gaonkari, later termed as Communidade system under Portuguese rule which functioned as an autonomous unit of village administration. The primary activity of the Gaonkari system consisted of administration of village land. The income was utilised for the common services for the village. Along with Communidades, Fernandes (1999) writes, the other forms of local self-governments were Senado de Goa, later known as Camara municipalities and Juntas de Fregueisias (rural self-governing bodies) established only in 1959, just two years before Portuguese were ousted from Goa which were allocated the responsibility of repair of village roads, drains, bridges, gutters and maintenance of street lights. After liberation, President of India promulgated Goa, Daman and Diu Village Panchayat Regulation (1962) under Article 240 of the Indian Constitution. This provided for a single tier Panchayati Raj system in the Union Territory of Goa and accordingly, village Panchayats were set up. Three types of panchayats were created, having five, seven and nine members respectively depending upon the population. However, these panchayats enjoyed limited powers because in a tiny state like Goa, giving more powers to panchayats means lessening the importance of Members of Legislative Assemblies(MLAs). After the passing of 73rd Amendment Act, Goa government adopted two tier Panchayati Raj as the population of Goa is less than 20 lakh. At present, Goa has 190 panchayats. Whereas functioning of *Communidades* displayed a notion of community, the gram panchayat has failed to evoke a similar sense of involvement and belonging (Fernandes, 1999).

With the passing of Goa Panchayati Raj Act, 1994 the powers of the panchayats were enhanced. The initial success of PRI Act which can be recorded was of Du Pont's Nylon 6, 6 plant set up in Querim village much to the dissatisfaction of the people. People demanded cancellation of this project due to environmental and other reasons. The project was cancelled when the panchayat and the villagers resolved not to permit the plant within the jurisdiction of the village. The environmental NGOs filed the writ petitions informing the Court that as a decision had been taken by the Panchayat not to permit the plant within its jurisdiction (Alvares, 2002). However, subsequent years had less to applaud for success of PRIs.

The devolution report prepared by Indian Institute of Public Administration (2012–13) based on six dimensions – framework, functions, finances, functionaries, capacity building and accountability – indicate Goa much below national average. Out of 29 subjects, 18 subjects are devolved to Gram Panchayat and 6 are devolved to Zilla Panchayat. While NGOs, activists and panchayats were demanding for more powers and finances to panchayats, the recent issues of Regional Plan and mega housing projects led to debate over more powers to gram sabha. With an increase in construction activities, land in village is coming under huge pressure. Panchayats' power of granting licenses and NOCs to the projects coming up in the village also became a source of corruption in panchayats.

Two Issues

Regional Plan

The issues of mega housing project and regional plan brought the debate over powers to panchayat and gram sabha to the forefront. In both these cases, land use planning became a matter of concern. Goa, after liberation, adopted land use planning in the form of Regional Plan (RP). Town and Country Planning (TCP) department was set up in 1964 to prepare the Regional Plan for Goa. In the year 1974, Goa Assembly passed Town and Country Planning Act. The Act provided for appointment of Chief Town Planner who has the responsibility of preparing Regional Plan of Goa. The Act provided for the stages by which development may be carried out, the network of transport and communication lines, the proposals for conservation and development of natural resources and such other matters as may have an influence on the development of the concerned area, including rural and urban areas. Apart from other things, the Act also provided for indicating the extent of anticipated growth of rural and urban centres both existing and new. With these initiatives there was a hope for planned development. The initial experiences with Regional Plans were not very encouraging. There were incidences when plans changed many times to suit the need of one or the other party, while the TCP Act provided for once notified Regional Plan cannot be changed for ten years. Though Regional Plan included plan for rural areas, local governments were never made part of the planning process. With protests intensified against Regional Plan 2011, there were also demands for making panchayats part of planning process.

When the Regional Plan 2011 was notified and kept open for public scrutiny, Goa Bachao Abhiyan (GBA), an NGO studied the plan and expressed concerns over its implementation in the original form. One of the major concerns in the Regional Plan was increase in the settlement area and commercial area. The RP-2011 showed 51 per cent of the land as settlement area. Which means loss of land for these purposes which once notified cannot be challenged. Large areas were demarcated for food parks, golf courses and others which cater mainly to the needs of tourists. There were also environmental concerns, concerns over influx of migrants and impact on natural resources and infrastructure. These issues were brought to the notice of people of Goa. The protest movement initiated by GBA against RP-2011 soon became a mass movement. People at various places in Goa and many non-governmental organisations demanded for scrapping of RP-2011. Bowing to the peoples' protest government of Goa scrapped RP-2011 in 2007.

After the scrapping of RP-2011 there was pressure on the government to make planning bottom-up process. GBA was forerunner in this demand.

Government agreed to constitute a Task Force to formulate RP-2021 which would consist of representatives of people. GBA also pushed for sending the draft plans of respective villages to panchayats for getting acceptance. RP-2021 was sent to villages for scrutiny. It was brought out in the Gram Sabha meetings the discrepancies in the plan. In some places canals, nallas, religious structures were not shown in the plan while in some places open areas were shown as major settlement areas and many such cases were identified. These incidences made GBA and others to demand for legally formalising participatory development. Though Congress government tried to make planning little more democratic but no action was initiated by the government to ensure participatory development by formally involving panchayats in the process of formulating Regional Plan. Even no efforts were made by the subsequent BJP government to make planning process more participatory. Governments were reluctant to give more powers to the people. After twenty years of passing of GPRA 1994 also Regional Plan, a major land use plan of Goa failed to ensure participatory planning.

Mega Housing Projects

The year 2007 saw an end of one issue i.e. scrapping of RP-2011 and emergence of another in the form of mega housing project. The years 2007 and 2008 saw uproar over mega housing projects in the meetings of gram sabha in most of the villages of Goa. Mega housing projects are massive residential projects that are promoted by big builders and are mainly sought to be constructed in village area, an area which have long been protected by the villagers and communidades.

Mega housing projects are constantly on the rise in many villages of Goa. Mushrooming of such housing projects with each project having capacity of more than 100 to 150 flats created anxiety among the people of Goan villages. In most of the cases people were unaware of such projects coming up in their villages as NOCs granted by the panchayats. Once sanctioned by the panchayat, villagers are finding it difficult to put a halt on the work. People in many villages like Benaulim, Aldona, Pilerne, Colva and others demanded that all the mega housing projects should be placed in the gram sabha meeting for approval. There were controversies over transparency in government dealings and transactions. In some villages, people were protesting against conversion of land in the Industrial area for housing projects. Hill cutting activities are also noticed to give way for mega housing projects.

Rapidly growing mega housing projects are attracting large number of migrant workers needed for the construction activity. On the other hand these mega housing projects are catering to the needs of outsiders as the cost of these flats are so high that common people of Goa cannot afford to buy. Thus, attracting people from outside Goa to buy these flats. Often these flats are used by outsiders as second homes. There is fear among the people that these massive construction works may result in demographic change in most of the villages. The villagers also expressed concern over garbage disposal and pressure on available resources such as water and electricity in the villages. Garbage disposal is the biggest challenge before the panchayats as they are finding it difficult to identify the place for its disposal. While identifying the place to dispose off garbage generated by this housing project is the responsibility of the villages, the villagers are not given a voice in sanctioning or rejecting these projects.

In most of the cases relating to mega housing projects, people of the villages were kept in dark over sanction given to these projects. When people come to know about them at the execution stage, they attempted to put a halt to these projects. The people tried to register their opposition by attending the gram sabha meetings in large number and demanded for revocation of construction licenses issued to these projects. In many villages, people formed groups and demanded that all high density mega projects be put on hold immediately and no permission should be given to any new projects. Similar resolutions were passed in many gram sabha meetings. In some villages, people kept a vigilant watch on Sarpanch and Panchayat Secretary so that they do not issue license to construction files. The incidents also reveal lack of trust in the elected representatives.

There is growing discontent among the people over the manner in which members of panchayat function. Growing corruption in panchayat has also become cause of concern. As brought out by Tomazinho Cardozo (2011), in the 1960s and 1970s people were reluctant to contest for panchayat posts. It was a social service in true sense. However, by projecting Goa as a tourist destination, hotels, motels, guest houses and huge building complexes started mushrooming in villages which required construction licenses, occupancy certificates and other certificates. To avoid delay, builders and developers started giving gifts in kind and cash thus corruption entered PRIs in Goa. The state has witnessed lot of uproar in the gram sabha meetings over mega housing projects with gram sabhas passing resolution opposing mega projects coming up in their village.

Inspite of all their efforts, people were finding it difficult to influence panchayat decisions. They started organising themselves and called for public meetings to fight against mega housing projects. Orlim Gavn Rakon Manch called for a public meeting to object proposed housing project in Orlim. Similarly, Goenkarncho Orixitt Avaz, Ganv Ghor Rakhonn Manch and Citizens Welfare Committee are few of such organisations formed to oppose mega housing projects coming up in their villages. They also stressed for need of unity to fight against such mega housing projects coming up in different parts of Goa.

Due to this huge uproars coming from all corners of Goa, the Directorate of Panchayats prepared a report on the mega projects in the state and 150 controversial projects were identified (Fernandes, 2013). The entire debate over powers to gram sabha is revolving around granting and revoking construction licenses. Mounting pressure from various gram sabhas to stop issuing NOCs to mega housing projects made TCP department to issue an advisory to the Directorate of Panchayats stating that gram sabha has no say in issuing and revoking construction licenses. This triggered a huge hue and cry over the matter. Though the opinion states that Sub-section 4 of Section 6 of (GPRA, 1994) declares that the decision taken by Gram Sabha is binding and final in so far as Panchayat is concerned, it put forth the argument there is no provision in Goa Panchayati Raj

Act permitting the gram sabha to grant permission to either construction or revoke or to interfere with the permission (over construction license) (GOACOM, 2013).

In a letter to the Director of Panchayats the TCP department reproduced the opinions of legal experts to state that the functions of the gram sabha, as mentioned in the Goa Panchayati Raj Act states that the Sarpanch has to place 'certain matters' for approval before the gram sabha but it does not expressly mention any development or construction activity (GOACOM, 2013).

The then Chief Minister said that gram sabhas enjoy merely advisory capacity within the Panchayat Raj system and best meant to be the watchdog over the functioning of panchayats. While opposing this statement, Council of Social Justice and Peace (CSJP) wrote letter to the CM demanding clarification, in response to which CM asserted that Gram Sabhas have no overriding powers over panchayat. CMs claim was supported by government officials as well as some lawyers who claimed that Goa Panchayati Raj Act does not provided Gram Sabha overriding powers over Panchayat. This shows reluctance on the part of government to give more powers to people.

The recent development raised question over transparency and accountability in the functioning of elected representatives. With growing corruption and panchayat members given overriding powers over gram sabha it will be hard for people to hold panchayat members accountable. Thus, participatory democracy is proving to be rhetorical. As observed by De Toqueville, 'The world has suffered more from leaders and authorities than from the masses. No government by experts in which the masses do not have the chance to inform the experts as to their needs can be anything but an oligarchy managed in the interest of the few' (Terchek and Conte, 2001).

Activists as well as members of gram sabha are demanding more powers to gram sabhas in deciding the development projects in their villages. Gram Sabha meetings across Goa are questioning the relevance of 73rd Amendment Act if Panchayat cannot be held accountable to gram sabha. What has been observed is time and again there are attempts made to dilute the functions of local self-governing bodies. Amidst demands for strengthening gram sabha, government proposed amendment to GPRA which generated massive public protest because of amendment at Section 47-B of the Act which stated that 'the secretary shall execute the order passed by any authority in any appeal or petition made before such authority under the provisions of this Act or Rules framed thereunder, if the panchayat fails to execute the same within the time limit as specified in such order and in case no time limit has been specified, within one month of passing of such order (*Times of India*, 2010). Social activists opposed the amendment stridently with Goa Bachao Abhiyan convener Sabina Martins arguing that by giving powers to the village panchayat secretary, the government in collusion with the director of panchayats, would bring in projects opposed by the public through the backdoor (*TOI*, 2010). While panchayats are struggling to retain and maintain their powers there is little attention given towards making people part of decision-making both by elected representatives of legislative assembly as well as members of panchayat.

John Dewey asserts that only by reclaiming public arenas for the practice of localised self-government can citizens hope to govern themselves freely and wisely. But such discussions must also proceed with the understanding that democratic objectives can never be realised without a commitment to democratic means and attitudes that is without tolerance, inclusiveness, and the protection of freedom (Terchek and Conte, 2001). Thus, while demanding more powers to Gram Sabha, what needs to be taken into consideration is ensuring inclusiveness.

What has also been noticed in Goa is most of the people are not aware of dates of gram sabha meetings. GPRA provides for 1/10th as quorum for gram sabha meeting but it also states in the absence of required quorum, Panchayat has to wait for half an hour and if after half an hour also there is no quorum then meeting can be continued without quorum. What it means is after with or without quorum meeting can continue after waiting for half an hour. No efforts are made by the members of panchayat to ensure quorum as it is not mandatory. Many panchas opine that the gram sabha is an advisory body and fear that making it a deliberative body would lead to intense conflict between gram sabha and elected members or rival groups within the village and emanate in a paralysis of policy and works execution (Fernandes, 1999).

In the light of these two issues the ongoing debate over power to gram sabha becomes relevant. With more powers in the hands of Panchayat members in whom people have lost trust there is a need to relook into the matter of powers to gram sabha. No doubt with the passing of 73rd Amendment Act and GPRA, a mechanism is put in place for people's participation. But the question is how far it has succeeded in ensuring participatory development in the village. In both the above-mentioned cases - may it be preparing Regional Plan or mega housing projects - have something to do with the land use in the village over which people are denied a say. There is need to rebuild trust between people and elected representatives by guaranteeing accountability and transparency.

References

Alvares, C. (2002), *Du Pont: Out of Goa*, The Goa Foundation, Goa.

Cardozo, T. (2011), 'Of Panchas, Sarpanchas and Developers', *The Navhind Times*, p. 3.

deSouza, P.R. (2003), 'The Struggle for Local Government: Indian Democracy's New Phase', *Emerging Federal Process in India (Autumn)*, Vol. 33, No. 4.

Devolution Index (2012-13), Retrieved October 10, 2014, from www.iipa.org.in/upload/panchayat_devolution_index_report_2012-13.pdf.

Dreze, J. and A. Sen (2006), *India: Development and Participation*, Oxford University Press, New Delhi.

Fernandes, A. (1999), 'Reconnecting Sabhas to Gram', paper presented at National Conference on Gram Sabha, NIRD, Hyderabad.

—— (2008), *Panchayatantra*, University Book House Pvt. Ltd., Jaipur.

Fernandes, S. (2013), 'Participation and Development: The Case of Goa', in P.P. Balan, S. George and T. Kenhikannan (eds), *Decentralisation and Development: Experiences and Experiments*, Kerala Institute of Local Administration, Kerala, p. 220.

Goa Panchayat Raj Act (GPRA) (1994), Retrieved May 5, 2014, from goaprintingpress.gov.in/uploads/panchayatrajactandrules.pdf.

GOACOM (2013), *TCP Faults Gram Sabhas*, Retrieved December 22, 2014, from http://www.goacom.com/goa-news-highlights/7166-tcp-faults-gram-sabhas.

Halarnkar, T.D. (1990), *Gram Panchayat in Goa: A Critical Study*, Rajhans Offset, Panaji.

Haragopal, G. (2003), 'Governance through Participative Development: The Role of People's Movement', in P. Sahni and U. Medury (eds), *Governance for Development*, Prentice-Hall of India, New Delhi, p. 56.

Salgaonkar, S. (2006), *Women, Political Power and the State*, Abhijeet Publications, New Delhi.

Terchek, R.J. and T. Conte (2001), *Theories of Democracy*, Rowman and Littlefield Publishers, Lanham.

Times of India (2010), *Goa Panchayati Raj Act Notified with Relief.* Retrieved December 22, 2014, from http://timesofindia.indiatimes.com/city/jaipur/goa-panchayat-raj-act-notified-with-reliefs/articleshow/6778128.cms.

22

Maharashtra Model of Panchayati Raj

Changes and Challenges after the 73rd Constitutional Amendment Act

Jitendra Wasnik

The three-tier structures i.e. Zilla Parishad, Panchayat Samiti and Gram Panchayat of Panchayati Raj Institutions (PRIs) were established in Maharashtra State in May 1962; which brought in a uniform pattern of Local Self-Government in the rural areas of all the regions i.e. Western Maharashtra, Vidarbha and Marathwada of the state. The history of local government institutions in present Maharashtra dates back to 19th century; when for the first time District Local Boards were established in 1862 in Bombay Presidency. They developed slowly from government created institutions to popularly elected bodies over a period of approximately 100 years. Other regions of the state had different starting points and passed through different stage of development in this area and hence had different patterns of their own. After Independence and especially after the recognition of States in 1956, when all these came together and became parts of bilingual Bombay Sate, efforts began to bring uniformity in the field of local government in the State. The Bombay Village Panchayat Act 1958 was the first such step in that direction.

Maharashtra as a separate State of Marathi speaking people was formed on 1 May 1960. By that time the report of Balwant Rai Mehta study team was already referred to the State government, which was seriously thinking about the matter. Subsequently, a committee under the chairmanship of V.P. Naik was constituted to study the Mehta committee report in all its aspects and recommend suitable model of PRIs for the State. Naik Committee studied the subject of establishing a new set of PRIs thoroughly and submitted its recommendations in a 1961. It is on the basis of the recommendations of the Naik Committee that a comprehensive legislation 'Maharashtra Zilla Parishad and Panchayat Samiti Act' was passed in 1961 and it came into force from 1 May 1962. Thus, Maharashtra became the eleventh state in the country to adopt three-tier system of Panchayati Raj.

For the review and evaluation of the status of Panchayati Raj in Maharashtra, two important committees appointed by the state were the *Bongirwar Committee* (1970) and the *Patil Committee* (1984). Both the evaluation committees have recommended more financial and administrative autonomy to the *Zilla Parishads*. Other significant reviews were the *Heble Report* (1971) and the report of the *Kale Committee* (1981).

73rd Constitutional Amendment Act

The enactment of 73rd Constitutional Amendment Act (73rd CAA) on 24 April 1993 gave an impetus to the concept of local self-government which till then suffered from lack of constitutional protection. It has certain pinpointed mandatory and discretionary provisions which, after the incorporation in the state Act, have streamlined the process for regular and timely Panchayats elections, ratio of reservation in respect of SCs, STs, OBCs, etc. and formation of State Finance Commission. *Nyayya Panchayats* and State Finance Commission ceased to exist subsequently in Maharashtra. Maharashtra which had held panchayats elections before the enactment subsequently brought out the changes as per the provisions of 73rd CAA; such as reservation and its respective Panchayati Act. Above all, it enjoins upon the State Government to switch over to a more or less uniform pattern of structure of PRIs across the country.

Before the 73rd CAA, the PRIs in Maharashtra were governed by two separate Acts, the Bombay Village Panchayats Act 1958 and the Maharashtra Zilla Parishads and Panchayat Samitis Act 1961. As a follow up action of the 73rd CAA, the Maharashtra Government has enacted a law for making amendments to its both Panchayats Act. The law is known as Bombay Village Panchayat and the Maharashtra Zilla Parishads and Panchayat Samitis Amendment Act, 1994 and came into force on 24 April 1994. It incorporates mandatory provisions of the 73rd CAA (Datye. 2002: 6–7).

Composition of Panchayati Raj

In Maharashtra, PRIs are mainly responsible for rural development. These institutions started functioning in the state from 1 May 1962. The state is second which started three-tier structure of PRIs. The structure has been so devised that the Zilla Parishad and Panchayat Samitis are organically linked together. A Panchayat Samiti in a similar manner is linked with the Gram Panchayats. According to 73rd CAA, the State Government took a decision to transfer subjects given in Article 243G (4) of Schedule 11 of the Constitution to PRIs. As per the Government decision, 122 schemes of nine administrative departments of the State Government are transferred to PRIs (Economic Survey of Maharashtra, 2000–2001: 153).

Zilla Parishads

Presently 33 *Zilla Parishads* have been constituted in Maharashtra, each district having one *Zilla Parishad*. There is no *Zilla Parishad* for Greater Mumbai and Mumbai suburban area which is entirely an urban area. Constitution: Total elected membership of a *Zilla Parishad* in Maharashtra is between 'not more than seventy-five and not less than fifty in number (*The Maharashtra Zilla Parishads and Panchayat Samitis Act, 1961:* 8) as may be determined by the State Election Commission depending upon the size of the district. Generally, a *Zilla Parishad* member is directly elected for the population of 36,000 to 40,000. All are the chairpersons of the Panchayat Samitis in the district, who were the ex-officio members. This establishes an organic link between a *Panchayat Samiti* and the *Zilla Parishad. Panchayat Samiti* acts as an agency of its *Zilla Parishad* for implementing development programmes. Therefore, such a link is of a vital importance. The reservation for SCs, STs and women has been provided in addition to 27 per cent reservation for the OBCs. This keeps the *Zilla Parishad* aware of its responsibilities in connection with women and the weaker sections so that social justice could be extended to them through the *Zilla Parishad*.

- *Committee System:* The *Zilla Parishad* works on a committee system. The committee system ensured the participation of elected members in the decision-making process. There are nine subject committees in each *Zilla Parishad:* Finance, Works, Agriculture, Social Welfare, Education, Health, Animal Husbandry and Dairy, Women and Child Welfare, Water Conservation and Drinking Water and a Standing Committee (ibid.: 47). The president and vice-presidents of the *Zilla Parishads* and the chairpersons of the committees were elected by the directly elected members as well as the ex-officio members. The president is ex-officio chairman of standing committee. The chairpersons (ibid.: 42) of the social welfare committees had to be from the SCs, STs, *Vimukta Jatis* or NTs. The President, the Vice-president and the Chairmen of various subject committees are full time functionaries. They are ex-officio members of the Standing Committee and responsible for the implementation of the decisions of the *Zilla Parishad*. As such, they are paid honorarium and are given accommodation facilities. The term of the *Zilla Parishad* is normally of 5 years.
- *Functions:* The list of subject of activities (ibid.: 131–37) given in the First Schedule of the *Zilla Parishad and Panchayat Samiti Act, 1961*. The subjects are: Agriculture, Forests, Social Welfare, Education, Medical, Ayurveda, Public Health, Buildings and Communications, Irrigation, Community Development, Social Education, Rural Housing and other miscellaneous functions.
- *Finance:* The most important sources of income of *Zilla Parishad* are government grants. Various grants are received by a *Zilla Parishad* and through the *Zilla Parishad*, by the Panchayat Samitis in its area. The main grants are: Grants of forest revenue, Purposive grants, Establishment grants, Local cess matching grant, Incentive grants, Grants for plan schemes, Block grants etc. Imposition of taxes is a potential source of revenue which *Zilla Parishads* and *Panchayat Samitis* can tap.

Panchayat Samiti

A *Panchayat Samiti* in Maharashtra works as an area committee of *Zilla Parishad*. It is a non-corporate body and cannot levy taxes. It, therefore, provides downward ex-officio membership for the elected representatives in the *Zilla Parishad* from the constituencies in the block (Nandedkar, 1979: 16).

The *Panchayat Samitis* are constituted in each block and elect members, ex-officio members, and associated members. The members of the *Panchayat Samiti* are elected from electoral colleges in the block for which each *Zilla Parishad* electoral division is divided into two electoral colleges for the term of 5 years. The Chairman and Deputy Chairman of a *Panchayat Samiti* are from the elected members of the *Panchayat Samiti* and are its full-time functionaries. The functions of the *Panchayat Samiti* are more or less the same as those of the *Zilla Parishad*, and related to the development work in their respected area. The *samitis* function under overall guidance and instructions of the *Zilla Parishads*. The BDO is the ex-officio Secretary of a *Panchayat Samiti*. Main source of income is the Block grant received by the *Panchayat Samiti* according to the schematic pattern.

Gram Panchayat

The Gram Panchayat is the important representative and elected body in the *panchayats* system at village level. It consists of such number of members not being less than seven and not more than seventeen (*The Bombay Village Panchayats Act, 1958:* 8) depending on population. The Gram Panchayat is formed for one or a group of villages. Its members are elected on the basis of adult franchise by the *Gram Sabha* through a direct vote. Seats are reserved for SCs and STs. The term of Gram Panchayat is also of 5 years. It has been given the power to constitute committees for the discharge of its duties. The Secretary of a Gram Panchayat belongs to the Class-III District Services.

The Panchayati Raj system in Maharashtra is unique in some respects. The fundamental unit of administration is the *Zilla Parishad* and not the *Panchayat Samiti*. The position of the *Zilla Parishad* in the Panchayati Raj system is pivotal, as it is the main executive body (Sirsikar, 1995: 176). The essence of Panchayati Raj is a three-tiered organic structure entrusted with a wide range of development functions and with popular participation as its modus operandi (Nandedkar, 1979: 17). The success of Panchayati Raj depends on the elected representative's dedication to the cause of grassroots development through grassroots democracy and their firm pledge to work tirelessly with compassion, social justice and equity for all, for the inclusive growth through inclusive governance (Fifteenth Anniversary Charter on Panchayati Raj, 2008: 21).

PRIs today have the basic commitment towards rural development. It is a strategy for the improvement in social, economic, and political life of the people, with special emphasis on the rural poor. These institutions have significant role to play in the planned development of rural India. Therefore, planning under and through Panchayati Raj is essential not only for the progress of rural development but also for the success of national planning (Deshmukh, 2005: 194). Thus, one of the ideas behind the introduction of PRIs is to strengthen the rural base with the primary motto of rural development.

Status of Panchayati Raj

A Panchayat is only one of the several units of government in which control over public resources is vested. The ideal of classical democratic theory is that in a democratic society every citizen should have equal access to these resources

(Lele, 1982: 81). Maharashtra had a tradition of strong Panchayats even before enactment of the 73rd CAA. The Bombay Village Panchayat Act, 1958 and the Maharashtra Zilla Parishad and Panchayat Samiti Act 1961 define the duties, responsibilities and powers of the Village Panchayats. The population of SCs is 0.99 crore and STs was 0.86 crore reported in census 2001. Since the SC communities have migrated to urban areas, while the ST communities have remained primarily rural, it reflects in the composition of PRIs, where the ST community have a larger representation compared to the SCs, as shown in the Table 1.

Table 1

Number of Elected Representatives at Panchayat Level in Maharashtra

Level	*Nos.*	*No. of Elected Representatives*							
		General	*SCs*		*STs*		*Women*		*Total*
			No.	*%*	*No.*	*%*	*No.*	*%*	
Gram Panchayat	2,7893	1,72,370	24,624	11	26,863	12	74,620	33.3	2,23,857
Panchayat Samitis	351	3,022	430	10	470	12	1,307	33.3	3,922
Zilla Parishads	35	1,482	215	11	264	13.46	654	33.35	1961

Source: Ministry of Panchayati Raj, Government of India, Annual Report, 2007–2008, pp. 73–75.

Financial Status of PRIs

PRIs are the prominent organisations playing an important role in development at local level. These are distinctly divided into rural and urban areas. The financial resources as well as the composition of expenditure of these institutions are given in Table 2.

Table 2

Income and Expenditure of PRIs in Maharashtra (₹ in crore)

PRI	*Item*	*1999–2000**	*2002–2003***	*2007–2008****
Gram Panchayat	Income	515.05	775	1,310
	Expenditure	380.33	544.39	938
Zilla Parishad	Income	6,132.27	6,619.34	12,582
	Expenditure	5,941.36	6,028.51	18,475

Source: *Economic Survey of Maharashtra, 2000–2001: 151. **Economic Survey of Maharashtra, 2003–2004: 23. *** Economic Survey of Maharashtra, 2007–2008: 165.

Maharashtra Model of Panchayati Raj: Major Features

The PRIs in Maharashtra have significant dimension and on the basis of that it is recognised as 'Maharashtra Model' for the PRIs in India. Some of the dimensions of this model are as follows:

Effective Devolution of Functions and Functionaries

Devolution of functions was done under the Bombay Village Panchayat Act, 1958 and the *Maharashtra Zilla Parishad and Panchayat Samitis Act, 1961*. The overall view of the functions performed by these institutions, highlights that the functions assigned to Gram Panchayat are of local nature performing the daily needs of the villagers. The *Panchayat Samiti* works as a sub-committee of *Zilla Parishad* and performs only those functions which are assigned to it. The *Zilla Parishad* being an apex body performs the function of coordination, control, supervision and serves as the link between the State Government and Panchayati Raj structure. In compliance with the First Schedule, Section 100 of the *Maharashtra Zilla Parishad and Panchayat Samitis Act, 1961* enumerates 129 subjects which fall within the purview of *Zilla Parishad*, which have been listed in Schedule 1st of the Act called 'District List'. Section 101 of the Act enlists the subjects which fall under the purview of *Panchayat Samitis*. In addition to the subjects listed in these schedules, the state government has transferred many more subjects and schemes to *Zilla Parishad* under the section 102 and 103 of the Act. The State Government has full liberty to delete or add any entry in the given schedule at any point of time.

Section 60 of *Bombay Village Panchayat Act 1958* provides for appointment of Panchayat Secretary for a group of Panchayats based on size and population of the village and income of the Panchayat. Under Section 61, Panchayats have the power to appoint such staff as may be necessary for the proper discharge of its duties under this Act and pay their salaries from the Village Fund. A Panchayat may, from time to time, by written order, fine or dismiss any servant appointed by it but an appeal shall lie against such order to the BDO within one month from the date of the communication of the order to the servant.

Class I/II Officers: The officers of class I and II working in the *Zilla Parishad* report to HOD and the Chief Executive officers of the *Zilla Parishad*. The powers of recruitment, promotion and disciplinary action of Class I/II officers working in the *Zilla Parishads* are vested in the State Government. Class III/IV Officers are recruited by the *Zilla Parishad*. Chief Executive officer who is the Administrative HOD writes Annual Confidential Report (ACR) of all Class I/II Officers of *Zilla Parishad* (*The Maharashtra Zilla Parishads and Panchayat Samitis Act, 1961*: 53). At Intermediate Level BDO writes ACR of Class III and IV working in *Panchayat Samiti*.

Effective Devolution of Finances

Gram Panchayats have been authorised to accord administrative approval and sanction expenditure for the work costing upto ₹ 3 lakh for which technical sanction of Junior Engineer is required. If the cost of work is more than ₹ 3 lakh and upto ₹ 10 lakh, administrative approval of *Panchayat Samiti* and technical sanction of Assistant Engineer is essential. In case of works costing more than ₹ 10 lakh administrative approval of *Zilla Parishad* and technical sanction of Executive Engineer is essential.

Gram Panchayats can levy taxes on buildings and land, shops, hotels, trade, fairs, festivals, fee for supply of water from wells and tanks and piped water supply, grazing cattle and car and *Tonga* stands (*The Bombay Village Panchayats Act, 1958*: 59–61). The *Zilla Parishad* can levy the property tax, *yatra* tax, water charge fees on *Melawas*, *Bazar* fee, permission fee and special tax on land and houses which includes Stamp Duty, Cess on Land Revenue, Cess on water charges, Forest Revenue, Water charges etc.

The Plan Grants to PRIs are separately budgeted and a budget document known as Appendix IV of the state Budget is presented in the Assembly. The funds are transferred through district treasuries to Panchayats.

Establishment of State Finance Commission (SFC)

The first SFC was set up in April 1994 and its report was submitted in November 1996. The State Govt. accepted the report with modifications in July 1997 and Action Taken Report was submitted to the State Legislature in April 1997. The Second SFC was set up in May 1999 and its report was submitted in October 2002. The State Govt. accepted the report in October 2002 and ATR was submitted to State Legislature during the Budget Session i.e. August 2003.

Maharashtra was allocated an amount of ₹ 65,672.90 lakhs by the Eleventh Finance Commission for PRIs. Out of this amount, an amount of ₹ 59,105.61 lakhs only was released to the State Government. Although, a matching contribution of ₹ 22,986.23 lakhs was provided by the State Government, the total utilisation by the PRIs as reported by the State Government was ₹ 82,064.32 lakhs which is 88.62 per cent.

The Twelfth Finance Commission has allocated an amount of ₹ 1,983 crore for the PRIs for the period 2005–10. The State has so far secured both the instalments of 2005–06 amounting to ₹ 198.30 crore each as well as the 1st instalment of 2006–07, which was released, on 15 September 2006. The State has, however, paid an amount of ₹ 1,23,86,958 as interest to the PRIs for delay in sending the allocations to the Panchayats beyond the stipulated 15-day period.

Activity Mapping

The Bombay Village Panchayat Act, 1958, lists 79 items; it may be seen from the above that land improvement and land consolidation have already been assigned to the Village Panchayat under the Act of 1958. Opening of fair price shops has been assigned to village Panchayats under the General Administration. Preparation of Plans for the development of the village and drawing up of programmes for increasing the output of agriculture and non-agricultural produce in the village has been assigned to Village Panchayat under General Administration in accordance with the Act of 1958. Zilla Parishad and Panchayat Samiti have been assigned 204 items in Schedules I and II of the Act 1961. Since these functions have been devolved by legislation, they should be treated as devolved regardless of the Heads under which they have been put in the Act. In fact, activity mapping has been done under both the Acts of 1958 and 1961.

Planning and Implementation

DPCs have not been constituted in accordance with Article 243 ZD. Instead, a nominated body called the DPDC has been constituted. Outlays are provided for various Centrally Sponsored Schemes in the District Plan as per the guidelines of the Central Government. Other resources include schemes for removal of regional imbalance, state pool schemes, credit plan, hill areas development programme and MLA fund.

Gram Panchayat shall place statement of expenditures incurred on development works, before the Gram Sabha every six months. Annual accounts and planning of proposed works are to be placed before first meeting of Gram Sabha. Gram Panchayats have to display information about the estimates of development works and expenditures incurred on the notice board.

Parallel Bodies

The main parallel body is District Rural Development Agency (DRDA). In spite of the fact that *Zilla Parishads* have been strong in Maharashtra, the DRDAs have not been abolished. President of *Zilla Parishad* is Chairman of Governing body, whereas CEO of *Zilla Parishad* is Chairman of Executive Committee of DRDA. In March, 2004, the post Project Director DRDA was upgraded to the level of Additional CEO. Now, a senior officer in the rank of Additional CEO is looking after working of DRDA.

Reservations for Women, SCs and STs

One-third of the seats of Village Panchayat/Block Panchayat/District Panchayat as the case may be, are reserved for women (including reserved seats for SC and ST women).

According to the provision contained in Section 12 and 58 of the *Maharashtra Zilla Parishad and Panchayat Samiti Act, 1961* and Section 10 of the *Bombay Village Panchayat Act, 1958* the seats are to be reserved for the persons belonging to the SCs and the STs in a Panchayats at all level. Maharashtra has also provided for 27 per cent reservation to OBCs.

Reservation for all categories has been given to each constituency by rotation. The manner of rotation has been prescribed in the rules i.e. The Maharashtra *Zilla Parishads* and *Panchayat Samitis* (Manner and Rotation of Reservation of Seats) Rules, 1996 and the Bombay Village Panchayat Act (Division of the Village into wards and Reservation of Seats for Women and SCs and STs (Rules 1966).

Annual Reports on the State of the Panchayats

It is obligatory for the *Zilla Parishads* and *Panchayat Samitis* to prepare annual administration reports under Section 142 of the *Maharashtra Zilla Parishad and Panchayat Samiti Act, 1961*. This report should include the audit note and the replies thereto and should be submitted to the State Legislature through the Rural Development Department of the State Government.

Elections

In Maharashtra, State Election Commission was established in April 1994. The Commission has been empowered to delimit the constituencies for elections. The elections are conducted by the District Collector under the control and supervision of the State Election Commission. The State Government provides budgetary support and required funds for the functioning of the Commission and the election process. Funds are provided to the Collector on the basis of the requirement projected by him and the State Election Commission.

Audit

A consolidated finance and revenue account with an audit review report is submitted by Chief Auditor, Local Funds Accounts, Maharashtra, for every financial year. The consolidated finance and revenue accounts are based on the annual accounts submitted by the respective *Zilla Parishads* after due scrutiny by audit. A critical review on the working of the PRIs and comments on points arising from the consolidated finance and revenue accounts are embodied in a separate report called the Audit Review Report. Annual Administration Reports of the *Zilla Parishads* are placed before the State Legislature. The State Legislature has appointed a Committee on Panchayati Raj to exercise the functions of the Public Accounts Committee and Estimates Committee in relation to the budgets and accounts of the *Zilla Parishads* and *Panchayat Samitis.*

E-Governance

The Government of Maharashtra has started the process of computerisation through the resources made available through 12th Finance Commission. All the *Panchayat Samitis* and *Zilla Parishads* have been provided with computers. Further, the PRIs have started the computerisation of several processes such as preparation of Pay Roll, GPF Account keeping, and Agriculture Pesticide/Insecticide and fertiliser licenses, Reference Monitoring Systems.

As per directive of Panchayat Raj Ministry, the process of collecting and entering the database for all the PRIs for the Panchayati Raj portal has been started. An e-Panchayats project for computerisation of all the Gram Panchayats is also under preparation. A large amount of official correspondence takes place through e-mail.

Capacity Building and Training

The Rural Development Department maintains a large infrastructure for training the PRIs representatives and officials. There are 11 Panchayati Raj Training Centres and 9 Gram Sevak Training Centres, and one Composite Training Centre in the State. Training programmes are organised for all the elected members of the PRIs, which include *Sarpanch*, *Upsarpanch*, and members of Gram Panchayats. A Special Action Plan has been launched for training all PRIs representatives from *Zilla Parishads* to Gram Panchayats. The Yashwantrao Chavan Academy of Development Administration (Yashada), the main training institution of the State Government, also includes the State Institute of Rural Development. From 2002–2003, in the training centres, on an average, 9,378 PRIs officials have been trained and in eleven Panchayat Raj Training Centres, 26,662 PRIs representatives have been provided with training.

During 2005–06, an amount of ₹ 2,13,59,500 was sanctioned and released to the YASHADA for Training of elected representatives by the Ministry of Finance. In addition, a programme funded by UNFPA for awareness of Health related issues in women elected representatives of PRIs is also being implemented by the YASHADA. Under this project, an amount of ₹ 17 lakhs was released to the academy during 2005–06.

Provisions of Panchayats (Extension to the Scheduled Areas) Act

For the development of scheduled area, the parliament passed a special act in 1996 called 'The Provisions of Panchayats (Extension to the Scheduled Areas) Act, 1996 (PESA)'. The Maharashtra *Zilla Parishads* and *Panchayat Samitis* (Extension to the Scheduled Areas and Amendments) Ordinance, 1997 was promulgated on 3rd January 1997 and on 12 April, 1997 it was replaced by Maharashtra *Zilla Parishads* and *Panchayat Samitis* (Extension to the Scheduled Areas and Amendments) Act, 1997 to bring the state law in conformity with it. On 29th December 1997, amendments were made to Bombay Village Panchayat Act, 1958, and to some other acts endowing upon the Panchayats in the scheduled areas the powers to function as institutions of self-government (Mathew, 1995: 193).

The history of PRIs had been one of ups and downs as existed in other pockets and states of the country. The main constraint on PRIs acquiring the desired status and emerging as agents of development in the State had been the lack of political will and the typical attitude of the bureaucracy which regarded them as subordinate and inferior institutions. Other constraints were of a technical nature and consisted of both shortage of trained staff, financial resources, and the lack of interest on the part of members of the institutions to strengthen the resources of the Panchayats. In spite of these constraints, PRIs had achieved better results as compared to local self-government institutions in other states. They had also proved to be the training ground for politicians aspiring to leadership at the state level.

References

Datye, S.N. (2002), 'Panchayati Raj in Maharashtra State', in G. Palanithurai (ed.), *Dynamics of New Panchayati Raj in India*, Concept Publishing Company, New Delhi.

Deshmukh, Neelima (2005), 'Women's Empowerment through Panchayati Raj Institutions: A Case Study of Wambori Gram Panchayat in Maharashtra', *The Indian Journal of Public Administration*, Vol. LI, No. 2, April-June.

Economic Survey of Maharashtra (2000–2001), Government of Maharashtra.

—— (2007–2008), Government of Maharashtra.

Fifteenth Anniversary Charter on Panchayati Raj (2008), Ministry of Panchayati Raj, Government of India, April.

Lele, Jayant (1982), *Elite Pluralism and Class Rule: Political Development in Maharashtra*, Popular Prakashan, Bombay.

Mathew, George (1995), *Panchayati Raj: From Legislation to Movement*, Concept Publishing Company, New Delhi.

Nandedkar, V.G. (1979), *Local Government: It's Role in Development Administration*, Concept Publishing Company, Delhi.

Sirsikar, V.M. (1995), *Politics of Modern Maharashtra*, Orient Longman, Bombay.

The Bombay Village Panchayats Act, 1958 (as modified up to 12 January 2006), Government of Maharashtra.

The Maharashtra Zilla Parishads and Panchayat Samitis Act, 1961 (as modified up to 18 October 1996), Government of Maharashtra.

Index